PSYCHOLOGY AND SOCIAL PROBLEMS

PSYCHOLOGY AND SOCIAL PROBLEMS

An Introduction to Applied Psychology

Edited by

Anthony Gale
Department of Psychology
University of Southampton

and

Antony J. Chapman
Department of Psychology
University of Leeds

JOHN WILEY & SONS
Chichester · New York · Brisbane · Toronto · Singapore

Reprinted March 1989
Reprinted June 1991

Library of Congress Cataloging in Publication Data

Main entry under title:

Psychology and social problems.
Includes index.
   1. Psychology, Applied—Addresses, essays, lectures.
   2. Social problems—Addresses, essays, lectures.
   I. Gale, Anthony.   II. Chapman, Antony J.
   BF636.A2P79   1984   158   83–16728

   ISBN 0 471 90313 2
   ISBN 0 471 90314 0 (pbk.)

British Library Cataloguing in Publication Data

Psychology and social problems.
   1. Psychology, Applied
   I. Gale, Anthony   II. Chapman, Antony J.
   158   BF636

   ISBN 0 471 90313 2 (cloth)
   ISBN 0 471 90314 0 (paper)

Phototypeset by Input Typesetting Ltd, London SW19 8DR
Printed in Great Britain by Antony Rowe Ltd, Chippenham, Wiltshire

DEDICATION

Liz, Michael and Maggie,
Siriol and family

LIST OF CONTRIBUTORS

A. T. Carr
Clinical Teaching Unit, Department of Psychology, Plymouth Polytechnic, Drake Circus, Plymouth, Devon, PL4 8AA

A. J. Chapman
Department of Psychology, University of Leeds, Leeds LS2 9JT

D. D. Clark-Carter
Department of Psychology, The University, University Park, Nottingham, NG7 2RD

A. D. B. Clarke
Department of Psychology, The University, Hull HU6 7RX

A. M. Clarke
Department of Psychology, The University, Hull HU6 7RX

C. L. Cooper
Department of Management Sciences, University of Manchester Institute of Science and Technology, P.O. Box 88, Manchester M60 1QD

C. J. Cox
Department of Management Sciences, University of Manchester Institute of Science and Technology, P.O. Box 88, Manchester M60 1QD

D. P. Farrington
Institute of Criminology, University of Cambridge, 7 West Road, Cambridge CB3 9DT

D. Fontana
Department of Education, University College Cardiff, P.O. Box 78, Cardiff CF1 1XL

A. Gale
Department of Psychology, University of Southampton, Highfield, Southampton SO9 5NH

H. Giles
Department of Psychology, University of Bristol, 8/10 Berkeley Square, Bristol BS8 1HH

M. R. Gossop
Drug Dependence Clinical Research and Treatment Unit, The Bethlem Royal Hospital and the Maudsley Hospital, Monks Orchard Road, Beckenham, Kent BR3 3BX

M. M. Gruneberg
Department of Psychology, University College, Singleton Park, Swansea SA2 8PP

M. Herbert
Department of Psychology, The University, Leicester, LE1 7RH

M. Hewstone
Laboratoire Européen de Psychologie Sociale, Maison des Sciences de l'Homme, 54 Boulevard Raspail, 75270 Paris Cédex 06, France

C. I. Howarth
Department of Psychology, The University, University Park, Nottingham NG7 2RD

D. Jehu
Psychological Service Centre, University of Manitoba, Winnipeg, Manitoba, Canada R3T 2N2

N. P. Sheehy
Department of Psychology, University of Leeds, Leeds LS2 9JT

R. Slater
Department of Applied Psychology, University of Wales Institute of Science and Technology, Llwyn-y-Grant Road, Cardiff CF3 7UX

C. D. Spielberger
Center for Research in Community Psychology, Human Resources Institute, University of South Florida, Tampa, Florida 33620, USA

S. R. Sutton
Addiction Research Unit, Institute of Psychiatry, 101 Denmark Hill, London SE5 8AF

D. Wallis
Department of Applied Psychology, University of Wales Institute of Science and Technology, Llwyn-y-Grant Road, Cardiff CF3 7UX

CONTENTS

FOREWORD

Charles D. Spielberger

Applications of psychology currently touch the lives of countless people. Nearly everyone has a relative or friend who has taken a psychological test or sought help for vocational or personal problems from a counsellor or psychotherapist. Indeed, as society has become more complex, and people have gained greater freedom and control over their lives and careers, the range of services offered by psychologists to both individuals and institutions has greatly expanded.

Given the pervasive influence of applied psychology in everyday life, understanding psychological principles and their applications has become a necessity for the enlightened citizen. In *Psychology and Social Problems*, Professors Gale and Chapman provide an authoritative and comprehensive introduction to applied psychology that will prove invaluable to the undergraduate student. To assist them in covering the massive subject matter, they have called upon highly qualified experts from different areas of applied psychology, and challenged them to examine their respective fields within a common framework that serves to integrate otherwise diverse domains.

Meaningful applications of psychology must be based on a sound scientific foundation. Consequently, ethical application of psychological principles to social problems must await the development of relevant theory that has been tested by empirical research. In addition to a thorough knowledge of scientific facts and theory, practitioners of applied psychology must also have the requisite personal qualities that will enable them to work comfortably and effectively with a wide range of clients.

While philosophers and theologians have speculated about human nature for many centuries, psychology is a relatively young scientific discipline, and applications of psychological principles are even more recent. The establishment of psychology as an experimental science is generally credited to Wilhelm Wundt, who founded the first permanent laboratory of psychology at the University of Leipzig in 1879 (Boring, 1957). Applied psychology owes a special debt to Sir Francis Galton of Great Britain, whose creative genius inspired and stimulated early investigations of individual differences.

In 1884, at an international health exhibition, Galton established an anthropometric laboratory, which many historians of psychology consider the first laboratory of applied psychology. Galton designed numerous instruments for making anthropometric and psychometric measurements. For the sum of threepence, an interested citizen could obtain accurate measurements of height, weight, breathing power, hearing, colour sense, strength of pull, and many other individual human abilities and characteristics. At the closing of the exhibition, Galton's laboratory was transferred to London's South Kensington Museum, where it was maintained for six years. During the operation of the laboratory, data were collected on more than nine thousand persons.

For historians of psychology the year 1890 marks the beginning point for applied psychology (Boring, 1957; Napoli, 1981). In that year, James McKeen Cattell, an American psychologist working at the University of Pennsylvania, coined the term *mental test*, and published the results of the first psychological testing programme. Strongly influenced by the work of Galton, who had previously developed a number of procedures that would now be called mental tests, Cattell was motivated by the very practical goal of selecting those applicants for admission to the university who had the best chance for success.

Cattell received his doctorate from Leipzig in 1886, and was well trained in Wundt's approach to experimental psychology, which involved seeking general laws about the structure of the mind. But, like Galton, Cattell considered individual differences to be the crucial variables in his experiments. The particular characteristics measured in his testing programme included reaction time, colour vision, keenness of hearing, sensitivity to pain, remote memory, and other qualities that reflected quickness of mind.

There is little current interest in Wundt's structuralism, but students of psychology must be aware of important differences in orientation between psychologists who search for general laws of behaviour and those whose major concern is in the measurement of individual differences. Psychologists who work in university settings are more likely to employ experimental methods to investigate general processes whereas applied psychologists are more likely to use psychological tests in the assessment of individual differences in their clients or patients. By the mid-1950's these differences in orientation were sufficiently pronounced for Lee J. Cronbach (1957) to refer to them as 'The two disciplines of scientific psychology', in his Presidential Address to the American Psychological Association.

Between 1890 and the First World War, psychology emerged as a respectable academic discipline in the universities of Europe and the United States. This period also witnessed important applications of psychology in clinical, industrial and educational contexts. Psychologists began to administer tests in institutions for the mentally retarded and in industrial settings where they were used in the selection of job applicants. A significant milestone occurred in 1896. The first psychological clinic was established by Lightner Witmer at the University of Pennsylvania in response to a school principal's request for assistance in helping an elementary pupil with a serious educational problem.

Applied psychology was also stimulated by advances in measurement and statistics. In addition to his many contributions to the psychology of individual differences, Galton was a pioneer in the development of statistical methods. He was among the first to utilize the bell-shaped, normal probability curve in describing the distributions of measures of human, social and biological characteristics, and to work out statistical methods for quantifying the relationship (correlation) between paired measures. Karl Pearson, Charles Spearman, Godfrey Thomson and Cyril Burt in Great Britain, and L. L. Thurstone in the United States, also made distinguished early contributions to the statistical foundations of psychological science and to the measurement of general intelligence and primary mental abilities.

The growth of applied psychology was greatly accelerated by the First World War, in which psychologists constructed tests for screening new recruits, and for classifying and selecting men for specific military jobs. The Army Alpha Test, a standardized measure of mental ability developed by the United States Army, was administered to more than 1.7 million men in the most massive testing effort ever undertaken up until that time. After the war, many American psychologists completed their enlistments working in Army rehabilitation hospitals, where they were involved in evaluating and treating individual patients, and thus extended the range of applications in clinical settings where few psychologists had previously worked.

Curiously, even the Great Depression of the 1930's contributed to the development of applied psychology. Massive unemployment, resulting in reduced numbers of academic positions, stimulated directors of USA graduate training programmes in psychology to assist their students in finding employment in applied settings, and to provide courses and appropriate field experiences to prepare them for such work.

The Second World War provided a major turning point for the widespread acceptance of applied psychology. Once again, psychologists became heavily involved in developing tests for screening and classifying military personnel, but had much more to offer in these fields, and others as well. In the United States, for example, the most prestigious experts in personnel evaluation and psychological testing contributed to the construction of the General Classification Test, which was administered to more than 9 million men. Perhaps the greatest success achieved by psychologists during World War II was in the selection of pilots. The utilization of psychological tests greatly reduced the failure rate in aviation training programmes, as compared with previous selection procedures based on educational requirements, psychiatric interviews, and physical examinations.

Hopefully, the preceding brief overview of the historical development of applied psychology will prove helpful in understanding current applications of psychology to a variety of social problems. In their introductory chapter, Gale and Chapman discuss the nature of applied psychology. They identify its core characteristics and make a convincing case for applied psychology as a unitary discipline that must be based on a broad foundation of psychological theory and research. They also describe what applied psychologists do in their work, examine the complicated moral and ethical problems that are encountered in applications of psychology to social problems, and give a number of meaningful examples of the interventions that they practise in a variety of environmental settings. The reader will find the *Checklist* for evaluating the outcomes of psychological interventions especially helpful in reviewing individual studies.

The contents of this volume give ample testimony to the continuing growth and vitality of applied psychology. Individual chapters provide a coherent analysis of fifteen different problem areas in which applied psychologists currently work. Clearly, the boundaries for the application of psychology to the solution of individual and social problems have been greatly expanded, and can no longer be defined in terms of the traditional professional activities of clinical, industrial and educational psychologists.

REFERENCES

Boring, E. G. (1957). *A History of Experimental Psychology* (Second Edition). New York: Appleton-Century-Crofts.

Cronbach, L. J. (1957). The two disciplines of scientific psychology. *American Psychologist*, **12**, 671–684.

Napoli, D. S. (1981). *Architects of Adjustment: The history of the psychological profession in the United States*. Port Washington, NY: Kennikat Press.

PREFACE

This volume results from a belief that Applied Psychology should be regarded as a unitary discipline. Ours is a radical approach to Applied Psychology, and we begin by examining the definition of social problems, moral implications for the practice of psychology, and issues intrinsic to the evaluation of interventions. A common analytic framework is then used for each of the 'social problems' addressed. Hence contributions are sectioned as follows:

The extent of the problem
Concepts of the person and models of human behaviour
Individual assessment
The immediate social and emotional environment
The wider social and organizational environment
Types of intervention
Is psychological intervention successful?
Methodological and practical problems
Problems of ethics and confidentiality
The role of other disciplines and professions
Future prospects

They conclude with annotated readings and reference lists.

Our approach helps to avoid the outmoded and unhelpful classifications apparent in more traditional texts: we believe, for example, that it is misguided to limit the use of psychological tools and instruments to the contexts in which they were originally developed. By demonstrating the unity of the discipline we seek to curtail and counteract the unfortunate fragmentation of psychology into sectional interests and divisions, into 'pure/applied', 'mechanistic/humanistic', 'social/biological' and 'phenomenological/behaviourist' psychology. Most of all we hope to show psychological practitioners, and potential practitioners, that Applied Psychology is best recognized as a single discipline. Whatever the 'applied problem' practitioners must select a strategy for intervention on the basis of information derived from *all* available sources of knowledge. Only then can they be confident that their intervention will be appropriate to the individual client or organization. The problems we have chosen to highlight are conspicuous examples of good contemporary practice.

Psychology and Social Problems was prepared for use by students at universities and colleges studying for first degrees in psychology and as a source of additional reading for courses in child development, educational psychology, organizational and social psychology, and clinical psychology. Much of the material will also be of interest to students of medicine, education, and the paramedical and caring professions. The lists of further readings following each chapter will enable the student to extend individual study through readily accessible books and review articles.

In preparing the final manuscript for the printer, we acknowledge with gratitude the help of Claire Jolly.

ANTHONY GALE   *Southampton*
ANTONY J. CHAPMAN   *Leeds*
August 1983

Psychology and Social Problems
Edited by A. Gale and A. J. Chapman
© 1984 John Wiley & Sons Ltd.

CHAPTER 1

THE NATURE OF APPLIED PSYCHOLOGY

Anthony Gale and **Antony J. Chapman**

Textbooks in applied psychology typically come in two varieties. One describes *techniques* which psychologists have devised; for example, mental tests, behaviour modification, job description, individual psychotherapy and group work. The other describes the work of different categories of *psychological professional*, the clinical, educational, community, industrial and prison psychologist. *Psychology and Social Problems* adopts a different approach. We think it useful to apply a psychological analysis to what applied psychologists do in their working lives. Such an analysis reveals many common features in applied psychological practice. Indeed we consider that most of the skills and techniques available to psychology could and should be deployed in a variety of contexts. They are not the preserve of a particular branch of expertise, and the particular titles which psychologists hold ('educational', 'clinical' and so on) owe more to historical accident and the nature of the funding agencies for which psychologists work than to actual differences in practice.

It may well be that a job description or job profile reveals that psychologists in different contexts apply certain skills at the expense of others. Thus a clinical psychologist working in a large psychiatric hospital may spend a good deal of time with *individuals* yet devote little time to the promotion of organizational change. Conversely the industrial psychologist may work as a *change agent* to facilitate efficiency in working groups and not be expected to offer individual *counselling* or *personal welfare* advice. But it is the values and priorities which operate in the working context which determine the job profile of the psychologist. Individual counselling and welfare work in a factory could well lead to increased productivity, reduced interpersonal frictions and increased personal satisfaction with work. Organizational changes in an institutional setting might well lead to improvements in staff morale and performance and the delivery of personal services to residents. But at present psychologists are rarely called upon to discharge such functions *in those contexts*.

A Psychological Analysis of Applied Psychological Skill

Our analysis of applied psychological skills and attributes leads us to identify the following core or common characteristics. As illustrated above, not all the skills are applied equally in different working situations.

- Psychologists are concerned with bringing about *change*.
- Typically the implementation of change is seen to be associated with a desire to improve the *quality of life* of other individuals.
- Psychologists are trained in special procedures and techniques for purposes of *observation*, *measurement* and *report*.
- They are presented with *problems* which are multiply determined and need to be analysed into their constituent parts.
- Psychological knowledge and emphasis shifts over time; thus psychologists need to be aware that the contemporary preferred *model of man* and *conceptions of the person* will influence the ways in which the psychologist and Society deal with the individual.
- Psychologists work within *organizational* settings, where characteristics of the organization may influence the ways in which people treat each other.
- The psychologist has no self-evident right to make decisions for others; yet the majority of the psychologist's working time is spent in dealing with people. Contemporary definitions of *the person* incorporate the view that individuals should be no less free to make choices about their own lives, than are psychologists.
- Clients are people who belong to *families* and other personally significant *emotional networks*; such networks will influence the ways in which clients perceive the world and their own roles within it.
- Clients also have other *affiliations* – for example, of a religious, political or ideological nature – whose values will be of personal significance to them. Again, it might be difficult to understand the *client's view of the world* without setting the client's problem within those contexts.
- Life is stressful and psychologists and their clients can be subject to *stresses* and *strains*; the psychologist needs to devise methods of coping and is expected to assist clients in the development of personal coping skills.
- Psychological interventions typically involve *education and training* and, in many cases, an attempt to transfer to the client personal autonomy and responsibility for change.
- Like other professionals, psychologists have a responsibility to *evaluate the efficacy* of the strategies devised to promote change.

- In most of their working lives and contexts psychologists have to *collaborate with members of other professional* groups (such as nurses, doctors, social workers, managers and administrators). Successful collaboration presupposes an understanding of the principles which guide the professional life of colleagues and a development of mutual respect.
- Most applied psychologists are employed by public agencies or are affected professionally by *legislation*; they need to keep in touch with, understand and maintain discourse with *government agencies*.
- Resources are never unlimited; thus it is necessary to learn to *allocate resources* in ways which reflect priority and maximize pay-off.
- Professional intervention does not occur in a vacuum and a variety of professional groups will compete with psychologists to acquire influence; thus psychologists need to be *politically aware* and vigilant.
- Finally, because the work of psychologists concerns *people* in such a direct way, there are immediate *moral consequences* of psychological interventions. This implies that psychologists need to be practised in *moral discourse* and in handling complex issues to do with ethics, privacy, consent, confidentiality, interpersonal influence and personal accountability.

Our list is a mixed collection of knowledge, skills, attitudes and values; and it is evident that to a certain extent the psychologist stands on shifting ground. We believe it is difficult to describe the work of the professional psychologist without encompassing all these domains. Nor is there necessarily an immediate coherence between different characteristics of psychological skill; for example, the need to *evaluate* treatments may involve the deception of clients (see page 16). Our notion of communality among the various applications of psychology has implications for the ways in which psychologists are educated and trained. Thus, if the skills in our list were treated as curriculum objectives, we suspect that the character of present training schemes would alter radically. However, training is not a focus of this book.

The analysis of applied psychological skill adopted above has enabled us to ask all the contributors to this volume to employ a common framework for presenting their expert knowledge. Thus each chapter in *Psychology and Social Problems* has headings as follows:

The Extent of the Problem This involves an appropriate estimate of the magnitude of the problem under consideration, including data on incidence and prevalence. The historical background to the problem is often of relevance to the contemporary evaluation of it.

Concepts of the Person and Models of Human Behaviour Alternative theoretical models (for example, psychoanalysis, personal construct theory, behavioural approaches, social psychological approaches, biological and medical models) will influence the ways in which a particular problem is conceptualized and handled. Thus the ways in which psychology in general views individual motivation and the causes of action will influence the practice of the applied psychologist.

Individual Assessment   Here we describe how the individual client, or the patient, or the 'problem' is assessed, and we include the use of particular instruments and techniques devised for measurement purposes.

The Immediate Social and Emotional Environment   The individual lives and works with intimates and workmates within a social context. Features of the immediate environment may serve to create or to exacerbate the problem in question, or the consequences of the individual's difficulties might include adverse effects upon those who surround and interact with the individual.

The Wider Social and Organizational Context   Under this heading we refer not only to social norms and public attitudes concerning appropriate and deviant behaviours but to the ways in which such broader aspects of society might act as a cause of problems for individuals. Society also responds to particular problems in different ways, and it varies in the degree of provision allocated to assist with problems.

Types of Intervention   The model of the person adopted, and the nature of the analysis of the problem in question, will determine the type of intervention considered to be appropriate. Some types of intervention (for example, directive and non-directive approaches) may be seen to be in contradiction with each other. In other cases, different varieties of intervention (for example, anxiety-reducing drugs and psychotherapy) may be seen to be complementary and appropriate to tackle different aspects of the individual's problem.

Is Psychological Intervention Successful?   Examples are given of key outcome or evaluation studies. This involves consideration of outcome criteria, duration of follow-up, changes which occur during the intervention process and identification of the specific variables within an intervention 'package' which are seen to be responsible for change. Intervention with individuals is likely to affect also the social networks to which they belong; intervention in groups and organizations should also have an impact on individual members. Thus the evaluation of outcome presents many difficulties.

Methodological and Practical Problems   When one works in the field it is rarely possible, convenient or ethically acceptable to engage in experimental manipulations available in the laboratory. Under this section, the problems considered in earlier sections are drawn together to provide the reader with an evaluative and critical framework to be used in reading new material and published reports in the area of interest.

Problems of Ethics and Confidentiality   Here our authors analyse the extent to which privacy and interpersonal relations have to be borne in mind by the practising psychologist. On occasion, such discussion involves consideration of changes which have occurred since psychology was first applied to the problem (for example, in the treatment of mental handicap) and shifts in the moral framework (explicit or implicit) within which the psychologist works. Broader political issues may determine the sort of problem to which psychological expertise is applied or even constrain the degrees of psychological intervention. Thus notions of priority, modes of intervention and even concepts of *blame* may be affected by non-psychological factors.

The Role of Other Disciplines and Professions   We have already seen that many professional groups can be involved in the process of helping or in bringing about change. Historical factors have led to a division of labour among different groups. In many cases, the role of the psychologist in relation to other colleagues in a team has altered over time. Quite often, the division of labour owes little to a functional analysis of the nature of the problems faced by the team.

Future Prospects   Psychological expertise is still developing and its application continues to extend across many contexts. It is therefore unlikely that the view of any social problem as seen in the 1980's will persist unaltered into the 1990's. It is a challenge to speculate about the view of life to come and to consider ways in which psychologists might improve their effectiveness in the future.

The presentation of individual topics within a common framework enables the reader to approach this book in various ways. Individual chapters may be read to gain an overview and coherent analysis of a particular problem domain, or cross-reference may be made *between* chapters, in relation to particular headings. Finally, the student may wish to refer back to the present chapter to confirm whether or not our conceptual analysis of psychological skill is appropriate in all cases. Although our contributors come from different backgrounds, and few have appeared together before within one volume, there are nevertheless a number of common issues which recur throughout the book. The remainder of this chapter is devoted to consideration of such general issues.

WHAT IS A 'PROBLEM'?

Let us begin with a straightforward view of psychological problems. People are functional or dysfunctional; if they are functional then they require no professional assistance; if they are dysfunctional then they will benefit from the intervention of an expert. The expert's role is to diagnose the problem, recommend an intervention and bring about change in the individual, who then becomes functional. Such an account may sound a most acceptable rationale for the existence of applied psychology and for the employment of psychologists within Society, wherever such problems arise.

However, this approach makes a number of assumptions about functional and dysfunctional living and we must immediately ask the question 'functional for what?'. The answer will call upon a set of *value* judgements about how people should live and how they should interact with each other. It is clear that styles of living vary within cultures, between cultures and within the same culture over time. For example, some twenty years ago in the Western World, homosexual behaviour between consenting adults was anathematized and legally prohibited in several societies. A change in our views of sexual relationships has served to remove some of the stigma which applied to the homosexual. We think it likely that psychologists nowadays will encounter fewer individuals whose personal difficulties arise from homosexual preference. In the UK and the USA the prevailing viewpoint has altered not only Society's view of the individual, but the views that individuals have of themselves.

Is it in fact the *individual* who presents the problem? If it is the person who is dysfunctional, then presumably the person should be the focus of treatment? The traditional approach of the educational psychologist, when advice was sought concerning an individual child's learning difficulties or unacceptable social behaviour, was to administer psychological tests to determine the origins of dysfunction. This strategy followed from the notion that the problem owed its origin to maladaptive characteristics *within* the child. A more contemporary view is that a complete picture of the problem will only emerge after considering not only the child's test scores, but the quality of the child's home background, the atmosphere, teaching style and modes of control which operate in the classroom and the general organizational climate within the school. Only then will the psychologist be able to locate the sources of the child's difficulties. Viewed in this way, the problem might prove to be not the child's problem, but the family's problem or the teacher's problem or the school's problem. The truth is that the problem is likely to be related to several variables both 'internal' and 'external' to the child. At the broader level, the child's failure to achieve certain desirable norms of behaviour reminds us that in other cultures *different* norms for achievement might apply. A child who starts formal schooling at the age of six or seven can hardly present a school-related problem at the age of five.

We are not denying that people differ. Rather, it is the society we live in which determines whether particular differences between people are (a) seen to be important and (b) seen to possess positive or negative evaluation. In one country, a challenge to the political system may be seen to be both desirable and acceptable within conventional modes of expression; in another, the political dissident may be treated as a psychiatric case. Nor do we deny that individuals in distress experience distress; but their distress arises from a *combination* of personal condition, social attribution and their own acceptance of social norms of desirable behaviour. Thus dysfunction needs to be defined in terms of *context*. Let us consider a further example. Nowadays, depression is regarded as an undesirable condition. Depressed people feel unhappy and induce despondency in those around them. Thus we search for explanations of and cures for depression. Yet we do observe under *some* circumstances—for example, the death of a loved one, or loss of employment, or severance of an intimate relationship—that depression is a 'natural' side effect. Are there then occasions when depression may be seen as functional or adaptive? Could depressive episodes be self-limiting and might the introduction of medication or the identification of someone as ill and in need of treatment serve to prolong or disrupt an adaptive process? If symptoms of depression were given a *positive* connotation—'time for reconstruction', 'time out', 'preparation for creativity', 'tooling up for new relationships or working conditions' and so on—would the individual who is depressed suffer from personal attributions of inadequacy and hopelessness?

We select this dramatic example to challenge the reader's assumptions about health and well-being. For a more radical view, the writings of Szasz (e.g., 1972) are usually guaranteed to provoke irritation and confusion. A further example is provided by data on sex differences in the recorded incidence of psychiatric disorder. This also presents an excellent demonstration of problems associated with defining a problem. Al-Issa (1980) and Miles (1981) show that while data do indicate a higher incidence of psychiatric disorder for females, it is not clear whether this reflects (a) greater opportunity for medical consultation, (b) social and medical stereotypes of what it is like to be a 'healthy' man or a 'healthy' woman, (c) shifts in diagnostic categories over time, (d) differential application of different diagnostic categories to men and women (e.g., psychosomatic disorders as opposed to personality disorders), or (e) elements in social structure or patterns of working and living which put women particularly at risk. Needless to say, not all authorities agree that there *are* true sex differences in the incidence of psychiatric disorder (Dohrenwend and Dohrenwend, 1974). Thus there is even controversy as to what data are required to convince us that a problem really is a problem.

Many of our authors raise similar objections to a straightforward definition of social problems. Society defines which problems call for priority allocation of resources, but politicians and other public leaders often assume a particular model of a problem and a particular set of causal mechanisms which are seen to contribute to it. Thus, for example, some may hold the view that children leave school with the 'wrong' qualifications or 'irrelevant' skills (the problem is *defined*). The cause of the 'problem' may then be selected from a number of favoured and plausible possibilities: decline in educational standards; the incompetence of teachers and working mothers; disintegration of family life; poor communication between school and industry and so on. The psychologist may then be called upon to examine the mechanisms underlying one of these alleged causal chains. Again, we are not denying that causal relationships *might* apply between correlated variables, but it is extremely difficult to ascribe appropriate weightings to different sources of influence.

What about the *facts*? Might these not be a secure and reliable starting point for our enquiry? Unfortunately, we discover that data are compiled for *administrative* reasons and not for purposes of psychological investigation. Thus the degree of provision of special resources – for example, for handicapped persons – will influence the statistics relating to incidence and prevalence of handicap (see the discussion of Clarke and Clarke in Chapter 15). In some cases, incidents are not recorded, either because of incentives to concealment or because of deficiencies in detection: thus true data concerning accidents and crime may be difficult to derive. Another confusing feature of basic information in certain fields of enquiry is that terms are used which appear to be 'psychological' in a technical sense, but which are vernacular or belong to a different set of technical terms. Thus *legal* notions like *intent* (which seem to be psychological) involve special legal definition and unobservable events which are not truly open to scientific enquiry. In the case of accident prevention, the notion of individual 'proneness' may owe more to popular belief that all events are *caused* than to solid empirical data on individual differences in liability to accidental behaviour.

Finally, we should note that Society appears to be very selective in identifying problems, even when two sets of phenomena bear a remarkable resemblance. Thus heroin addiction, alcoholism, smoking and legal drug abuse in the form of prescribed minor tranquillizers, all bear similar features. Individuals absorb substances which are known to have damaging physical consequences. Deaths attributable to smoking and alcohol outstrip those attributable to heroin by a factor of many hundreds. Moreover, legal prohibition on aspects of tobacco and alcohol sales could have dramatic consequences, much greater than any known psychological intervention. But it is heroin addiction which attracts public concern and public stigma. Very few general practitioners can have paused to consider the consequences for health of the annual level of prescriptions for popular drugs such as Librium and Valium.

Psychologists should beware lest they also become drawn into a social categorization of problems. There is no reason why the psychologist should not be concerned about *any* aspect of drug abuse.

To summarize our view, we do not deny that there are many problems in Society and we believe that the psychologist has a special and unique role to play in helping to relieve personal distress and in improving personal experience and the quality of life. However, problems are typically multiply-determined and complex, incorporating a mixture of facts, opinions and wishes. Frequently a problem encompasses not only the way things are, but the ways people think things ought to be or ought not to be. We are not suggesting that the careful analysis of a problem causes the problem to disappear; rather, upon analysis, many psychological problems can change character. Moreover, while we may wish that the condition of many of us will improve as a result of changes of social policy and a variety of interventions, we consider it unlikely that we shall ever reach a utopian state of universal happiness. Indeed, some theorists believe that tension and conflict can actually *assist* in the adjustment to new conditions.

Man's history so far has been associated with constant innovation, not only in terms of technical change, but in terms of social organization. The present expectations in terms of future opportunities for universal employment offer a powerful example. Such changes are likely to have an impact on the way people view each other and themselves and, as a result, will be associated with psychological stress during the process of readjustment. In such circumstances, presumably there will always be a place for psychological intervention or its equivalent. However, we cannot predict that psychology will necessarily continue to exist as an identifiable profession in the longer term, and the functions which psychologists serve may be taken over by others.

Having considered the difficulties involved in defining what is truly a social problem, we now turn to the courses open to psychologists in helping to alleviate problems. Earlier we noted that psychologists deal largely with *people* in the process of conducting their professional life as psychologists. If psychologists were committed to making *machines* work their professional life would be relatively straightforward. Once you understand how the machine works and how it has gone wrong, you should be able to identify a remedy and apply it. However, in dealing with people, rather special considerations apply and these impose severe constraints upon the unlimited practice of professional skill and the application of knowledge.

PROBLEMS OF ETHICS AND CONFIDENTIALITY

The difficulty with moral problems is that they never cease to be problems. Sartre's injunction that we are 'condemned to be free' reminds us that we will always be faced with moral choices and moral decisions. In such cases our actions are likely to affect the lives of others and to be in accordance with one set of socially accepted norms yet in conflict with another set. Such conflict is the very essence of moral dilemmas. Even those of us who belong to organized religious groups, where moral guidelines tend to be set out in more explicit form than Sartre thought possible, are accustomed to the conflicts which moral decisions can impose in particular situations.

The psychologist's professional life is bound up with the lives of others and the psychologist's practice of expertise directly influences the actions and experiences of clients. Yet there is nothing particular or special about *psychological* knowledge or skill *per se* which makes the psychologist an expert in moral affairs, nor is there any rulebook which prescribes what actions should be taken in particular circumstances. Thus there will always be doubt about what action is appropriate or acceptable. A moral decision usually involves the weighing up of relevant facts; but such facts are considered in the light of the individual's set of values or superordinate moral principles. Is there a set of superordinate principles to which psychologists can subscribe? The *Ethical Principles for Research with Human Subjects*, published by The British Psychological Society (see Chapman and Gale, 1982), begin with the following assertion:

> Psychologists are committed to increasing the understanding that people have of their own and others' behaviour in the belief that this understanding ameliorates the human condition and enhances human dignity. These ethical values must characterize not only applications of psychological knowledge, but also the means of obtaining knowledge. (p. 511).

These are bold words, as befits a declaration of this nature but, without wanting to sound harsh to our colleagues, we must confess to some difficulty in deriving from these Principles any clear understanding or definitions of key words such as 'understanding', 'ameliorates', 'the human condition', or 'human dignity'. The meaning of such crucial terms is partially dependent upon the contemporary *Zeitgeist* and processes of social definition.

Let us take a practical example. Who would have imagined twenty years ago that an Act of Parliament would be passed in Britain which gave the parents of educationally retarded children the right to have full access to the child's educational and psychological records, to confer with teachers and educational psychologists about the appropriate means of educating their child, or to call in an independent informed person to provide advice and guidance? Yet these are clear implications of the 1981 Education Act which arose from recommendations of the Warnock Report (Department of Education and Science, 1978). The notion of 'human dignity' has surely been redefined and extended, as it applies to the handicapped? In contrast, students at British universities may well ask why they typically have *no* access to assessment grades, confidential reports or other materials kept in their personal files. The vulnerability of educationally retarded persons seems for once to have operated to their advantage in contrast to the educationally privileged.

Such examples serve to demonstrate that the psychologist works within a context which is defined by the prevailing culture; a culture which is constantly changing. The value system of the culture influences the ways in which we think about and interact with others, whether in a personal or professional capacity. It influences the theories we develop, the types of investigation we conduct and the sorts of data we derive from the world. In professional practice, the value system influences our view of what is desirable or undesirable behaviour. Thus a minimal condition of competence for the professional psychologist is a demonstrable awareness of social influences and their impact on individual behaviour. Our understanding of the development of moral judgement itself is far from complete and authorities in the field (e.g., Wright, 1971) have demonstrated quite clearly that simple everyday notions like 'conscience', 'fear of transgression' and 'guilt' become complex and elusive when studied in the laboratory. Thus the *psychological* aspects of moral debate can be as complicated and difficult to resolve as are issues of judgement.

We may have given the impression that the psychologist is somehow a prisoner to inexorable forces over which the individual has virtually no control. But some have argued that psychology *contributes* to public ways of thinking about human beings and that society at large borrows or is influenced by the models of the person developed within psychology. Thus psychology itself makes an active contribution to the *Zeitgeist* (Shotter, 1975).

As psychological knowledge becomes progressively well-founded and psychological interventions are shown to be influential in creating change, there will be debates concerning the propriety of applying psychological techniques, just as there are debates concerning the use of knowledge derived from medicine, engineering and physics. Thus the use of intelligence tests and even the very dissemination of information concerning test results, has created as much public debate as have issues relating to spare-part surgery, pollution and nuclear power.

At a more immediate level, the interface between psychologist and client has altered, particularly in the clinical field, as the psychologist has changed role from *technician* providing test data, to *expert* providing therapy and advice on intervention strategies. Such a shift in role implies a shift in personal responsibility. What has changed is the nature and extent of the information revealed to the psychologist and the willingness of others to heed the psychologist's advice and take action upon it. Such access to information and influence implies status and power. In our culture it is understood that power, in its turn, implies responsibility and accountability.

The Notion of Informed Consent

In many contexts, the psychologist seeks the permission of others to participate in an experimental or therapeutic procedure. It is the giving of such
permission, under certain conditions, which is called 'informed consent'. The
notion of informed consent implies *knowledge*, *competence* and *voluntary
choice*. We need to consider this notion in some detail because its ramifications cut across all the key topics discussed in this book. Say you want to
ask Person X to serve as a subject in your experiment, or you advise Person
X to take part in a programme of treatment, to what extent can you convey
knowledge of what is entailed? You can inform X about procedures, but you
can hardly inform X of what it will be like to *experience* the procedures
involved. Indeed, the relationship with you is such and the circumstances of
the encounter so special, that X is unlikely to have had equivalent or similar
experiences from which to extrapolate in the process of making a decision.
Thus a decision to participate might depend more on your relationship with
X and status differences between you than on direct knowledge of what is
to happen to X. The issue is, can one know in advance what it is like to
have a novel experience? Nor is there a guarantee that you, as a psychologist,
have undergone the experience *yourself*, rather than administer the procedures which lead to the experience for others. It is suggested by some authorities, that the psychologist's own experience of a problem conveys to the
client a sense of authenticity and trust. That is one of the reasons why in
Britain experience as a working teacher is seen as a pre-condition to being
able to give advice on problems relating to teaching. Such views have not
gone unchallenged (see, for example, the Summerfield Report, Department
of Education and Science, 1968).

The uncertainties concerning what *knowledge* means have led psychologists
to recommend that the subject or client should always be free to withdraw
consent under any condition which changes the person's conception of what
is involved in the procedure. Thus Carr (in Chapter 9) gives the example of
a housewife who finds that her family resents changes which have come about
as a result of her undergoing therapy. In such circumstances, the psychologist
might be aware that the client's behaviour is actually sustained by complex
processes of reinforcement within the family context, that is that the family,
in a sense, 'needs' the wife's disorder. The processes involved may be more
compatible with the family's wishes than the consequences of 'successful'
treatment as defined by the *therapist*, or as defined by the therapist in
consultation with the client at the outset, and at a time when those consequences were not fully appreciated. Similarly, we should expect that subjects
taking part in experiments would also feel free to withdraw consent.
However, our discussion of *voluntariness* below, indicates that free withdrawal may not always seem possible.

How does the psychologist decide *how much* to reveal? In the case of experiments there is sufficient evidence available to support the claim that subjects behave differently when they know what hypotheses are under investigation (Silverman, 1977). Thus the transmission of complete information can be incompatible with the very aims of the experiment. In the case of psychological treatments or interventions, is the psychologist obliged to offer the client an account of controlled trials, contradictory findings and degrees of statistical significance? Again, we have sufficient evidence to support the claim that *faith* in the change agent is itself part of the therapeutic process (Garfield and Bergin, 1978). In such circumstances, revelations concerning the limitations of the therapist's supposed omniscience can be seen to run counter to the very purposes of the procedure.

There can be no straightforward prescription for entering values into some cost/benefit equation which the psychologist needs to compute on each individual occasion and in differing circumstances, and the reader will note that in our discussion we tend to raise questions rather than produce answers. The British Psychological Society recommends that on occasions of personal doubt concerning the ethical virtue of proposed courses of action, the psychologist should confer with colleagues, with the aim at least of clarifying issues and maximizing the probability of viewing the problem from all possible angles (see Chapman and Gale, 1982).

Our discussion of problems associated with the concept of *knowledge* serves to undermine the notion of informed consent, illustrating yet again the complexities of issues involving moral choice in professional practice.

The notion of *competence* implies the ability to make use of knowledge in coming to a decision. However, the persons with whom psychologists have professional contact include young children, the elderly, the infirm, the handicapped and those in deep distress. In such cases it is unlikely that detailed discussion of procedures, experimental designs or levels of statistical significance will have any meaning for the person concerned. Paradoxically, if such persons *were* seen as fully competent to make choices, they might well not have come into contact with the psychologist in the first place. Typically, decisions about actions in relation to such persons are made *by others*. Such transfer of personal responsibility presupposes several assumptions about the awareness and/or level of understanding of the individuals involved and their capacity to share in the range of human emotions and feelings which the 'normal' population enjoys. Quite often psychologists have discovered that they have been drawn, perhaps unwittingly, into sharing such assumptions. Both Clarke and Clarke (in Chapter 15) and Slater (in Chapter 16) show how the treatment of the educationally retarded and the elderly, within institutionalized settings, has in the past supported the notion of *incompetence* rather than competence on the part of residents. The very vulnerability of many client groups imposes special responsibilities upon the practitioner.

We do not need to engage in complex philosophical discussion of the concept of 'free will' to see that the notion of voluntary consent is difficult to specify in certain circumstances. Children, persons in custodial care, and those considered by the authorities to be a potential danger to themselves or others are hardly in a position to give free consent to psychological intervention. Similarly, a person in extreme emotional distress can hardly engage in dispassionate consideration of alternative courses of action. In such cases the psychologist is in the position of one who is charged with knowing what is 'good' for others. A guiding principle may well be the reduction of distress. This might even justify short-term aversive treatment for longer-term positive benefits. The individual who engages in destructive behaviour or self-mutilation can become involved in a progressive cycle of isolation, rejection and punishment. The breaking of this cycle can lead to social acceptance and the positive regard of others. Thus the means (aversive treatment) may be seen to justify the ends (social acceptance and approval).

But the change agent must always consider the questions 'change *for* what or *to* what?'. Notions of socially acceptable behaviour are socially defined. Some of the critics of behavioural methods suggest that psychologists have become unthinking agents of institutionalizing authority. One answer to such a charge is that behavioural treatments can be focused on creating a sense of autonomy and self-control for the individual, thereby releasing the client from unwanted external controlling conditions. Such autonomy of action would hardly be compatible with institutionalized behaviours.

In the case of empirical research, subjects might find themselves in a state of forced compliance. Residents in an institution are rarely called to a consultative meeting to seek their permission to participate in a research project. They might be observed or be subjected to novel arrangements, without any formal consent being sought or given. What is it, we may ask, that distinguishes persons living in their own homes from persons living in a hospital? Current conventions would not allow us to enter people's homes without their consent nor to install microphones in their living-rooms without extended discussion.

Undergraduate students might express surprise at the view that psychology departments in higher education can have *some* features in common with the characteristics of institutions described by Goffman (1961). But we may well ask how free the student is to refuse to participate in experiments or to withdraw if the procedures prove to be unacceptable? Just as the elderly resident might wish to please the hospital staff, so may the student wish to please (or not displease) the tutor. The restraints on voluntary actions and decisions can come from *within* the person as well as from *external* sources.

The individual's *perception* of the consequences of non-compliance may be a powerful force in securing agreement to participate.

Thus the notions of *knowledge*, *competence* and *voluntariness* involve some subtlety of interpretation if they are to be applied in particular circumstances to the notion of informed consent.

Finally, we should note that some psychological procedures, by their nature, do not involve consent in any meaning of the term. Methods involving observation in public places or in working situations can involve deriving 'data' from many persons without their knowledge. It would be difficult to assert that the 'rules' of sitting on a park bench or drinking in a public house incorporate the possibility of hidden psychologists or concealed recording equipment. Some forms of observation actually involve *joining* a particular group and becoming a pseudo-member. For example, Hewstone and Giles point out (in Chapter 13) that our understanding of intergroup conflict is always limited by access to data and constraints upon manipulations. Say, as a means of overcoming such difficulties, you join an extreme racist political group in order to observe its behaviour. Note that the following moral consequences ensue: (a) you confirm the status of the group by adding to its membership; (b) you deceive its members as to your purposes for joining; (c) you could be seen to be an accessory to extreme actions taken by the group – for example, a premeditated attack on an ethnic minority; and, (d) you could place yourself, your close relatives or your workmates at jeopardy if your deceit is discovered and your deception provokes anger and retribution. It may seem strange that a psychologist should express concern at the deception of persons whose views many would condemn; but there is no immediate logical or moral link between the act of disagreement and the decision to deceive.

Confidentiality

Psychologists, by virtue of their various roles as counsellors, therapists, advisers, teachers and researchers are in receipt of personal and private information. Sometimes the client may not even realize that information is being revealed. Even when the individual completes psychological tests, we cannot assume that the purpose or content of the test are understood or that the individual will always appreciate the use to which the information will be put. In many contexts, when the individual reveals personal information, it is on the assumption that it is confidential and will not be revealed to others without express consent. The psychologist will then need to seek that consent before revealing the information, say to another family member or another professional or to an employer.

But there are contexts where the information does not belong to the psychologist or to the client. The psychologist is not free to conceal from the authorities (the police, prison staff or the courts) information given by a prisoner and, in Britain, the notes made in a patient's records are the property of the Health Service. There may well be some occasions when psychologists fail to record information for fear that it may be abused. Thus the psychologist has to ask, '*who* is my client?'. The answer can offer a conflict, given the psychologist's accustomed role as a helper of individuals. It is customary when providing consultancy advice to management to insist that the content revealed by interviews with employees will not be transmitted to employers. Similarly, in research, data from individuals should always appear in an anonymous form or as aggregated among group data. However, when working for the prison service in Britain, the psychologist has no right to conceal information, however derived.

In the case of minors or persons unable to give informed consent, the psychologist will need to consider the *consequences* of revelation. For example, it is not necessarily the case that revelation of a child's test score to parents will have positive effects; for it could have an adverse influence on the parents' view of the child and the child's sense of self-esteem.

We indicated earlier that information implies power and that power implies responsibility. Personal information and its potential abuse provide salient illustrations of this general principle.

CONTROL GROUPS AND THEIR CONSEQUENCES

No treatment should be used with an individual without adequate demonstration of its efficacy. However, to demonstrate efficacy, controlled trials are essential. To conduct controlled trials (a) some patients must receive treatment whose efficacy, by definition, is not yet demonstrated; (b) some patients must have treatment withheld; (c) some patients must be led to *believe* they are receiving treatment when in fact they are not; and, (d) individuals must be allocated, independent of their wishes, to randomized and/or matched groups. Thus potentially, to conduct proper trials, one might cause harm by delay, by deception or by use of a substance which proves to be ineffective or even damaging. In a sense individuals are being used and deceived for what the therapist or interventionist considers to be a higher goal, namely the potential benefits to *others*. The therapist cannot assume that such altruistic ideals are shared by the population under study. Such considerations have made some therapists reject the notion of controlled trials, but then they also become caught on the horns of a dilemma and are behaving illogically, for they still lack justification for use of the treatment in the first place. The solution of one moral dilemma typically creates a further dilemma.

When a patient gives consent to participate in such trials, what exactly is understood and can such understanding actually work against the purpose of the trial and the treatment? If you ask yourself 'am I on the real drug or the placebo?', what influence will your concerns have upon outcome? And it is not only the patients, but colleagues also, who need to be deceived, or at least misled, if the trials are to be conducted properly. Silverstone and Turner (1974) in reviewing a set of drug trials show that claimed per cent efficacy drops dramatically, from uncontrolled trials, to control trials, to double-blind controlled trials, ranging from some 70% through 50% to 30%. Not only the client, but the professional dealing with the client, is affected by processes involving faith, belief and placebo.

MORAL VALUES AND PSYCHOLOGICAL INTERVENTIONS

The psychologist is a human being whose actions are guided by personal beliefs. Such beliefs owe their origin to developmental experience, religious and political convictions, the rational analysis of moral problems and relations with intimates and working colleagues. It would be naïve to assume that such a value system, with all its consistencies and inconsistencies, would not influence professional practice or the nature of interaction with clients. The client's value system might actually conflict with those of the psychologist and it may prove necessary to refer the individual to someone else. Or the moral and personal beliefs of the client might make certain actions out of the question; for example, particular treatments in sex therapy might not be acceptable to a couple. Such situations are concerned with *explicit* differences of viewpoint. But there is always the danger of values being transmitted in an *implicit* mode; that is why psychologists and therapists are trained to be accepting and non-evaluative of the views and experiences of clients or subjects in experimental investigations or respondents in interviews or surveys. We should not forget that the other person's perception of us may include assumptions about our beliefs and reactions, which we ourselves may be unaware of or even deny. Each of us can be a stimulus which triggers expectations and stereotypes in others.

There is also a danger that psychologists might themselves become caught up in value systems and their consequences, without even appreciating the fact. We have already referred to the dangers of confirming institutional practices, which are typically at odds with notions of individual autonomy and independence. But clients often identify their problem as the one which they would like to *believe* it to be, rather than the *real* problem as perceived by an outsider. Thus a therapist might become drawn into the scapegoating of an individual family member or of a social group, or a researcher become focused upon a particular population (drug addicts or football 'hooligans'), at the expense of a detailed analysis of the whole context. For example, as we indicated earlier, smoking and alcoholism present enormous problems in terms of human pain and suffering, yet provoke much less public outrage than other forms of minor drug abuse. In many contexts, psychologists, like other scientists, need to ask themselves whether it is their role to sustain the *status quo* or to challenge and criticize the social order or to make positive attempts to redirect public concern. In the final analysis, this must be a personal decision, for the displacement of one state of affairs will presumably lead to *another* state of affairs to which *someone* will find personal objection. The present focus on health education and a support for anti-smoking campaigns will not necessarily lead to a *totally* positive outcome. Currently we are witnessing the progressive stigmatization of the smoker. Formerly, heroes and public figures smoked on stage and screen, and the male smoker was seen as masculine and socially desirable. Now smokers are not to be associated in advertisements with positive attributes; they must sit in special compartments in public transport and in special seats in public places. In public health advertisements, smokers are projected as weak, antisocial and undesirable. Following Goffman's notions of stigma, individual personality characteristics and interpersonal differences among smokers have disappeared and all that is left are the appropriate criteria and discriminative stimuli for the imposition of an apartheid.

ARE PSYCHOLOGICAL INTERVENTIONS SUCCESSFUL?

The acid test for any professional is whether they are seen to be competent and successful by the client. In the case of psychology, clients are not only individuals or groups, but public agencies. Thus there is both a responsibility and a pressure to evaluate the efficacy of particular intervention strategies and, in the extreme case, the very future existence of psychology as an applied discipline can be seen to depend on evidence that psychology works. Psychologists are in an unusual profession: they have been trained in experimental design, the application of statistical techniques and the interpretation of data. Their skills may be applied not only to the evaluation of *psychological* interventions, but to interventions of a variety of types, the principal criterion of relevance being whether the intervention is designed to change the beliefs, attitudes or behaviours of human beings. Each of our authors has provided examples of interventions in the field under discussion, the evidence in favour of particular interventions, and the practical and methodological difficulties which apply in setting up research or in evaluating data derived from practice.

We conclude this chapter with a checklist, which will enable you to evaluate any individual study or review of studies, whether they be applied to individuals or to groups. The intention is that you may use our checklist as a tool kit, not only for gauging the efficacy of interventions described in *Psychology and Social Problems*, but to assist in the comprehension and interpretation of evaluation studies elsewhere, in books and scientific journals. Our checklist is subdivided into seven headings; typically, however, it is difficult to separate the items given in the case of any individual study, for they tend to be interrelated. The items are not explained, for to do that would require a monograph: we would recommend that you analyse the items with your tutors and fellow students and that you seek illustrations from within the following chapters.

A CHECKLIST FOR EVALUATING PSYCHOLOGICAL OUTCOME STUDIES

Defining the Problem

Who *defined* or *identified* the problem in the first instance, the client or the change agent?

What *route* was followed by the client to gain access to the change agent?

How did the client *select* him/herself, or how was the sample selected, and could the mode of selection make the sample exceptional or special?

Were there similar potential clients who did *not* request an intervention? Why? What *distinguishes* the two groups and might it be important?

What sorts of *bias* may have operated on the sample and might such biases have a bearing on the interpretation of the outcome?

What *model* of the person or of organizations was favoured by the change agent (for example, behavioural, medical, biological, moral, psychoanalytic, trait, personal construct, rational/economic, and so on)?

Did the change agent have a formal *taxonomy* of the problem domain?

Was the intervention under consideration a *primary* factor or a *secondary* factor or a *consequence* of other purposes or intervention targets?

Were notions of 'blame' and/or 'responsibility' incorporated into the client's conception of the problem and did these serve to obfuscate the design of the intervention or the evaluation of outcome?

Did the change agent attempt to *change* the conception of the problem as perceived by the client?

Selecting the Intervention

Did the investigator or change agent have a *theoretical* orientation?

Was the intervention based on 'rule of thumb' principles or derived directly from theoretical principles?

Had *other* forms of intervention been attempted beforehand and were they successful or unsuccessful?

What characteristics did the intervention share *in common* with other intervention strategies?

Were *alternative* strategies for the intervention considered but rejected? If so, on what grounds?

Were specific *objectives* defined in advance of the intervention?
Were the *criteria* for estimating change specified in advance?
What were the client's *expectations* of outcome?
Were some client problems considered unsuited to the particular intervention employed and/or were some clients excluded on that ground?

Design Features

Was the intervention carried out within the *context* or natural setting (for example, the home, the classroom, the work situation or an accident black spot) where the problem arose, or in a simulation or special setting (for example, the laboratory, a simulator, the surgery or the consulting room)?

Were control groups incorporated into the design to examine: (i) the effects of *different* interventions; (ii) effects of *level* of intervention (within treatments); (iii) the *absence* of intervention (no treatment); (iv) pretence of intervention (*attention/placebo*); (v) the effects upon different *client* groups; and, (vi) effects of different change agents?

Was *sample size* sufficient (in group designs or within-group designs) to satisfy the requirements of sampling theory?

Were there independent estimates or special groups within the design, to enable measurement of '*spontaneous*' recovery or change, that is in the absence of any formal intervention?

Were *randomized* designs employed and/or what variables were employed for matching purposes?

Were there controls to estimate the effects of *any* intervention (i.e., the 'Hawthorne' effect)?

Was the 'untreated' group *truly* untreated?

In *multiple* group designs, were different change agents assigned to different groups and how?

When more than one change agent was involved, were all *trained* to an equal degree of competence?

Was there a control for *withdrawal* of intervention?

Were '*contracts*' undertaken between the change agent and the client and on what grounds and on what terms?

What was the *duration* of the intervention?

Was time of *contact* controlled for?

Can the intervention be broken down into its *constituent* parts or processes?

Can different types of intervention be seen to have *additive* or multiplicative effects? (Note that additive effects can lead to improvement, deterioration or no absolute aggregate effect.)

Was the evaluation study carried out by the change agents themselves or by an *independent* investigator?

In longitudinal studies, was the same research team employed over time, and were the *instruments* used equally reliable and valid as the sample changed over time?

What was the duration of *follow-up*?

Procedures Employed and Measurements Taken

Were the instruments used to measure baseline variables and change variables *reliable* and adequately *validated*?

Where *specially* devised instruments were used, were precautions taken to estimate their reliability?

What *baseline* measures were obtained, when and in what domains (e.g., behavioural, objective/subjective, interview, questionnaire, productivity measures, client opinion, expert opinion, social relationships, contact with social agencies, physiology, simulations and so on)?

Were the techniques employed *specified* in detail and in full?

What actually *happened* during the change process or intervention?

How did the *change agent* behave during the intervention process?

How did the *client* react during the intervention process?

Were *changes* introduced into the intervention procedures and/or the intervention objectives, *during* the course of the intervention? On what grounds?

Were *criteria* of outcome altered during the intervention process? On what grounds?

Who implemented the change? Is there any guarantee that the procedures were followed as specified?

Where clients were expected to carry out part of the intervention procedures for *themselves*, is there a guarantee that they complied with the requirements specified for them by the change agent?

Was there evidence that the clients or the organization involved *resisted* the attempts to implement the changes specified by the change agent?

How and why were *decisions* made to *terminate* the intervention?

When the 'client' was *more than one individual* or group, how far did the measures of outcome extend and to what variables did they apply?

Did the investigator or change agent include measures for possible *negative* effects as well as positive effects?

What *assessment* methods were used to estimate *change*? Were they the same methods as employed in the baseline assessment?

Did baseline or follow-up samples include *all* appropriate categories of data?

Results of the Investigation

Did changes occur in the *target* behaviours?

Did changes occur also in *other* behaviours?

Were proper distinctions drawn between measures of correlation (a *ranking* method) and measures of absolute change (*levels*) over time? (The inferences allowed are somewhat different.)

Were the variables under study the *only* variables to be altered during the period under investigation?

Was attention paid to *correlated* variables, which may have had as much or more influence as the variables under study?

Was there any *drop out* during the intervention and why? For example, did *particular* clients or groups drop out and what implications might this have for the interpretation of outcome?

What was the *criterion* of success accepted by the *change agent*?

What was the *criterion* of success accepted by the *client*?

Did the change agent *and* the client *agree* on the degree of estimated success or failure of the intervention?

Where *multiple* criteria of outcome were employed, did they intercorrelate?

Where *clients* were asked for their *opinion* of the degree of success of the intervention, were their views as expressed, stable and free of bias and error?

Inferences and Conclusions to be Drawn from the Study

Were the characteristics of the sample well-specified in terms of *salient* variables, thereby enabling a direct comparison with other studies?

Were the *classifications* and *procedures* employed sufficiently well-specified to allow for direct comparison with other cases or studies?

Where data were obtained for *non-research* purposes, were they subject to bias, selectivity, distortion, deficiency or other *contaminating* influence?

Where variables have been shown to be *correlated*, were careful attempts made by the investigator to disentangle possible *alternative* causal relationships, before inferences were drawn about particular causal chains or mechanisms?

Was the client under the influence of *other* factors over which the change agent had no control?

Did the data enable a partitioning of *specific* variables and their selective influence on outcome?

Was it possible to partial out differential effects for different *client* characteristics?

Were the *outcome criteria* employed sufficiently standardized to enable comparison between the study in question and other studies?

Where extreme groups were employed, were precautions taken to estimate possible *regression to the mean* effects?

Since bias is potentially present in all studies, did the person reporting an individual study or data from several studies show clear evidence of *systematic* consideration of *alternative* interpretations of the data?

Implications for Future Practice

Where statistically significant findings have been shown to apply to *group* data, can clear implications be drawn for application to the *individual* client?

What are the implications in practical and theoretical terms if one problem disappeared as a result of intervention, only to be *replaced* by another problem?

Can one set up estimates of the *costs* and *benefits* (in terms of time, individual effort and money) associated with particular interventions or levels of intervention and their outcomes (in terms of individuals, groups and savings)?

What are the implications for *future* intervention strategies?

Could *non-psychological* intervention (e.g., welfare, housing or government restrictions on advertising of harmful substances) have achieved equivalent or even greater effects upon the target variables?

Is there *exchange* of information and *integration* of effort between the various agencies involved with the client or population in question?

CONCLUSION

We began this chapter with the claim that Applied Psychology may be viewed as a unitary discipline containing a number of invariant features which cut across all exemplars of applied psychological practice. This is not a standard view and to some degree we profess to have a revolutionary standpoint. For example, if our view were generally acceptable than applied psychologists would all be trained in similar ways and would be taught to utilize similar methods and approaches. We hope that the various examples given in this book illustrate our claim that there is more in common among the various applications of psychology than surface differences might lead us to believe.

Howarth (1980) adopts a similar analysis to our own. He conceives of human beings as 'problem-solvers'. Problem-solving involves three elements: (i) an agreed purpose to be achieved; (ii) well-understood resources to be brought to bear in solving the problem; and, (iii) an effective strategy for making the best use of the resources available. In considering the implications of this model for the application of psychology, he identifies eight rules for practice:

(i)   Help individual clients to clarify their purposes. Try to understand how they see their own problems and what they would regard as solutions.

(ii)   Discover the nature of the psychological and other resources available to individual clients.

(iii)   Seek to understand a client's habitual strategies and life-style.

(iv)   In investigating these things, do not work in conceptual or social isolation. Draw on as many sources of information as possible, using a wide range of mechanist and humanist techniques in a pragmatic fashion.

(v)   Bear in mind the principle of generalization and study the problem in 'real life' rather than in a special clinic or laboratory.

(vi)   Formulate with the client possible modifications of his/her strategic behaviour. This depends on agreeing with him/her the appropriate level of analysis at which strategic modification can be achieved.

(vii)   Help the client to practise these modifications in the situation in which the problem exists and as extensively (in time) as possible. Almost always, this will involve working with and through non-professional help.

(viii)   Finally, the effects of the intervention should be evaluated with as much statistical scepticism as possible. But the ultimate criterion used in the statistics must be that the client and his/her associates are satisfied with the solution, provided it does not harm other people. In other words, the solution must meet culturally acceptable standards.

It will be apparent that, in its essential features, Howarth's analysis is similar to ours. The reader will have observed that there are, however, differences of emphasis in our approach and that each of Howarth's 'rules' requires a degree of clarification and extension before application is possible. Nevertheless, such unity of viewpoint is encouraging and serves to justify the general approach which we and our authors have adopted in *Psychology and Problems: An Introduction to Applied Psychology*.

ANNOTATED READINGS

Bulmer, M. (1982). *Social Research Ethics: An Examination of the Merits of Covert Participant Observation*. London: Macmillan Press.

Contributors to this volume tackle questions about the right and proper behaviour for the social scientist, what is permitted in the name of 'social science', and the primary responsibility and principles governing the behaviour of the researcher in relation to the people being studied. In the light of their experience as researchers, the contributors evaluate the researcher's responsibilities for the well-being of subjects and for obtaining their informed consent to research. In a lively debate, focused primarily on covert participation, much light is thrown on general ethical problems.

Chapman, A. J. and Gale, A. (1982). *Psychology and People: A Tutorial Text*. London: The British Psychological Society and Macmillan Press.

This book meets the needs of a broad spectrum of newcomers to Psychology –

school pupils, first-year degree students, and students preparing for professional examinations. The coverage is biased towards topics and issues which hold direct and immediate significance within everyday life and personal experience. Established authorities treat the life span from biological underpinnings to ageing, motivation and intellect, social influences including interviewing, bargaining and mass communications, and finally special problems and their treatments, including psychopathology, institutions and counselling. Each of 24 chapters is followed by a set of examination questions, annotated readings and practical exercises. The final pages of the book present ethical principles for research with human subjects.

Chapman, A. J. and Jones, D. M. (1980). *Models of Man*. Leicester: The British Psychological Society. Hillsdale, New Jersey: Erlbaum.

Some of the most eminent British psychologists debate fundamental conceptual questions and, in so doing, cast light on the research strategies and assumptions which they use in their work. The contributions demonstrate how conceptual models employed by psychologists have influenced the way people in general, not just psychologists, think and act. Many contributors show how their particular models illuminate reality as we know it or believe it to be; others show how models allow parallels and relationships between systems to be drawn up; still others show that models can be useful intellectual tools when starting to think about a problem but could become misleading if applied too rigidly to later conceptual and empirical enquiries. Points of view, agreement and discord are highlighted in edited discussions following each of the first 20 chapters; and, in the second section of the book, there follow a further 13 critical essays.

Eiser, J. R. (1982). *Social Psychology and Behavioral Medicine*. Chichester: Wiley.

Conceptual critiques, reviews, and empirical studies identify social psychological approaches to the development of behavioral medicine. Hence the book demonstrates many of the ways in which social psychology is relevant to problems of health and illness and the wide range of opportunities for research. Twenty-two chapters are divided into 5 sections: the development of behavioral medicine; antecedents of illness and injury; smoking, alcoholism, and addiction; communication and influence; reactions to illness, treatment, ageing and bereavement. Specific topics in common with *Psychology and Social Problems* include accidents, smoking, alcoholism, drug-dependence, and ageing.

Feldman, P. and Orford, J. (1980). *Psychological Problems: The Social Context*. Chichester: Wiley.

This book presents some aspects of the development of social psychology in dealing with psychological problems. It is shown that social variables play a major part in the occurrence of problems, in their effective management, and in their prevention. The first Part of the book focuses on basic theory and research findings in social psychology, with current or future implications for the solution of psychological problems. The second Part concentrates on the practical applications of social and community psychology in changing either the behaviour of individuals or the environment in which they live.

Warr, P. B. (1978). *Psychology at Work*. Second Edition. Harmondsworth: Penguin.

Sixteen specially prepared chapters follow a brief but excellent introduction by the

Editor. He shows that the barriers between 'pure' and 'applied' psychology may be bridged to the benefit of both, and he shows how applied psychologists are striving to develop theory and taking practical steps to improve health and efficiency at work. He argues that 'applied psychology' differs from 'pure psychology' in terms of features such as the population studied, the research setting, and the intended outcomes of the work. The problems for the applied researcher tend to emanate from real-life situations: they are external to psychology. Following Sir Frederic Bartlett, Warr maintains that the development of psychology rests upon involvement in day-to-day problems: theory has to be built upon practical reality.

REFERENCES

Al-Issa, I. (1980). *The Psychopathology of Women*. Englewood Cliffs, NJ: Prentice Hall.

Chapman, A. J. and Gale, A. (1982). *Psychology and People: A Tutorial Text*. London: The British Psychological Society and Macmillan Press.

Department of Education and Science (1968). Psychologists in Education Services. (The Summerfield Report). London: Her Majesty's Stationery Office.

Department of Education and Science (1978). Report of the Committee of Enquiry into the Education of Handicapped Children and Young People. (The Warnock Report). London: Her Majesty's Stationery Office.

Dohrenwend, B. P. and Dohrenwend, B. S. (1974). Social and cultural influences on psychopathology. *Annual Review of Psychology*, **25**, 417–452.

Garfield, S. L. and Bergin, A. E. (1978) (Eds.). *Handbook of Psychotherapy and Behavior Change*. (Second Edition). New York: Wiley.

Goffman, E. (1961). *Asylums: Essays on the Social Situation of Mental Patients and Other Inmates*. New York: Doubleday.

Howarth, C. I. (1980). The structure of effective psychology: Man as problem-solver. In: A. J. Chapman and D. M. Jones (Eds.). *Models of Man*. Leicester: The British Psychological Society. Hillsdale, NJ: Erlbaum.

Miles, A. (1981). *The Mentally Ill in Contemporary Society: A Sociological Introduction*. Oxford: Martin Robertson.

Shotter, J. (1975). *Images of Man in Psychological Research*. London: Methuen.

Silverman, I. (1977). *The Human Subject in the Psychology Laboratory*. New York: Pergamon.

Silverstone, T. and Turner, P. (1974). *Drug Treatment in Psychiatry*. London: Routledge and Kegan Paul.

Szasz, T. S. (1972). *The Myth of Mental Illness*. St. Albans: Paladin.

Wright, D. S. (1971). *The Psychology of Moral Behaviour*. Harmondsworth: Penguin.

Psychology and Social Problems
Edited by A. Gale and A. J. Chapman
© 1984 John Wiley & Sons Ltd.

CHAPTER 2

PROBLEMS OF CHILDHOOD

Martin Herbert

I.–THE EXTENT OF THE PROBLEM

The generic term 'childhood problems' refers to a large and heterogeneous collection of disorders ranging from depression, anxiety, inhibition and shyness to non-compliance, destructiveness, stealing and aggression. All sorts of terms (or euphemisms) have been used to refer to psychological disorders in the growing child. There is the popular and ubiquitous expression 'maladjusted child' and other designations such as 'nervous', 'highly strung', 'emotionally disturbed', 'difficult', to mention but a few. In essence, these problems represent exaggerations, deficits or disabling combinations of feelings, attitudes and behaviours common to all children.

There is a remarkable consensus among clinical and statistical studies for a meaningful distinction between those disorders which primarily lead to emotional disturbance or distress for children themselves (e.g., anxiety, shyness, depression, feelings of inferiority and timidity) and those which involve mainly the kinds of antisocial behaviour (e.g., destructiveness, aggression, lying, stealing and disobedience) which disrupt the well-being of others, notably those in frequent contact with the child (Achenbach, 1974). The former category, the so-called 'emotional disorders', are manifested by about 2½% of pre-adolescent children; their prevalence increases somewhat by adolescence. Boys and girls are about equally prone to emotional problems.

For most children these kinds of problem manifest themselves briefly at certain periods and then become minimal or disappear completely (MacFarlane, Allen and Honzik, 1954). We know as a result of longitudinal studies that for the most part, children who suffer from emotional disorders become reasonably well adjusted adults; they are almost as likely to grow up 'normal' as children drawn at random from the general population. In a sense these difficulties are the emotional equivalent of 'growing pains'. But that is not to deny that they sometimes persist and reach levels of intensity which cause all-round suffering.

There is another category of difficulties which declines at a rather later stage, and at a slower rate than most others; for example, over-activity, destructiveness and tempers. In fact, one-third of boys still have temper explosions at thirteen. In their *severe* forms these and other types of aggressive, antisocial behaviours constitute a constellation of problems referred to as 'conduct disorders'. They involve physical and verbal aggressiveness, disruptiveness, irresponsibility, non-compliance and poor personal relationships; delinquent activities, early drug and alcohol use and substance abuse may also feature as part of the syndrome. This behaviour pattern is notable for the fundamental inability or unwillingness on the part of the youth to adhere to the rules and codes of conduct prescribed by society at its various levels: family, school, and indeed the community at large.

It is difficult to obtain reliable estimates of the prevalence of conduct disorders. Of all the childhood problems, these ones, giving rise as they do to social disapproval because of their antisocial qualities, involve social judgments of a relative kind, and subjective personal definitions. We do know that approximately one-third of the referrals made by parents and teachers to clinics are diagnosed as conduct problems. There are at least three times as many males as females manifesting conduct disorders, although the incidence in girls is on the increase.

Antisocial activities tend to disrupt and hinder the acquisition of crucial adaptive skills. Their presence in childhood is predictive of problems of adjustment in later adolescence and adulthood. The empirical results of several investigations suggest that children with more extreme forms do not 'outgrow' their problem behaviours; the case histories of delinquents repeatedly indicate the onset of serious antisocial behaviour when they were very young. Attempts have been made to identify with special screening devices, those children (indeed, even infants), who are at risk of developing conduct, delinquent or other disorders (Herbert, 1982).

We have touched upon the fact that the judgement of what is 'ab-normal' (i.e., a *deviation* from a norm or standard) is largely a social one; the child fails to meet certain of society's expectations of what constitutes appropriate behaviour. Unfortunately, terms like 'normal' and 'abnormal' are commonly applied to children as if they are mutually exclusive concepts like 'hard' and 'soft'. But in reality we are referring to behavioural continua (matters of degree): quantitative judgements of what constitutes abnormality, rather than qualitative differences in kind. The labels 'normal' and 'abnormal' are also used in the manner of trait-attributes; thus the label 'abnormal' attached to a particular boy seems to suggest that he is maladjusted in some absolute and generalized sense. This is misleading; the most that can be said of any child is that certain of his or her actions or attributes are more or less abnormal, and they tend to be associated with particular circumstances and situations. The issue of generalized traits *versus* situational-specificity has been examined by Bowers (1973). He reached the conclusion from his review of published studies that both trait theorists and situationists have overstated their cases.

This issue also highlights a major difference in the theoretical models put forward to explain problematic phenomena: notably the trait theories of the psychoanalysts and the situational specificity emphasized by behavioural theorists.

II.—CONCEPTS OF THE PERSON AND MODELS OF HUMAN BEHAVIOUR

It is common for the two clusters of problems we have identified to be thought of as either over-controlled (internalized) or under-controlled (externalized) patterns of behaviour. These 'directional metaphors' are illuminating, but also misleading if applied too rigidly or literally to individual cases. As we see later they contain theoretical assumptions.

We all have pet theories as to why some children do not develop in what society regards as a desirable manner: the breakdown or the social isolation of the family, the decline in parental discipline, too much violence on television, the rejection of moral values and of religion, the size and nature of today's schools, and so on. It is difficult, however, to substantiate (despite painstaking research) that any one of these particular factors does have a crucial influence, let alone to construct a coherent general theory explaining problem behaviours.

Social Learning Perspective

Socialization　There are at least some conclusions to which we can point, arising from a multitude of studies of the family and society and the manner in which the asocial neonate gradually learns to adapt to living life as a social being. Society delegates its most crucial functions to the family. The precise organization of the family may vary, but the *tasks* which it performs are unique. Among them are the protection and the social training of the young. Parents set out to 'civilize' the child in their care; in short, the family transforms a biological organism into a social being by the process usually called 'socialization'. Notions of right and wrong, a code of behaviour, a set of attitudes and values, the ability to see the other person's point of view – all of these basic qualities which make an individual into a socialized personality – are nurtured in the first instance within the family setting.

Socialization is sometimes portrayed as a long drawn-out battle of wills, as a confrontation between young children wanting to go their own way and parents wishing them to *adapt* to the family's (and society's) ways. Undoubtedly 'battles' do take place. But there is a basic readiness on the part of most children to be trained—an inbuilt bias towards all things social. The sight of the mother's face automatically elicits a smile from the baby; that produces a happy reaction in the mother and causes her in turn to smile back and to talk or tickle or touch it; in this way she elicits further responses from the baby. A chain of mutually rewarding interactions is thus initiated, very often initially by the baby, who is a proactive as well as reactive being. Parents and child learn about each other in the course of these interactions, and more often than not mutual adjustment is brought about by a kind of negotiation process in which parent and child are required to show some flexibility. Sadly some babies get off to a bad start. Mutually aversive interactions can set in when an infant is temperamentally difficult, unmalleable and resistant to social training (Thomas, Chess and Birch, 1968) or where parents are depressed, over-anxious or too rigid.

We have referred to the requirement that a child should adapt to the expectations of the family and society. The contemporary Western nuclear family of parents and offspring introduces children first of all to their kin and then to their wider community and society; it introduces them to social mores and rules—the ones to which they must 'adjust' or adapt themselves. Psychological problems are very much bound up with the favourable and unfavourable perceptions that children have of themselves as individuals—their self-images—and their perceptions of, and relationships with, other people. So many of the hurdles which youngsters have to overcome are social ones—the problems of getting on with other children of the same age, with teachers, with parents, and, by no means least, being on good terms with themselves as individuals. Positive self-attitudes are the basic ingredients of positive mental health and negative self-concepts among the critical predispositions to maladjustment (Coopersmith, 1967).

The concept of adaptation has proved useful if somewhat elusive to clinical psychologists in evaluating their clients. There are many and varied definitions of positive mental health (Jahoda, 1958). Certainly most parents have a picture of the sorts of persons their children 'ought' to be, and of the society they are being fitted for. The youngsters who fail, or resist the adjustment—usually parents want a compromise not a capitulation—of their individual natures to the prescribed social standards, are thought to be maladjusted, or 'maladapted' to use a more contemporary term. Obviously we are dealing here with value judgments not objective universal medical criteria! What is also obvious is that the presence of a weak link in the chain—a disturbed or neglectful family—can engender serious harm, not only to the individual, but also to the fabric of society itself.

Learning The child's learning occurs within a social setting; rewards, punishments and other events are mediated by human agents and within attachment and social systems, and are not simply the impersonal consequences of behaviour. In the learning theory canon, much (by no means all) of a person's 'normal' (i.e., prosocial, adaptive, functional) behavioural repertoire is acquired, maintained and regulated by its effects upon the natural environment, and the feedback it receives with regard to these consequences. This notion is extended to accommodate the 'abnormal' (i.e., antisocial, maladaptive, dysfunctional) behaviours, thoughts and feelings. The very processes which help the child adapt to life can, under certain circumstances, contribute to maladjustment. An immature child who learns by imitating an adult is not necessarily able to comprehend when it is undesirable (deviant) behaviour that is being modelled. The child who learns (adaptively) on the basis of classical and instrumental conditioning processes to avoid dangerous situations can also learn in the same way (maladaptively) to avoid the dentist or social gatherings. A teacher may unwittingly reinforce disruptive behaviour by attending to it. The development of fears is, of course, influenced by the child's history, and by the setting in which the fear-provoking situations occur; that is to say, there are significant experiential and learning components at work. However, the tendency of a child to over-react with fear is also closely related to the inherited sensitivity of the autonomic nervous system.

Social Learning Let us now elaborate the perspective which combines both *learning* and *social* components by examining conduct disorders in this context. Social learning theorists suggest that children with serious conduct problems are maladjusted because, for a variety of reasons, their early social conditioning has been ineffective. As a consequence they have failed to negotiate adequately the early stages in the internalization of adequate behavioural controls—what some would call (conveniently, but simplistically) *conscience*. There is an absence of a strong emotional aversion to antisocial acts, a diminished capacity to resist temptation and a lack of feeling of remorse when harm has been inflicted (Herbert, 1978). The commonly held view (see Wright, 1971) is that anxiety about threatened withdrawal of parental love and approval is the major contributing factor to the child's internalization of parental values and to making the child more susceptible to adult influence. A series of actions might be considered to be internalized to the extent that their maintenance has become independent of external outcomes—that is, to the extent that their reinforcing consequences are internally mediated, without the support of external events such as rewards and punishments. Norm-abiding behaviour ultimately depends not only on avoidance of externally imposed consequences but, more importantly, on the avoidance of anxiety or guilt, which has its source within the individual.

Conduct disorders are often conceptualized in terms of the child's inability or reluctance to comply with rules. We need to remember that such persistent flouting of codes and conventions in the seriously disturbed child is not only related to frequent lapses of poorly established controls nor to the failure to learn these controls in the first place; there is also the possibility that the behavioural standards a child has absorbed in the family or neighbourhood do not coincide with the norms of that section of society which enacts and enforces the rules.

Unlike children in more traditional Eastern families who are instructed in the rules, conventions, laws, ethics and religious practices of the community and the importance of traditional beliefs, these matters are conveyed rather haphazardly to many Western children. Where Eastern children are told in no uncertain terms that if they perform the religious rituals incorrectly, they will displease the Ancestral spirits to whom the ceremonies are dedicated, irreverence or indifference to the old and traditional is not uncommon in the West. Children in a Western society have no such clear-cut *rites de passage* to which they can refer. If a boy's parents are practising Catholics or Jews, the child – at an appropriate age – will probably make his first Communion or celebrate his Bar Mitzvah. Both ceremonies are comparable to an initiation rite in a primitive society. They announce the child's new status to other members of the group (in this case church or temple) and give a sense of identity with that group, the members of which have all undergone the same experience. Yet one would be hard pressed to find ceremonies in secular society which are so generally recognized.

Developmental Perspective

In an urbanized society there remain few rituals or ceremonies which are generally recognized by the whole community as special marks of the various stages in a child's development. On the other hand, in isolated rural or peasant communities and isolated tribal societies, formal initiation rites are a principal means of demonstrating to the community and to children themselves that they are socially as well as physically accepted as adults. These rites have a traditional order. They may have gone on for generations with little change; their meaning is clear to all. This is in complete contrast to the industrialized societies of Western Europe and the United States, where a striking feature of life is the diversity of ethnic groups. Class differences, occupational and kinship groupings cut across each other, often resulting in a confusion of roles, expectations and tasks for the individual child.

Proponents of a 'stage' theory of childhood development (e.g., Ausubel and Sullivan, 1970) suggest that although they may be more or less unformalized, there are very real stages in the socialization of the child; furthermore, the child's attempts to negotiate successive developmental stages and tasks can lead to crisis. A developmental task arises at a certain period in the life of an individual, successful achievement of which leads to happiness in the individual, disapproval by society and difficulty with other tasks. The tasks might be ones such as learning to talk or to control elimination; or they may involve the development of self-control over aggressive and sexual inclinations, acquiring moral attitudes and social skills, adjusting to school-life and mastering academic competencies, becoming self-directed and self-confident. Each stage of development is thought to correspond to a particular form of social demand; the child must deal with and master a central problem.

Erikson (1965) is a major proponent of such a developmental timetable. At each stage a conflict between opposite poles in a pattern of reciprocity between the self and others has to be resolved. The crises are related to trust *versus* mistrust; autonomy *versus* shame; initiative *versus* guilt; industry *versus* inferiority; identity *versus* identity diffusion; and so on. Danziger (1971) sees a connection between the bi-polar pairs (e.g., trust *versus* mistrust) described by Erikson, and Piaget's ideas (Piaget, 1932) concerning assimilation and accommodation. The Piagetian description of cognitive development in terms of the interplay of accommodatory and assimilatory processes is analogous (according to Danziger) to the interplay of 'ego' and 'alter' in personality development—namely the achievement of a balance between the poles of recognizing and adapting to the needs of others and imposing self-centred demands on the social environment. An extreme lack of balance in reciprocity between self and others in either direction gives rise to unsatisfactory social relationships: an egocentric nonentity at one extreme and a self-abasing nonentity at the other.

The newborn infant (to take one example of Erikson's schema) needs to develop a sense of trust, and later, a growing autonomy. A lasting sense of trust, security, confidence or optimism (as opposed to distrust, insecurity, inadequacy or pessimism) is thought to be based upon affection, a degree of continuity of care-giving and the reasonably prompt satisfaction of the infant's needs (see Seligman, 1975). The major hazards to the development of a perception of a benign, trustworthy and predictable world in which the children initiate their own independence-seeking and perceive their actions as having meaningful consequences, are neglect, abuse, indifference, extreme inconsistency and other conditions—social and physical—which interfere with the child's sense of personal adequacy or which hinder the acquisition of skills. Such contingencies are likely to produce a child who behaves dysfunctionally. Incidentally, physically handicapped children are massively over-represented in the population of youngsters with behaviour problems. If such children can be helped to become more competent, then they may have less recourse to problem behaviour.

Treatment Implications of the Social Learning and Developmental Perspectives

Behaviour therapy is based upon a model which states that since abnormal behaviour is learned and maintained in the same way as normal behaviour, as opposed to being a manifestation of inferred intrapsychic conflicts, it can be treated directly through the application of social learning principles rather than indirectly by 'working through' these underlying problems. If it is accepted that problematic behaviours of childhood are acquired, largely as a function of faulty learning processes, then there is a case for arguing that problems can most effectively be modified where they occur, by changing the 'social lessons' the child receives and the reinforcing contingencies supplied by the social agents. The so-called 'triadic model' or 'triadic approach' recognizes the profound influence that parents and other significant caregivers have on children's development and mental health, an influence far greater than that which any professional could exert even with extensive and intensive intervention. As parents and teachers exert a significant founda-tional influence during the impressionable years of early childhood, they are usually in a strong position to facilitate prosocial learning and adjustment, and moderate the genesis of behaviour problems. Additionally, they are on hand and therefore in a good position to extend the beneficial changes (brought about in therapy) over time, and to generalize them across various life-situations.

Psychoanalytic and Neo-psychoanalytic Perspectives

Psychoanalysis, with its concentration on instincts, is a motivationally based theory which assumes determinism in all human behaviour. It assumes the existence and significant influence of unconscious mental processes, and the perennial nature of psychological conflict and anxiety in both normal persona-lity development and in the evolution of psychopathology. Sigmund Freud, the founder of psychoanalysis, treated no children directly, although his report on 'Little Hans', a child analysed vicariously, proved highly influential. His views of childhood and its aberrations were based largely upon recon-structions of the early years derived from the free associations, dreams and memories of adult neurotic patients (Freud, 1932).

Freud was very much an exponent of *verstehende* or 'understanding' psych-ology. The classical Freudian theory is primarily a doctrine about mental energy (psychic energy). There is a metaphor in Freud's exposition, in which the person is like an energy system in which energy flows, gets side-tracked, or becomes damned-up. In all persons there is a limited amount of energy, and if it gets discharged in one way, there is that much less energy to be discharged in another way. This mental energy serves to determine the psycho-sexual stages—oral, anal and phallic—through which the human mind and personality develop and become partitioned. The structural aspects of personality, *ego*, *id*, *super-ego*, were introduced by Freud in an attempt to deal with the central problem of psychological conflict; the theme of 'man divided against himself'.

The id contains the blind striving of both the life and death instincts and is the source of all our motives, drives and energies. The ego is the rational section of the personality, and the superego is the moral and ethical part of the person's being, akin to conscience. The mind, Freud theorized, is cut across by a critically important barrier, separating the unconscious from the conscious elements. The ego has at its command several 'defence mechanisms'—repression, rationalization, fantasy, sublimation and regression—with which to control the balance and distribution of energy. If this control has not been satisfactorily achieved in the past, the repression barrier, which has kept the unconscious impulses of the mind at bay, may break down under stress or frustration. As a result, the unconscious elements may then come to the surface to the accompaniment of anxiety, and in the compromise form of neurotic symptoms, in the child internalizing emotional problems or (alternatively) 'acting-out' conduct disorders (see Lee and Herbert, 1970).

Freud went on to say that abnormal mental phenomena are simply exaggerations of normal phenomena, and that a patient's symptoms represent, in essence, the outcome of his or her attempts to meet personal problems as well as possible; in this way Freud bridged the gap between normal and abnormal behaviour. The practical implications of the psychoanalytic or neo-psychoanalytic approaches to childhood problems (the latter exemplified by Anna Freud, 1946, and Melanie Klein, 1954) is that treatment usually takes the classical one-to-one (so-called 'dyadic') approach in which the therapist works directly with the child.

It should be noted that classical Freudian psychoanalysis has, over the years, become elaborated, modified, and in the hands of some of its cross-disciplinary practitioners, attenuated. It is often referred to as the *psychodynamic* approach. Whatever it is called, the conventional methods of psychoanalytic psychotherapy used with adults are not very suitable for children. Children are not always able to put their anxieties into words; for one thing in the early stages of cognitive development they are not reflexive or introspective. They are not always interested in exploring their past life. They are too close to the episodes that are thought by some psychoanalysts to be crucial in the development of neuroses, to enjoy talking about them. They will not always cooperate in the method of free association. The main problem is that the motivation to participate in therapy is missing, because children are usually unaware of 'having' any problem and often are brought to the clinics against their will.

III.—INDIVIDUAL ASSESSMENT

Basically the function of psychological tests is to measure differences between individuals or between the reactions of the same individual on different tasks or on different occasions. Psychometric methods such as check lists, questionnaires, rating scales, and IQ tests, have proved useful (if not relied on extensively) in the assessment of problem children. There is a number of techniques available (e.g., the Q-sort technique, the Semantic Differential and the Repertory Grid Test) which allow for the direct expression of the child's personal conceptual system—the manner in which the individual 'sees' or construes him/herself, other people and the world he/she lives in. They may reveal concepts or 'constructs', and relationships between constructs, that the person is barely aware of, or which function normally at the emotional rather than the verbally explicit level. For example, a girl may be construing her teacher in much the same punitive terms as her father, and a test like the Repertory Grid helps to point out such connections.

However, in trying to learn about the behaviour of other persons, the two principal ways are through questioning and observation. Interviewing (because of the opportunity it gives to question and observe a patient) is one of the prime instruments of psychological assessment, and for this reason it is used by behaviour therapists and psychodynamic workers alike. In the case of children the interview (or part of it) may take place in a playroom. Interviews may vary from the *highly structured* (representing little more than an orally administered questionnaire) through what are termed *patterned* or *guided* interviews covering certain predetermined areas of the person's behaviour, to *non-directive* and *depth* interviews in which the interviewer merely sets the stage and encourages the subject to talk as freely as possible. The latter are most favoured by psychodynamically-orientated clinicians.

A particularly important function in a psychiatric setting is to elicit life-history data. What individuals have done in the past is thought to be a good indicator of what they may do in the future, especially when interpreted in the light of concomitant circumstances, and of their subject's comments on their actions; and it also has an explanatory function—an attempt to relate the child's present psychological status to earlier experiences. A vast clinical and research literature has sought to put flesh on the bones of Wordsworth's aphorism that 'the child is father to the man'. The findings of research studies, most of which are retrospective or cross-sectional, typically generate evidence telling us (for example) that there are links between the experience of an unhappy, disharmonious and disrupted family life in childhood and later behaviour problems, teenage pregnancy, extramarital conception, marriage breakdown, less satisfactory neonatal care, and delinquency (Rutter, 1977).

The fact is that very rarely can current problems be traced to *specific* past experiences with any degree of confidence. What is clear from broadly based epidemiological surveys, is that among all the allegedly harmful factors blamed in the literature for this or that psychopathology (be they prenatal or perinatal pathology, noxious parental characteristics, family problems, etc.), it is possible to identify significant numbers of children who developed normally, despite being subjected to these influences.

Sadly, the psychologist's knowledge of causality in behaviour development is modest, and therefore his/her conjectures about the outcome of conditions far removed in time from present manifestations of dysfunctional behaviour—combinations of parental attitudes, home and school circumstances, reinforcement contingencies, genetic influences, temperamental and other intrinsic factors—are tenuous at best.

Behavioural Assessment

Behaviourally orientated psychologists will lose little sleep over the doubts and uncertainties about early precursors of childhood problems. Their gaze is firmly fixed on the 'here-and-now', on the immediate antecedents and consequences of problematic episodes, which for them are the controlling contingencies of note. And they work on the assumption that it is necessary to have highly detailed and specific information (based on specially designed 'sharp focus' interviews and direct observation) about the child's behaviour in various life situations (see Herbert, 1981).

The behaviour of any child tends to be highly specific to circumstances, places, and people. Assessment techniques designed to identify and gauge generalized attributes (e.g., personality traits) in a child, have poor predictive value (Mischel, 1968), and thus find little favour with behaviour therapists. The behaviour therapist works from the premise that prediction is best from behaviour in one situation to behaviour in similar situations (Bandura, 1969).

Identification and Specification of the Problem

Thus the first step is to obtain information about all aspects of a child's behaviour which are considered to be problematic by the parents, any other persons (e.g., teachers), agencies (e.g., medical or educational), or the child him/herself. The process of labelling behaviour as 'deviant' occurs in a social context; in any group, be it a school, a family, marriage, or a work team, each member will have different perceptions of the 'real problem' in that system. Social learning theorists attempt to conceptualize the problem not as an encapsulated entity but as a process. A longitudinal perspective is adopted which views the client and the behaviours of the client as part of a complex network of interacting social and learning systems, any aspect of which may have a bearing on present troubles. Thus, in attempting to reach some kind of assessment and plan a programme of treatment, the unit of attention is broadly conceived; the focus of help is no longer simply on the child brought for assessment. Rather, attention is on the whole human being within a fluid, 'real-life' situation. The analysis is *functional*, in that it provides a description of the child-in-situation and the interrelationship of child and his/her setting. It is based on the concept of a functional relationship with the environment in which changes in individual behaviour produce changes in the environment and vice versa.

The key word in the early phase of assessment is 'what'. Graziano (1971) provides a list of the 'what' questions that need to be asked. *What* is the child doing? Under *what* conditions are these behaviours emitted? *What* are the effects of these acts? *What* desirable acts should be encouraged? These questions tell us about the specified problem and its effects (pay-off) for the child; they also elucidate the circumstances under which the problem occurs and those under which it does not.

The clinician also tries to find out about the child's skills and prosocial behaviour patterns. Parents are encouraged to think about them and indeed record them. They are provided with appropriate record forms and explanations about how to observe, to code behaviour and to record. Clinicians usually find it is advantageous to observe for themselves what is happening currently in order to set realistic treatment goals or make plans for achieving them. There are several aids to observations: coding categories, instruction manuals for parents, and methods for keeping objective records by therapists themselves and/or by the parents, child, or some other person in the child's environment.

Identification of the Conditions Influencing the Problem Behaviour

The second component of the behavioural assessment reflects the behavioural model of psychopathology in that it provides the data for a formulation of explanatory hypotheses about the current factors which influence the initiation and maintenance of the problem.

A behavioural classification can be specified in terms of the following four components (see Kanfer and Saslow, 1969):

(i) *Prior stimulation* (S). These are the antecedent stimulus events which reliably precede the criterion behaviours. They may be functionally related to the response by setting the stage for them ('discriminative stimuli') or evoking them ('eliciting stimuli').

(ii) *Organismic variables* (O). These include motives and the biological and psychological states of the organism.

(iii) *Response* (R).

(iv) *Consequent events* (C). Consequent events refer to the new conditions which the criterion behaviours were instrumental in bringing about. The effects of these behaviours on the person's internal and external environment are crucial determinants of whether or not the behaviour will recur.

The Elements of a Behaviour Analysis

It is possible to indicate the relative temporal relationships of the elements mentioned above as follows: S→O→R→C. The complete description of any behavioural sequence requires the specification of each of these influences and their interaction with the others. Jehu, Hardiker, Yelloly and Shaw (1972) summarize the approach to the explanation of problem behaviour as follows:

> It is regarded as a function of somatic factors, previous learning experiences and contemporary events. The assessment of these events is directed towards the precise identification of the antecedent, outcome and symbolic conditions which control the problem behaviour . . . First certain antecedent conditions may be eliciting or reinforcing problem responses, especially those of an emotional kind, while other such conditions may involve some lack of appropriate discriminative stimulus control over the client's instrumental responses. Second there may be outcome conditions which either reinforce problem behaviour or punish or extinguish desirable responses. Finally, any of these inappropriate forms of antecedent or outcome control may be operating in the client's symbolic processes, rather than in his external environment or psychological changes, or there may be an impairment of his problem-solving capacity. (p. 76).

Psychodynamic Assessment

Psychodynamic therapists tend to use play and play-based interviews for assessment. Such an approach makes use of children's familiar and spontaneous mode of expression—play—and this provides a background against which the therapist can discuss their problems with them. The first person to advocate studying the play of children in order to understand and educate them was Rousseau, in the eighteenth century. Since then, several theories have been put forward to explain the meaning and utility of play in childhood; they generally emphasize its function as a means of preparation for the future, as a natural process of learning, as a means of release (catharsis) from tensions, and as an outlet for excess physical energies. In many ways, play, for the child, is life itself.

Freud's daughter, Anna, used children's play in a manner which is analogous to the use of the interpretation of dreams with adults. Play is analysed so as to uncover unconscious conflicts. This involves the interpretation of the symbolic meanings and the unconscious motivations underlying drawings, paintings, games and other forms of imaginative play (Freud, 1946). Anna Freud was the first theorist systematically to transpose classical psychoanalytic theory into a system of child analysis.

Therapists and theorists of a psychoanalytic or (as it is more widely designated) psychodynamic persuasion, are interested in historical factors—the early determinants of problems, and also intra-psychic factors such as the relationships between ego, id and superego. It is postulated that from a very tender age, people discover and make use of complex defensive reactions (Lee and Herbert, 1970). These are evolved to protect and enhance the gradually evolving self-image (ego). The strategies and tactics soften anxieties and failures and guard the integrity of the ego by increasing the feeling of personal worth. They also serve to fulfil the needs of the individual. When used to excess, involving as they do a degree of self-deception, they may be labelled 'neurotic' (e.g., excessive escapism or fantasy).

The so-called 'projective techniques' are used to assess defence mechanisms, conflict areas and psychosexual fixations. They comprise many different tasks such as interpreting inkblots (Rorschach Test), telling stories in response to pictures (Thematic Apperception Test), completing unfinished stories (Geneva Story Completion Test), devising dramatic plots (Make a Picture Story), making 'worlds' out of miniatures (Lowenfeld World Game), giving associations to words (Word Association Test), etc. The tasks (stimuli) tend to be relatively unstructured in order to stimulate idiosyncratic material.

IV.—THE IMMEDIATE EMOTIONAL AND SOCIAL ENVIRONMENT

When the family fails in providing appropriate and consistent socialization experiences the child seems to be particularly vulnerable to the development of conduct and delinquent disorders. This is reflected in empirical studies (see West and Farrington, 1973). Typically the children with persistent disorders come from families where there is discord and quarrelling; where affection is lacking; where discipline is inconsistent, ineffective and either extremely severe or lax. In a sense, as we said earlier, children are 'antisocial' from birth. Patterson (1975) observes that the average 3-year-old in American society has learned all of 14 noxious behaviours. Usually, such coercive behaviours display a steady decline in performance rates from a high point in infancy down to more moderate levels at the age of school entrance. The identified 'aggressive' youngster, according to Patterson, displays coercive behaviours at a level commensurate with a 3- to 4-year-old child and, in this sense, is an example of arrested socialization. He lists the following possibilities for the child's failure to substitute more adaptive, more mature behaviours for his primitive coercive repertoire: (a) the parents might neglect to condition prosocial skills (e.g., they seldom reinforce the use of language or other self-help skills); (b) they might provide rich schedules of positive reinforcement for coercive behaviours; (c) they might allow siblings to increase the frequency of aversive stimuli which are terminated when the target child uses coercive behaviours; (d) they may use punishment inconsistently for coercive behaviours; and/or (e) they may use weak conditioned punishers as consequences for coercion.

The family is a dynamic system. This means that it is susceptible to movement and change. It is not a static entity oblivious to the personality, developments and relationships of its members; nor is it resistant to the pressures of history. One might think of it as a system with its individual members as elements or sub-units within it. Whatever happens to one or more of its elements—say, mental illness in the mother, or serious marital disharmony—affects the entire system.

According to some research workers there is a blurring of age and sex roles in certain families, and the combination of instability at home and ambiguous role-relationships hinders the development of appropriate forms of behaviour and a stable sense of identity in the child. According to these theorists, verbal interactions between parents and child tend to be stereotyped with almost no outlet for spontaneous expression. Frequently they fail to respond to their child's communications or to the child's demands for a recognition of his/her own point of view. Their own statements tend to be intrusive and take the form of interventions rather than replies to the child. The replies they do make tend to be selective, being responses to those of the child's expressions which have been initiated by themselves rather than to any expressions originated by the child. The child's spontaneous utterances and self-expression are restricted as if he or she were being denied the right to an independent point of view. There are theorists who contend that the complexities of language and logic are such that a condition as serious as schizophrenic thought disorder may be a consequence of the child having received a faulty grounding in the agreed (consensual linguistic) meanings of society. These deficiencies are thought to limit the child's adaptive capacities and permit him/her to escape from insoluble contradictions by abandoning the 'meaning system' of the prevailing culture. The child takes refuge in irrationality and withdrawn behaviour.

While most adults show sensitivity to children quite naturally, some parents unfortunately are devoid of this vital component of parenting. Why this is so we still do not know for certain; it does seem, however, that parents who themselves had a deprived childhood and did not themselves experience sensitive care are more likely to show the same attitudes to their own children.

Behaviourists and classical psychoanalysts have, in the past, tended to treat the family and the wider social environment to which it introduces the child, in a somewhat cavalier fashion. However, several eminent psychoanalysts broke away from Freudian orthodoxy because of various kinds of dissatisfaction with Freudian theory. Common themes in the repudiation of parts of the Freudian doctrine were: a desire to focus on cultural influences and interpersonal relationships (i.e., the social context); and a related emphasis on the conscious aspects of personality, self or ego (self-evaluation, self-esteem, the need for security, etc.).

There have been modifications in therapeutic practice to reflect this change in orientation. Karen Horney (1947) differs from many psychanalytic writers inasmuch as she does not consider it justified to focus attention on childhood in a one-sided manner and to consider later reactions essentially as repetitions of earlier ones. She recognizes that neuroses are generated not only by incidental individual experiences, but also by the specific cultural conditions to which people are exposed. Indeed, the cultural conditions not only lend weight and colour to the individual experiences, but in the last analysis determine their particular form. Horney singled out for analysis a characteristic conflict of present Western culture—the contradiction between the high evaluation of success in our competitive society and the Christian principle of neighbourly love and need for affection. In her book *The Neurotic Personality of Our Time* she describes the neurotic person as the victim of this pervasive conflict of values.

V.—THE WIDER SOCIAL AND ORGANIZATIONAL ENVIRONMENT

In modern Western societies the State has considerable rights in the health and education of children. The school constitutes the most important environment for the child outside the family.

Children spend some 15,000 hours at school. Here then is another environment of critical importance in helping families to meet children's needs and to shape their thinking and personalities. The findings of Rutter, Maugham, Mortimore and Ouston (1979) demonstrate this very clearly. To give a few illustrative examples, their data showed that the most immediate and direct feedback in terms of praise or approval had the strongest association with pupil behaviour. The amount of punishment showed only weak, and generally non-significant, associations with outcome, and when the associations did reach significance, the trend was for higher levels of punishment to be associated with *worse* outcomes. The researchers found outcomes to be better when both the curriculum and approaches to discipline were agreed and supported by the staff acting together. Thus, attendance was better and delinquency less frequent in schools where courses were planned jointly. Group planning provided opportunities for teachers to encourage and support one another. In addition continuity of teaching was facilitated. Much the same was found with regard to standards of discipline. Examination successes were more frequent and delinquency less common in schools where discipline was based on general expectations set by the school (or house or department), rather than left to individual teachers to work out for themselves. School values and norms appear to be more effective if it is clear to all that they have widespread support. Discipline is easier to maintain if the pupils appreciate that it relates to generally accepted approaches and does not simply represent the whims of the individual teacher. Rutter *et al* state that the particular rules which are set and the specific disciplinary techniques which are used, are probably much less important than the establishment of some principles and guidelines which are both clearly recognizable, and accepted by the school as a whole.

VI.—TYPES OF INTERVENTION

Traditional

The traditional (often eclectic) treatment of problem behaviour takes place in a clinic or a hospital. Parents bring the child to the professional (a psychiatrist, psychologist or social worker) who works primarily with the child as the 'target' patient with 'target' problems to be modified. The setting for the therapy is the consulting room and the expert 'treats the patient'. This is a situation far removed from the child's experience of life and occupying a minuscule proportion of it. Frequently, therapists are unable to see parent-child (or teacher-child) interactions in their natural settings, and indeed they may not even observe directly in the artificiality of their consulting rooms the problem behaviour patterns for which the child was referred. Although the parents and teachers are sometimes advised to be more consistent, warm, loving or understanding, they are often left to their own devices to translate such instructions into action. As a result, many do not know specifically how they should change their handling of the child.

The Triadic Model (Behaviour Modification)

As behaviour is seen as a function of the total learning environment, behaviour modification is not only about changing the undesirable behaviour of 'problem children' but also about altering the behaviour of the persons—parents, teachers and others—who form a significant part of the child's social world. Help is directed to the modification of that environment. This would seem preferable to withdrawing the child from it. The parents become the real agents of change in what may be a long-haul operation (in the case of the conduct disorders), thus contributing to the problem of extending positive changes over time.

The last 15 years or so have seen major advances in the behavioural treatment of children's problems. There is a wide range of empirically based therapeutic procedures from which to choose in planning an intervention. Among the more optimistic developments in recent years has been the application of behavioural treatments to the alleviation of emotional disorders and, indeed, even the intractable conduct disorders; methods such as *differential reinforcement*, *time out* from positive reinforcement, *response-cost* and *over-correction* procedures, have been applied to good effect. Incentive systems (*token economies*) are negotiated and contracted between parents and children, and some are linked to behaviour at school.

In the case of older children and adolescents, therapists tend to use more cognitively orientated methods (see Herbert, 1981) including *self-control training* (assertion and relaxation training, desensitization of anger, role-play, behaviour rehearsal); *problem-solving skill-training* and *social skills training*. A technique which has proved to be invaluable with hyperactive, impulsive children is *self-instruction training*—the development of children's skills in guiding their own performance by the use of self-suggestion, comments, praise, and other directives.

Psychodynamic Play Therapy (derived from ego-psychology)

Most psychoanalysts no longer study only isolated manifestations of repressed mental content; they place these manifestations in the context of the complex dynamic system—the total personality—that Freud liked to call the 'mental apparatus'. Although the integrative and synthesizing functions of the ego are mentioned by Freud, they were not much developed by him. The adaptational nature of ego development was presaged by him when he distinguished between the reality and the pleasure principles. The ego psychologists have developed these important aspects of ego functions; they postulate an autonomous ego which is a rational institution responsible for intellectual and social achievements, and whose functioning is not solely dependent on the wishes of the id—it has its own motives, interests and objectives and its own origin and development. Such a view focuses on those ego functions which do not deal with the resolution of internal conflicts, but with the adaptation of the individual to his/her environment. In this tradition, various forms of play therapy—relationship therapy and non-directive therapy—have also evolved and continue to be used.

Axline (1947) in her book, *Play Therapy*, describes the non-directive form. She says that this approach is based upon the fact that play is the child's natural medium of self-expression. An opportunity is given to the child to 'play out' feelings and problems, just as, in certain types of adult therapy, an individual 'talks out' or 'works through' difficulties. Non-directive therapy is based upon the assumption that individuals have, within themselves, not only the abilities to solve their own problems satisfactorily, but also a growth impulse that makes mature behaviour more satisfying than immature behaviour.

Here, the basic principles which guide therapists are as follows: therapists develop a warm, friendly relationship with the child; they accept the child exactly as he is; they establish a feeling of permissiveness in the relationship so that the child feels entirely free to express his feelings; in addition they are alert to recognize the feelings expressed by the child and to reflect those feelings back to him in such a manner that he gains insight into his behaviour.

Family Therapy

There is no space in this chapter to describe adequately the vast subject matter of family therapy. However, family therapy is not so much a school or system of therapy as a basic redefinition of the therapeutic task itself. The target for assessment and intervention is far broader than the child himself. Whereas the conventional treatment model tends to identify the 'nominated client' (viz. the child) as the unit of attention, diagnostic thinking has since been considerably influenced by interactional frames of reference explicit in systems theory. Family therapists attempt to conceptualize the problem in a more horizontal (rather than vertical-historical) manner, viewing the client as part of a complex network of interrelating social systems, any aspect of which may have a bearing on the present predicament and indeed may provide the clue to the 'real' problem—often formulated in terms of unsatisfactory patterns of dominance, poor communication and ineffective decision making (Haley, 1972; Skynner, 1964). There are few satisfactory studies of family therapy or of improvements in child and/or family functioning subsequent to family therapy (see Alexander and Parsons, 1973; Epstein, Sigall and Rakoff, 1972; Gale, 1979; Gurman, 1973; Gurman and Kniskern, 1978; Wells, Dilkes and Trivelli, 1972). Family therapists may have a behavioural, psychodynamic, or indeed some other theoretical orientation. As we have seen, home based (triadic) behavioural work takes account of the family as a complex and dynamic system and focuses not only on the individual but on the system of relationships in which that individual interacts.

VII.—IS PSYCHOLOGICAL INTERVENTION SUCCESSFUL?

A major problem in answering this question is the paucity of hard evidence about the effectiveness of treatment with regard to childhood problems. There is an absence of large, well-controlled, rigorously designed, studies. Most evaluative work has been conducted on adults; and in this respect Bergin (1978) asserts that the technical claims of the diverse schools have never been adequately vindicated. Such an assumption that there are no differences between therapeutic approaches with regard to outcome, would be hotly disputed by behaviour therapists. Nevertheless, it is just such an assumption which leads some theorists to argue that the effective factors are the same for all therapies and they can be identified with the common components of all types of influence and healing (warmth, respect, kindness, hope, understanding, provision of 'explanations'). It is important to remember that the *outcome* of therapy is not a unitary variable. It differs according to the perspective of the client, relatives, therapist, work colleagues and others.

Gelfand and Hartmann (1975) claim that children are particularly responsive to behaviour-orientated therapeutic interventions. They are frequently referred to clinics for help with circumscribed problems such as enuresis, phobias, temper-tantrums and the like. These are the types of problem which are most amenable to behaviour therapy (Rachman, 1971). These therapeutic techniques require careful control over the client's environment, something more easily achieved in the home and classroom with youngsters than for people, namely adults, living in a more open-ended world.

There is some evidence (Herbert, 1982) that an approach which educates significant adults in the child's environment is more effective than traditional psychotherapy. The triadic model—the involvement of parents—has been adopted by the present author in work with hyperactive and conduct disordered children and adolescents at the Child Treatment Research Unit, University of Leicester. The methods elaborated, for the task of enhancing or making good the socialization process (described above) when it is going wrong, have been applied with encouraging effectiveness by parents (cf. Herbert and Iwaniec, 1981).

In a sample of 117 children (aged two to sixteen) with conduct disorders accepted for treatment, a majority (83 per cent) was causing *serious* disruption within the family; these children were often perceived by their parents to be 'out of control'. The outcome of treatment was as follows: 61 per cent were evaluated as successful (improved on several criteria); 21 per cent were moderately improved; and 18 per cent showed no improvement. A median figure of three months (and some 33 hours) of intervention to termination—but not including follow-up—was required. Similar results were obtained in a replication study of a sample of conduct disorders drawn from 36 consecutive mixed cases referred to the Unit. Twelve of the sixteen children who improved with treatment, maintained this improvement over a six-month period. Three of the four who deteriorated over this period responded to booster behavioural programmes.

These results are at least encouraging. As we mentioned earlier it is difficult to provide a base rate for conduct problems or long-term success rates for their treatment, because of difficulties of definition and a paucity of longitudinal evidence. But unlike the development of fears and many other problems of childhood, there is not the same tendency for the conduct problems to be transitory. Researchers such as Robins (1966) suggest that by ages seven or eight years the child with extreme antisocial aggressive patterns of behaviour is at quite considerable risk of continuing into adolescence and indeed adulthood with serious deviancy of one kind or another.

Eighty per cent of her large sample of conduct disordered children appeared before a juvenile court and of these fifty per cent were committed to correctional institutions. Only one in six of the seriously antisocial children was completely free of psychiatric disorder in adult life and over a quarter showed sociopathic personality disorder.

With regard to the wider spectrum of child problems the results of behavioural treatments are also favourable. O'Leary, Turkewitz and Taffell (1973) found (for the behavioural treatment of 70 cases in an out-patient training clinic) that the average improvement rate as reported by therapists (87 per cent) and parents (90 per cent) was substantially higher than that reported by Levitt (1963) in his survey of child-clinic psychotherapeutic schemes (65 per cent) or his estimate of spontaneous remission rates.

VIII.—METHODOLOGICAL AND PRACTICAL PROBLEMS

It has to be faced that there are many practical difficulties in working with parents and teachers as the primary mediators of change—and in natural (which often means experimentally 'unnatural') settings. Behaviour therapy is characterized by its brave attempts to achieve rigorous assessment and experimental evaluation of treatment—a tradition nurtured in experimental psychology. A variety of experimental research methods is used; between-group research designs and intra-subject-replication designs, the latter originating in operant conditioning research. Kazdin and Wilson (1978) provide a review of the issues and of research strategies. Most of the single subject (N=1) designs involve a pre-treatment period of measurement (baseline) of target problems (dependent variables) followed by the intervention or some systematic variation of the treatment (the independent variable). These variations include reversal designs, multiple baseline designs, changing criterion designs and multi-element baseline designs.

Psychodynamic workers have been accused of neglecting evaluative studies of their interventions. A common rejoinder involves the argument that it is difficult to operationalize the subtle, elusive, not to mention unconscious 'psychic entities', which are the subject of psychoanalytic treatment. For a review of some of the issues see Lee and Herbert (1970).

Problems in the Evaluation of Change

Much of the confusion over evaluating therapeutic change can be blamed on a lack of precise specification of therapeutic outcomes. The assessment of outcomes is heavily dependent on one's choice of criteria (see Herbert, 1981). A particular source of obfuscation is the definition of a 'problem'; the criteria of an effective outcome in the treatment of a neurotic phobia might be very different as between the psychoanalyst and behaviour therapist.

There are widely divergent views as to the purposes of psycho-therapy (behaviour therapists tending to accept that the 'presenting' or stated problem is usually the 'real' problem). Differing conceptualizations of objectives lead inevitably to different therapeutic *operations*. Different goals lead to divergent *outcomes*. Global questions such as 'Is *x* therapy effective?' and 'Does therapy of the *y* variety work?' are meaningless. They beg several further questions: effective for whom; to what purpose; in what context; for how long?; and so on. Failure to specify clearcut objectives in therapy means one cannot validate or (more important) invalidate the way one is working.

Critics suggest that psychodynamic approaches to children's problems do not improve on the rate at which they would get better without treatment (i.e., the so-called 'spontaneous remission' rate). These views have not gone unchallenged.

A major problem of scientific (nomothetic-type) studies of therapeutic outcomes is, allegedly, the 'averaging-out' of the therapeutic effect. Bergin (1978) argues that when improved and unimproved cases are all lumped together in an experimental group, they cancel each other out to some extent and the overall yield in terms of improvement is no greater than the change occurring in a control group. And, although reports and studies show little difference in the average amount of change occurring after treatment, a significant increase in the variability of criterion scores appears at post-testing in the treatment groups. This spread of criterion scores, Bergin concludes, implies that treatment has a beneficial effect on some clients and an *unfavourable* effect on others. It is being said, then, that some therapists have a benign effect on their clients' problems while other have a deleterious effect.

IX.—PROBLEMS OF ETHICS AND CONFIDENTIALITY

A critical issue in work with children is the moral foundation of its therapeutic armamentarium. This issue is of concern throughout medicine, of course, but it is a particularly sensitive one in child psychology and child psychiatry because of the vulnerability of its clientele and the controversial nature of some of its methods. Child patients are not always a voluntary clientele, in the sense of seeing themselves as patients, of choosing to come to the clinic, or of consenting to treatment.

Behaviour therapy, too, seems to generate ethical controversy, and, indeed, much heated opposition. The domain of behaviour therapy modification is not infrequently broadened out of all recognition to include any method whose end-goal is behaviour change and modification. Thus, behaviour modification, psychosurgery, electro-convulsive-therapy (E.C.T.) and brainwashing are merged to conjure up a scenario which combines images of Anthony Burgess' *A Clockwork Orange* and Aldous Huxley's

Brave New World. However, the sillier or ill-informed extrapolations should not provide an excuse to dismiss the serious reservations of people who are aware of the defining attributes of the behavioural approach (see Erwin, 1978, for an excellent review of the issues). Therapies, of whatever persuasion, are in the business of producing change; all involve social value judgements about undesirable and desirable behaviours. To the extent that they change people, they can all be accused of being presumptuous, manipulative, and open to abuse. Proponents of a behavioural approach claim that a particular feature of behaviour therapy is the respect paid to the integrity of the client by its democratic (as opposed to authoritarian) and participant (as opposed to unidirectional) therapeutic basis. Good practice is, or should be, like this—not simply on ethical grounds but for good theoretical reasons. Behaviour therapy is nothing if it is not about self-management. It respects the client: by focusing on observed behaviours (there is an absence of the 'hidden agendas' of some depth-therapies); by limiting treatment to helping diminish maladaptive functioning (rather than seeking to change 'deep structures' of personality); and by carefully negotiating treatment goals with the client.

X.—THE ROLE OF OTHER DISCIPLINES AND PROFESSIONS

Behaviour therapy or modification, unlike psychoanalysis (which is the domain of a very small group of specialists) is increasingly being used by trained psychiatrists, psychologists, social workers, nurses and teachers. Sadly, appropriate training is still hard to come by in the UK, although it features increasingly in the curricula of courses for various helping professions.

The point is often made that by providing non-professionals with methods and skills to cope with or prevent future problems, behavioural work has moved the focus of therapy towards a preventive model of mental health. There is a grave shortage of professional people with relevant training. This can be mitigated by the fact that clinicians do not have a monopoly of helping skills or such therapeutic qualities as common sense.

The fact that this approach has been taught to parents more often than other more traditional approaches may be due to certain advantages that behaviour modification is assumed to have: persons without a considerable amount of psychological knowledge can grasp the concepts; many persons can be taught at one time; a relatively short training period is needed. Then there is the consideration that parents often prefer a model of problem development and resolution that does not assume 'sick' behaviour based on a medical model. In addition, many childhood problems consist of well-defined behaviours that are conducive to behavioural treatment.

Of interest is the absence of substantive differences in the results of professional as opposed to non- or para-professional therapists. Durlak (1979) reviewed 42 studies comparing the effectiveness of professional and para-professional therapists/helpers. Para-professionals, overall, achieve clinical outcomes equal to or significantly better than those obtained by professionals.

XI.—FUTURE PROSPECTS

The high hopes of preventive parent education have never been fulfilled, probably because of its focus on content rather than on process, on finding techniques and formulae designed to satisfy an abstract principle of 'good adjustment' in the child, rather than providing parents with a broad theoretical framework within which to analyse, and act upon, unique personal and familial disposition.

The complex interactions of person and social context have also conspired to make a nonsense of the simple classical linear causality which is so pervasive in the literature on parent education and preventive work. Parent education has too often been a passive didactic exercise in which the objective is to mould the children in such a manner that they will eventually become well-adjusted adults, 'well-adjusted' in terms of the theoretical value system of the educators or therapist. Available evidence suggests that what is important in childrearing is the general social climate in the home—the attitudes and feelings of the parents which form a background to the application of specific methods and interactions of child-rearing. For example, the mother does best who does what she and the community to which she belongs believe is right for the child (Behrens, 1954). The important fact that parent education is an active process, involving the interdependence and interaction of various dynamic personal and social forces, tends to be overlooked. It can fruitfully be conceived as a partnership with a family, requiring debate and negotiation over goals (Herbert, 1978), rather than the unilateral provision of *ex cathedra* doctrines about child care.

It would be a quantum leap forward if we could identify the periods when children are most vulnerable to emotional problems, and concentrate our efforts and resources so as to help them (and their parents) through such crises. In the case of the potentially long-term conduct disorders, it is important that maladaptive learning processes are disrupted and prosocial actions encouraged in a manner that will persist over long periods of time. The therapeutic perspective is a long one. And herein lies the possibility of doing preventive work (Herbert, 1978, 1981). New adaptive behaviours need to become part of a child's life-style. This means that they must be functional, having 'survival' value, and receiving environmental support. Simplistic 'either-or' schemes aimed at changing the child (e.g., at the intra-psychic level) or the child's environment, are likely to have limited success.

XII.—ANNOTATED READINGS

Axline, V. M. (1966). *Dibs in Search of Self*. London: Gollancz.

An excellent study of play therapy in practice.

Herbert, M. (1974). *Emotional Problems of Development in Children*. London: Academic Press.

The problems which most commonly beset children at certain ages and stages are discussed within a framework of normal development. The reader's attention is drawn to the child's stage of cognitive, moral, ego and social development at particular ages, and the developmental tasks and crises with which he/she has to cope.

Herbert, M. (1981). *Behavioural Treatment of Problem Children: A Practice Manual*. London: Academic Press.

Available in paperback, this is a 'how-to-do-it' manual (with many caveats) for the helping professions. Illustrated with flow charts and case studies.

McAuley, R. and McAuley, P. (1977). *Child Behaviour Problems: An Empirical Approach to Management*. London: Macmillan Press.

A fine account for undergraduates and professionals of the 'nitty gritty' of work with children.

Rapoport, R., Rapoport, R. N. and Strelitz, Z. (1977). *Fathers, Mothers and Others*. London: Routledge and Kegan Paul.

A comprehensive review of the role, tasks and needs of parents through history and in modern times.

Review of Child Development Research.

An invaluable storehouse of research data on children—normal and abnormal—in a series of volumes published by Russell Sage Foundation, New York.

Rutter, M. (1975). *Helping Troubled Children*. Harmondsworth: Penguin.

A highly readable, simple (but not simplistic) account of the problems of childhood; it includes case histories illustrating diagnosis and treatment.

Rutter, M. and Hersov, L. (1977). *Child Psychiatry: Modern Approaches*. Oxford: Blackwell.

An excellent compendium of psychiatric approaches to childhood disorder.

XIII.—REFERENCES

Achenbach, R. M. (1974). *Developmental Psychopathology*. New York: Ronald Press.

Alexander, J. F. and Parsons, B. V. (1973). Short-term behavioral intervention with delinquent families: impact on family process and recidivism. *Journal of Abnormal Psychology*, **81**, 219–225.

Ausubel, D. P. and Sullivan, E. V. (1970). *Theory and Problems of Child Development*. (2nd Edition). London: Grune and Stratton.

Axline, V. M. (1947). *Play Therapy: The Inner Dynamics of Childhood*. Boston Massachusetts: Houghton-Mifflin.

Bandura, A. (1969). *Principles of Behavior Modification*. New York: Holt, Rinehart and Winston.

Behrens, M. L. (1954). Child rearing and the character structure of the mother. *Child Development*, **25**, 225–238.

Bergin, A. E. (1978). The Evaluation of Therapeutic Outcomes. In: S. L. Garfield and A. E. Bergin (Eds.) *Handbook of Psychotherapy and Behavior Change*. (Second Edition). New York: Wiley.

Bowers, K. S. (1973). Situationism in psychology: an analysis and a critique. *Psychological Review*, **80**, 307–336.

Coopersmith, S. (1967). *The Antecedents of Self-Esteem*. London: Freeman.

Danziger, K. (1971). *Socialization*. Harmondsworth: Penguin.

Durlak, J. A. (1979). Comparative effectiveness of paraprofessional and professional helpers. *Psychological Bulletin*, **86**, 80–92.

Epstein, N. B., Sigall, J. J. and Rakoff, V. (1972). Methodological problems in family interaction research. In: J. Framo (Ed.) *Family Interaction: A Dialogue Between Family Researchers and Family Therapists*. New York: Springer.

Erikson, E. (1965). *Childhood and Society* (Revised Edition). Harmondsworth: Penguin.

Erwin, E. (1978). *Behaviour Therapy: Scientific, Philosophical and Moral Foundations*. Cambridge: Cambridge University Press.

Freud, A. (1946). *The Psycho-analytic Treatment of Children*. London: Imago.

Freud, S. (1932). *New Introductory Lectures on Psychoanalysis*. London: Hogarth Press.

Gale, A. (1979). Problems of outcome research in family therapy. In: S. Walrond-Skinner (Ed.). *Family and Marital Psychotherapy: A Critical Approach*. London: Routledge and Kegan Paul.

Gelfand, D. M. (1969). *Social Learning in Childhood*. Belmont, California: Brooks/Cole.

Gelfand, D. M. and Hartmann, D. P. (1975). *Child Behaviour: Analysis and Therapy*. Oxford: Pergamon Press.

Graziano, A. M. (1971) (Ed.). *Behavior Therapy with Children*. New York: Aldine Atherton.

Gurman, A. S. (1973). The effects and effectiveness of marital therapy: a view of outcome research. *Family Process*, **12**, 145–170.

Gurman, A. S., and Kniskern, D. P. (1978). Research on marital and family therapy: Progress, perspective, and prospect. In: S. L. Garfield, and A. E. Bergin (Eds.) *Handbook of Psychotherapy and Behavior Change*. (Second Edition). New York: Wiley.

Haley, J. (1972). Critical overview of present status of family interaction research. In: J. Framo (Ed.) *Family Interaction: A Dialogue Between Family Researchers and Family Therapists*. New York: Springer.

Herbert, M. (1978). *Conduct Disorders of Childhood and Adolescence: A Behavioural Approach to Assessment and Treatment*. Chichester: Wiley.

Herbert, M. (1981). *Behavioural Treatment of Problem Children: A Practice Manual.* London: Academic Press.

Herbert, M. (1982). Conduct Disorders of Childhood. In: B. Lahey and A. E. Kazdin

(Eds.) *Advances in Clinical Child Psychology*. Volume V. New York: Plenum Press.

Herbert, M. and Iwaniec, D. (1981). Behavioural psychotherapy in natural home-settings: an empirical study applied to conduct disordered and incontinent children. *Behavioural Psychotherapy*, **9**, 55–76.

Horney, K. (1947). *The Neurotic Personality of Our Time*. London: Kegan Paul.

Jahoda, M. (1958). *Current Concepts of Positive Mental Health*. New York: Basic Books.

Jehu, D., Hardiker, P., Yelloly, M. and Shaw, M. (1972). *Behaviour Modification in Social Work*. Chichester: Wiley.

Kanfer, F. H., and Saslow, G. (1967). Behavioral Diagnosis. In: C. M. Franks (Ed.) *Behavior Therapy: Appraisal and Status*. New York: McGraw-Hill.

Kazdin, A. E., and Wilson, G. T. (1978). *Evaluation of Behavior Therapy: Issues, Evidence and Research Strategies*. Cambridge, Massachusetts: Ballinger.

Klein, M. (1954). *Psychoanalysis of Children*. London: Hogarth Press.

Lee, S. G. and Herbert, M. (1970) (Eds.). *Freud and Psychology*. Harmondsworth: Penguin.

Levitt, E. E. (1963). Psychotherapy with children: a further evaluation. *Behaviour Research and Therapy*, **1**, 45–51.

MacFarlane, J. W., Allen, L. and Honzik, M. (1954). *A Developmental Study of the Behavior Problems of Normal Children*. Berkeley: University of California Press.

Mischel, W. (1968). *Personality and Assessment*. New York: Wiley.

O'Leary, K. D., Turkewitz, H. and Taffell, S. J. (1973). Parent and therapist evaluation of behaviour therapy in a child psychological clinic. *Journal of Consulting and Clinical Psychology*, **41**, 279–283.

Patterson, G. R. (1975). The Coercive Child: Architect or Victim of a Coercive System? In: L. Hamerlynck, I. C. Handy and E. J. Mash (Eds.) *Behavior Modification and Families*. New York: Brunner Mazell.

Piaget, J. (1932). *The Moral Judgement of the Child*. New York: Harcourt and Brace.

Rachman, S. (1971). *The Effects of Psychotherapy*. Oxford: Pergamon Press.

Robins, L. N. (1966). *Deviant Children Grown Up*. Baltimore, Maryland: Wilkins and Wilkins.

Rutter, M. (1977). Prospective studies to investigate behavioural change. In: J. S. Strauss, H. M. Babigian and M. Roff (Eds.) *The Origins and Course of Psychopathology*. New York: Plenum.

Rutter, M., Maughan, B., Mortimore, P. and Ouston, J. (1979). *Fifteen Thousand Hours: Secondary Schools and their Effects on Children*. London: Open Books.

Seligman, M. E. P. (1975). *Helplessness*. San Francisco, California: Freeman.

Skynner, A. C. R. (1964). A group-analytic approach to conjoint family therapy. *Journal of Child Psychology and Psychiatry*, **10**, 81–106.

Thomas, A., Chess, S. and Birch, H. G. (1968). *Temperament and Behaviour Disorders in Children*. London: University of London Press.

Wells, R. A., Dilkes, T. C. and Trivelli, N. (1972). The results of family therapy: a critical review of the literature. *Family Process*, **11**, 189–207.

West, D. J., and Farrington, D. P. (1973). *Who Becomes Delinquent?*. London: Heinemann.

Wright, D. S. (1971). *The Psychology of Moral Behaviour*. Harmondsworth: Penguin.

Psychology and Social Problems
Edited by A. Gale and A. J. Chapman
© 1984 John Wiley & Sons Ltd.

CHAPTER 3

DELINQUENT AND CRIMINAL BEHAVIOUR

David P. Farrington

I.—THE EXTENT OF THE PROBLEM

Before discussing the extent of delinquent and criminal behaviour, it is necessary to discuss its definition and measurement. Delinquency and crime are usually defined by reference to the criminal law, but this varies over time and place. Delinquency and crime are heterogeneous concepts, covering acts as apparently diverse as theft, vandalism, violence against the person, drug use and various kinds of heterosexual and homosexual indecency. The relativity and heterogeneity of these legal concepts seems likely to hinder their scientific study.

Despite this, most research has been designed to investigate delinquency and crime rather than more specific legal concepts such as theft or non-legal concepts such as antisocial behaviour. There are many problems with legal definitions. For example, they usually rely on unobservable constructs such as intent (determined according to legal criteria), which behavioural scientists prefer to avoid. Also, the boundary between what is legal and what is illegal may be poorly defined and variable, as when school bullying gradually escalates into criminal violence. Also, legal categories are so wide that they may include acts which are behaviourally quite different. For example, robberies may range from armed bank robberies carried out by gangs of masked men to thefts of small amounts of money perpetrated by one school child on another.

It could be argued that the concentration on delinquent and criminal behaviour is appropriate, since it is this behaviour which is generally regarded as a 'social problem' to be prevented and/or treated. An alternative view is that delinquency and crime are defined by groups who have sufficient political power to have their interests (for example, in the protection of unequally distributed private property) embodied in the criminal law. According to this view, psychologists who accept current legal definitions are at best technicians or handmaidens of the ruling classes and at worst agents of capitalist oppression.

These kinds of argument cannot be resolved by empirical research, and some definitions have to be accepted before research can begin. There are empirical reasons for studying crime and delinquency in general rather than more specific concepts. In practice, most socially disapproved acts tend to be associated, in the sense that people who commit one kind of deviant act relatively frequently tend also to commit others relatively frequently. For example, West and Farrington (1977) reported that there was little evidence of specialization in offending, since most youths convicted of aggressive crimes, damaging property or drug use had also been convicted of crimes of dishonesty. The most common delinquent acts (thefts, burglaries and taking vehicles) were associated with more marginal deviant activities such as heavy drinking, heavy gambling, reckless driving and sexual promiscuity. Therefore, it seems reasonable to attempt to explain, prevent and treat delinquent and criminal behaviour in general.

Most of the conclusions reached in this chapter are based on research using legal definitions of delinquency and crime. Furthermore, most research uses legally generated methods of measurement, especially official records collected by the police and other criminal justice agencies. These records have many well-known defects (see, e.g., Farrington, 1979c). For example, acts appearing in official records are a biased and under-representative sample of all delinquent or criminal acts committed, records are kept for the benefit of agency personnel rather than researchers, and they are often kept inefficiently and unsystematically. There are many reasons why delinquent acts fail to appear in an official record, such as failure to define the act as delinquent, failure to report the act to the police, failure to record the act by the police, and failure to apprehend any offender. A major problem is that official records of crime reflect the behaviour both of offenders and of official agencies, and it is difficult to disentangle these.

The most important alternative methods of measuring crime involve self-report and victim surveys, in which people are asked to say if they have committed specified acts, or if they have been the victims of specified acts, within a specified period. Victim surveys are of only limited use in providing information about offenders, partly because some crimes have no identifiable victim (e.g., drug use) and partly because victims often do not know the identity of offenders. The key question arising in self-reported delinquency surveys is validity. To what extent are people able and willing to give accurate reports on their delinquent behaviour, and to what extent are they prone to exaggerate, conceal or forget? The major method of establishing validity has been to compare self-reports with official records. For example, West and Farrington (1977) found that only 6% of convicted youths did not admit being convicted, and only 2% of unconvicted youths claimed to have been convicted. Furthermore, among unconvicted youths, large numbers of admitted offences predicted future convictions. These and other tests have been taken to show that self-reports of offending are reasonably valid.

Both self-reports and official records are essentially indirect methods of measuring offending. In the long term, psychologists should aim to develop methods of directly observing crimes, which would almost certainly require behavioural rather than legal definitions of crimes. This desirable state of affairs is some way off, although some observational research on shoplifting has been carried out (Buckle and Farrington, 1983).

Even using legal definitions and official records, surprisingly little is known about incidence and prevalence. Official criminal records from the British Home Office (1982) show that the peak age for convictions in 1981 was 18 for males, with 7.7 convictions for indictable offences per 100 persons. The corresponding peak age for females was 17, with 1.0 convictions per 100 persons. The indictable offences are the more serious ones, primarily consisting of thefts and burglaries, excluding minor offences such as motoring infractions, drunkenness and common assault. Unfortunately, the official statistics do not give the number of *different* people convicted at each age.

Farrington (1981) was able to estimate the life-time prevalence of convictions. He calculated that, if 1977 conviction rates were maintained, about 44% of males and 15% of females in England and Wales would be convicted at some time during their lives. He forecast that, if the existing increasing conviction trends continued, the time was not far off when the majority of males would be convicted of indictable offences at some time during their lives. Therefore, it is clear that, even on the basis of official records, criminal behaviour is not restricted to a tiny deviant minority of the population.

Self-report studies reveal far more crime than official records. For example, West and Farrington (1973) reported that, by the age of 17, the majority of their urban working class youths had committed minor indictable crimes such as travelling without a ticket (90%), breaking windows of empty houses (82%), receiving stolen property (65%), stealing from school (59%) and stealing from small shops (53%). However, the incidence of most crimes declined as the youths got older. Whereas 10.9% admitted burglary between ages 15 and 18, only 4.5% admitted it between ages 19 and 21, and only 2.6% between ages 22 and 24 (Farrington, 1983a). It seems that, for many young males, the commission of minor crimes of dishonesty is a normal part of growing up, but very few persist in committing serious crimes after the age of 20.

According to official records, many more males than females commit offences. For example, in 1981, there were 5.4 males found guilty or cautioned for indictable offences for every female (correcting for the population at risk: see Home Office, 1982, Table 5.18). This ratio has declined from 6.1 in 1971. Sex ratios in self-report surveys frequently appear to be much lower. For example, Campbell (1981) reported a sex ratio of only 1.3 to 1, apparently because each act was admitted by about 34% of boys and 26% of girls on average. This ratio, based on prevalence, cannot easily be compared with the official ratio based on numbers of acts committed. However, even this prevalence ratio was high for the more serious acts such as breaking into a shop and using a weapon in a fight (both 5.7 to 1). The most plausible conclusion is that, while males are far more likely than females to commit serious crimes such as burglary and violence, males and females do not differ greatly in the commission of minor deviant acts such as truancy and taking money from home.

While crime and delinquency are widespread, it is nevertheless true to say that the real social problem of crime and delinquency stems from the 5% (approximately) who are the most frequent and serious offenders. Farrington (1983a) reported that 5.8% of the youths accounted for about half of all the convictions, just as earlier West and Farrington (1977) had found that 4.6% of the families accounted for about half of all the convictions of family members (fathers, mothers, sons and daughters). The concentration of serious offending in a relatively small group of multiproblem families is remarkable.

II.—CONCEPTS OF THE PERSON AND MODELS OF HUMAN BEHAVIOUR

In general, theories have been proposed to explain either the occurrence of criminal acts or the development of people with criminal tendencies. Of course, these two things could be linked, for example by suggesting that a person with a certain level of criminal tendency had a certain probability of committing a criminal act in a given situation. Theories designed to explain the occurrence of criminal acts have, in general, concentrated on immediate or situational factors, whereas those designed to explain the development of criminal people have concentrated on historical or individual factors.

A very general theory designed to explain the occurrence of criminal acts was put forward by Clarke (1977). He argued that offending should be viewed as a decision reached in a particular set of circumstances rather than as a generalized behavioural disposition. He proposed that a criminal event depended on (a) early environment and upbringing (e.g., broken home, inconsistent discipline, criminal father); (b) socio-economic and demographic status (e.g., young, male, black, unskilled); (c) current living circumstances (e.g., inner city residence, delinquent associates, truant, football fan, weekend drinker); (d) crises and events (e.g., loses job, beaten up, quarrels with wife, friend arrested); (e) the person (cognitive processes such as perception of risk, and motivational states such as bored or fed up); and (f) the situation (e.g., poorly lit street, no police patrols, unlocked car, self-service shop). The criminal event arose from the interaction between the person and the situation, which were influenced by factors (a) to (d). Clarke was doubtful about whether heredity or personality should be included in this model.

Traditional legal theories dating back to Jeremy Bentham also propose that offending should be viewed as a decision made in a particular situation. Bentham thought that people acted rationally and hedonistically, weighing the pleasure of the crime against the pain of the legal punishment, and that it was necessary to increase the severity of the punishment to tip the scales in favour of law-abiding behaviour. He also realized that there was an interaction between certainty and severity of punishment and concluded that, as a punishment became less certain, it should be made more severe to maintain its deterrent effect. Farrington (1979b) developed a version of this theory, proposing essentially that offending was a rational decision depending on perceived costs, benefits and probabilities, and using the ideas of the subjectively expected utility model of risky decision making.

Theories designed to explain the development of criminal people almost all have the conscience as their central concept. They are essentially social learning theories aiming to explain why people learn to inhibit delinquent behaviour. It is suggested that children are naturally selfish and hedonistic, trying to maximize their pleasure and minimize their pain. Delinquency arises naturally in the pursuit of hedonism, so the problem is to explain why people refrain from delinquent or criminal acts. The answer, according to these theories, is because the tendency to commit delinquent acts is opposed by an internal force—the conscience.

The two most influential versions of this theory were put forward by Trasler (1962) and Eysenck (1964). They agreed that the crucial factor in building up the conscience was punishment imposed by the parents. After the child committed an act which the parent considered to be socially undesirable and for which the child was punished, the child had an anxiety reaction. After the behaviour was followed by the punishment a number of times, the contemplation of the act by the child led to an involuntary resurgence of the anxiety, which tended to block the commission of the act. Therefore, the conscience was essentially a conditioned anxiety response. In this theory, the punishment did not have to be physical punishment, but could be withdrawal of love, for example.

In explaining why some people were more likely to commit delinquent acts than others, Trasler and Eysenck differed in emphasis. Trasler emphasized different methods of child rearing used by parents, while Eysenck emphasized inherited differences in the ability to build up conditioned responses, which were linked to his personality factors. According to Trasler, it was necessary to have a consistent association between the disapproved behaviour and the punishment in order to build up a strong conscience. Hence, laxity, poor supervision and inconsistency, which were more common among lower-class parents, tended to produce delinquent children. According to Eysenck, more extraverted people were less able to build up conditional responses than more introverted ones. Hence, more extraverted people had weaker consciences and committed more delinquent acts. Those who were neurotic as well as extraverted were even more delinquent, because neuroticism acted as a drive which amplified any existing behaviour tendencies.

Despite superficial differences, the social learning theories have many similarities to psychoanalytic theories. According to Freud, personality was divided into three mechanisms—the *id*, *ego* and *superego*. The id contained instinctual drives which were conducive to delinquency. The ego controlled behaviour and was the seat of consciousness, trying to achieve the wishes of the id while taking into account the demands of reality. The superego performed two functions, namely opposing antisocial instincts (the conscience) and representing ideal behaviour (the ego-ideal). It essentially consisted of the internal representation of the standards of the parents. Whether a person committed a delinquent act depended primarily on the strength of the superego, which in turn depended on the type of upbringing the person enjoyed during the first few years of life. People were likely to have strong superegos if they enjoyed a warm, loving relationship with their parents, if their parents consistently discouraged antisocial behaviour, and if their parents consistently acted in accordance with the ideals of the criminal law. (Detailed discussion of developmental theories is provided by Herbert in Chapter 2.)

As an example of a somewhat different psychological theory, Kohlberg (1976) proposed that people become delinquent because their moral reasoning powers have failed to develop. Some sociological theories are quite similar to the psychological ones outlined above. In particular, the social control theory of Hirschi (1969) was similar to social learning theory in suggesting that people commit delinquent acts because they do not have a strong bond to society. Other sociological theories, such as the delinquent subculture theory of Cohen (1955) or the differential association theory of Sutherland and Cressey (1974), assumed that conforming behaviour was normal and that the problem was to explain why people became delinquent. Both of these theories laid great emphasis on the norms and values to which people were exposed.

None of these theories has been verified in a programme of well-controlled empirical research.

III.—INDIVIDUAL ASSESSMENT

In attempting to test the theories outlined above, or in carrying out and evaluating prevention or treatment methods based on them, it is necessary to measure a wide variety of theoretical constructs. Methods of measuring the key dependent variable of delinquent or criminal behaviour have been described in Section I above. Methods of measuring other theoretical constructs include self-report questionnaires, other psychological tests, interviews, ratings by other people, physical and physiological techniques, and direct observation of behaviour. The methods used by West and Farrington (1977) in a study of young males are now described as illustrative examples.

Self-report questionnaires and other psychological tests have the advantages of ease of administration and comparatively objective scoring. In this research, non-verbal IQ was measured using the Progressive Matrices test, vocabulary using Mill Hill Synonyms, and personality by the New Junior Maudsley Inventory (at the ages of 10 and 14) and the Eysenck Personality Inventory (at 16). Psychomotor clumsiness was measured using three tests, the Porteus Mazes, the Spiral Maze and the Tapping Test. Self-concept was measured using the Semantic Differential, and projective techniques such as the Picture Frustration Test and the Hand Test were also used (primarily as measures of aggressive tendencies). Self-report questionnaires were also used to measure social attitudes, and delinquent acts by friends and acquaintances.

A great deal of information was derived from interviews. Interviews with the boys' parents provided details about such things as family income, family size (also checked against school records), the social class of the family breadwinner, the parents' degree of supervision of the boy, their child-rearing attitudes and behaviour, and their degree of conflict with each other. Interviews with the boys provided details about their job histories and leisure habits, such as spending time hanging about, drinking and sexual activity. Ratings were obtained from the boys' teachers about such things as troublesome behaviour in school, truancy and school attainments. Peer ratings were also collected, about the boys' troublesomeness, daring, dishonesty and popularity.

The major physical and physiological measures were of height and weight at different ages, grip strength and pulse rate. Ratings of physical appearance were made by the interviewers, regarding such things as racial characteristics, wearing glasses, tattoos, nail biting and hair length. Finally, a small number of direct behavioural measures was taken, for example by systematically giving youths opportunities to smoke and to gamble part of their interview fee.

In this research, the two major measurement problems were validity and objectivity. Regarding validity, it is essential to try to verify that an empirical variable really was measuring the intended theoretical construct and not something else. This can only be achieved by having a large number of different measures of different theoretical constructs, and by investigating the intercorrelations. It is then possible to demonstrate, for example, that self-report, psychological test, interview and offical records measures of X are more closely related to each other than to self-report, psychological test, interview and official records measures of Y.

Objectivity is especially a problem in interviews, and it is desirable to investigate the effects of different interviewers. This was done in the present research by randomly allocating youths to interviewers and by having all interviews with the youths fully tape-recorded and transcribed. The interviews were structured, and the interviewers were given detailed instructions. Problems of objectivity arose in the earliest interviews conducted with the families by psychiatric social workers. In order that they might work in their accustomed way, and to elicit the maximum cooperation, the psychiatric social workers were given a list of topics to be covered, but were allowed to conduct unstructured interviews. They took a few written notes during the interviews, but mainly relied on dictating into a tape-recorder afterwards. A good deal of this information proved to be too subjective and too much influenced by halo effects to be of use for research purposes.

IV.—THE IMMEDIATE SOCIAL AND EMOTIONAL ENVIRONMENT

It seems clear that family interaction is an important factor in the development of delinquency in children. West and Farrington (1973) found that children who had experienced cruel, passive or neglecting parental attitudes, harsh or erratic parental discipline, parental disharmony and lax parental supervision tended to become the most delinquent. In addition, children who were brought up by parents who had themselves been convicted, or who had convicted older siblings, tended to become the most delinquent. These results are consistent with social learning theory, especially if it is suggested that children become delinquent either because of inefficient social training or because of their exposure to delinquent models or delinquent values.

It may be that official and self-report measures of delinquency peak between ages 15 and 19 because young people are most under the influence of their peers at these ages. All the evidence suggests that juvenile delinquency is a group phenomenon. For example, West and Farrington (1973) reported that about five-sixths of burglaries and three-quarters of thefts from shops were committed with (typically two) other persons, usually other boys of similar age. Later research was designed to compare convicted youths who gave up criminal behaviour after the age of 20 with those who persisted. Two important factors seemed to be that those who gave up had broken away from their delinquent associates and had previously committed offences for excitement or enjoyment (as opposed to rational or utilitarian reasons). It is plausible to suggest that those who commit delinquent acts in small groups do so primarily for excitement and tend to give up after the age of 20, whereas those who commit such acts alone do so primarily for rational reasons and tend to persist. The peer group facilitation of delinquency may operate by making it an exciting, boredom-reducing activity, perhaps through the medium of dares and challenges.

After the age of 20, the peer group tends to give way to marriage and family influences once again, and it is widely believed that marriage is one of the factors leading to a reduction in criminal behaviour with age. In the present research, married men thought that they were less criminal than single men, married men were more likely to have given up going round in a small group of males, and married delinquents were less likely to be reconvicted than matched unmarried delinquents (West, 1982). However, it was also noticeable that convicted men had a greater tendency to marry convicted women than did unconvicted men, and that delinquents who married convicted women were more likely to be reconvicted than those who married unconvicted women. Therefore, the effect of marriage on men seems to depend to some extent on characteristics of the marriage partner.

There has been a great deal of recent work on the importance of the immediate physical environment on offending, emphasizing criminal opportunities and surveillance. For example, Wilson (1978) studied vandalism on London housing estates, and found that most damage occurred in places which were easy to reach (at ground level) and not continuously observed (e.g., lifts, stairs, garages). However, the best predictor of vandalism rates was not a physical factor but child density. For more details of this series of studies, see Clarke and Mayhew (1980).

V.—THE WIDER SOCIAL AND ORGANIZATIONAL ENVIRONMENT

Some of the psychological theories have tried to explain how larger social structural factors have an effect on criminal behaviour. For example, Trasler (1962) suggested that delinquency was greater in the lower social classes because lower-class parents used less efficient methods of child rearing. This theory is wide ranging, trying to relate societal factors such as social class to social psychological factors such as family interaction, individual psychological factors such as strength of conscience, and physiological processes (e.g., in the autonomic nervous system). It seems likely that a complete explanation of criminal behaviour will have to include theoretical constructs at all these levels, so that a distinction between psychological and sociological theories may not be helpful.

Some sociological theories also include constructs at several different levels. For example, the labelling theory of Lemert (1972) explained how official labelling by society might produce an increase in deviant behaviour, because the individual's self-concept (a psychological construct) was changed by interaction with agents of social control (a social psychological process) and by the stigmatization of societal labelling. In agreement with this theory, Farrington (1977) found that youths who were convicted tended to increase their delinquency afterwards, in comparison with matched unconvicted youths.

One social institution which is often thought to influence delinquent behaviour is the school. In the 1960s, Power, Alderson, Phillipson, Shoenberg and Morris (1967) showed that apparently similar London schools had dramatically different delinquency rates. However, Farrington (1972) found that the major reason for these different rates was because the schools had different intakes, and that the schools themselves had no significant effect over and above intake factors. In more recent research, Rutter, Maughan, Mortimore, Ouston and Smith (1979) showed that, while intake factors were indeed the most important, the schools themselves also had a significant additive effect. Delinquency rates were high when there was a high amount of punishment given to pupils, and a low amount of praise. Unfortunately, it is impossible to know whether frequent punishments and rare rewards produce delinquency (perhaps through alienation from the school) or whether frequent punishments, rare rewards and delinquency are all consequences of having a high proportion of troublesome children in a school.

Crime and delinquency are clearly greater in some areas than in others, and in particular are greater in urban areas (and especially in inner-city areas) than in rural ones. Moving out of an inner-city area seems to lead to a decrease in delinquent and criminal behaviour (West, 1982). How areas have effects on individuals is not entirely clear. It could be that inner-city living produces increased tensions and frustrations, which in turn produce increased crime. Alternatively, it could be that local authority housing practices lead to a concentration of problem families in certain areas, and that there is more opportunity for crime in an inner-city area than in the country.

It might be expected that criminal and delinquent behaviour would be affected by societal changes such as increasing divorce rates or increasing unemployment rates. At the individual level, it is clear that divorce and unemployment are associated with high delinquency, but this is much less clear at the societal level. In other words, unemployed individuals are more delinquent than employed individuals, but it is less clear (and more difficult to demonstrate) that periods of high unemployment produce high crime rates.

VI.—TYPES OF INTERVENTION

The response of the criminal justice system to crime and delinquency is most commonly intended to achieve the aim of retribution. It is thought that offenders should suffer in proportion to the gravity of their crimes and also in proportion to the gravity of their criminal records. Responses are also intended to achieve the aims of individual and general deterrence, based on the rational Bentham theory of crime outlined in Section II above. In recent years, the aim of incapacitation, or preventing crime by keeping offenders out of circulation, has become more prominent, especially in connection with dangerous offenders. Other notable aims are reparation and denunciation (see Farrington, 1978).

Emphasis on rehabilitation, which is the penal aim most closely associated with psychological interventions, has declined in the last decade. This is partly because of the belief, widespread at least in government agencies, that rehabilitation is difficult or impossible (e.g., Brody, 1976). After describing the theory outlined in Section II above, Clarke (1977) concluded that the best hope of reducing crime is to concentrate on reducing opportunities by physical or situational crime prevention, and this view is still popular in the Home Office. My own view is that the abandonment of rehabilitation is premature, because much of the research on which it is apparently based has serious methodological difficulties, some of which are mentioned in Sections VII and VIII.

The major psychological interventions used with offenders can be divided into 'talking therapies' (counselling, psychotherapy and social skills training) versus 'behavioural' ones (behaviour modification and behaviour therapy). These therapeutic methods can be used with individuals or with unrelated or related groups (for example, the family). They are difficult to evaluate because of the heterogeneity and variability of the treatments, including the common use of more than one treatment (e.g., social skills training plus behaviour modification). Another problem is that psychological interventions may be confounded with non-psychological ones; for example, when social skills training is used as part of an intermediate treatment programme.

In many cases, the talking therapies are roughly based on the psychoanalytic theory described above. The aim of the treatment is to build up relationships with clients, to help them understand their problems, and to help them adopt non-criminal solutions. With social skills training, there may be explicit teaching (perhaps involving role-playing) of how to resist peer pressures to commit offences, how to interact with the opposite sex, how to deal with authority figures, etc. The behavioural therapies are roughly based on the social learning theory outlined above. They aim to change the offender's behaviour by the systematic and explicit use of rewards and punishments. A detailed account of behavioural interventions is given by Herbert in Chapter 2.

VII.—IS PSYCHOLOGICAL INTERVENTION SUCCESSFUL?

For reasons which are explained in Section VIII, it is desirable to evaluate psychological interventions (or indeed any interventions) with offenders by means of randomized experiments, randomly assigning not less than about 50 subjects to each condition and having a follow-up measure of offending during a reasonably long period (at least two years). This assumes that the main aim of the intervention is to reduce subsequent offending by the treated people. Farrington (1982) has provided a detailed review of randomized experiments in criminology.

The experiments reviewed can be divided into those carried out in institutions and those in the natural environment, and into those carried out in Great Britain and those in North America. The term 'psychological' is interpreted very liberally here to include any counselling, whether carried out by psychologists or not. Even with this liberal definition, it is hard to find experimental evaluations of the effect of psychological interventions in the natural environment on offending in Great Britain. The nearest study is probably the IMPACT experiment (Folkard, Smith and Smith, 1976), which showed that intensive probation was no better than regular probation in preventing reconvictions in a two-year follow-up period.

There have been four British experiments on talking therapies in institutions. Williams (1970) compared three borstals with different regimes, based respectively on individual casework, group counselling, and the more traditional approach of hard work, firm discipline, and the inculcation of personal responsibility. Those treated in the casework institution had a lower reconviction rate during a two-year follow-up period than those treated in the others. Cornish and Clarke (1975) compared two living units within an approved school, one run as a therapeutic community and the other more traditionally, but found no difference in reconviction rates between them. Shaw (1974) and Fowles (1978) both studied the effects of special pre-release counselling in prisons, but unfortunately obtained contradictory results. The counselling was effective in reducing reconvictions in the Shaw experiment, but not in the Fowles one. These results are difficult to summarize, other than to suggest that talking therapies can sometimes be effective.

Clearly, more research is needed. There is a special need for randomized experiments on behavioural therapies, especially in the natural environment. In reviewing delinquent behaviour modification attempts in the natural environment, Farrington (1979a) noted that behaviour modification was based on the theory that the likelihood of any act depended on the rewards and punishments for that act in the environment. The reinforcement system in an institution was likely to be different from that in the outside world. Therefore, even if a person were totally non-delinquent in an institution, the theory would not lead us to expect that this non-delinquent behaviour should persist in the changed contingencies of the outside world.

Moving on to North American research, evaluations of talking therapies in the natural environment suggest that, in general, they are ineffectual in reducing offending (see the review by Farrington, 1982). The most impressive experiment is the Cambridge-Somerville study evaluated by McCord (1978). In this, the boys who were randomly assigned to the treated group were given an average of five years regular friendly attention by counsellors, while those in the untreated group were left to the usual resources of the community. Thirty years later, McCord found little difference between the treated and control groups, except that more of the treated group had committed two or more offences, and more of the treated group had become alcoholics, become mentally ill, or died at an early age. She speculated that the treated group might have become dependent on the treatment and then resentful when it was withdrawn.

Perhaps the most interesting North American evaluation of behavioural therapy in the natural environment was carried out by Binder and Newkirk (1977). In this, the treated group was helped using contingency contracting within families. The aim was to change patterns of communication within families, to teach parents effective ways of giving rewards and punishments, and to change environmental conditions which caused trouble. This programme was effective in reducing arrests during a one-year follow-up period, but a later unpublished report showed that the effect was obtained only in one town out of two.

North American evaluations of talking therapies in institutions, of which the most famous was by Kassebaum, Ward and Wilner (1971), tend to show no effect on recidivism. The experiment by Adams (1970) is interesting, because he investigated the desirability of matching the treatment to the clients. Institutionalized delinquents were divided into those thought to be amenable and those thought to be non-amenable to the individual counselling treatment, and both groups were then randomly assigned to the treatment and control conditions. The 'treated amenable' group had the lowest recidivism rate, while the 'treated non-amenable' group had the highest. This experiment shows the possibility of an interaction between types of treatment and types of people.

The last North American experiment to be mentioned was carried out by Jesness (1975). In this, delinquents were randomly assigned to two institutions similar in size, organizational structure, staffing patterns and physical layout. The main difference was that one had a behavioural regime in which points were earned for reinforcers such as recreational opportunities and early parole, while in the other the treatment strategy was based on psychodynamic principles and group therapy. A two-year follow-up showed no difference between the institutions in recidivism.

The only conclusion which can be drawn from this body of literature is that psychological interventions are sometimes but not always successful. The key parameters which distinguish the effective from the ineffective treatments are not yet clear. However, the past experiments have drawn attention to a number of methodological problems which need to be overcome in future research (for more details see Farrington, 1982).

Beginning with the independent variable, the exact nature of the treatments given is often unclear. When they are described in detail, there is often disagreement about what underlying theoretical constructs were being manipulated. For example, did the Cambridge-Somerville study involve 'individual psychotherapy' or 'friendly visiting'? In addition, information about the extent to which the treatments were carried out as intended is often missing. Treatments specified at the beginning of an experiment may change over time, perhaps because administrators wish to correct perceived defects or make possible improvements. Attempts may be made to select staff who are sympathetic to the particular treatment they are giving, but this makes it difficult to disentangle the effects of the treatment from the effects of the staff. Few researchers have attempted to control for the possibility of a 'Hawthorne' effect, namely that *any* kind of special attention given to clients might lead to an improvement in their behaviour.

Very few experiments have been able to arrange a truly 'untreated' control group. It is more feasible to compare two varieties or strengths of the same treatment, but then there may be insufficient variation in the independent variable to produce a detectable effect. If two treatments are compared and the first proves better than the second, it is impossible to know whether either is better or worse than no treatment. Similarly, if two treatments are equally effective, it is impossible to know whether they are both better than, both worse than, or both just as good as no treatment.

Moving on to the dependent variable, the most common measures of offending have been based on official records, which have many problems (see Section I). Official records should be supplemented by other measures, such as self-reports. There are problems surrounding the length of the follow-up period and when it should start. In situations where there can be a delay of several months or even a year between arrest and conviction, it is important to lengthen the follow-up period so that the offence-conviction interval is relatively small or to define reconvictions according to the date of the offence rather than the date of the conviction. Experiments measuring reconvictions during a one-year follow-up period seem unsatisfactory, because they exclude people who have re-offended quite soon after the treatment but have not yet been reconvicted.

Problems arise when institutional and community treatments are compared, in regard to the start of the follow-up period. If this begins on release for the institutional group and on sentence for the community group, the groups will be at risk during different age ranges and time periods. This difficulty can be avoided if the treatment period is the same in each case and if the follow-up period begins at the end of the treatment, but there is then the problem of what to do about those in the community group who offend during the treatment period. There is no easy solution, but one possibility is to extend the aims of the treatment to include crime prevention for any reason (including incapacitation). The follow-up period can then include time spent in an institution and can start on the date of sentence for both groups.

VIII.—METHODOLOGICAL AND PRACTICAL PROBLEMS

There are or should be two stages in any research enterprise—generating and testing hypotheses. Hypotheses can be generated by a variety of methods, including armchair speculation, literature reviews, searches of records, participant observation research and unstructured interviews. The hypotheses which are of most interest to a scientist are those which can be tested in empirical research and which predict the effect of one factor (the independent variable) on another (the dependent variable). Testing such hypotheses may be part of the assessment of the adequacy of a theory, if they are derived from it. Alternatively, testing such hypotheses may be part of the assessment of methods of preventing or treating delinquency, which may or may not be derived from explicitly formulated theories about the causes of delinquency.

The best method of testing a causal hypothesis is to carry out a randomized experiment. There are many problems of interpretation arising in non-experimental research. For example, imagine a correlational study which shows that poor parental supervision is associated with high self-reported delinquency. Does this mean that poor parental supervision produces delinquent behaviour? Or that parents whose children commit large numbers of delinquent acts give up trying to supervise them as a result? Or that there is no causal relationship between poor parental supervision and delinquency, but that they appear to be related because both tend to occur especially in low income families? These are only some of the possibilities. The only way to establish if parental supervision does produce (or conversely prevent) delinquency is to carry out an experiment in which parental supervision is deliberately varied as the independent variable and delinquent behaviour is measured as the dependent one.

The best kinds of experiments in this area are those in which people are assigned at random to different conditions of the independent variable. Providing that a reasonably large number of people is assigned at random, those in one condition will be equivalent (within the limits of statistical fluctuation) to those in another, on all variables extraneous to the experiment. The control of extraneous variables by randomization is similar to the control of extraneous variables in the physical sciences by holding physical conditions (e.g., temperature, pressure) constant. Non-randomized experiments, for example those involving matching, can never ensure equivalence on all extraneous variables. Hence, in non-randomized experiments it could always be argued that some uncontrolled variable was responsible for any observed change in the dependent one.

Despite the methodological advantages of randomized experiments, they are difficult to carry out on real-life problems such as the prevention of delinquency. Some ethical objections to them are considered in Section IX. One practical problem arises from the prospective nature of experiments. Allowing time for pilot work, randomly assigning a sufficient number of cases, an adequate follow-up period, data analysis, and writing up a report, it is doubtful if a worthwhile criminological experiment could be completed within five years. This time scale may make funding difficult. A major problem is to get permission for experiments from criminal justice administrators, and even when randomization has been agreed, administrators may find ways of circumventing it (see, e.g., Conner, 1977). Ideally, the programme administrators and the subjects should be ignorant of the experimental conditions and hypotheses, to avoid problems such as experimenter expectancy and demand characteristics. But this is usually difficult to arrange.

When a randomized experiment is impossible, the next best method is to carry out a prospective longitudinal survey and to analyse it as a quasi-experiment (see Cook and Campbell, 1979). An example of this kind of approach is the Farrington (1977) study of the effect of official labelling on delinquent behaviour, mentioned in Section III. In prospective research, problems of retrospective bias are avoided. In longitudinal research, it is possible to establish if changes in one factor precede changes in another, which helps in trying to establish causal order. If a large number of variables is measured, it is then possible to achieve statistical (as opposed to experimental) control of extraneous variables. Of course, prospective longitudinal surveys have practical problems, for example in keeping contact with subjects over a long period, but they have many advantages (for a review of longitudinal research on crime and delinquency, see Farrington, 1979c).

IX.—PROBLEMS OF ETHICS AND CONFIDENTIALITY

Ethical problems are discussed here first in connection with psychological research on crime and delinquency and, second, in connection with the roles of psychologists as professionals in the criminal justice system.

Beginning with research, it has already been pointed out that, from a methodological standpoint, it is desirable for subjects to be ignorant about experimental conditions and hypotheses. This clashes with the requirement that subjects should give their informed consent to participate in psychological research. The extent to which incarcerated subjects can freely consent to participate has sometimes been doubted. A problem arising, especially in experiments, centres on the denial of treatment to certain people. This would be difficult to justify if there were sufficient resources to treat everyone and if the treatment was known to be beneficial. However, if the effects of the treatment were known, it would be unnecessary to carry out an experiment to investigate them. Furthermore, resources are often insufficient to treat everyone, and in these cases randomization may be the fairest method of selecting clients for treatment.

A useful rule is that subjects should not be harmed by participating in research. Many experimenters randomly assign subjects either to the usual treatment or to something believed to be better (or preferred by the subjects). For example, people who would normally be committed to an institution might be randomly assigned either to an institution or to some kind of counselling treatment in the community. One problem with this is that what is best for the individual is not necessarily best for the community. Ethical issues arise if people who would normally be in institutions commit offences while in the community as part of an experiment. Overall, the best way to evaluate whether a project is ethical is probably to consider whether its likely benefits (usually consisting of, or consequent upon, advancement of knowledge) outweigh its likely costs (e.g., in terms of deception, invasion of privacy, social harm or harm caused to subjects).

Moving on to ethical issues affecting professional psychologists in the criminal justice system, this topic has been discussed by a task force of the American Psychological Association (1978). In Britain, a large number of these psychologists are employed in the prison system (see, e.g., Farrington, 1980), and others are employed by the Department of Health and Social Security in such institutions as Community Homes, and Observation and Assessment Centres. Another important group of psychologists are those who appear in court as expert witnesses (see Haward, 1979). Other professional psychologists (mainly clinical or educational) work with offenders in Special Hospitals or in the child guidance services. Few British psychologists are as yet employed by police departments (unlike North America) and few by the probation service.

A major ethical issue is whether the psychologist's client is the offender or the criminal justice system. In penal institutions, this is unclear. In courts, because of their adversarial nature, the psychologist as an expert witness is called (and paid) by one side only, and in practice spends a great deal of time trying to refute police evidence. It might be more in accord with their scientific ideals if psychologists could give evidence dispassionately as 'friends of the court'. A related issue is the degree of confidentiality of information given by offenders to psychologists. How far information given by prisoners to prison psychologists can be kept confidential from the prison authorities is unclear. In court, there is no statutory provision which would allow a psychologist to withhold confidential information given by a client. This lack of confidentiality should be made clear to offenders or defendants at the outset of any interview, even if it may interfere with therapeutic efforts.

Because prison psychologists are employees of the Home Office, they may find it difficult in practice to refuse to carry out instructions which they

regarded as unethical. For this reason, it is important for prison psychologists
to belong to The British Psychological Society, which has its declared ethical
codes. With the backing of the BPS, it may be more possible for prison
psychologists to refuse in such circumstances. One rather worrying recent
development centres on the issue of competence. Ethically, professional
psychologists should only carry out tasks which are within their sphere of
competence (as established by their training and qualifications). However, it
is noticeable that the roles of prison psychologists in recent years have
widened considerably, to include for example advice to the governor about
the planning of prison buildings and the design of security techniques. In an
era of lessening emphasis on rehabilitation in the prison system, it may make
a great deal of tactical sense to change from being treatment professionals
to being senior management advisers; but it is less obvious that the latter is
always within the sphere of competence of individual psychologists. As
Trasler (1974) pointed out, there are dangers in blurring the distinction
between advice based on systematic research and that stemming primarily
from the armchair. No doubt such considerations will affect the pattern of
training of psychologists for work within the prison service.

X.—THE ROLE OF OTHER DISCIPLINES AND PROFESSIONS

In discussing this, it is wise to distinguish between psychology as an academic
discipline and psychologists as professionals in the criminal justice system.
Psychology as an academic discipline overlaps considerably in subject matter
with other social and behavioural sciences, and especially with sociology
and psychiatry. There are more differences between psychology and other
disciplines in methodology than in areas of interest. For example, a good
deal of sociological research is essentially of the hypothesis-generating kind,
based on participant observation, interviews, searches of records and other
correlational techniques. In contrast, most psychological research is designed
to test hypotheses using the experimental method, and this is often the
unique contribution of psychologists. Because of the considerable overlap in
areas of interest, psychologists interested in crime and delinquency have to
be familiar with the sociological, psychiatric and legal literature (research
and theories).

Psychologists as criminal justice professionals are likely to come into
conflict particularly with psychiatrists. In courts, for example, the role of
psychiatrists is much better established and has a longer history than that of
psychologists. It is quite common for a psychiatrist to give expert witness
testimony consisting of clinical opinions based on assessments by a psychologist. Many psychologists feel that they, and not psychiatrists, should present
these kinds of psychological assessments in court. Psychologists in courts are

also likely to conflict with lawyers, who try to convert their scientific concepts into legal terms such as 'disease of the mind' and 'beyond reasonable doubt'.

XI.—FUTURE PROSPECTS

To my mind, the major role of psychologists interested in crime and delinquency or employed in the criminal justice system should be to carry out quantitative, and especially experimental, research. This is not to argue that they should not be involved in other activities (e.g., rehabilitative treatment) as well. However, more than any other group, they are trained and qualified to carry out methodologically sophisticated research. The extent of our ignorance about the relative effectiveness of different penal treatments is appalling, and there is not enough hard evidence about the causes of delinquency or about the best ways of preventing or treating it. It seems unethical of the British government to continue using a range of penal treatments whose effects are essentially unknown, and to introduce new laws, new penal treatments and large-scale social programmes without attempting to evaluate their likely effects beforehand in small-scale experiments.

It is easy to specify the ideal model of scientific progress. Ideally, a series of testable causal hypotheses should be derived from each theory. These should then be tested in research projects involving randomized experiments, prospective longitudinal surveys, and direct behavioural measures. Such projects could be concerned with the prevention or treatment of delinquency since, if a factor causes delinquency, it should be possible in principle to vary that factor to prevent delinquency. Ideally, each experiment should be one link in a chain of cumulative knowledge, guided by theory. Methods of prevention and treatment of delinquency should be based on empirically validated theories. It may be that attempts at an early age to prevent delinquency would have more success than attempts to treat it later; that the most effective method of rehabilitating offenders is by means of behaviour modification in the natural environment; and that crime can be reduced more effectively by changing the physical environment than by trying to change people. These kinds of question need to be investigated in a programme of well controlled research.

The ideals stated above seem quite far off at present, but psychologists should not lose sight of them. There are many problems in achieving them at present. Conservative governments in Britain seem hostile to research and more interested in retribution, deterrence and incapacitation than in rehabilitation or prevention. As Farrington (1983b) has argued, the 1980 White Paper (Home Office, Welsh Office, Department of Health and Social Security, 1980), which led to the Criminal Justice Act 1982, seriously distorted and misrepresented existing research findings in justifying the new legislation. Ironically, it may be that more rioting, in prisons and in the streets, is the best stimulus for government funding for crime and delinquency research. Unfortunately, the kind of research which is stimulated is usually *ad hoc* and short-term rather than the cumulative long-term fundamental programme which is needed. I can only hope that it will be possible to educate some future government about the need for methodologically adequate research. At that happy time, psychologists would be able to make an important contribution to our knowledge about the explanation, prevention and treatment of delinquent and criminal behaviour. That would surely be to everyone's advantage.

XII.—ANNOTATED READINGS

Clarke, R. V. G. and Cornish, D. B. (1972). *The Controlled Trial in Institutional Research*. London: Her Majesty's Stationery Office.

This reviews existing randomized experiments on the treatment of delinquents and criminals. It also describes an experiment carried out by the authors in Kingswood Approved School, comparing a living unit run as a therapeutic community with a more traditional unit. It is especially useful in detailing the methodological and practical problems which arise in these kinds of experiments.

Farrington, D. P., Hawkins, K. and Lloyd-Bostock, S. (1979) *Psychology, Law and Legal Processes*. London: Macmillan Press.

This collection, which contains chapters by lawyers and psychologists, reviews British research on the contribution of psychologists to law and legal processes. There is a review chapter by the editors and substantive chapters on such topics as the psychologist as an expert witness, jury decision making, magistrates' sentencing, eyewitness testimony and identification parades.

Feldman, M. P. (1977). *Criminal Behaviour*. Chichester: Wiley.

This is a wide-ranging introductory textbook on criminological psychology. It contains chapters on such topics as: socialization, moral development and child-rearing methods; experiments on transgression and aggression; helping behaviour; chromosome abnormalities and genetic factors; personality; psychopaths and sexual offenders; and behaviour modification techniques.

Rutter, M. and Giller, H. (1983) *Juvenile Delinquency*. Harmondsworth: Penguin.

This is the most recent comprehensive review of knowledge about juvenile delinquency. It covers measurement problems, historical trends and correlates of delinquency. It goes on to evaluate the major theories and the major methods of prevention and treatment.

West, D. J. (1982). *Delinquency*. London: Heinemann.

This is a non-technical review of the major results obtained in the longitudinal survey of delinquency referred to in the text. It discusses the nature and extent of delinquency, the identification of potential delinquents, and the effects of such things as schools, marriage and getting caught, on the course of delinquency careers.

West, D. J. and Farrington, D. P. (1977). *The Delinquent Way of Life*. London: Heinemann.

This is a more technical report on the longitudinal survey concentrating on the state of affairs at age 18–19. It documents how a constellation of adverse family background factors (including poverty, large families, marital disharmony, ineffective child-rearing methods and parental criminality) leads to a socially deviant life style in late adolescence and early adulthood (including heavy drinking, gambling, drug use, reckless driving, sexual promiscuity, aggression and criminal behaviour).

XIII.—REFERENCES

Adams, S. (1970). The PICO project. In: N. Johnston, L. Savitz and M. E. Wolfgang (Eds.) *The Sociology of Punishment and Correction* (Second Edition). New York: Wiley.

American Psychological Association (1978). Report of the task force on the role of psychology in the criminal justice system. *American Psychologist*, **33**, 1099–1133.

Binder, A. and Newkirk, M. (1977). A programme to extend police service capability. *Crime Prevention Review*, **4**, 26–32.

Brody, S. R. (1976). *The Effectiveness of Sentencing*. London: Her Majesty's Stationery Office.

Buckle, A. and Farrington, D. P. (1983). An observational study of shoplifting. *British Journal of Criminology*, **23**, in press.

Campbell, A. (1981). *Girl Delinquents*. Oxford. Blackwell.

Clarke, R. V. G. (1977). Psychology and crime. *Bulletin of the British Psychological Society*, **30**, 280–283.

Clarke, R. V. G. and Mayhew, P. (Eds.) (1980). *Designing out Crime*. London: Her Majesty's Stationery Office.

Cohen, A. K. (1955). *Delinquent Boys*. Glencoe, Illinois: Free Press.

Conner, R. F. (1977). Selecting a control group. *Evaluation Quarterly*, **1**, 195–244.

Cook, T. D. and Campbell, D. T. (1979). *Quasi-Experimentation*. Chicago, Illinois: Rand McNally.

Cornish, D. B. and Clarke, R. V. G. (1975). *Residential Treatment and its Effects on Delinquency*. London: Her Majesty's Stationery Office.

Eysenck, H. J. (1964). *Crime and Personality*. London: Routledge and Kegan Paul.

Farrington, D. P. (1972). Delinquency begins at home. *New Society*, **21**, 495–497.

Farrington, D. P. (1977). The effects of public labelling. *British Journal of Criminology*, **17**, 112–125.

Farrington, D. P. (1978). The effectiveness of sentences. *Justice of the Peace*, **142**, 68–71.

Farrington, D. P. (1979a). Delinquent behaviour modification in the natural environment. *British Journal of Criminology*, **19**, 353–372.

Farrington, D. P. (1979b). Experiments on deviance with special reference to dishonesty. In: L. Berkowitz (Ed.) *Advances in Experimental Social Psychology*, volume 12. New York: Academic Press.

Farrington, D. P. (1979c). Longitudinal research on crime and delinquency. In: N. Morris and M. Tonry (Eds.) *Crime and Justice*, volume 1. Chicago, Illinois: University of Chicago Press.

Farrington, D. P. (1980). The professionalization of English prison psychologists. *Professional Psychology*, **11**, 855–862.

Farrington, D. P. (1981). The prevalence of convictions. *British Journal of Criminology*, **21**, 173–175.

Farrington, D. P. (1982). Randomized experiments on crime and justice. In: M. Tonry and N. Morris (Eds.) *Crime and Justice*, volume 4. Chicago, Illinois: University of Chicago Press.

Farrington, D. P. (1983a) Offending from 10 to 25 years of age. In: K. Van Dusen and S. A. Mednick (Eds.) *Prospective Studies of Crime and Delinquency*. Boston: Kluwer-Nijhoff.

Farrington, D. P. (1983b). The juvenile justice system in England and Wales. In: M. Klein (Ed.) *Western Systems of Juvenile Justice*. Beverly Hills, California: Sage.

Folkard, M. S., Smith, D. E. and Smith, D. D. (1976) *IMPACT*, volume 2. London: Her Majesty's Stationery Office.

Fowles, A. J. (1978) *Prison Welfare*. London: Her Majesty's Stationery Office.

Haward, L. R. C. (1979) The psychologist as expert witness. In: D. P. Farrington, K. Hawkins and S. Lloyd-Bostock (Eds.) *Psychology, Law and Legal Processes*. London: Macmillan Press.

Hirschi, T. (1969). *Causes of Delinquency*. Berkeley, California: University of California Press.

Home Office (1982). *Criminal Statistics, England and Wales, 1981*. London: Her Majesty's Stationery Office (Cmnd. 8668).

Home Office, Welsh Office, Department of Health and Social Security (1980). *Young Offenders*. London: Her Majesty's Stationery Office (Cmnd. 8045).

Jesness, C. F. (1975). Comparative effectiveness of behaviour modification and transactional analysis programmes for delinquents. *Journal of Consulting and Clinical Psychology*, **43**, 758–779.

Kassebaum, G., Ward, D. and Wilner, D. (1971). *Prison Treatment and Parole Survival*. New York: Wiley.

Kohlberg, L. (1976) Moral stages and moralization. In: T. Lickona (Ed.) *Moral Development and Behavior*. New York: Holt, Rinehart and Winston.

Lemert, E. M. (1972). *Human Deviance, Social Problems and Social Control* (Second Edition). Englewood Cliffs, New Jersey: Prentice-Hall.

McCord, J. (1978). A thirty-year follow-up of treatment effects. *American Psychologist*, **33**, 284–289.

Power, M. J., Alderson, M. R., Phillipson, C. M., Shoenberg, E. and Morris, J. N. (1967). Delinquent schools? *New Society*, **10**, 542–543.

Rutter, M., Maughan, B., Mortimore, P., Ouston, J. and Smith, A. (1979). *Fifteen Thousand Hours*. London: Open Books.

Shaw, M. (1974). *Social Work in Prison*. London: Her Majesty's Stationery Office.

Sutherland, E. H. and Cressey, D. R. (1974). *Criminology* (Ninth Edition). Philadelphia, Pennsylvania: Lippincott.

Trasler, G. B. (1962). *The Explanation of Criminality*. London: Routledge and Kegan Paul.

Trasler, G. B. (1974). The role of psychologists in the penal system. In: L. Blom-Cooper (Ed.) *Progress in Penal Reform*. Oxford: Clarendon Press.

West, D. J. (1982). *Delinquency*. London: Heinemann.

West, D. J. and Farrington, D. P. (1973). *Who Becomes Delinquent?* London: Heinemann.

West, D. J. and Farrington, D. P. (1977). *The Delinquent Way of Life*. London: Heinemann.

Williams, M. (1970). *A Study of Some Aspects of Borstal Allocation*. London: Home Office Prison Department, Office of the Chief Psychologist.

Wilson, S. (1978). Vandalism and 'defensible space' on London housing estates. In: R. V. G. Clarke (Ed.) *Tackling Vandalism*. London: Her Majesty's Stationery Office.

Psychology and Social Problems
Edited by A. Gale and A. J. Chapman
© 1984 John Wiley & Sons Ltd.

CHAPTER 4

FAILURES OF ACADEMIC ACHIEVEMENT

David Fontana

I.—THE EXTENT OF THE PROBLEM

We can define academic failure as occurring where an individual's standard of performance falls below a certain specified level in a given activity. Such a definition begs a number of questions of course, such as *who* determines the 'specified level'; *who* decides whether or not it has been achieved; and *what* kinds of criteria are employed or should be employed by those responsible for these decisions? We return to these issues later, but our definition would probably be accepted by the majority of those involved in academic work as a fair description of the way in which the term 'academic failure' is most generally used. Certainly it allows us, once we have said what particular 'specified level' we are going to take as our yardstick, to identify with reasonable precision the extent of this failure. In the main, our references are to the UK since the UK gives us access to a coherent body of statistical research data within a sizeable population. Much of what we have to say however is applicable generally to developed countries throughout the Western world, and also has bearing upon what is happening elsewhere.

The obvious starting point, in view of their wide incidence, their supposed objectivity, and their significance for career prospects, is with public examinations such as the General Certificate of Education (GCE) and the Certificate of Secondary Education (CSE). Taking these as our specified level of performance, we make the unexpected discovery that failure, rather than success, appears to be the norm. Though the figures vary a little from year to year, some 12.3 per cent of children (Department of Education and Science, 1979a) attending maintained schools in England, leave school at the statutory age without being entered for a single public examination. That is, one child in every eight is not considered capable of attempting even one CSE or GCE Examination. Since the possession of CSE and/or GCE passes at age 16 is a necessary requirement for entry into higher education or into courses leading to skilled occupations, this means that one child in every eight (the figure is as high as one in four in Wales) is destined, unless very fortunate, to spend the rest of his/her career in an unskilled or at best a semi-skilled vocation. Bad as this is, it forms only the first part of the picture. Although every child entered for a CSE Examination is awarded a pass, only those obtaining a *graded* pass (Grades 1 to 5) obtain qualifications of relevance to prospective employers. Since some 11.4 per cent of children taking CSE fail to gain a graded pass in any subject, they end up hardly better off than those who were not even entered for the examination. And since only Grade 1 at CSE is regarded as equivalent to a pass at the GCE Ordinary (or 'O') Level, very few CSE condidates (probably under 10 per cent each year) end up with the five or more 'O' Level equivalents necessary if they are seriously considering pursuing their studies into the sixth form at 16+ or entering some form of skilled or professional training.

Turning to GCE 'O' Level proper, statistics show (Department of Education and Science, 1979a) that only a little over half (54.4 per cent) of children in the 16+ age group are entered for one or more examinations, and less than half this number 9.6 per cent overall) obtain five or more passes. Indeed, as some GCE Examination Boards allow only 60 per cent of those children sitting each examination to pass per year, and vary the pass mark up or down accordingly (we have more to say about this practice in due course), some 40 per cent of the children who have struggled this far are doomed to failure before they put pen to paper. The nature of this statistic, plus the low percentage obtaining five or more passes, justifies our earlier statement that, judged by the yardstick of public examinations, failure rather than success appears to be the norm at school level.

If we stay within the school context for a moment, and look at those children who choose to stay on after the statutory school leaving age and embark upon GCE Advanced (or 'A') Level Courses, we find that the pattern improves, but only marginally. Of those entering 'A' Level examinations at 18 years of age, 68 per cent can expect to pass, though only 34 per cent overall will achieve the A, B or C Grades likely to make them attractive to universities, and only 9 per cent overall will achieve the coveted A grade. Twenty per cent will achieve the two or three passes with good grades necessary actually to obtain places in universities and polytechnics, while approximately double this number will proceed to courses at non-degree level. To put these figures in perspective, of the whole population of school leavers (16+ through to 18+) currently less than 8 per cent will embark on degree courses, and only a further 15 per cent will go on to other forms of Further and Higher Education. This figure compares adversely with the figures in certain other developed countries such as the USA and Japan, where the participation rate approaches forty per cent.

These figures are bleak enough to those who value the benefits of higher education for the individual, but if we consider the 15 per cent or so of children who, it will be recalled, are not entered for public examinations of any kind it will be found that they face other, additional kinds of academic failure. Although the children concerned are singled out with the laudable intention of helping them satisfy special needs, 1.8 per cent of the school population has to cope with the experience of attending schools for the physically and mentally handicapped, while a further 4.7 per cent (494,248 in Britain at the most recent count) spend at least some part of the school day in remedial classes within the normal school, due to learning or emotional difficulties (Department of Education and Science, 1978). Thus something approaching three-quarters of a million children have to live with the knowledge that they are unsuited for the normal pattern of education offered to their peers.

Even these figures are only part of the story, for many children, although educated in the normal classroom, nevertheless have to face their inability to cope with the work tackled effectively by their peers. Exact figures on the number of backward children in normal classes are hard to come by, but in a survey of the population of 9- to 11 year-old children on the Isle of Wight, Rutter, Tizard and Whitmore (1970) established that 16 per cent of them showed either intellectual retardation (IQ scores of 70 or below) or educational retardation in the basic subjects (usually defined as performance on tests of attainment which lags 28 months or more behind chronological age). Since the Isle of Wight is a relatively prosperous area, it is probable that these figures are an underestimate for Britain as a whole, and they may also be an underestimate for older age groups where children have had even more opportunity to fall behind. It is interesting, in any case, to set such assessments against the 15 per cent of the school population who are not entered for public examinations and the 11 per cent who, though entered for the CSE, fail to gain a graded pass in any subject. Working from such figures, there are probably some 20 per cent of the school population who are intellectually or educationally retarded in some significant form or other. That means one child in every five must come to terms with the reminders of personal academic failure every school day, which may be one reason why truancy or school refusal is estimated to be as high as 25 per cent amongst the 16+ age group in some parts of the country.

Failure in Higher Education is rather more difficult to assess than it is at school level. Is every student who fails to gain a first class honours degree a 'failure' in some sense, or should we only use this term for those who are unable to obtain any kind of degree? Or is the cut-off point to be located between those who obtain first or second class honours and those who do not, or between those who obtain any kind of honours and those who are awarded only ordinary degrees? The figures themselves show that in Britain roughly one student in every eight who starts a degree course will drop out or will fail his or her final examinations. Of the remainder, just over 6 per cent will obtain first class honours, 28 per cent second class honours (upper division), 44 per cent second class honours (lower division or undivided), 11 per cent third class honours, and approximately the same number, pass degrees (Department of Education and Science, 1979b). Without commenting upon the desirability of classifying first degrees in this or any other way, we have to accept the fact that one third of degree students will either fail to obtain any degree at all or will fail to obtain a good honours classification. When we consider that all these individuals will have obtained good GCE 'A' Level results (leaving aside the small number of mature students who may enter without the usual matriculation requirements) we may well wonder what has gone wrong.

II.—CONCEPTS OF THE PERSON AND MODELS OF HUMAN BEHAVIOUR

Decisions as to what shall be termed 'failure' and what shall be termed 'success' are highly subjective things. Thus the concepts of the person entertained by those responsible for making academic and assessment decisions are of vital importance. Put at its simplest, if I refuse to accept the notion that individual differences between people can be adequately measured, or if I believe that everyone must be allowed to choose their own activities for themselves free from the judgement of others, then I am very unlikely to see anyone as having failed in whatever they set out to do. Or, to be rather more realistic, if I consider student failure to be a sign of bad teaching rather than of student inadequacy, then I am likely to regard such failure as a sign that I must improve my teaching methods rather than as a sign that my students are lacking in ability.

The important part played by teachers' concepts of children in assessing and determining children's academic progress is demonstrated by a number of studies in various fields. When streaming was more prevalent in the British primary school (equivalent to school grades 1 to six in the USA) than it is today, Jackson (1964) showed that teacher decisions on which children should be assigned respectively to A and B streams seemed to depend far more upon children's dress and speech and general behaviour than upon any measurable difference in cognitive ability. Since he also demonstrated that the A-streamers in his sample showed enhancement of measured intelligence over their primary school careers while the B-streamers showed deterioration, it can be seen what a far-reaching effect such decisions may have had upon child performance. Quite apart from the poorer academic and linguistic environment in which the B-streamers had to work, it seems probable that the very act of labelling them as 'B-streamers' served to lower both their own expectations as to future performance and the expectations of their teachers. Both sets of expectations, together with their combined effects, would have consequential effects upon standards of child attainment.

Similar evidence for the deleterious effect of labelling children as academically inferior comes from Hargreaves (1967) and from Lacey (1970). In the course of their separate investigations, they detected the existence of distinct 'A-stream' and 'C-stream' mentalities in both non-selective and selective secondary schools, with C-streamers across schools appearing to have more in common with each other in terms of self-concepts, work habits and attitudes to school and to teachers than they had with the A-streamers within their own schools. The C-streamers in both types of school were negatively orientated on these variables and the A-streamers positively orientated. We may conclude that if children think their teachers conceptualize them in academically unfavourable terms, then they are more likely to lower their own academic expectations and to fail to identify with the aims and objectives of the school than if they think these conceptualizations are favourable.

In a sense, we are probably observing the working here of what is known as the *self-fulfilling prophecy* (see, for example, Nash, 1976). If the teacher conceptualizes a child as being of low ability, then the teacher's very behaviour towards the child (in terms of academic expectations, general attitude, provision of educational opportunities) will be a potent factor in producing the prophesized low level of performance. We can see the operation of the self-fulfilling prophecy (albeit in a positive rather than a negative direction) if we turn to a much publicized and earlier study by Rosenthal and Jacobson (1968). The authors showed that when a group of teachers were told in confidence that certain of their children had been identified as likely to show above average academic improvement over a set period, the expected improvement did indeed take place. Unknown to the teachers, the children concerned had been selected not on the basis of the claimed psychological tests but purely at random, and their improved performance appeared to be due therefore to the (perhaps quite subtle) differences in the way in which their teachers now related to them. Rosenthal and Jacobson's study has been criticized on methodological grounds, and it is probable that the effect noted by them would not be so marked in all learning environments; but it remains an important indication of the influence that a teacher's conceptualization of a child can have upon the child's academic progress, even when based upon misleading evidence.

On a broader canvas, we can see the self-fulfilling prophecy at work in a different way if we look at the policy decisions of the administrators and politicians who control the general application and management of the formal educational system. These decisions have traditionally depended upon the 'pool of ability' notion; that is, upon the notion that there is only a limited number of children within the total population who can benefit from higher education, or who can cope with particular school courses or attain a particular standard of performance. Once this notion is accepted, it is allowed to determine the actual number of places made available in higher education, the number of places on particular courses and so on. Entry requirements to these avenues are fixed at a level that excludes all candidates over and above the number concerned. We are not necessarily suggesting that the 'pool of ability' notion is mistaken. We are suggesting that once children are conceptualized by educators and administrators as sharply marked off from each other in terms of ability (and in ways which cannot be changed by educational provision), then this conceptualization is allowed to determine the structure and extent of the kinds of educational opportunities offered. Examinations are then manipulated so that only the predicted number of children is allowed to emerge successfully. We should note that the 'pool of ability' notion, owes its existence in part to historical accident, since in Britain much of both secondary and higher education developed out of a fee-paying system which catered only for a relatively small elite. This historical fact later combined with some very debatable psychological evidence as to the hereditability of cognitive abilities such as intelligence (see Kamin, 1974) to produce a limited number of available educational opportunities.

III.–INDIVIDUAL ASSESSMENT

Thus academic failure is essentially a judgement passed upon performance. When discussing assessment, therefore, it is important to repeat the point that the threshold at which failure can be said to occur in any given performance is often at the discretion of the assessor. The assessor may decide to engineer assessment measures so that each child obtains what are deemed to be 'satisfactory' marks. Or, alternatively, decisions on how well children have done could be made simply by comparing each individual's results with those he/she obtained in the previous test. Again, each child's performance may be compared with that of the rest of the class or with that of the rest of his/her age group, leaving the child with the knowledge that he or she comes out of these comparisons rather well or rather badly as the case may be. Whatever strategy is used, children are usually left with few opportunities to monitor their own performance and draw their own conclusions as to its merits.

In general, the majority of assessment measures used in education are classed either as tests of *ability* or tests of *achievement*. Tests of ability are generally thought of by teachers as providing some measure of a child's 'potential', and in many schools (primary schools in particular) verbal reasoning tests are administered annually and children's scores noted down as part of school records. With the autonomy enjoyed by local education authorities in Britain in such matters, the decision as to which tests to use—or indeed whether to use any such tests at all—is left to the individual authorities, who often leave it in turn to individual headteachers. Where verbal reasoning tests are used, these are sometimes tests developed locally by the school psychological service. Essentially they yield a *v:ed* (verbal and educational) score, and this is used to help schools identify both those children with apparently low ability and those children whose school performance seems to lag behind their ability scores.

More specialized ability testing is carried out by members of the school psychological service, who are invited into the school by headteachers to assess and advise on children whose work is giving cause for concern. Unlike the group tests of verbal reasoning administered by the schools themselves, the psychologist will usually employ an individual intelligence test, such as the Wechsler Intelligence Scale for Children (WISC). The WISC yields both a *v:ed* (verbal and educational) and a *k:m* (mechanical and spatial) score, and in diagnosing backwardness the psychologist looks for major discrepancies between the two, and also for a total score which is significantly below the norm for the child's chronological age. Usually a total score which converts to an IQ score of below 80 is taken together with evidence of poor overall verbal fluency and of school work which lags two years or so behind chronological age) as evidence that the child is educationally subnormal (ESN) and in need of some form of special educational provision. At one time, subject to parental consent, such a child would have been transferred to a special school, but in recent years the policy has been to move the child for all or part of the school day to a remedial class within the normal school. This policy has received an extra boost with the publication of the Warnock Report (Department of Education and Science, 1978), which recommends that in the future, special schools should in fact be used to provide intensive expert short-term help rather than long-term care. The Report also contains a number of further recommendations designed to facilitate the provision of specialist help in normal schools for the one child in every five whom it estimates will need this help in some form at some point during school life.

It is important to realize that a distinction exists here between ESN children and those classified as SSN (Severely Sub-Normal). The latter children usually have IQs of below 50, and are normally diagnosed as in need of specialist help while they are still at the pre-school stage. By virtue of their degree of handicap, such children would usually find normal schools quite unsuitable, and in consequence they attend schools specially geared to meet their needs. An intermediate classification of ESN(M) (Moderately Educationally Sub-normal) is sometimes used for children with IQs of between 50 and 70 (see Chapter 15 by Clarke and Clarke). In the future it seems likely that the terms ESN, SSN and ESN(M) will be replaced, as recommended in the Warnock Report, by the terms 'children with learning difficulties', 'children with severe learning difficulties' and 'children with moderate learning difficulties' respectively.

Tests of achievement are very much more widely used within education than tests of ability. Every time a teacher gives a class test, he or she is in fact administering a test of achievement. Such tests (also known as tests of attainment) are designed simply to establish the extent of a child's knowledge of a given subject at a given point in time. Whatever the child's ability, if he has neglected to learn anything about the subject, he will obtain poor marks for attainment. Public examinations such as the GCE and the CSE are essentially tests of attainment, as are university first degree examinations and the examinations administered by professional bodies to control admission to their ranks. It is important to recognize (a point too often neglected) that attainment tests are in part tests of the teacher's diligence in teaching as well as the student's diligence in learning. Thus there are three sources of the variations in examination marks, namely the abilities and diligence of the student, the competence of the teacher, and the selection of questions and grading schedules.

Most schools carry out routine attainment testing, from the class tests to which we have already referred to standardized tests of attainment in which children's performance is compared to the norms for their age. At primary school level standardized tests for reading and number work are in particular widely used. These yield scores for 'reading age' and 'arithmetical age' rather like the 'mental age' scores used in IQ testing; more recently, standardized tests of progress in a number of curricular areas (such as the Bristol Attainment Guides) have been developed for British use. At secondary school level, routine attainment testing is if anything more popular, though less use is made of standardized tests and more use made of tests developed by individual teachers and geared towards syllabuses for public examinations.

The arguments in favour of attainment tests are that they help teachers to monitor children's progress, to identify those who may need special help and to give children useful practice in examination techniques. But tests present children with frequent opportunities for comparing marks and general achievement levels, inevitably to the disadvantage of large numbers of them. Tests also serve to distract attention away from the intrinsic interest of a school subject and to emphasize instead its role as a prompter of anxiety and uncertainty.

IV.—THE IMMEDIATE SOCIAL AND EMOTIONAL ENVIRONMENT

Many of us will probably recall that a large number of our most intense emotional experiences in childhood were associated in some way with school. The majority probably stemmed from occasions when we were particularly successful at some task or other, and received the rewards of praise and social esteem, or from occasions when we performed badly and were punished by disapproval and social censure. Without wishing to enter a debate on the formative influence of childhood experiences upon the mature personality, it seems that children, especially young children, are particularly vulnerable to social forces, and develop many of their self-concepts in response to the relationships that they have with authority figures and significant others.

Thus the attitudes that teachers and parents adopt towards children, and the general emotional atmospheres of the school and of the home, appear to be of critical importance in determining the way in which children tackle many of the academic tasks that face them. Children who are exposed to an environment which is encouraging, supportive, and not overly judgemental are more likely to develop positive and confident attitudes towards themselves and towards their work than are children placed in environments in which the reverse is the case. Pioneering research such as that by Coopersmith (1967) into the development of self-esteem suggests that it is also advantageous if the environment is perceived by the children as fair-minded and consistent, and as accepting of them as people. Such an environment seems to give children a sense of personal worth and significance, and the confidence that plays such an important part in academic success.

In a number of publications Rutter (e.g., Rutter, 1975) has drawn attention to more specific factors in the child's immediate emotional environment that appear to contribute to symptoms of academic failure such as school refusal (truancy), maladjustment, and backwardness in the basic subjects. Within the home, these include poor stress-coping strategies by parents (e.g., maladaptive aggression or passive resignation), unsatisfactory parental marital relationships, very severe or very lax standards of discipline, parental overprotectiveness, parental criminality, long or particularly abrupt periods of parent-child separation, and poor patterns of communication between family members. At school level, important factors seem to include high turn-over of staff and of pupils (which presumably give individual children a sense of social and academic insecurity) and the presence of large numbers of immigrant and economically impoverished children who, through no fault of their own, tend to impede the development of a sense of community, by virtue of the disparate social and cultural backgrounds which they bring with them.

The part played by the emotional atmosphere of the school in fostering academic failure is starkly demonstrated by studies such as that of Power, Benn and Morris (1972), which indicate that there are highly significant differences in delinquency and maladjustment rates between schools, even when schools are matched for catchment area variables. Differences between schools appear unrelated to such formal factors as age of school buildings and school size and resources, and Rutter (1973) has shown that these differences also obtain in academic variables such as reading skills. Though he concedes that it is difficult to pin-point the precise causal variables, he considers that sharp formal demarcation between 'valued' and 'less-valued' children (e.g., in streaming and setting) within the school system, clashes of values between the school and the immediate community (the home-school conflict), and variations in teaching styles, may all be implicated.

The subject of teaching styles is too extensive to be more than touched on here, but available evidence suggests that both children and higher education students work best in an atmosphere of relatively low stress (Fransson 1977; Wade, 1981), and that children also benefit from an atmosphere in which there is sufficient structure to give them guidance and security (Bennett, 1976), and in which firm quiet commands are used instead of angry punitive ones (Kounin, 1970). All these add up to an emotional environment that is relatively calm, consistent and accepting, and which contains teachers who provide children with socially effective role models.

V.—THE WIDER SOCIAL AND ORGANIZATIONAL ENVIRONMENT

We have already indicated that decisions as to what constitutes success and failure in any given level of performance are open to debate. Often we can only understand this debate if we acknowledge the wider social background against which it takes place. This means looking at the beliefs and value systems entertained by society and by sub-groups within society, and seeing how they influence the demands and expectations placed upon individuals. Such an exercise involves philosophical and sociological issues as well as psychological ones, but for the present purposes we can at least show how certain widely entertained social presuppositions can operate to limit the opportunities for academic success offered by society to some of its members.

One of the clearest ways of illustrating such limitations is to look at sex-role stereotyping, where we find that within both the school and the family different success-related and failure-related criteria are shown for the sexes, with these criteria usually (though not invariably) working against the inter-ests of women and in favour of those of men. Stein and Bailey (1973), together with other researchers in the field, have shown that even in early childhood more boys than girls are encouraged by parents to develop high expectancies of success, to establish high aspirations, and to learn to deal satisfactorily with the experience of failure should it occur (i.e., to remain confident and ready to try again). These male-orientated lessons are further emphasized by the books and stories to which children are exposed, with far more books having male than female heroes, and containing illustrations of male rather than female characters (Weitzman, Eifler, Hokada and Ross, 1972). In addition books are more likely to portray males as active, physical, independent and as part of a group, while females are more likely to be shown as inconspicuous, passive, solitary, and subordinate. Further, males are more likely to be shown outdoors than females, and engaged in exciting occupations (if adults), and in the giving of treats to children.

In view of the publicity which sex-stereotyping in children's books has received in recent years, some attempt is now being made to redress the balance, but there is little evidence that it has as yet made much impact upon authors and publishers. Nor is there much evidence that, in spite of the spread of co-education, girls are being given the same success-orientations in school as are boys. This is graphically illustrated in research reported by Kleinke (1978) in which some of the subtleties behind the different treatments meted out to boys and girls at school level (often unwittingly) are teased out. The research showed that although the *level* of positive and negative evaluations given to boys and girls in the classroom may be the same, the pattern behind them contains interesting and potentially highly significant differences. In the samples studied, the positive evaluations received by the boys tended very markedly to be based upon intellectual conduct and the negative evaluations upon general behaviour, while for the girls the position was exactly reversed. Thus the boys appeared to learn to perceive positive evaluations from teachers as an indication of their intellectual ability, and negative evaluations as irrelevant to it; while the girls learnt that positive evaluations simply indicated their classroom conduct was good, and negative evaluations cast doubt on their intellectual ability.

Lessons of this kind appear to help boys to discount past failures and emphasize past successes when setting their present and future expectations, while girls are left to emphasize their failures and discount their successes. This may be one of the reasons why even academically sophisticated people like college students tend to attribute female success on male tasks to luck, while attributing male success on both male and female tasks to ability (Deaux and Emswiller, 1974). Similar double standards are seen to operate even amongst supposed experts on human psychological characteristics such as psychiatrists, who appear to associate mental health in males with aggression, independence, competitiveness and high levels of skill and ambition, while mental health in females is more often associated by them with submissiveness, dependency, lack of objectivity, and a readiness to be influenced by others (Broverman, Broverman, Clarkson, Rosenkrantz and Vogel, 1970).

If we turn to the vast research associated with vocational world, we see that once again women are perceived in a less flattering light than men. A good example is reported by Kleinke (1978). The research involved inviting a broad sample of male management staff in the USA to list respectively the characteristics they associated with men, the characteristics they associated with successful company managers, and the characteristics they associated with women. Results showed that their views as to the characteristics of men and the characteristics of successful managers were much in agreement (aggression, leadership qualities, emotional stability, self-reliance), while their view as to the characteristics of women and those of successful managers bore very little relation to each other. In other words, these highly influential business*men* entertained stereotyped views on the abilities of men and women likely to favour men strongly when it came to matters of job selection and promotion (Schein, 1973).

The various research findings summarized above indicate some of the ways in which society generally tends to conceptualize the male sex in more achievement-orientated terms than the female. Rather along the lines of the self-fulfilling prophecy, males are expected to achieve more both academically and vocationally than females, and this expectation serves as an agent towards its own realization. We get some idea of the extent of this realization within the academic world from the fact that although the number of males and females qualified to enter degree courses does not differ significantly, in Britain nearly two-thirds of those who actually start degree work (64 per cent) are males (Department of Education and Science, 1979b). Heavily as this 2:1 ratio favours males, it widens even further at postgraduate level, with over three times as many men as women obtaining higher degrees (and nearly five times as many if we look at doctorates alone). Small wonder, perhaps, that nearly ninety per cent of university posts and a similar percentage of secondary school headships go to men.

Another major area in which social presuppositions operate to limit the opportunities for academic success enjoyed by many children is that of the school curriculum itself. In Britain the Newsom Report (Ministry of Education, 1963) and the Warnock Report (Department of Education and Science, 1978), which are the most relevant government reports in the areas concerned, stress that the material taught in schools is far too 'academic' in content, and too closely geared towards the more able pupils and towards hurdles such as university entry. Though the reasons for this are complex and stretch back into the last century, in part they seem to reflect the higher valuation that society places upon the professions than upon commerical and manufacturing industries. Thus the curriculum favours the 'thinkers' as opposed to the 'doers', and neglects to provide the kind of vocational training relevant to the needs of large sections of the school population. The forces against change are of course enormous. We have a vast army (and are adding to it every year) of teachers trained in the 'traditional' subjects, and it would require courageous and far-seeing decisions by policy makers to re-orientate the curriculum drastically. For example, while we have teachers of history and geography, they will continue to create historians and geographers, some of whom will enter teaching and thus continue the cycle. Even within subjects, such as some of the sciences, which are potentially more vocational in nature, the syllabuses are still largely geared toward 'pure' rather than 'applied' knowledge. Non-academic children once again end up as apparent failures, and with insufficient qualifications to pursue their studies at a post-school level.

VI.—TYPES OF INTERVENTION

Since examinations figure so largely as criterion variables in academic success and failure, one obvious method of intervention is to change the format of examinations so that more children are able to cope with them satisfactorily. At the level of public examinations, an obvious start has been made in Britain by introducing Mode III GCE and CSE. Whereas Modes I and II are marked by the Regional Examining Board, either to a syllabus drawn up by the Board (Mode I) or approved by the Board (Mode II), Mode III is set and marked by the individual schools themselves, and is only moderated by the Board. As a consequence, Mode III allows schools to devise syllabuses suited to the particular needs of their pupils, and to employ assessment procedures that take more account of their particular strengths. According to a recent report prepared for the Schools Council (Torrance, 1982), Mode III improves pupil motivation, raises standards, and allows pupil merit to emerge that would be masked by externally administered examinations. Unfortunately, only one per cent of GCE entries and only 25 per cent of CSE are through Mode III. The reason seems to lie partly in the extra financial costs involved in Mode III and partly in the extra workload which it imposes upon the school staff.

If greater use is made of Mode III, and if the new 16+ examination (which is planned to replace GCE and CSE with a single common syllabus) incorporates some of Mode III's apparent strengths, then examinations for school leavers will be used increasingly as ways of allowing pupils to demonstrate their knowledge rather than their lack of it. Examinations could then have less of a determining influence upon the curriculum. In consequence, the curriculum will be allowed to develop a less narrowly 'academic' bias, and will be able to reflect the vocational and personal developmental needs of the less gifted as well as of the more gifted child.

At the individual level, the main strategy for intervention shown in schools takes the form of special remedial help for those children who are clearly unable to cope with important areas of their work. It is unfortunate that, due to limitations of staffing, such help can normally only be offered to children who are either formally classified as backward or are close to this classification. Far too often there is little that can be done by way of specialist individual help for the child who simply finds it a struggle to keep up. Such a child becomes part of the close on 50 per cent of children who, as we have seen, are not entered for a single GCE 'O' level examination.

For the child who does receive special help, the first rule of remedial intervention is that the child should be allowed to experience success at *however low a level*. Having been allowed to fail consistently in his or her academic career so far, the child is in need of the experience of success to enable him development of academic self-esteem and a more positive attitude towards school. This applies whether children's problems are associated mainly with school work or whether they show the broader personal and social problems that may lead to their being classified as maladjusted. There is evidence (see, for example, The Warnock Report, 1978) that maladjustment and poor school work often shown signs of a causal relationship, with anti-social behaviour leading to problems with child-teacher relationships and with academic work, and failure in academic work leading to frustration and anti-social behaviour. Thus the experience of success often has a beneficial effect upon maladjusted behaviour, which in turn leads to further improvements in school work.

Sometimes, especially in closed communities like residential special schools, remedial programmes are built into what are known as performance contracts (see, for example, Merrett, 1981). The performance contract is essentially a behaviour modification programme in which the child agrees with the adult to produce certain kinds of carefully specified desirable social or academic behaviours in return for equally carefully specified rewards. Thus the aggressive child may agree to eschew violence or the recalcitrant child agree to hand in work assignments at specified times in return for rewards such as extra helpings of food and special outings. The rule is that the desired behaviours should be broken into small units well within the child's capacity, and the rewards be scaled accordingly and administered promptly. Thus initially the contract might be for one hour's non-violent behaviour or one line of written work at a time, and the rewards might take the form of small tokens which the child has to accumulate until enough are held to exchange for the promised treat. The child thus experiences success at each point, and also receives incidental reinforcers (such as increased friendliness and esteem from other children and teachers) as a consequence of improved behaviour, which serve to make that behaviour persist even when the original contract has been fulfilled. (A more detailed account of such contracts is given by Herbert in Chapter 2).

Maladjusted children can also be referred to the child guidance unit of the school psychological service for specialist assessment and counselling. Where their problems embrace—or perhaps stem from—disturbed relationships within the family, help may also be sought from family therapy. The family therapist (who is usually a psychologist or psychiatrist) interviews the family as a whole unit, observes the ways in which family members interact with and conceptualize each other, and attempts to bring problems to the surface where they can be examined and discussed by all concerned. Unfortunately, family therapy units are still few and far between, and tend to be supported by voluntary agencies rather than by public money.

VII.—IS PSYCHOLOGICAL INTERVENTION SUCCESSFUL?

Although evidence on the relative success rates of different kinds of intervention is surprisingly difficult to come by, there can be little doubt that carefully structured and administered remedial programmes do produce marked improvement in academic performance. Such successful programmes appear to ensure the crucial experience of success to which we have already made reference by employing (a) careful assessment procedures and record keeping by the remedial specialist, so that he or she knows as precisely as possible the extent of the child's problems and of his existing knowledge; (b) the organizing of learning into very small steps, so that the child is aware both of what is expected of him and of the fact that he is making progress; (c) adequate feedback for both teacher and child so that achievements and areas of difficulty can be recognized; and (d) systematic rewards (praise, progress charts, material reinforcers) at each appropriate point. Thus school comes to be seen by the child as a place where one gains skills and knowledge, rather than as a place where one demonstrates their absence.

The main immediate obstacles in the way of intervention strategies of this kind appear to be twofold. First and most obviously, there is a lack of sufficient public money, with the result that remedial personnel are far too few in number to attend to more than the most desperately needful cases. Ideally one would wish to see a remedial specialist (either a teacher or a psychologist) trained in assessment and intervention procedures attached to each primary school with the task of identifying and helping children with special difficulties, from school entry upwards. The argument that this would only serve to draw children's attention to their difficulties is untenable; most of them are all too painfully aware of these difficulties already. At the same time the number of specially trained remedial staff at secondary school level needs to be greatly increased, and school counsellors appointed to all schools as a matter of course. Unfortunately, such counsellors are regarded as a dispensable luxury by most schools, since they count against the staff-student ratio and mean the school loses a subject specialist as a consequence.

The second obstacle in the way of intervention strategies is the much larger issue of social deprivation. Here only massive programmes of educational enrichment directed at children who are identified as academically at risk in view of their socio-economic background are likely to produce significant improvements on a national scale. Longitudinal studies such as the National Child Development Survey (see, for example, Davie, Butler and Goldstein, 1972) indicate that there is a clear association between lower socio-economic status and lower measured IQ and educational attainment, and the clear indication is that resources should be made available to compensate such children educationally for their environmental handicap. Programmes such as the American Head Start and the British Educational Priority Area Schemes (see, for example, Midwinter, 1972) have yet to be fully evaluated, but the signs are that although there may not be obvious immediate gains in variables such as IQ scores and reading attainment, in the long term children show significantly enhanced self-esteem, academic confidence, and willingness to learn (see, for example, Abelson, 1972).

VIII.—METHODOLOGICAL AND PRACTICAL PROBLEMS

One of the biggest problems, however, lies in evaluating intervention strategies, whether they be of the macro kind (like Head Start) or of the micro, classroom-based variety. The lack of any real evaluatory framework seems to be due in part to the absence of satisfactory coordination between the bodies responsible for funding research and between the various projects that they fund, and in part the absence of any formal agreement on the parameters defining academic success. To take these in turn, it has to be said that the relatively large sums of money dispensed by the Schools Council, for educational research in England and Wales, the Social Science Research Council, and the Department of Education and Science, have produced disappointingly little by way of the kind of findings that feed back directly into classroom practice. Perhaps the major problem here is that teachers have insufficient knowledge of psychological research to be able to articulate their professional difficulties in a form recognizable to the funding agencies, while few psychologists have sufficient first-hand knowledge of classroom practice to be able to mount research projects that produce findings recognizable to the class teacher. As a consequence, the funding agencies tend to support a wide range of self-contained projects on the strength of their respectability as research exercises, rather than mounting a concerted attack on the general issues that teachers insist really matter. This leads to the frequent charge of 'irrelevance' levelled by teachers at research evidence.

Teachers are as much at fault as are psychologists in failing to reach formal agreement on the parameters defining academic success. Throughout the educational world there is a lack of any real consensus as to what constitutes success and failure. Even if we take apparently objective criteria such as the passing of public examinations we have to ask where the line is drawn between success and failure. Is it the possession of five 'O' levels, of six, of seven? And should they all be 'A' grades, or will 'B's' and 'C's' do? Is a child a success if he gets into the sixth form, or must he pass some GCE 'A' levels to prove himself still further? And is a university student who obtains a third class honours degree a failure when some 93 per cent of the population fail even to start degree courses? However, many teachers would deny that examinations are the real measure of the education they provide. In place of examinations they frequently bring forward the elusive concept of 'potential'. A child is a success if he reaches his 'potential' whether that potential be represented by outstanding achievements or simply by the ability to read and write. But how can we measure this 'potential'? By tests of ability such as intelligence tests? Hardly, since measured intelligence appears to be dependent in no small degree upon the very experiences we give to a child to help him realize his 'potential'. By attainment tests? Certainly not, since these pretend to do nothing other than to measure what he already knows. The answer is that we have no clear way of assessing potential, nor even of defining precisely what we mean by the term. In the absence of such precision, psychologists have no easy task in planning educational research and in assessing the relative merits of different intervention strategies. As a further complication, it is probably harder to eliminate contaminating variables or to hold them constant in educational research than it is in almost any other area of applied psychology, since children are bombarded in and out of school with a bewildering range of experiences that might loosely be termed educational, and that might influence the outcome of any research designed to examine the efficacy or relative efficacy of various teaching skills and techniques. Small wonder that many educationalists, particularly in special education, fall back (like the psychoanalysts) on the presentation of individual case studies when discussing intervention strategies.

It must be said that there is often a strong resistance amongst both teachers and parents to the thesis that the responsibility for academic failure does not lie primarily with the child. Acceptance of this thesis means acceptance of the fact that children who consistently fail are usually children who have been presented with academic problems inappropriate to their current level of understanding, and for this the responsibility in some measure must lie with the people who formulate the problems, namely the teachers and parents themselves. Such a fact is not a particularly palatable one, and ego defences not surprisingly are raised against it. But if the interests of children are to be best served, the first requisite is that those adults involved in any way with guiding child development should look carefully at their own behaviour and try to assess the influence it has upon such development. Psychologists themselves, whether of the 'pure' or 'applied' kind, are, of course, no more exempt from this exercise than anyone else.

IX.—PROBLEMS OF ETHICS AND CONFIDENTIALITY

One of the most contentious issues concerning confidentiality is whether or not parents (and children themselves) should have access to ability and attainment scores kept in school records. These records often follow children as they move up within a school and indeed as they transfer from school to school and, as may be inferred from our references to the self-fulfilling prophecy earlier in the chapter, can influence a teacher's attitude towards a child even before the two have really met. In view of the potential power of school records it is often argued, therefore, that parents should have access to them (together with access to reports drawn up by school psychologists, counsellors and the like) in order to challenge anything that they consider to be false or misleading. Against this it is argued that if parents are informed (say) that their child has a relatively low IQ score, the knowledge may influence their behaviour towards the child in much the same way as it may influence the teachers.

A problem of a different kind is raised by the fact that during interviews children may confide in the psychologist or the counsellor material relating to their academic or social progress that is of a very private and personal nature, and that they wish to keep from their parents or teachers. Should a confidence of this kind be broken, even on those occasions when it appears to be in the best interests of the child that it should? Unfortunately there is no agreed ethical code governing the psychologist's decisions on such matters, nor is it clear that the psychologist's right to secrecy is safeguarded under the law as it is in the case of medical and legal practitioners and ministers of religion. Since in such matters the psychologist can hardly remain ethically neutral, it is apparent that final decisions on how much parents (or indeed teachers and professionals in related disciplines) should be told regarding a child's problems must be left to professional judgement. This judgement must be subject to the provisos firstly that the child's interests are paramount, and secondly that if a child's confidences have to be broken the child must be informed of this in advance, together with the necessary reasons, and given the psychologist's full support in whatever might follow.

X. – THE ROLE OF OTHER DISCIPLINES AND PROFESSIONS

Where problems of neglect or violence within the home are contributing towards a child's failure in school, psychologists may well find themselves liaising with social workers and child care officers (and perhaps probation officers if the child has been before the courts). School welfare officers may also be involved, and their task is mainly to look into problems of school refusal and to investigate the more obvious symptoms of economic hardship. In addition to these agencies (who are all employed by the Local Authority) voluntary services such as the National Society for the Prevention of Cruelty to Children can also be drawn in, as can the clergy who, particularly in Roman Catholic communities, often have an excellent knowledge of local families and their problems. In extreme cases, children may be removed for varying periods from their homes and taken into the care of the Local Authority, and here foster parents (if children are placed with families) and house parents (if children are placed in hostels) can also be involved.

On the more strictly academic level, in Britain the Local Authority also employs a team of educational advisors, whose function it is to enter schools and advise on all aspects of the curriculum and of remedial provision, and who often work closely with the school psychologist and (though more rarely) with local HMIs (Her Majesty's Inspectors of Schools) who are employed directly by the DES. Such co-operation can lead to the devising and monitoring of special remedial programmes, and to the development of new assessment procedures designed to meet local needs. Where children show extreme behaviour problems in addition to academic failure, school counsellors, family therapists, and even clinical psychologists and psychiatrists may all be involved, together with any other agency, lay or professional, which knows the child well and has something to contribute.

If all this makes it sound as if the psychologist is part of a high powered team beavering away efficiently to help the problem child, this is sadly far from the case. Often the team lacks an overall policy maker and co-ordinator, and invariably it lacks sufficient funds and trained personnel to make much real impact on the complex and extensive problems with which it is faced.

XI.—FUTURE PROSPECTS

It may be thought that in this chapter we have taken the part of the child too assiduously, that we have ignored the fact that children can be lacking in motivation and reluctant to learn the kind of things that lead to academic success. Yet there is no denying that it is we adults who hold the cards. It is we who decide what to teach, how to teach it, and how to examine whether it has been learnt, and it is strange therefore, that when failure happens we assume it is the fault of the child. For the child, this is rather like acting in a play written and directed by someone else, and then being blamed because the play is a failure.

As to the future, it may be that new examinations like Mode III and the new syllabuses that support them will change the script of the play so that it makes more sense to the people who have to use it; but the outlook is not an optimistic one. Society is changing so rapidly, in terms of its technological complexity and its employment patterns, and educational change takes so long to filter down to the classroom that it is hard to see how an educational system that cannot cope with present problems will be able to adapt quickly enough to tackle the much greater challenges that lie ahead. Some estimates suggest that by the end of the century, manufacturing industry will be employing less than half the people it employs at present, and that the emphasis upon high level skills within the workforce will be much greater than it is now. Where (and how) will the 50 per cent or so of children who currently fail to be entered for even one 'O' level fit in? It looks as if psychologists (to say nothing of teachers and politicians) have a lot of hard thinking to do.

XII.—ANNOTATED READINGS

Kleinke, C. L. (1978). *Self Perception: The Psychology of Personal Awareness*. San Francisco, California: Freeman.

An excellent survey of the whole field of self perception, with particularly good chapters on self perception of success and failure and on learned helplessness and self control.

Rutter, M. (1975). *Helping Troubled Children*. Harmondsworth: Penguin.

A comprehensive text summarizing much of the research evidence on failure at school level. It includes case histories illustrating diagnosis and treatment.

Ryle, A. (1973). *Student Casualties*. Harmondsworth: Penguin.

A short but authoritative account of some of the factors associated with failure in higher education.

Department of Education and Science (1978). *Special Educational Needs: Report of the Committee of Enquiry into the Education of Handicapped Children and Young People*. London: Her Majesty's Stationery Office.

Although an official government report on children with learning difficulties, it is extremely readable, comprehensive and thought-provoking. (Known as The Warnock Report).

Wolff, S. (1973). *Children Under Stress*. Harmondsworth: Penguin.

One of the best short books on the general stress factors which operate upon children and predispose them to failure at all levels.

Holt, J. (1964). *How Children Fail*. New York: Pitman.

A well-known text which is still one of the best accounts of the nature and causes of failure at school level.

XIII.—REFERENCES

Abelson, W. (1972). Head Start graduates in school. In: S. Ryan (Ed.) *A Report on the Longitudinal Evaluation of Preschool Children*. Washington, D.C.: DHEW Office of Child Development.

Bennett, N. (1976). *Teaching Styles and Pupil Progress*. London: Open Books.

Broverman, I. K., Broverman, D. M., Clarkson, F. E., Rosenkrantz, P. S. and Vogel, S. R. (1970). Sex-role stereotypes and clinical judgements of mental health. *Journal of Consulting and Clinical Psychology*, **341**, 1–7.

Coopersmith, S. (1967). *The Antecedents of Self-esteem*. San Francisco, California: Freeman.

Davie, R., Butler, N. and Goldstein, H. (1972). *From Birth to Seven*. London: Longmans.

Deaux, K. and Emswiller, T. (1974). Explanations of successful performance on sex-linked tasks: What is skill for the male is luck for the female. *Journal of Personality and Social Psychology*, **29**, 80–85.

Department of Education and Science (1978). *Special Educational Needs: Report of* the Committee of Enquiry into the Education of Handicapped Children and Young People (The Warnock Report) London: Her Majesty's Stationery Office.

Department of Education and Science (1979a). Statistics of Education Vol. 2: School Leavers. London: Her Majesty's Stationery Office.

Department of Education and Science (1979b). Statistics of Education Vol. 6: Universities. London: Her Majesty's Stationery Office.

Fransson, A. (1977). On qualitative differences in learning: IV—Effects of intrinsic motivation and extrinsic test anxiety on process and outcome. British Journal of Educational Psychology, 47, 244–257.

Hargreaves, D. (1967). Social Relations in a Secondary School. London: Routledge and Kegan Paul.

Jackson, B. (1964). Streaming: An Educational System in Miniature. London: Routledge and Kegan Paul.

Kamin, L. J. (1974). The Science and Politics of I.Q. Potomac, Maryland: Lawrence Erlbaum.

Kleinke, C. L. (1978). Self Perception: The Psychology of Personal Awareness. San Francisco, California: Freeman.

Kounin, J. S. (1970). Discipline and Group Management in Classrooms. New York: Holt, Rinehart and Winston.

Lacey, C. (1970). Hightown Grammar. Manchester: Manchester University Press.

Merrett, F. E. (1981). Studies in behaviour modification in British educational settings—a review. In: K. Wheldall (Ed.) The Behaviourist In The Classroom: Aspects of applied behavioural analysis in British educational contexts. Birmingham: Educational Review Publications.

Midwinter, E. (1972). Projections: An Educational Priority Area at Work. London: Ward Lock.

Ministry of Education (1963). Half Our Future. (The Newsom Report) London: Her Majesty's Stationery Office.

Nash, R. (1976). Teacher Expectations and Pupil Learning. London: Routledge and Kegan Paul.

Power, M. J., Benn, R. T. and Morris, J. N. (1972). Neighbourhood, school and juveniles before the courts. British Journal of Criminology, 12, 111–132.

Rosenthal, R. R. and Jacobson, L. (1968). Pygmalion in the Classroom. New York: Holt, Rinehart and Winston

Rutter, M. (1973). Why are London children so disturbed? Proceedings of the Royal Society of Medicine, 66, 1221–1225.

Rutter, M. (1975). Helping Troubled Children. Harmondsworth: Penguin.

Rutter, M., Tizard, J. and Whitmore, K. (Eds.) (1970). Education, Health and Behaviour. London: Longmans.

Schein, V. E. (1973). The relationship between sex-role stereotypes and requisite management characteristics. Journal of Applied Psychology, 57, 95–100.

Stein, A. H. and Bailey, M. M. (1973). The socialization of achievement orientation in females. Psychological Bulletin, 80, 345–366.

Torrance, H. (1982) Mode III Examining: Six Case Studies. London: Longmans for the Schools Council.

Wade, B. E. (1981) Highly anxious pupils in formal and informal primary classrooms; the relationship between inferred coping strategies and: I—cognitive attainment. British Journal of Educational Psychology, 51, 39–49.

Weitzman, C. J., Eifler, D., Hokada, E. and Ross, C. (1972). Sex-role socialization in picture books for preschool children. American Journal of Sociology, 77, 1125–1150.

Psychology and Social Problems
Edited by A. Gale and A. J. Chapman
© 1984 John Wiley & Sons Ltd.

CHAPTER 5

OCCUPATIONAL GUIDANCE AND UNEMPLOYMENT

Don Wallis

1.—THE EXTENT OF THE PROBLEM

Prominent among the topics which occupational psychologists study is the relationship between experience of the world of work and psychological well-being (Warr and Wall, 1978). They have traditionally paid more attention to human performance and efficiency than to the *quality* of working life. But nowadays the emphasis has perceptibly shifted towards the latter. There are pragmatic grounds for this as well as humane ones. For there is evidence that our expectations and attitudes about work, together with the rewards and satisfactions obtained, affect not only the way we behave at work but also at home and in the community at large.

Though interpretations of this evidence are scarcely uniform, there is a general consensus among psychologists that it is better for people to enjoy their work than not. A more controversial inference is that even a relatively 'poor' quality of working life (in the sense used here of *work as paid employment*) is more likely to promote psychological fulfilment and harmony than is a lack of any work at all. The two topics which we take up in this chapter may at first sight appear unrelated. Nevertheless they both impinge upon the wider issue of applying psychology to the quality of life in general and working life in particular.

Occupational guidance is one of several terms currently in use to designate the process of helping people choose occupations that will prove congenial and rewarding to them. That people want this help is indisputable. Every year in Britain, over 400,000 young persons leave school hoping to enter the world of work for the first time. At least 50,000 adults consulted the national Occupational Guidance Service annually during the 1970s. Disabled and disadvantaged people who attend Employment Rehabilitation Centres, as many as 14,000 clients a year, also receive occupational guidance. Why should such assistance be sought? And why apply specifically psychological knowledge and techniques to what may seem to be primarily an economic and social issue?

The answer to one question lies in the bewildering variety of occupational options theoretically on offer to those entering or already engaged in the labour force. Work in an 'advanced' modern society imposes an endless array of demands for different human activities in dissimilar environments, spanning different epochs during which the occupations may themselves change. Some order can be imposed upon this variety through a more-or-less coherent grouping of like characteristics into occupational categories. Around 3,500 of these occupations are described in the standard British Classification of Occupations and Dictionary of Occupational Titles. (The American counterpart lists over 21,000.) Now let us assume for a moment the quite improbable circumstance that a class, say, of 16-year-old school-leavers was fully conversant with the details of these 3,000-plus occupations. Suppose too that their choices were made only according to the criteria of economic rewards and career prospects, availability, possession of prescribed educational qualifications, and personal preferences regarding the nature of work. Their selection of the few most suitable options for each person would present them with a formidable task of discrimination and choice. Assistance from knowledgeable careers advisers or vocational counsellors would seem to be highly advantageous if not well-nigh indispensable. In practice an even wider range of sometimes conflicting criteria may need to be taken into account, balancing enlightened self-interest and realism against the shifting uncertainties of the future world of work.

We shall return to the second question of a 'strictly psychological' contribution to occupational guidance. For the moment we may note that it hinges upon three components. First there has to be a translation of current and anticipated occupational demands into estimates for each occupation of how wide a range of personal qualities, skills, and potential for self-development, may be expected to meet them adequately. Second there have to be techniques of assessment from which individuals may be helped to appraise their own chances of suitability and success in their preferred occupations. A third component is psychological awareness of how occupational preferences are influenced and formed; how firmly they are embedded in an individual's lifestyle and aspirations; how compatible they are with the two former categories. A further consideration, cutting across all the others, is that people seeking occupational guidance fall into a number of sub-groups with some distinctive needs of their own. Among these, school-leavers and disabled people have been explicitly singled out for distinctive treatment in the past. Adult women, and unemployed people of both sexes, are large minorities with current claims for special help.

Our other main topic is *Unemployment*. At a time when registered unemployment in Great Britain has risen to about 14% of the total labour force, with close on 3,300,000 people out of work, one-third of them without work for more than a year, no-one will dispute that here is a social problem of chilling proportions. There is every indication that it will persist, and may get worse. What is its significance for applied psychologists? Can they contribute an understanding of how individuals respond to the experience of unemployment? Can they contribute in any way to the adjustments in life-style and attitudes which so many people will have to seek in the face of frustrated aspirations and fruitless attempts to find employment?

Until quite recently there had been no psychological research on unemployment to speak of, since a small but nonetheless significant amount in America and Austria during the worldwide depression of the 1930s (Jahoda, 1979). We have relatively little empirical data yet about the contemporary experience of unemployment, let alone of its longer-term effects. What is available, however, broadly agrees with earlier findings, despite differences in the economic circumstances of today and an alleged decline in the influence of the so-called 'protestant work ethic'. Moreover, the psychological impact on most people who cannot find or regain employment is what we might predict from the vastly greater research literature based on the experience and behaviour of people who are working.

For the great majority of us, even under present economic circumstances, about one-quarter of our entire waking hours from early adulthood until retirement are spent at work. Our personal identity and social standing is very largely bound up with the nature of our occupation and the level at which we practise it. It is only to be expected, therefore, that an informed choice of occupation will be a significant factor in the quality of our whole life experience. Neither should it surprise us that an involuntary lack or loss of work is a psychologically distressing and sometimes permanently debilitating intrusion upon our customary or anticipated life-styles. This can be so even when the victim of unemployment is afflicted by less than the usual burden of financial deprivation.

II.—CONCEPTS OF THE PERSON AND MODELS OF HUMAN BEHAVIOUR

Concepts and Models of Guidance

Occupational guidance is one among several terms found in the literature to denote procedures that help people choose work that is satisfying and within their competence to perform satisfactorily. *Vocational* and *careers guidance* are more-or-less synonymous alternatives. These terms may, however, convey overtones of selfless dedication throughout life to a single occupation. Such implications are wholly inappropriate for guidance in the modern idiom.

Two other terms, *careers* or *vocational counselling*, are also related; but they refer to procedures that many psychologists advocate as preferable to those characteristically practised in occupational guidance. Counselling entails a more protracted, empathic, and non-directive, relationship between practitioner and client.

Procedural differences between a 'guidance' and a 'counselling' approach tend to be associated with differences in the psychological theories that underpin them. In British psychology there is a long (though currently unfashionable) tradition of concentration upon individual differences. Occupational psychologists have concerned themselves with differences in cognitive abilities, personality variables, and motivation, which have a bearing on achievement and contentment in the working environment. This 'differentialist' tradition, sometimes discussed pejoratively as 'trait-and-factor' theory, has nevertheless been the dominant influence until quite recently upon the aims and practice of virtually every major occupational guidance service in Britain. Not only has this been true of private agencies like the National Institute of Industrial Psychology, but it applies equally to the three nationwide public services: the Employment Rehabilitation Service (ERS) for disabled and disadvantaged adults, the Careers Advisory Service for school-leavers and young adults, and the short-lived Occupational Guidance Service for adults (. . . born in 1966 and sacrificed on the altar of governmental spending cuts in 1980).

Broadly speaking, the 'differentialist' model rests upon two assumptions. The first is plausible enough. Psychological satisfaction from one's working life, and satisfactory achievement in one's job, are directly proportional to the closeness of fit between one's own distinctive 'mix' of work-related talents, inclinations, and expectations, and the accumulated demands and rewards of one's occupation. Therefore the best occupational choices for a client are those which reflect the most evident 'matches'. The second assumption is much less easy to defend. It amounts to a claim that the likelihood of future satisfaction and performance in a chosen occupation can be confidently predicted from assessments of what the client is like now, what the occupation is like now and what the occupation may become.

On the face of it, this model of guidance suggests a forlorn attempt to urge square plugs into corresponding square holes. Such is the limitless range of variation among people *and* occupations that the attempt would surely fail. Fortunately a more sophisticated interpretation operates in practice. The guidance practitioner's aim is first to steer a client away from unattainable and other clearly unsuitable choices. Then information is retrieved about as wide a range of possibilities as seem to be compatible with the client's circumstances and capabilities, taking full account of that person's already-formed interests and inclinations (Rodger and Cavanagh, 1968). Finally, clients are expected to arrive at their own realistic and committed choice among the feasible opportunities.

This differentialist and matching (or 'congruence') approach to guidance came under heavy fire during the 1960s. Psychologists who followed Super's (1957) lead, regarded occupational choice as an essentially developmental process. It was interwoven with the progressive growth of an individual's personal identity and preferred life-style throughout the whole of adolescence and adulthood. Indeed the steadily maturing ideas which the individual develops about his or her own nature and psychological make-up (the 'self-concept', as the approved psychological expression has it) are reckoned to be a crucial formative influence upon that individual's preferences and motivation towards the world of work. Choosing an occupation, on this view, is essentially part of the process of implementing your self-concept in real life.

Developmentalists therefore deprecate the practice of guidance as a once-only and possibly directive occurrence, tied only to crises like the transition from school to work or the threat of an impending redundancy. Not only should it be continuously available in the guise of a proper programme of 'careers education' during the years of secondary schooling. It should be supplemented periodically by recourse to vocational counselling throughout one's career, and preferably before any significant change of level or direction of occupation is in the offing.

Developmentalists are also critical of what they see as an undue emphasis in the differentialist matching model, upon a static assessment of separate psychological traits. A portrait of someone which is composed of apparently independent measures from psychological tests and rating scales cannot, they would say, adequately represent the dynamic, individualistic, 'wholeness' of that person. Even when coloured by supplementary information from a guidance interview, it must appear somehow static and incomplete. Moreover, unless people can be persuaded to *perceive themselves* as painted thus, and to accept the implications of their portrait willingly and with insight, it will have little significance for them in arriving at occupational decisions.

The following table brings together for comparison some of the characteristics of guidance we have been describing (see Table 5.1).

Concepts and Models of Unemployment

We have already hinted that in a society like ours, work in the sense of paid employment has a special psychological and social significance. Note that other kinds of working activity like unpaid housework or 'do-it-yourself' jobs fall outside this concept of work. Let us now return to the question of the psychological significance of *unemployment*. A formal definition of this has been stated by Hayes and Nutman (1981) as '. . . a state of worklessness

TABLE 5.1

TWO APPROACHES TO OCCUPATIONAL GUIDANCE	
Differentialist/Matching Model	**Developmental/Self-Concept Model**
Concentrates on	*Concentrates on*
measured individual differences	developmental theories of personality
traits and abilities theory	self-concept theory
use of tests and assessment norms	non-directive counselling
information about occupations	careers education, especially in schools
Tends towards	*Tends towards*
practitioner as occupational 'expert'	avoiding involvement in occupational
once-only 'crisis' guidance	decisions
advising clients about choices	relative neglect of economic and socio-logical factors

experienced by people who see themselves or are seen by others as potential members of the work force.' On this basis, unemployed people '. . . are those who are available for work, but are unable to secure work.' (pp. 1 and 2).

In a seminal paper on this topic, Marie Jahoda (1979) drew upon her own and others' research findings from the depressed years between 1929 and 1935. Interpreting these results in the light of subsequent knowledge about people's behaviour and attitudes with respect to paid employment, she concluded that despite the dissatisfactions and frustrations so many experience in their work, people are still motivated more positively towards working than not working. As she put it '. . . people want to work even while they hate it.' (p. 312). Jahoda went on to distinguish 'manifest' consequences of working, the objective and intended consequences such as earning a living, from the '*latent*' ones which are less tangible and generally unplanned. It is the latter which provide us with clues to the underlying psychological appeal of being employed and, conversely, to the destructive impact of unemployment.

These 'latent' consequences are worth spelling out. They confer benefits from working which nearly everyone seems to need and value highly. In Jahoda's estimation they comprise the following.

  (i) Employment imposes a *time structure* on the working day. Without the discipline and regularity of having to get up, go to work, and apportion one's time among various job-related routines, there can be a distortion of time scales and a loss of differentiation within periods of time. For example, weekends, working days, and holidays, are all the same.

 (ii) Employment implies regularly *shared experiences* and *contacts* outside the family. The importance of social contacts and interpersonal relationships at the work site has been attested by many researchers.

(iii) Employment links an individual to *goals and purposes* which extend beyond one's own immediate needs. Without it, the individual feels unused and useless, severed from any means of contributing to society at large.

(iv) Employment confers *status* and *personal identity*. A person's occupation is probably the clearest indicator, in our society, of social standing. Loss of work can seriously undermine that person's self-esteem. We have already noted the importance of the self-concept in choosing and sustaining an occupational role; destruction of that role can only be damaging to the self-concept.

(v) Employment requires one to be *active*; to exercise skill, perhaps to excel and to innovate. Awareness of one's own achievements in work can be intensely satisfying. Removing the opportunities for such satisfactions is a further source of psychological deprivation.

Unemployment evidently removes some powerful supports to our psychological well-being. Does it therefore bring about debilitating and lasting after-effects? As Jahoda pointed out, there had been very little empirical enquiry by psychologists to supplement data like her own from the 1930s. This is surprising, given that seasonal and cyclic unemployment has never completely disappeared, even under so-called 'full employment'. However, a re-awakening of interest was already taking place by 1979; and results from a number of contemporary studies are now to hand. With some reservations (cf. Gurney and Taylor, 1981; Sinfield, 1981; Hartley, 1980), researchers have been obtaining results which agree substantially with what we should expect from Jahoda's analysis. Certainly some of the psychological effects observed in the 1930s are showing up again.

Hill (1977) has drawn attention to the particular vulnerability of young persons, notably school-leavers, to the onset of listlessness and feelings of failure and rejection when jobs are not forthcoming. Acquiring an adult occupational identity is seriously impeded under these circumstances. Other evidence on unemployment and health, particularly mental health, suggests that involuntary and prolonged loss of work is associated more frequently and strongly with various symptoms of reduced psychological well-being (Hepworth, 1980; Stafford, Jackson and Banks, 1980), or with physical ill-health and with serious anxiety or depressive states, than would be expected by chance. But just how progressive and long-lasting, perhaps even irreversible, is the full psychological impact of protracted unemployment, it is too early yet to say. For example, the extent of psychological and practical support from one's family, friends, and social community, is a moderating influence upon outcomes.

Yet there is now a large measure of agreement among recent investigators as to the nature of the transition from the onset of an enforced job-loss and the eventual acceptance of unemployment as a normal, possibly permanent, way of life. A recently-published review of the psychology of unemployment

by Hayes and Nutman (1981) gives the best account of this. The stages
through which a person 'progresses' seem to be remarkably similar nowadays,
despite a very different economic and social climate, to those observed 50
years ago. Briefly (and here we are adopting the model put forward by
Harrison, 1976), it appears that a sequence like this is likely to be
experienced:

$$\text{Shock} \rightarrow \text{Optimism} \rightarrow \text{Pessimism} \rightarrow \text{Fatalism}$$

After the initial blow to morale and the sense of shock accompanying
notice of redundancy or dismissal, even when the news of this is conveyed
as sensitively as possible, most individuals recover with feelings of optimism
and expectation that they will soon find other acceptable jobs. But as the
harsh reality is brought home to them, through rejected applications, fruitless
appeals to employment agencies, and despite a desperate willingness to
change place of residence if necessary, morale falls away again. Acute distress
or all-pervasive boredom intrudes, and deep pessimism about the future sets
in. Eventually, perhaps not until a year after the first shock, a psychological
adjustment to the new situation takes over. Serious efforts to find work may
be abandoned. The individual settles down to permanent unemployment,
still psychologically and perhaps socially inert compared with the former self,
but relieved of the acute anxieties and depressed morale of the 'pessimistic'
phase. There is a reluctant adjustment to, if not enjoyment of, a fresh self-
image and life-style.

Though this model is now supported by several documented accounts,
there should be no need to remind psychologists that individual differences
may reveal quite wide departures from it.

III.—INDIVIDUAL ASSESSMENT

Assessment in occupational guidance is customarily shaped by the assumption
that occupational demands can be phrased in the same psychological terminology as is used to describe the personal qualities, motivation, and social
characteristics of individuals. A common system of classification is therefore
implied for individuals and occupations. The most widely used system in
Britain is attributable to the late Alec Rodger (Rodger, 1952). He devised
it for the National Institute of Industrial Psychology (the NIIP) along the
lines of an earlier ('psychographic') assessment plan drawn up by Cyril Burt
in the 1920s. The *Seven-Point Plan*, as it is known, calls for clients to be
assessed under the following headings, each reckoned to be significant for
success and satisfaction in employment.

(i)   *Physical Make-up*: including health, appearance, and speech.
(ii) *Attainments*: educational qualifications, previous occupational training
      or experience.

(iii) *General Intelligence*: not only 'measured' intelligence, but also an estimate of how effectively intelligence is used in everyday life.

(iv) *Special Aptitudes*: regarded as capacities or talents for excelling in mechanical, manually dextrous, artistic, linguistic, and other distinctively skilled occupations.

(v) *Interests*: preferred sorts of activity; for example of a constructional, 'practical', nature; or for more intellectual tasks; or, instead, for interpersonal, socially-oriented kinds of work.

(vi) *Disposition*: personality variables such as sociability, dependability, and emotional stability, are broadly what is relevant here.

(vii) *Circumstances*: this 'catch-all' category is intended mainly to allow for sociological and economic factors. Examples are mobility, expectations regarding earnings and career progression, and domestic circumstances in so far as these constrain acceptance of occupational features like irregular hours, shiftwork, extensive travel.

There is undoubtedly an old-fashioned aura about these labels for psychological characteristics. Indeed the *Seven-Point Plan* has often been criticized as overly pragmatic and atheoretical. That it singles out something called 'general intelligence' as a requirement for assessment is sufficient ground for many psychologists to dismiss it as reactionary too. Yet such is the need and appeal for practitioners to have systematic guidelines on what to assess and how to record and coordinate the data for interpretation to or by a client, that alternative schemes are remarkably more derivative, than different from, Rodger's *Plan*. Thus the general adult Occupational Guidance Service assessed clients under six headings: (i) Physical, Quality of Speech, and Health; (ii) Circumstances; (iii) Attainments; (iv) Abilities; (v) Disposition; (vi) Aims and Aspirations. Similarly the psychologists working in Employment Rehabilitation Centres for disabled and disadvantaged people, assess and report on their clients in terms of (i) Appearance, Fitness, and Health; (ii) Circumstances; (iii) Work History; (iv) Intelligence, Aptitudes, and Work Performance; (v) Adjustment and Disposition; and (vi) Preferences, Aims, and Plans.

Ever since the first professional service was set up in 1922 by the NIIP, individuals have been assessed through a combination of *interviewing* (usually structured according to a schema like the *Seven-Point Plan*) and *psychological testing* (usually of general intellectual ability, i.e., intelligence; plus special abilities like verbal fluency, numeracy, and mechanical aptitude). Before the first interview, information is normally obtained from a client about educational and occupational history. Indeed the guidance interview is much more than just an occasion for supplementing information already to hand from a client's biographical data and test results. It is the medium through which the constituent parts of a total assessment are inter-related, brought together into a coherent and personalized whole, and then fully discussed with the client in the context of his or her emerging preferences for work and under-standing of occupational demands. In a guidance context, rather more so than is likely in a vocational *counselling* relationship, a further objective will be to help the client towards an informed choice among occupations, with a fair degree of commitment to take action accordingly.

There has always been controversy over the place of psychological testing in personal assessment. On the whole psychologists tend to be more cautious about using tests than are other practitioners who may have been trained to use them. However it is still quite common practice for psychologists to invite their clients to complete a battery of 'general ability' tests. Examples of widely-used tests are the Birkbeck 1-4 series, the AH4 Test of general intelligence, and the DEVAT battery (Department of Employment Voca-tional Aptitude Tests). The latter is the most recently developed assessment battery in Britain for guidance purposes, specially designed and evaluated in the early 1970s by psychologists in the Department of Employment for the Careers Advisory Service to use with school-leavers. Modified versions have been prepared for complementary use in adult guidance procedures. The DEVAT battery comprises 6 sub-tests: Arithmetic; Shapes; Same Word; Reasoning; Mechanical Comprehension; and Mathematics. For details of these tests, and for a well-documented account of how the DEVAT battery was constructed and standardized, readers should consult the DEVAT Manual (Employment Services Agency, 1977).

These tests can sometimes yield unsuspected clues to cognitive capacities relevant to occupational success. But no assessment would be acceptable, let alone valid, which took any less account of occupational preferences and 'interests'. Therefore perhaps the most relevant and helpful form of psycho-logical 'testing' to have found a regular place in guidance procedure is that which reveals the pattern of an individual's occupational interests. 'Testing' is really an inappropriate description in this context. Instruments like the Kuder Preference Record (completed as a matter of routine by all clients of the short-lived Occupational Guidance Service) and the Edinburgh APU Occupational Interests Guide (developed in the first place for use by school-leavers and young adults) are really adaptations of the paired-comparisons technique to questionnaires about occupational activities and preferences. There are no 'right' or 'wrong' answers. Nor are these instruments used to assess individuals in relation to norms, or to each other. They are examples of 'ipsative' rather than 'normative' procedures. For example, the Occupational Interests Guide provides a profile assessment for an individual showing the relative strengths, within himself, of his interest in each of eight or nine occupational activities; for example, of a scientific, computational, clerical-sales, or social service, nature (Closs, 1975).

Though the amount of psychological research on unemployment may be gaining ground compared with that directed to guidance, there is still very little in the way of direct psychological involvement in remedial action. So it is only to be expected that the assessment of individuals has hitherto been envisaged as a means of collecting aggregated data for research objectives, rather than a basis for diagnosis and remedial action for those particular individuals. Since research workers have shown more interest in emotional and attitudinal characteristics (rather than cognitive ones) of unemployed people, instruments which figure prominently in the UK literature are exemplified by Goldberg's General Health Questionnaire and the Life Satisfaction Scale (e.g., Hepworth, 1980). Specially drawn-up questionnaires, often incorporating items to assess 'self-esteem', are usually the main instruments for assessing the psychological state of jobless individuals.

IV.—THE IMMEDIATE SOCIAL AND EMOTIONAL ENVIRONMENT

Two issues stand out here. Each has to do with psychological interactions between participants. With respect to guidance we have to take account of the adviser-client relationship. In relation to unemployment there is the emotional state of an individual to consider and its effect upon family and other intimate social relationships.

At the core of guidance procedure lies an appraisal of the client. No doubt self-appraisal in this context is to be preferred. Even so, it is likely to be supplemented by someone else, skilled at assessment and competent to suggest various forms of suitable training or employment. This 'expert' role should perhaps be no more than informative. In practice it is likely to become frankly advisory. To a young, inexperienced, and even bewildered client, it may even appear mildly directive though not necessarily unwelcome on that account. However, guidance practitioners try to avoid inducing a dependent and passive stance from their clients. They try instead to arrive *jointly* at an agreed appraisal of the circumstances, and at recommendations for action to which the client feels personally committed. It is only fair to say, though, that most guidance advisers find it impracticable to adopt the strictly empathic and non-directive style to which vocational counsellors so often claim adherence.

As we suggested earlier, the psychological impact of losing or failing to get a job is moderated by one's personal self-image and social attitudes, which are themselves at least partially constructed from expectations or experience of work. Hayes and Nutman (1981) have described vividly how unemployed people are inclined to devalue themselves and to worry over what they perceive (albeit wrongly) as a loss of esteem from family, friends, and the wider community. They speak of the 'identity strain' which may be brought on by unemployment. The unfortunate individual feels that he or she can no longer fulfil the self-image through social roles which matter. Social interactions with others can become strained and discomforting, especially if those people are still employed. The individual will probably avoid frank discussion of his or her new and disconcerting status. He or she may try to hide behind a facade of defiant acceptance of the situation or an equally vehement rejection of it. Or there may be a retreat into comparative social isolation, defending what is now perceived as his or her own relative inadequacy.

Small wonder, therefore, that research workers have sometimes reported great difficulty in making contact with and securing cooperation from unemployed people. The latter may very well not perceive such intrusion upon their time and their psychological defence as being either materially rewarding or wholly benign.

Symptoms of psychological stress do not, however, always accompany unemployment. It probably depends upon individual differences in emotional stability and perhaps upon the level of previous employment. There is evidence that stress is moderated by the degree of familial and social supportiveness extended to the unemployed person. For example, Fineman (1979) found in a study of 25 unemployed managers that stress (defined as '. . . a psychological state of experienced high anxiety') did not necessarily appear. Where it did, the amount was not simply predictable from measures of predisposition towards anxiety. Fineman was nevertheless able to infer useful clues as to how counselling can benefit an unemployed person. Both anxiety and strain are reducible if the person is encouraged to confront personal circumstances and problems; through supportive counselling, the person may come to perceive them as less threatening to one's self-esteem than formerly.

V.—THE WIDER SOCIAL AND ORGANIZATIONAL ENVIRONMENT

In Western (or, as some would have it, 'post-industrial') societies, the contemporary scene is peculiarly significant both for guidance and for unemployment. First there is the pervasive impact of advanced and constantly-changing technology. This affects not only manufacturing industries, which now employ less than 33% of the labour force in Britain. It impinges also upon the practice of government and local administration, and the so-called 'service' or tertiary sector of public utilities, health, education, and social services. Most remarkable of all is the growth of 'information technology'—computer-based communication and control systems—and its potential effects upon virtually every occupational category from process control workers to secretaries and clerical staff. The consequence of technological change, exacerbated by persistent economic recession, is structural unemployment on an unprecedented and possibly irreversible scale. Though new occupations are emerging to parallel fresh technological and social development, many more have been lost or drastically pruned. Paradoxically, all this has heightened the problem of occupational choice for young people.

Not only are they confronted by serious restrictions on the scope of available openings. They have also to face uncertainties regarding the precise demands for skill, not to mention the durability and career prospects, of new and unfamiliar occupations.

Secondly, there are signs of changing attitudes towards work in our society. As Shimmin (1980) cautioned, evidence of this is neither comprehensive nor unambiguous. But the indications are persuasive. Legislation, which usually reflects rather than initiating a shift in societal values, has recently been directed towards further enhancing the health and safety of workers (Health and Safety Act, 1974), and removing restrictions upon the employment of certain minority groups and women (Sex Discrimination Act, 1975; Race Relations Act, 1976). Though statutory measures have not yet been taken to enhance the *quality* of working life, there has certainly been pressure upon managements and trade unions alike to pay greater attention to it. Work can and should be designed and organized for maximal human satisfaction as well as maximal efficiency; or, so it has been insistently claimed, by organizational psychologists among others.

A third factor, associated with changing attitudes about work, is the growing public awareness that a high rate of structural unemployment is probably here to stay. It encourages a softening of society's traditional disapproval of people without work. The idea that to be jobless is also to be worthless dies hard. But as we grow accustomed to losses of job opportunities for school-leavers, more redundancies and early retirements, where so many people become and stay unemployed involuntarily, it must undermine the puritanical view that not to be working is somehow improper and negligently self-indulgent.

Just what is the effect in Britain of abandoning the Occupational Guidance Service (the OGS) can only be guessed at this stage. There does not seem to have been an outbreak of new private agencies, nor a rush of clients to those already operating when the OGS ceased. Parents of school-leavers, even among the professional middle-classes, have always shown more interest in a job *placement* service than in one which offers disinterested assistance towards making occupational and careers choices. Now that employment prospects for the under-21s are so diminished, it is only too likely that seeking guidance has an even lower priority, especially if it costs parental money.

So far there has been no curtailment of the Careers Service for young persons. The emphasis here has always been upon placement into jobs, however, rather than upon serious occupational or careers guidance. With jobs in such short supply, the Careers Service is now taking over a major role in promoting and organizing compensatory schemes for unemployed school-leavers, like the government's Youth Training Scheme which opened in 1983.

VI.—TYPES OF INTERVENTION

Public sector provision for vocational guidance is now only available in Britain to school-leavers and young adults (through the Careers Service administered by local authorities), and to disabled and some categories of 'disadvantaged' adults who are admitted to the 27 Employment Rehabilitation Centres. The latter are operated through the Employment Services Agency of the Manpower Services Commission. Psychologists have only rarely been employed as such in the Careers Service, but there is a small group of them that provides modest research and development support for the Service as a whole. It may not be widely appreciated that each Employment Rehabilitation Centre has an occupational psychologist on its staff contributing vocational guidance and some counselling to the clients, who spend around eight weeks at a centre. The guidance draws heavily upon observation of how the disabled person is adjusting to handicaps, aided by the experience of trying out various kinds of semi-skilled vocational activity in the simulated industrial environment of a Centre.

Other than through these 'national' organizations, informed and professional guidance is only available at the sixteen or so small, fee-charging, private agencies. Most of these are in London. Moderate provision is also made for university and polytechnic students through their own careers and appointments centres.

Supportive services of a distinctively therapeutic and counselling nature do not yet exist specifically for people who are involuntarily out of work. Nor is it self-evidently appropriate on therapeutic, social, or economic, grounds to institute them. However, one possibility to which some psychologists have given serious thought is the establishment of local centres for unemployed persons. As Winfield (1981) says, these are places where '. . . people can go and obtain information about all aspects of unemployment, meet other unemployed and even engage in a variety of social, cultural, or learning experiences' (pp. 353). Most of these centres are still at a planning or formative stage. The precise style and range of services they will offer is uncertain. Objectives for starting them up may be political as well as humanistic, avowedly functional (for example, explaining obscure official guidelines about job-seeking strategies) as well as supportive (for example, providing social, recreational, and learning experiences, in an inexpensive but congenial setting). But from a psychological standpoint, anything which helps to restore the daily structure of activities and interpersonal relationship that paid employment formerly guaranteed, should be beneficial to psychological health and well-being. We might expect benefits particularly for individuals who may be susceptible to, or already displaying, clinical symptoms of depression and even more serious disorders (Shepherd, 1981).

Winfield is clear that psychologists can help distinctively in this context:

not, however, as well-meaning, charitably-minded consultants, whether voluntarily or not; nor, he insists, as observational or manipulative researchers! Rather psychologists should adopt a catalyst's role '. . . operating as a sort of self-effacing subversive. The role is to define, shape and help install self-adapting psychological support systems: systems designed to promote, not decrease, user self-management' (pp. 353). Winfield stresses the importance of surveying the needs of local unemployed groups as they themselves perceive them, before planning the amenities and organization of a centre. Perhaps applied psychologists could be helpful in this diagnostic role.

VII.—IS PSYCHOLOGICAL INTERVENTION SUCCESSFUL?

Predicting vocational success has been a captivating objective for applied psychologists from the earliest days of personnel selection and occupational guidance. Not that much in the way of reliable and valid prediction has been unequivocally demonstrated, except in military organizations. It is arguable that methodological difficulties in follow-up research are as much to blame as any inherent weaknesses in guidance or selection procedures.

The earliest enquiry into its efficacy was carried out in 1923 by Burt, who was then in charge of vocational guidance at the NIIP. Several other large-scale studies were mounted by NIIP staff during the 1930s. According to Frisby (1970), the number of their clients from whom adequate data could be elicited about subsequent careers, was generally too small for definitive conclusions. Yet it was claimed that '. . . If a correct prediction is taken to be a case in which an individual followed the advice and succeeded or rejected it and failed, the proportion of correct predictions . . . was between 75% and 80%'(pp. 41). With small numbers, proportions like this can be misleading. Moreover the 'measures' of vocational success were open to criticism. For example, 'success' and 'happiness' in their work were self-rated on 3-point scales, as an index of adjustment to their employment, by clients followed-up in one of the studies. Even if such ratings were free of misinterpretation and bias by the respondents, their reliability and validity as *criterion* measures must be suspect, in view of the likelihood that powerful factors besides the soundness of occupational choice will influence one's success and satisfaction as a worker.

All clients of the Occupational Guidance Service were asked to return a simple self-completion questionnaire mailed to them six months later. One study of 1,000 cases in 1968 revealed that 49% of clients had changed their occupation radically whilst another 32% had changed jobs within the same occupational setting; 19% were still in their former employment. It is not clear to what extent these outcomes were the direct result of guidance, or even whether they were in accordance with it. However, 72% of the sample claimed to be 'well satisfied' or 'fairly well satisfied' with the guidance (White, Raphael and Crinnion, 1970).

Evidence of this kind can scarcely be regarded as conclusive of anything. Indeed there are grounds for doubting if hard evidence of whether guidance actually 'works' is attainable in practice. So it is not surprising that most research since the 1930s has in fact concentrated upon development and evaluation of more refined techniques for practitioners to use. On the whole it appears that a discrete and sophisticated use of psychological tests (of occupational interests and attitudes, as well as cognitive and personality factors) is advantageous. It sharpens the edge of assessments which advisers may be asked to make. In addition, clients can use interpreted test results to heighten awareness of their own capabilities and to exercise informed judgement about their occupational aspirations.

In more recent evaluations of occupational guidance, British investigators (e.g., Lancashire and Cohen, 1970) have adopted criteria which reflect the influence of developmental theories. Rather than just using 'snapshots' of how clients are currently employed and their reactions to their jobs, researchers have examined whole career patterns in relation to earlier guidance consultations. There is certainly some support for the conclusion that individuals whose occupational patterns more or less follow the advice given earlier, are the more likely to tread satisfactory career paths. 'Satisfactory' implies 'vertical progress' towards increasing qualifications, and responsibility, and promotions. (For an informative review of recent and early evaluative research in this area, readers may like to consult Watts and Kidd, 1978).

Whether such encouraging results will be sustained in future, assuming that technological change and uncertain employment trends continue, remains to be seen.

VIII.—METHODOLOGICAL AND PRACTICAL PROBLEMS

Some of these have been identified in the previous section. As in so much of applied psychology, the ubiquitous 'criterion problem' is the most serious one for anyone wishing to evaluate the worth of occupational guidance. What outcomes constitute 'success'? And how can we measure them? There are no simple answers. If guidance is conceived as a procedure for seeing that individuals choose to use their talents and develop their potentialities for maximal economic gain, the criterion of stable employment, high earnings and productive performance, may be appropriate. Probably not, however, if the objective of guidance is to ensure that occupational and career patterns are in harmony with personal values and desires. In that event, 'satisfaction' or 'commitment' to one's work may be more relevant, though hardly sufficient alone.

Deciding that a suitable criterion is *predicting* the vocational success of our clients, as so many of the earlier investigations did, will not relieve us of the problem of agreeing how that success is to be judged. Nor will it resolve the question of how to determine, if individual clients *are* successful in their working lives, that this success is attributable wholly or indeed at all to the guidance they received. Even if the successful clients have chosen jobs which accord with recommendations during guidance, and if the unsuccessful ones have acted in contrary fashion, we have still to establish that the former group was not just fortunate in meeting unusually favourable circumstances at work; whilst the latter was not just unlucky in encountering the reverse. Naturally, in principle we can also follow-up a matched or randomly chosen control group, in which no-one has experienced any guidance whatever. The scarcity of studies where this has been done is indicative of the practical difficulties that researchers encounter in designing and completing follow-up research of this kind.

We have noted also that more effort has been devoted since the 1950s to improving the range and quality of procedures actually used by guidance practitioners. For example, when the DEVAT test battery was being introduced (Employment Services Agency, 1977), its utility was assessed partly in terms of *how* its results were used by careers officers and school-leavers, and how useful the participants judged it to be in the guidance context. Nevertheless, a problem arises here too. Just as the value and effectiveness of occupational guidance cannot easily be evaluated simply in terms of vocational success among clients, so too it should not be judged simply in terms of the particular techniques its practitioners employ. There is no *inherent* reason why a non-directive counselling interview should be preferable to a computer-based interactive programme or to a battery of diagnostic psychological tests; or *vice versa*. It depends upon the objectives of the total procedure, and the theoretical system which underpins it.

One of the difficulties confronting the researcher into unemployment is the accessibility of subjects and data appertaining to them. Very properly, but unfortunately for research workers, all 'official' information recorded about unemployed people is confidential and inaccessible, except perhaps in aggregate form. Moreover, but not unexpectedly, unemployed people tend not to promote themselves as available for interviewing, observation, or other means of collecting psychological data. Indeed one of the author's own students who had embarked on a study of redundant and unemployed executives, was unable (despite appeals via the press and radio) to identify and contact more than a very small sample of individuals among the substantial numbers actually known at the time (1976) to be registered with the Professional Executive of the Manpower Services Commission. Random, quota or representative sampling is out of the question under these circumstances. Researchers very often have recourse to 'opportunity sampling'—which is a euphemism for saying that you will use those subjects who happen to be available—unsatisfactory though that alternative may be.

Other problems for the theoretician include the well-known one of disentangling causal relationships among correlated observations. For example, we know that the lack of structured time and activity which accompanies a lack of employment is often associated with an accentuation of symptoms like anxiety, loss of self-esteem, and so forth. But which is cause and which effect? Are they consistently interactive? There is a further difficulty regarding the effects of prolonged unemployment. It is known that many moderating variables affect responses indicative of mental health. They arise from differential social support systems which may operate at a family or community level; not to mention individual differences in personal stability and social or occupational history. Psychological measures of health and well-being are on the whole insufficiently sensitive in the presence of these moderators to discriminate clearly among effects over long periods.

Finally we should remember that the psychological impact of unemployment has been studied almost entirely through instruments of *self-report*, with repeated measures as the respondents go through the successive stages of continuing to be out of work. Recent work at the Medical Research Council/Social Science Research Council, Social and Applied Psychology Unit at Shcffield University and elsewhere has indeed drawn upon more refined and well-constructed questionnaires and rating scales than were readily available to earlier researchers. But the relationship of these measures to the concurrent or future *behaviour* of unemployed respondents is neither self-evident nor firmly established empirically.

IX.—PROBLEMS OF ETHICS AND CONFIDENTIALITY

There are no issues of principle which are uniquely confronted by applied psychologists working with unemployed people or clients seeking occupational guidance. They are subject to the same ethical guidelines and appropriate professional practices as other psychologists. Unnecessary or unwelcome intrusions upon privacy must therefore be eschewed. Particular care should be taken with the choice of any psychological tests which may be administered to clients.

Information volunteered by clients or respondents must always be treated as confidential, and not revealed in reports or publications unless in aggregated form which effectively protects the anonymity and safeguards the trust of individuals. No personal information should ever be yielded to a third party without the individual's specific consent, or prior knowledge that such information may be passed to other professional advisers or named 'official' channels. This can sometimes involve the practitioner or consultant in resisting pressure from, say a parent, to reveal the nature of or grounds for recommendations arrived at with a young person who does not wish to discuss them within the family.

Respect for the sensitivities, personal integrity, and self-esteem of one's client or 'subject' must always be the hallmark of an applied psychologist's relationship with other persons. Preservation of a neutral attitude towards moralistic issues, and the fostering of an empathic relationship without emotional or paternalistic overtones, will contribute to this ideal. This is just as important for a research worker's interaction with unemployed respondents as it is for a professional guidance consultation.

X.—THE ROLE OF OTHER DISCIPLINES AND PROFESSIONS

It happens to be true that psychologists have supplied the theoretical frameworks, technical instruments, and research expertise, which underpin systems of vocational guidance and counselling. The majority of practitioners are not, however, psychologists; though most of them will have received at least part of their training from psychologists.

By far the largest group in Britain are careers officers. (Careers teachers in schools, though they are becoming increasingly identifiable as specialists in *careers education* and *educational guidance*, are not specialists in occupational guidance). Most careers officers are graduates and have additionally to complete up to a year's professional training in assessment, guidance, job analysis, and communication of occupational information. They are employed by local authorities, which administer the Careers Service, to help school-leavers and young adults to shape their occupational choices and effect a smooth transition from school to work.

Vocational guidance is an integral feature of employment rehabilitation in Employment Rehabilitation Centres but the rehabilitative process as a whole is much more than this. It aims to help disabled people adjust to their handicaps, restore their self-confidence, and build positive and realistic attitudes towards going back to work. Whilst occupational psychologists bear the main responsibility for guidance, they share the other aspects of rehabilitation with social workers, medical practitioners, and industrial craftsmen-supervisors.

Where unemployment is concerned, psychologists are currently operating only in a research context. Sociologists and economists have a comparable interest in this area, though a quite different orientation towards it.

XI.—FUTURE PROSPECTS

The dominant questions about guidance and unemployment must surely stem from the gloomy prospects facing each of them. It has been predicted by the Warwick Institute of Employment Research that unemployment in Britain will remain well above the three million mark at least until 1990. Those still employed may well continue to be as many as twenty-four million. However there are likely to have been profound changes in the composition of the labour force. The contemporary scene in which 'blue-collar' jobs account for about 52% of the total will have changed to tip the balance by at least the same proportion in favour of 'white-collar' ones. As many as three-quarters of a million more of the latter are anticipated. Managers, technicians, health care, sports and entertainment workers will figure prominently among them. On the other hand 'manual' jobs in traditional industries will have declined by possibly one-and-a-quarter million. Forecasts of rising regional unemployment are grim indeed for already badly-hit areas like South Wales and North East England. Under these circumstances, does it really matter that guidance services are contracting? In so far as occupational choice and unemployment are regarded as variables associated with economic and manpower planning, rather than as phenomena demanding social and psychological support, the future for them certainly looks bleak. It is only too easy to argue that when employment is a scarce and valued resource, when occupational choice and planning for a career is even more curtailed for the majority of working people than it always has been, then public guidance services are a low priority luxury. Nor is it very likely that many more people, even potential clients, will be keen to pay the charges which are necessary to sustain private sector agencies.

Maybe this is overly pessimistic. Just possibly, the current economic pressures will be conducive to a serious development of guidance objectives and practices that are more closely attuned to modern psychological thinking than has been the case in Britain hitherto. In which case, significant forward steps could be along the following lines.
 (i) The nation-wide introduction of occupational and careers education programmes in all schools. Applied psychologists of the 'developmental' persuasion have advocated this for years. Implementation has so far been remarkably sporadic.
(ii) Development of a national service for adults in which the job-oriented 'crisis' guidance so characteristic of practice in Britain, is supplemented if not replaced by a professional system of vocational and personal *counselling*. The aim would be to help clients resolve a much wider range of personal problems than just those related to occupational choice.
Proposals of this kind, together with examples of well-founded practice, are common enough in the literature. (See, for example: Holdsworth, 1982; Newsome, 1977; Watts, Super and Kidd, 1981; Sundal-Hansen, 1981, for a powerful American scenario).

None of these prospects is likely to be fully realized without recourse to modern information technology. No doubt there are still many enthusiasts for guidance to whom the idea of computer-aiding as a necessary prop to human client-centred counselling is both abhorrent and threatening. The compelling advantages of computers for storing, searching-out, and retrieving personal and occupational data are nevertheless beginning to overcome such prejudices. Readers who want to explore this promising new territory will find Wallis, Jackson and Sneath (1978) a useful point of departure.

The recent upsurge of interest in research on unemployment seems certain to be sustained. Helping some people to adjust psychologically to involuntary and prolonged lack of employment may turn out to be as high a priority for our professional expertise as helping more fortunate people to choose their occupations wisely. There are plenty of gaps in our knowledge to be filled before we can contribute much credible expertise in this direction. For example, too little is known yet about individual differences among those who are out of work, differences which could be associated systematically with differential attitudes and reactions to the situation. It is as psychologically inept to think of unemployed people as homogeneous as it is not to distinguish differences among those who are working. Some evidence is already to hand from sociological and psychological research projects to suggest that many young people without regular work may be learning to live indefinitely with that disadvantage. If the government's Youth Training Scheme fails to increase the chances of many school-leavers getting employment it may at least equip some of them with enhanced skills to survive as part-time, self-employed, workers or even as beneficiaries of the 'informal' economy.

As Gurney and Taylor (1981) observed, we may be moving into an era where work is more of a privilege than a necessity or duty, as now. Anticipating this 'post-industrial' world, applied psychologists who want to provide the most effective and beneficial assistance for people entering or leaving the world of employment, will have to acquire an understanding of fresh patterns of working; patterns which may even become the norm eventually, though currently less common or socially disavowed. Unemployment may even become an option to be voluntarily selected. Part-time employment, or job-sharing, delayed entry into the labour market, and earlier retirement: all these are at least conceivable alternatives to be chosen advisedly rather than experienced unwillingly.

Psychological insights have still to be established into how these patterns may affect the quality of working life generally, yet prove differentially appealing or inimical to the well-being of particular individuals.

XII.—ANNOTATED READINGS

Hayes, J. and Nutman, P. (1981). *Understanding the Unemployed*. London: Tavistock.

An informative review of research data and theoretical models appertaining to the psychological effects of unemployment. Brings vividly to life what the experience of being jobless is like.

Holdsworth, R. (1982). *Psychology for Careers Counselling.* London: The British Psychological Society and Macmillan Press.

An authoritative text covering all the main psychological aspects of vocational guidance and counselling. Contains a palatable account of theories, technical data, and research-based experience. Chapters 13 and 14 present detailed accounts of where psychological tests and assessment procedures fit in.

Peters, H. J. and Hansen, J. C. (1977). *Vocational Guidance and Career Development. Selected Readings.* (Third Edition). London: Collier Macmillan.

Offers a reasonably eclectic range of papers by prominent American theorists and practitioners. The greater sophistication of practice and theory in the United States is evident from these papers.

Wallis, D., Jackson, C. R. S. and Sneath, F. (1978). Computers in Vocational Guidance. *Journal of Occupational Psychology (Special Issue)*, **51**, 1–117.

A collection of papers reviewing technical possibilities, advantages, and limitations of using computers for occupational guidance and counselling. Several computer guidance systems being developed or evaluated in Britain at the time are described in detail. Interactive as well as data storage and processing systems are included.

Watts, A. G., Super, D. E. and Kidd, J. M. (1981). *Career Development in Britain.* Cambridge: Hobsons Press for CRAC.

Examines in great detail the theory, practice, and empirical evaluation, of careers education and guidance. British research is given due prominence. Whilst the emphasis is firmly upon developmental theories of occupational choice and careers progression, criticisms and alternative explanations are contributed by two sociologists.

XIII.—REFERENCES

Closs, S. J. (1975). *Manual of the Occupational Interests Guide.* London: Hodder and Stoughton.

Employment Services Agency (1977). *The DEVAT Manual.* London: Her Majesty's Stationery Office.

Fineman, S. (1979). A psychological model of stress and its application to managerial unemployment. *Human Relations*, **32**, 323–345.

Frisby, C. B. (1970). The development of industrial psychology at the NIIP. *Occupational Psychology*, **44**, 35–50.

Gurney, R. and Taylor, K. (1981). Research on unemployment. Defects, neglect, and prospects. *Bulletin of the British Psychological Society*, **34**, 349–352.

Harrison, R. (1976). The demoralising experience of prolonged unemployment. *Department of Employment Gazette*, April, 339–348.

Hartley, J. (1980). The impact of unemployment upon the self-esteem of managers. *Journal of Occupational Psychology*, **53**, 147–156.

Hayes, J. and Nutman, P. (1981). *Understanding the Unemployed.* London: Tavistock.

Hepworth, S. J. (1980). The psychological impact of unemployment. *Journal of Occupational Psychology*, **53**, 139–146.

Hill, J. (1977). *The Social and Psychological Impact of Unemployment*. London: Tavistock Institute of Human Relations.

Holdsworth, R. (1982). *Psychology for Careers Counselling*. London: The British Psychological Society and Macmillan Press.

Jahoda, M. (1979). The impact of unemployment in the thirties and seventies. *Bulletin of the British Psychological Society*, **32**, 309–314.

Lancashire, R. and Cohen, B. J. (1970). Developments in vocational guidance. *Occupational Psychology*, **44**, 223–228.

Newsome, A. (1977). Counselling the student: the place of vocational counselling in a British student counselling service. *International Review of Applied Psychology*, **26**, 95–100.

Rodger, A. (1952). The Seven Point Plan. London: National Institute of Industrial Psychology, Paper No. 1.

Rodger, A. and Cavanagh, P. (1968). Personnel selection and vocational guidance. In: A. T. Welford (Ed.) *Society: Problems and Methods of Study*. London: Routledge and Kegan Paul.

Shepherd, G. (1981). Psychological disorder and unemployment. *Bulletin of the British Psychological Society*, **34**, 345–348.

Shimmin, S. (1980). The future of work. In: K. D. Duncan, M. M. Gruneberg and D. Wallis (Eds.), *Changes in Working Life*. Chichester: Wiley.

Sinfield, A. (1981). *What Unemployment Means*. Oxford: Martin Robertson.

Stafford, E. M., Jackson, P. R. and Banks, M. H. (1980). Employment, work involvement and mental health in less qualified young people. *Journal of Occupational Psychology*, **53**, 291–304.

Sundal-Hansen, L. (1981). New goals and strategies for vocational guidance and counseling. *International Journal of Advanced Counseling*, **4**, 21–33.

Super, D. E. (1957). *The Psychology of Careers*. London: Harper and Row.

Wallis, D. (1978). Some pressing problems for research in vocational guidance. *Journal of Occupational Psychology*, **51**, 7–18.

Wallis, D., Jackson, C.R.S. and Sneath, F. (1978). Computers in vocational guidance. *Journal of Occupational Psychology*, **51**, 1–117.

Warr, P. B. and Wall, T. D. (1975). *Work and Well-Being*. Harmondsworth: Penguin.

Watts, A. G. and Kidd, J. (1978). The effectiveness of careers guidance. *Journal of Occupational Psychology*, **51**, 235–248.

Watts, A. G., Super, D. E., and Kidd, J. M. (1981). *Career Development in Britain*. Cambridge: Hobsons Press for CRAC.

Winfield, I. (1981). Psychology and Centres for the Unemployed: challenge or chimera? *Bulletin of the British Psychological Society*, **34**, 353–355.

White, G. C., Raphael, L. H. and Crinnion, J. (1970). Vocational guidance and the Department of Employment: the work of Psychologists. *Occupational Psychology*, **44**, 229–236.

Psychology and Social Problems
Edited by A. Gale and A. J. Chapman
© 1984 John Wiley & Sons Ltd.

CHAPTER 6

SATISFACTION AT WORK

Michael M. Gruneberg

I.—THE EXTENT OF THE PROBLEM

Given that the great majority of adults will at some stage in their lives take paid employment, the importance of satisfaction at work is one which has almost universal significance, at least in the developed world. However the importance that job satisfaction has for each individual's quality of life is only one aspect of the importance of the topic. Another major factor which makes the study of job satisfaction significant is that it is often thought that job satisfaction leads to greater productivity, greater involvement in the job, less absence and less job turnover—all matters of considerable economic importance. Whilst some of these assumptions have come to be questioned, the fact that many people think that such relationships exist makes it important to establish exactly what the true state of affairs is.

The study of job satisfaction within the context of modern psychology can perhaps be traced to two major influences in the 1920's and 1930's, the Hawthorne study at the Western Electric Company, and a study by Hoppock (1935), which represents one of the first major attempts to study job satisfaction using survey methods and attitude scales.

The Hawthorne studies (see Roethlesberger and Dickson, 1939) began as a conventional study of the relationship between physical working conditions and productivity. The first studies involved changing the level of illumination and produced the extraordinary finding that no matter whether levels of illumination were increased or decreased, productivity improved. Indeed in one study illumination was reduced to the level of moonlight, yet productivity improved. Clearly there was more to the relationship between illumination and productivity than met the eye! What had in fact happened was that a group of employees had been specially selected to take part in an experiment, they had been treated as individuals of importance to the experimenters, and they had been put in a situation where they were the subject of attention and interest. The resulting improvement in performance, therefore, as a result of experimental manipulation could have been due to these 'special' experimental factors—a phenomenon now known as the Hawthorne effect. Whatever the exact reason for performance improvement as a result of illumination changes, the Hawthorne investigators decided to examine the strange effect in a further series of experiments.

The first of the new experiments involved placing a small group of female employees in a relay assembly test room, and carrying out a number of experimental manipulations on factors such as rest pauses, hours of work, payment systems and so on. After a two-year period, productivity had increased by 30% but despite the fact that a large number of factors had been simultaneously varied, the Hawthorne investigators attributed the improvement to *human relations* factors in the work situation.

Among the most important of these factors was friendly supervision. The human relations school of industrial psychology was born, and it sought to increase productivity by improving satisfaction at work. The Hawthorne investigators saw a poor working context as providing frustrations to good working practices and argued that where these were overcome, satisfaction would improve and with it productivity.

Whilst the value of Hawthorne has been questioned for a variety of reasons, including the inadequacy of its experimental design, its pro-management bias, and defects in the interpretation of findings in view of the wider cultural context in which the study took place, there is no doubt about its historical importance in focusing the attention of organizational psychologists on the value of studying satisfaction at work. At the same time, Hoppock (1935) using survey techniques, was also showing the importance of studying job satisfaction. His studies showed that only a third of employees expressed dissatisfaction with their jobs, and this led him to question whether in fact people were too easily satisfied with their jobs. Since the original Hoppock study, other findings on the extent of satisfaction have also tended to find the expression of job dissatisfaction to be in the region of about 15–20% of employees.

A reaction to both the human relations approach to satisfaction at work, and the Hoppock approach came with the work of Herzberg (1966). Herzberg attacked the view that context factors such as friendly supervision and pay had any real effect on job satisfaction; rather, he claimed, they affected the context in which satisfaction could take place. Herzberg also attacked the view that job satisfaction could be assessed by merely asking individuals whether or not they were satisfied with work. There is an important distinction between being satisfied with something and deriving satisfaction from it. One can be very satisfied with one's office desk, yet derive little job satisfaction from it. Satisfaction, according to Herzberg can only be derived from those factors such as achievement, recognition and growth which allow the individual to gain self-fulfilment.

These three approaches, then, can be regarded as landmarks in the study of satisfaction at work. Whilst no one individual school is generally adhered to at present, there is wide acceptance of the view that physical context, social context and the job itself all interact with the needs and values of individuals to give rise to both job satisfaction and dissatisfaction.

II.—CONCEPTS OF THE PERSON AND MODELS OF HUMAN BEHAVIOUR

The most influential early model of human behaviour as far as job satisfaction is concerned is that provided by Maslow (1943). Maslow's need theory proposed a hierarchy of needs, in which the lower order biological needs are at the bottom and the higher order needs are at the top. The needs are:

(i)   Self actualization needs.
(ii) Esteem needs.
(iii) Social (affiliation) needs.
(iv) Safety and security needs.
(v)   Basic physiological needs.

According to Maslow, only after the lower-order needs are satisfied are individuals in a position to seek the satisfaction of higher or esteem and self actualization needs. An analogy might be drawn with someone shipwrecked on a desert island, who first ensures that he has food and water and shelter. He or she will then examine the island for other humans, in the hope that they are friendly and will fulfill social needs. Only then will the individual concentrate on higher-order needs of achievement, recognition and so on within a society. The theory has been applied within a job context to argue that the employee first seeks satisfaction of basic needs for security and pay, as well as social satisfactions, before going on to seek satisfaction of higher-order needs for achievement and recognition.

Herzberg (1966) made Maslow's hierarchy the basic aspect of his theory. Herzberg divided needs into two, the lower-order needs (iii, iv and v) and the higher-order needs (i and ii) and argued that satisfaction at work came only from the fulfilment of higher-order needs. The fulfilment of lower-order needs (the 'hygiene' factors) according to Herzberg, led not to job satisfaction, but rather to *no dissatisfaction*. In other words, Herzberg proposes a theory of job satisfaction, known as the *two factor theory*, in which the causes of job satisfaction and job dissatisfaction are separate and distinct. The factors which make for job satisfaction are those higher-order factors (the 'motivators') which allow the individual to enjoy work through achievement, recognition, the exercise of a skill. Inadequacies in these factors do not lead to job dissatisfaction, merely to a lack of satisfaction. On the other hand, context factors, such as pay, supervision, poor working conditions and so on, cause job dissatisfaction when they are defective, but when they are satisfactory they do not lead to job satisfaction.

Herzberg's theory, like that of Maslow, has intuitive appeal, and provides an implicit and indeed even explicit theoretical basis for practice for many managers. Yet it would also be true to say that very few organizational psychologists are convinced by either Maslow's or Herzberg's theory. As Locke (1976) points out, Maslow's theory has no real evidence to support it and it is in the nature of things that even low level needs are not satisfied by one, or indeed many consummatory acts. Indeed success in satisfying some lower-level needs can lead to reinforcement of behaviour carried out in the process of satisfying such needs.

As far as Herzberg's theory is concerned, the matter is much more complex, partly because of the ambiguous way in which Herzberg states his theory. King (1970) for example, in an analysis of Herzberg's theory, notes five different interpretations of the theory.

If one examines the evidence, then it is quite clear that even within the data provided by Herzberg (1968) motivators when they are defective, can lead to dissatisfaction and hygiene factors when they are 'adequate' can lead to satisfaction. Thus factors such as achievement failure are sometimes reported to be dissatisfying whilst factors such as salary are reported as satisfying. Herzberg accounts for this evidence by arguing that it is the *relative* frequency of motivators causing dissatisfaction and the *relative* infrequency of hygiene factors causing satisfaction which supports his theory. One is therefore left with what King describes as a 'weak form' of the theory, that motivators are more likely to cause satisfaction than dissatisfaction and *vice versa* for hygiene factors.

It has to be said that when Herzberg uses his own method, the 'critical incident' technique, for investigating job satisfaction then many studies support his view. The critical incident technique involves asking respondents to describe the occasions when they felt particularly good, or particularly bad about their job. The usual finding is that when this technique is used, findings do support Herzberg. However, when practically any other technique is used, such as questionnaires, then a different pattern of results emerges. Studies such as those of Wall and Stephenson (1970) indicate that motivators are more important both to satisfaction and dissatisfaction than are hygiene factors. As many writers have pointed out, the problem with the critical incident technique is two-fold. First, it induces respondents to blame bad events on their surroundings, and take credit themselves for good events; and second, it almost certainly misses factors of importance which although they have a material effect on job satisfaction do not occur in the normal course of events as critical incidents.

Despite its limitations, Herzberg's theory has been, and continues to be, of considerable importance within organizational psychology. The emphasis on the importance of motivators rather than hygiene factors in understanding job satisfaction has wide support and has had a major influence in practical schemes of job redesign aimed at improving both job satisfaction and productivity.

Apart from Maslow and Herzberg, however, there have been a number of theoretical models which have been applied to job satisfaction. Among the most important of these are *equity theory* and *expectancy theory*, although the latter is more properly thought of as a theory of motivation rather than of satisfaction.

Equity theory assumes that we try to make sense of our environment by having our psychological world in balance. Basically, equity theory argues that we have expectations of what our inputs to and outputs from a situation ought to be. When these expectations are violated we are unhappy and dissatisfied. When our expectations and reality coincide on the other hand, we are satisfied. In a job context when we are to decide whether or not we are happy with pay, for example, we have expectations of what is reasonable and will be satisfied only if we receive what is reasonable. Our expectations are based on a comparison with what *others* put into a job on the one hand, and what they receive on the other. If others with whom we compare ourselves seem to be putting less effort or skill into a job than we are, but are receiving the same financial reward, we will become unhappy. But equity theory also argues that if others put the same effort into a job as we do ourselves, yet receive less than we do, then this *also* will lead to dissatisfaction, as again we will perceive rewards as being inequitably shared.

The evidence for equity theory is equivocal. There certainly is evidence that where individuals feel under-rewarded they will switch from quality of production to quantity (Lawler and O'Gara, 1967); and various studies (e.g., Pritchard, Dunnette and Jorgenson, 1972) have found perceived under-reward to lead to dissatisfaction. On the other hand, the evidence for dissatisfaction following *over-reward* is to say the least, equivocal, as Pritchard, Dunnette and Jorgenson (1972) note. They cite several studies which have failed to find overpayment effects when piece rates are used; and in their own study, Pritchard, Dunnette and Jorgenson did not find a decrease in performance with over-reward, as predicted by the theory. It does seem intuitively likely that it is easier to live with over-reward as opposed to under-reward.

The evidence relating to equity theory is clearly not straightforward, and at best it seems able to account only for some aspects of satisfaction. It seems most applicable when applied to dissatisfaction with underpayment.

Perhaps the most influential model of behaviour in relation to satisfaction at work is expectancy theory. Basically, expectancy theory argues that individuals will be motivated to act to the extent that they see a relationship between effort and performance and between performance and reward. When the rewards offered are what the individual feels is equitable and valued, there will be satisfaction. One major implication of the theory, therefore, is that performance leads to satisfaction, and not as the Human Relations School advocates, satisfaction leads to performance.

There is certainly evidence to support the view that effort will vary according to the perceived effects on performance. Arvey (1972), for example, varied expectancies between effort and performance and found those with low expectancies to perform less well than those with high expectancies. As far as the relationship between performance and reward is concerned, there is considerable evidence that the more closely performance is tied to reward, the greater is performance (see, for example, Campbell and Pritchard, 1976). Unfortunately, from the point of view of job satisfaction, the theory tells us little of what rewards individuals will find satisfying, and how rewards relate to each other.

It is probably fair to say that no theory of job satisfaction has universal empirical support, although all theories seem useful in explaining some aspects of the problem. In fairness, the situation within the realm of satisfaction at work is not much different from any other area of psychology. Nevertheless it is clear that how job satisfaction is viewed depends on the model of human behaviour which is held in the first place. For the Human Relations School, man is essentially seen as a social animal seeking basically social satisfactions, hence the emphasis on social satisfactions at work. For Herzberg, man is seen as a growing, individually achieving animal, and for Herzberg, therefore, social satisfactions at work clearly take second place to the individual's desire to satisfy higher order needs for achievement and success.

III.—INDIVIDUAL ASSESSMENT

As we saw in the case of Herzberg's theory, the problem of measuring the satisfaction of individuals is fraught with controversy. The most common method, involves designing questionnaires which try to examine job satisfaction in a *particular* situation. This has the advantage of taking account of local factors which might be important in one situation and unimportant in another. In one study, for example, Gruneberg, Startup and Tapsfield (1974) found by initial questioning that the geographical location of a university was an important factor in the job satisfaction of university teaching staff. This was because the university was felt to be geographically isolated on the one hand and yet set in beautiful surroundings on the other. Such geographical considerations would presumably be unimportant in a university which felt itself to be less geographically isolated. Of course, whilst questionnaires specifically designed to throw light on specific situations have a useful practical function, they can make it hard to compare the results of one study with the results of other studies.

All questionnaires, whether specific or general, suffer from a number of drawbacks. In the first place the manner in which individuals respond to job satisfaction questionnaires will depend to some extent on the perceived purpose of the study. For example, where there is a possibility that level of payment might be thought to be affected by responses on satisfaction with pay, it could be expected that this would have a major effect. Indeed Opsahl and Dunnette (1966) report on a study of job applicants, where pay was rated as of relatively little importance in relation to job satisfaction. It is obvious however, that this response is likely to be subject to bias. Anyone applying for a job who states that pay is a greater attraction than the job itself is unlikely to be appointed.

There are a number of other problems common to all questionnaire studies. Respondents will often take little time to think about their responses, will often give socially desirable rather than 'genuine' responses and are often influenced by the way the questions are phrased. These and other problems led Herzberg to use the critical incident technique in his studies of job satisfaction. As noted earlier, however, the critical incident technique also has major problems of interpretation.

Nevertheless, despite the drawbacks of any one technique of assessment, it would clearly be foolish to cease to examine the question of job satisfaction. Provided the reader is aware that many studies of job satisfaction are approximations to the truth, rather than cast iron pieces of evidence, considerable consistencies of behaviour can be seen in many studies. Where there are differences these can often be attributed to subtle differences in the *context* of studies, rather than in the unreliability of the measuring instruments themselves. Furthermore there is clear evidence that whatever job satisfaction investigations do measure, this can sometimes be related to factors of economic significance, such as job turnover. Furthermore there are standardized forms of job satisfaction questionnaire, such as the Job Descriptive Index (see Smith, Kendall and Hulin, 1969), which allow for direct comparison between studies. All that is required is a little common sense and caution in the interpretation of any one individual study.

IV.—THE IMMEDIATE SOCIAL AND EMOTIONAL ENVIRONMENT

The view that the immediate social environment is critical in job satisfaction has been a potent force in the development of ideas on job satisfaction. Human relationships at work, particularly friendly superiors and congenial work-mates were considered by the Human Relations School to be critical in job satisfaction and indeed productivity. With Herzberg came a reaction against this view, seeing human relationships as a 'hygiene' factor, where only lower level needs were being fulfilled, and where at best a state of no dissatisfaction could be achieved through the fulfilment of social needs. Apart from the implicit arrogance of Herzberg, that individuals in a work situation should seek rewards which he thought they should seek, it remains an empirical question as to whether social relationships do relate to job satisfaction.

There is in fact little dispute that the nature of supervision can have considerable effects on an individual's job satisfaction. One of the major distinctions made in discussing supervisory style is that between *democratic*, employee-orientated supervision, and *autocratic*, task-orientated supervision. A democratic, employee-orientated supervisor is one who establishes a good personal relationship with subordinates, takes an interest in them and likes to ensure that they achieve their goals. This approach therefore involves consultation and balancing the needs of the organization against the needs of the individual. An autocratic, task-orientated leader, on the other hand, regards his group as instrumental in achieving objectives set by the organization, and regards his function as ensuring that the group is organized in such a way as to achieve this aim. Thus individual preferences and needs are important only in relation to the attainment of group goals.

Many studies do in fact show that subordinates prefer employee-orientated leaders. Warr and Wall (1975), for example, note a number of studies which found that employee-orientated leadership related positively to job satisfaction. They note such findings are hardly surprising as employee-orientated leadership involves notions of consideration and pleasantness and most people prefer others to be considerate and pleasant to them, other things being equal.

In fact, the issues are more complex than at first sight appears. In the first place, not all individuals want to be consulted about decisions. Some individuals regard the job of a supervisor as that of decision-maker, and feel it is inappropriate that employees should have to take decisions for which they are not paid. More important, however, is the finding that as one goes from low level to high level jobs, the role of the supervisor is seen differently. For those in high level jobs, a supervisor who can use his skills to attain resources and influence the organization to help group members attain their goals is desired more than someone who is pleasant and considerate but incompetent. In other words, the preference is for someone who is 'A Bastard, but our Bastard' (see House, 1971).

The other aspect of social relationships emphasized by the Human Relations School and their co-workers, has also been found to be related to job satisfaction. Herzberg, Mausner, Peterson and Capwell (1957) in their review of the literature, found social aspects of the job were rated as first, on average, in response to the question of what made individuals most satisfied or dissatisfied with their jobs. Even allowing for the inadequacies of many studies, it is not surprising that social relationships should be important. After all it is through our social relationships that we receive and give many of life's pleasures. How many individuals for example, would regard high job achievement as complete if they did not have a family to share it with?

There is a considerable literature showing the effects of social interaction on job satisfaction. Walker and Guest (1952), for example, found that individuals who were socially isolated from others because of the physical design of the job were more likely to be dissatisfied, and Van Zelst (1952) found that when individuals were allowed to choose their own work mates, and therefore presumably those with whom they mixed well socially, job satisfaction improved.

Another important study showing the effects of social interaction on job satisfaction, is that of Trist and Bamforth (1951). They studied the effects of introducing new technology into British coal-mines. The effect of the new technology was to disrupt long-established social relationships, and led quickly to a lowering of morale, increased absence, conflict, and falling productivity. When social aspects of the work situation were later changed to take account of the importance of social relationships at work, job satisfaction and productivity again improved.

These social aspects of job satisfaction are of course only one aspect of the emotional context in which jobs are set. How individuals feel about the job is affected by a considerable number of other factors, such as the nature of the job itself and the rewards for job performance, both in terms of recognition and financial incentive.

As far as the job itself is concerned, a seminal study by Hackman and Lawler (1971) established at least four job aspects which were related to job satisfaction. These were the degree of *feedback* the individual obtained, the degree of *freedom* and *responsibility* to make decisions, the *variety* of operations involved in the job and the importance and meaningfulness—the *significance* of the job.

It is perhaps not surprising that these factors, termed 'core' job factors by Hackman and Lawler, should be related to job satisfaction. Feeding back to individuals knowledge about their progress is likely to have two effects. It provides information on how the individuals can improve their performance. For those individuals interested in achievement of satisfactory performance on the job therefore, it is essential to their progress that they receive feedback. Feedback also has a motivational function. Where individuals are fed back information that they are progressing well and achieving satisfactory performance, this is likely to be satisfying in its own right and lead to greater interest in the task. A study by Gebhard (1948), for example, found that feelings of liking a task increased where there had been success previously.

It is hardly surprising that freedom to make decisions (autonomy), variety, and task significance are related to satisfaction. The more significant the individual regards his job the greater are likely to be his feelings of self esteem and worth at the successful completion of the job. Feelings of self esteem are also likely to be enhanced where the individual is seen as responsible enough to make important decisions concerning the nature of the job. Autonomy is also likely to be related to the level of skill which an individual can exercise. If the individual is not free to make judgements about the way to tackle a job, then the skill which he can exercise is also limited, and success in job performance is someone else's success.

As far as job variety is concerned, there is little doubt that, other things being equal, the more operations an individual has to perform, the greater is likely to be the application of skill, the less the job is likely to be seen as boring, and the greater is likely to be the feeling of achievement on successful completion of the task. Walker and Guest (1952), in their study of automobile workers, found a major difference in job satisfaction according to whether individuals had one operation or five operations to perform; and Hackman and Lawler (1971) found a positive correlation of 0.38 between job satisfaction and variety.

Findings such as those of Hackman and Lawler have been replicated in a number of subsequent studies, and there seems little doubt, therefore, that emotional states concerning the job are affected by the nature of the job itself. Feelings about one's job are also affected by rewards which flow from job performance. Achievement and recognition are seen by Herzberg as being intrinsic motivators rather than external rewards, whereas financial rewards are seen as external to the job itself, a hygiene factor. Yet it is not at all clear that a neat distinction is possible. Recognition, for example, often takes the form of promotion, and is an externally signalled reward—a reward held out by the organization in return for good performance—as financial rewards often are. Indeed financial reward often goes with recognition. Achievement, too, whilst it flows from the performance of a job, is often based on organizationally imposed criteria rather than on what the individual might personally regard as achievement. Monetary reward, on the other hand, often signals recognition and achievement, higher status and evidence of the regard in which the organization holds an individual. Thus recognition, achievement and financial reward seem sometimes to be inextricably bound together.

Achievement in relation to job satisfaction has been studied by Locke (1965), who found a positive correlation between success and liking of a task, a finding similar to that of Gebhard (1948) noted earlier. Locke (1965) also showed that where individuals were allowed to set their own standards for achievement, their satisfaction was greater than when standards were imposed. Such findings have been used to support the view that individuals should participate in decisions concerning standards of achievement; but the evidence is somewhat ambiguous. Ivanecevich (1976), for example, found that the achievement of imposed goals was more satisfying than goals which individuals set themselves. It may be that in some circumstances, such as when goals are set by a respected expert, achievement is felt to be greater and more satisfying than when the individual sets goals which may be only of significance to himself.

As noted earlier, achievement, if it is to be sustained, often requires external validation (recognition). Recognition can come through means such as promotion or salary increase, or as Locke notes, through verbal praise from superiors and peers. Locke (1976) argues that all employees value being praised by superiors and colleagues, and that this is such a common experience that it hardly needs empirical support.

The effect of financial incentives on satisfaction, on the other hand, is subject to controversy. Despite Herzberg's assertion that financial rewards do not lead to job satisfaction, and despite the often reported finding that money is not considered important in relation to job satisfaction in questionnaire studies, individuals *do* act as if money is important. The majority of strikes for example, appear to be about money (Lawler, 1971) and individuals do appear to murder, rob and blackmail for money. Of course money is not necessarily salient in relation to a job which is otherwise adequately rewarded, such as university teaching! Then it is claimed to be possible to derive satisfactions from other job aspects such as being 'creative'. Possibly the most useful theoretical approach to pay is taken by equity theory, which, as noted before, regards pay satisfaction to be determined, not by the *absolute* level of payment, but by what individuals receive in relation to others. Pay bargaining by groups of individuals involves comparisons with pay awards for other similar groups.

It must be said, however, that equitable treatment in relation to what others are paid is unlikely to be the whole story. Some individuals at least, are likely to seek high financial gains because of their individual desires for wealth, power and possessions, no matter how well they are paid, even as low level workers.

V.—THE WIDER SOCIAL AND ORGANIZATIONAL ENVIRONMENT

As with authoritarian or democratic supervisory styles, whole organizations can be described in terms of whether or not they are authoritarian and task-oriented at the expense of individual needs and values. Such authoritarian organizations are known as *bureaucratic* structures.

Bureaucratic structures are organizational structures in which there is a hierarchy of authority from top to bottom, normally large numbers of individuals with little power at the bottom, and a small group with considerable power at the top exercising overall control. One characteristic of a bureaucratic structure is that the bottom jobs should be as deskilled as possible, so that people can easily be moved sideways from one job to another.

A moment's thought will lead to the conclusion that bureaucratic structures of this kind are unlikely to lead to job satisfaction. It was noted earlier that individuals receive much of their job satisfaction from liking jobs which give variety, utilize skill, are meaningful and give a chance of achievement. Job satisfaction is also affected by pleasant social interaction and the opportunity to have a say in decision making. These are aspects which bureaucratic structures seek to minimize.

Because of the pressure within bureaucracies to create job dissatisfaction, a large number of writers such as Herzberg (1966), and Hackman and Oldham (1976) have advocated redesigning organizational structures to the extent that the job structure of individuals will allow participation in decision making, individual growth and achievement. Such strategies are discussed in the next section.

VI.—TYPES OF INTERVENTION

Psychologists have a long history of poking their noses into other peoples' businesses, with varying degrees of succcss. From Taylor (1911) onwards, there have been any number of psychologists willing (but not always able) to tell mere business people how their organizations should be run. Often these psychologists have been consultants who have been happy to take their fees and run when desired improvements failed to materialize; and whilst it is undoubtedly true that psychological intervention can sometimes be successful, any review of the literature will quickly show that there is no magic wand which psychologists can wave to ensure desired improvements in every situation.

Perhaps the best known psychological intervention in organizations is *job enrichment*. This kind of job redesign aims at increasing job variety, autonomy, responsibility and meaningfulness, not only by increasing the number of jobs that individuals do, but by giving them the opportunity to participate in decision making concerning their job. Job enrichment should be distinguished from other job redesign strategies such as *job rotation* and *job enlargement*. Job rotation involves the same individual undertaking a number of different jobs in succession, rather than having just one job to perform. The idea behind job rotation is that it increases job variety. If employees want this then there is little objection to it, but job rotation can have the effect of disrupting established social groups and can therefore decrease rather than increase satisfaction.

Job enlargement involves increasing the variety and complexity of a job by giving the individual a number of different operations to perform at the same time. Whilst Herzberg argues that such job redesign is unlikely of itself to improve satisfaction, as it is just the adding together of a number of boring jobs, there is evidence that job enlargement may well be effective. Walker and Guest (1952) in their famous study of automobile workers, found that the number of operations which each individual performed was highly related to job satisfaction.

Job enrichment concentrates very much on the individual and his needs and problems. Another and related approach to job redesign is outlined by *socio-technical systems theory* (SST). In SST the unit of interest is the work group, and SST sees satisfaction and productivity being optimized where technical and social factors are jointly taken into account. SST emerged with the work of Trist and Bamforth (1951) who investigated the effects of the introduction of new technology on the efficiency and morale of coal-miners. As we saw in Section IV the new technology changed the job from one in which miners worked together in groups, to one involving the individuals specializing in their own particular isolated task. The result of the new technology was to reduce efficiency and morale. As a consequence, the job was again redesigned to take account of social factors, including the advantages of group working, and both productivity and satisfaction improved.

SST differs from job enrichment in seeing the individuals fulfilling their work role within a group context. Both see it as important to increase job variety and autonomy and indeed SST sees as a prerequisite of its philosophy the introduction of autonomous working groups which decide for themselves the nature of each individual's role within the group, and seek to share out skills so that there is greater individual flexibility in job performance. Indeed it is often the case that SST is 'job enrichment with groups added on'.

One specific application of job redesign, the Scanlon Plan (see, for example, Gruneberg and Oborne, 1982), involves giving employees a much greater say in matters of improved efficiency. Any suggestions of employees which result in improved productivity are rewarded by group bonuses, and group interaction is encouraged as a means of participation in decision making. The basic philosophy behind the Scanlon Plan is that in any organization there are many employees who are able to contribute to their work situation when they are consulted and motivated, so that organizations which do not consult their employees or motivate them are wasting considerable resources. Suggestion boxes, where employees are encouraged to inform management of improvements which could be made, are often a total failure, because they fail to grasp the essential aspect of Scanlon, that employees will not be motivated where they do not feel equitably treated in the first place.

VII.—IS PSYCHOLOGICAL INTERVENTION SUCCESSFUL?

It must be said at this point that in many cases job redesign is not introduced into organizations to improve satisfaction at work, but to improve efficiency. Lupton and Tanner (1980), for example, found that many of the well known European job redesign studies came about because management was introducing new equipment and needed different methods of operating more sophisticated machinery. It may be of course that with job redesign, increased productivity goes hand in hand with increased satisfaction—a case of love and money going together!

In fact the evaluation of job enrichment studies is fraught with problems. Whilst a large number of empirical studies show increased satisfaction as a result of job enrichment, it is unfortunately the case that a great many studies are so defective in either design or presentation of results that they must be discounted as evidence for the value of job enrichment. As Locke, Feren, McCaleb, Shaw and Derny (1980) point out, for example, several studies have inadequate controls. Many studies select those who are going to be job enriched on a *volunteer* basis, many studies have too few employees for adequate statistical analysis, and indeed many studies fail to provide statistical evidence that is of any value whatsoever.

In spite of these drawbacks to job enrichment studies, however, it still remains true that reviewer after reviewer is led to the conclusion that job enrichment does improve job satisfaction. Warr and Wall (1975), for example, in their review state 'we are still left with the feeling that most reported studies in this area support the conclusion that jobs which offer variety and require the individual to exercise discretion over his work activities lead to enhanced well being and mental health' (p. 137). Cummings and Molloy (1977), too, found job satisfaction to have improved in 64% of the 28 studies they examined. Certainly, even on this evidence, there is a considerable number of failures as far as improving job satisfaction is concerned.

A similar picture emerges with SST. Cummings and Molloy (1977), in their review, point out the problems of interpreting SST studies. In almost all studies, for example, more than one variable is manipulated at a time. Payment systems, new group structures, participation procedures, new work layouts, increased training and so on are often changed *simultaneously*, and it may well be that in some instances improved satisfaction has as much to do with improved pay as it has to do, for example, with greater job variety. Such difficulties in interpretation are additional to problems of poor experimental design and statistical analysis found in many SST studies. Nevertheless, as with job enrichment studies, a number of reviewers do agree that SST does 'work' in the sense of improving satisfaction at work. Cummings and Molloy (1977), for example, reviewed sixteen SST studies and found

70% to report improvements in job attitudes. Exactly why SST 'works' is not clear. It seems reasonable to suppose, though, that it can improve satisfaction at work.

The Scanlon Plan at least has the advantage over other job redesign systems of having been tried, in some cases over long periods of time, of itself an indication that it is 'working'. However, like all other job redesign schemes it suffers from difficulties in evaluation. As with other schemes, it is almost always the case that a number of changes are made simultaneously, and Hackman (1977) notes that in one review of 44 studies, fourteen were unsuccessful. Nevertheless, this does indicate that a considerable number are reported to be successful, and it might be argued that the reason for success is not as important as the fact that it does somehow 'work'. Success is admittedly often assessed in terms of increased productivity, but in a review of eight Scanlon Plan studies, Cummings and Molloy found all to report increases in quality of working life. As with other studies in other areas of job satisfaction, the balance of evidence certainly would lead one to believe that the Scanlon Plan is a worthwhile technique for improving job satisfaction.

VIII.—METHODOLOGICAL AND PRACTICAL PROBLEMS

It is clear that the whole area of job redesign is unsatisfactory from the point of view of scientific evaluation. Few experiments reach criteria of acceptability in terms of experimental design, statistical analysis or indeed presentation and interpretation of findings. Yet to accept these arguments as grounds for the total rejection of job redesign studies seems unreasonable for at least two reasons. First, there are some studies which do appear to have reasonable standards of scientific design (see, for example, Locke, Fereen, McCaleb, Shaw and Derny, 1980) and these studies also point to the value of job redesign. More importantly, many studies are carried out in practical situations where the application of strict scientific controls is not appropriate and indeed not even scientifically desirable. Take, for example, a real-life job enrichment study reported by Alderfer (1969). Ideally one might like to allocate employees to a job enrichment and a control group on a random or matched basis, and to make sure the only difference between the job enriched and control group was in terms of job design changes. In real life this is not only impracticable, it is undesirable. If the individuals who are having their job redesigned are going to be given expensive new machinery, are going to be required to learn complex new skills and are going to be expected to put more effort into their job in order to produce more, then there is good reason in terms of equity, for paying such individuals more for giving them advanced training, and above all for selecting those individuals who appear most likely to benefit from training: that is, those who are most competent. In Alderfer's study, this is precisely what was done. Yet if one is going to judge the effectiveness of a new procedure, it is reasonable to select those most competent to test such a procedure. If one were to investigate a new opening gambit in chess, after all, one would ask a chess master to analyse it, not a number-six board player from your local Chess Club! In other words, in practical situations there is conflict between academic stringency and practical requirement. It must always be borne in mind, however, that in this area the major purpose of scientific investigation is to have something to say of *practical* significance.

Rather than demanding the precision of the natural sciences, therefore, or even the rigour of experimental psychology, it is more reasonable to ask at this stage of job satisfaction and job redesign research whether it has advanced our understanding and improved our capacity to help individuals. Even allowing for all the reservations pointed out above, there is general consensus among reviewers that it has. So many studies point in the direction of improvements in satisfaction as a result of job redesign that it would be more unwise to dismiss the findings than to accept them with limitations.

IX.—PROBLEMS OF ETHICS AND CONFIDENTIALITY

The major ethical problem facing the psychologist interested in improving job satisfaction within an organizational context is that in practical terms it almost always has to be justified in the context of improved efficiency. As noted before, many major 'quality of working life' programmes aimed at improving job satisfaction started life in response to an organizational need to adapt to the introduction of new machinery. Quite clearly the claim that what is being changed is for the welfare of the workforce when in reality it is for the welfare of management is a considerable ethical problem. At the same time, it so happens that job redesign does often seem to benefit *both* productivity *and* satisfaction, so the conflict between employee welfare and management needs is not as great as it might be. Indeed it might be argued that in the real world management is not going to make changes which benefit employees *per se*, so that it makes sense for psychologists interested in employee welfare to sell job enrichment as improving productivity, knowing that it also improves satisfaction.

Perhaps a more serious ethical problem for consultant psychologists is that there is no guarantee that job redesign will work in any given situation. Any psychologist with even the most rudimentary contact with industry will know that countless psychologists have left a path strewn with unfulfilled promises and large bills! There is a great deal which psychologists can do in industry, and a great deal they cannot yet do; reasonable and ethical behaviour demands that potential clients should be made aware of this.

The day might come when trades unions and employees' organizations recognize the potential contribution which psychologists can make to the quality of working life. Until that time, the client will invariably be the employer, and the primary declared motive will be to increase efficiency. But whether the formal client is the employer or the employee, the psychological consultant must recognize that difficulties arise over confidentiality, access to privileged information, the uses to which such information might be put, and the potential for the breach of formal codes of professional practice. The employer may be the client, and the workforce within the organization will be employed by the client. But the client does not *own* the workforce and members of the workforce may have private thoughts, feelings and reactions which are salient to the efficient running of the organization. From the outset, therefore, it is necessary for the consultant to make it clear to all parties, that any information gained directly from interviews or even casual encounters, will not be identified with particular individuals. In making his report, the psychologist will need to incorporate such information within a general framework. Apart from issues of ethics and professional practice, the need to respect confidence may also be justified even at the level of expediency. For respondents will be unwilling to provide information if they believe that its revelation could do them harm. Thus a reputation for integrity and a willingness to respect the views of the groups with which he comes into contact, will enhance the professional standing of the psychologist. Finally, the psychologist, in the course of his discussions and investigations, will have access to information of commercial value. Again it must be understood that such information is available only within the context of the relationship between consultant and client.

X.—THE ROLE OF OTHER DISCIPLINES AND PROFESSIONS

Not only psychologists, of course, but sociologists, anthropologists, and engineers have been concerned with the welfare of individuals at work. Sociologists have, for example, been interested in organizational structure and its effects on behaviour, and engineers have been concerned with designing the work place and work instruments so that they can be best suited to the human operator. The science of ergonomics or human factors is a mixture of inputs from engineers and psychologists amongst others, and clearly has a considerable part to play in enhancing satisfaction at work (see, for example, Oborne, 1980).

XI.—FUTURE PROSPECTS

There is little doubt that psychology is reaching the stage where it has some sensible and useful things to say about human behaviour in the work situation. The problem is not now psychology, but psychologists. No amount of sound empirical background is helpful if psychologists throw all their caution to the wind and claim that their expertise can do for industry what it patently cannot do—transform poor management with poor ideas and a poor work-force into a world beater overnight. And yet satisfaction at work and efficient productivity is so vital to so many people that sooner or later the sound application of psychology in industry must be taken seriously. Leaving the application of psychology to consultants who have an interest in maximizing their own profits does not seem the only possibility. In the United Kingdom the Work Research Unit gives advice to firms seeking to introduce job redesign, and this writer at least would like to see a rapid expansion of such disinterested psychological advice to industry.

As far as seeing into the future in terms of academic developments is concerned, it is obvious that the future will bring a greater understanding of those situations in which different aspects of job redesign are appropriate and in which they are not. At a theoretical level, it is possible to see the development of more coherent and data based theories, although it is not clear that such theories will have any practical significance. On the other hand it is in the nature of things that what is in the future cannot be predicted by those projecting forward.

There are two areas, however, where one does not need a crystal ball in order to see that there will be major differences between what has gone before and what is to come. The first is the depressed economic outlook for many employees. The second is new technology.

For the last 30 years or so, most western economies have looked forward to unlimited expansion, and with it a job context in which organizations had a self interest in the welfare of their employees. After all, if employers were not 'nice' to employees, they could easily leave. Again, planning for improved productivity in the context of an expanding economy would benefit the employee, as he would receive a share of the benefits of improved perform-ance. Where the market for products is declining, improved efficiency means less jobs are needed, and this can result in the employees losing their jobs. Clearly, patterns of co-operation between employers and employees will vary considerably in different economic contexts. The same problem holds true for new technology. It always has been the case, of course, that new technology threatens jobs, but there never has been a time in history when technology threatened so many jobs of a particular kind—low level, mass production jobs employing large numbers of relatively unskilled people. The effects of technological changes on a major scale can only be guessed at.

XII.—ANNOTATED READING

Duncan, K. D., Gruneberg, M. M. and Wallis, D. (Eds.). (1980). *Changes in Working Life*. Chichester: Wiley.

This book consists of a number of papers presented at a N.A.T.O. conference on the quality of working life. Of particular interest is the section on job satisfaction and motivation, where a number of papers explore the nature of job satisfaction in its various aspects. Of interest, too, is the section on job redesign, where a number of papers discuss ways in which the quality of working life can be improved by some of the job redesign changes discussed in the present chapter.

Gruneberg, M. M. (1979). *Understanding Job Satisfaction*. London: Macmillan Press.

This is an introductory book, written for the student and manager, and covering an area in greater detail than the present chapter.

Gruneberg, M. M. and Oborne, D. J. (1982). *Industrial Productivity: A Psychological Perspective*. London: Macmillan Press.

This book includes a discussion of the kinds of job redesign which have been shown to help improve not only productivity, but also job satisfaction.

Hackman, J. R. and Suttle, J. L. (Eds.). (1977). *Improving Life at Work*. Santa Monica, California: Goodyear.

This book consists of a number of chapters contributed by experts in the field of job redesign. A chapter by Alderfer, for example, looks at groups; a chapter by Lawler examines payment systems; and a chapter by Beer and Driscoll looks at strategies for organizational change. The book is written at a level which any student should be able to cope with.

Locke, E. A. (1976). The nature and causes of job satisfaction. In: M. D. Dunnette (Ed.) *Handbook of Industrial and Organizational Psychology*. Chicago, Illinois: Rand McNally.

This chapter on job satisfaction is one of the standard reviews of the nature and causes of job satisfaction, and should be consulted by anyone seriously interested in the topic. Locke examines the theoretical background to job satisfaction, pointing to the weaknesses and strengths of almost all accounts of the nature of job satisfaction. He emphasizes the difference between values and expectations in understanding job satisfaction, although in the present writer's view he considerably undervalues the role of expectations in an understanding of job satisfaction.

XIII.—REFERENCES

Alderfer, C. P. (1969). Job enlargement and the organizational context. *Personnel Psychology*, **22**, 418–426.

Arvey, R. D. (1972). Task performance as a function of perceived effort-performance and performance-reward contingencies. *Organizational Behavior and Human Performance*, **8**, 423–433.

Campbell, J. P. and Pritchard, R. D. (1976). Motivation theory in industrial and organizational psychology. In: M. D. Dunnette, (Ed.) *Handbook of Industrial and Organizational Psychology*. Chicago, Illinois: Rand McNally.

Cummings, T. G. and Molloy, E. S. (1977). *Improving Productivity and the Quality of Working Life*. New York: Praeger.

Gebhard, M. E. (1948). The effects of success and failure upon the attractiveness of activities as a function of experience, expectation and need. *Journal of Experimental Psychology*, **28**, 371–388.

Gruneberg, M. M. and Oborne, D. J. (1982). *Industrial Productivity: A Psychological Perspective*. London: Macmillan Press.

Gruneberg, M. M., Startup, R. and Tapsfield, P. (1974). The effects of geographical factors on the job satisfaction of university teachers. *The Vocational Aspects of Education*, **26**, 25–29.

Hackman, J. R. (1977). Work design. In: J. R. Hackman and J. L. Suttle (Eds.) *Improving Life at Work*. Santa Monica, California: Goodyear.

Hackman, J. R. and Lawler, E. E. (1971). Employee reactions to job satisfaction characteristics. *Journal of Applied Psychology*, **55**, 259–286.

Hackman, J. R. and Oldham, G. R. (1976). Motivation through the design of work: Test of a theory. *Organizational Behavior and Human Performance*, **15**, 250–279.

Herzberg, F. (1966). *Work and the Nature of Man*. Cleveland, Ohio: World Publishing.

Herzberg, F. (1968). One more time. How do you motivate employees? *Harvard Business Review*, **46**, 53–62.

Herzberg, F., Mausner, B., Peterson, R. O. and Capwell, D. F. (1977). *Job Attitudes: Review of Research and Opinion*. Pittsburgh, Pennsylvania: Psychological Services of Pittsburgh.

Hoppock, R. (1935). *Job Satisfaction*. New York: Harper.

House, R. J. (1971) A path-goal theory of leader effectiveness. *Administrative Science Quarterly*, **16**, 321–338.

Ivanecevich, J. M. (1976). Effects of goal setting on performance and job satisfaction. *Journal of Applied Psychology*, **61**, 605–612.

King, W. (1970). Clarification and evaluation of the two factor theory of job satisfaction. *Psychological Bulletin*, **74**, 18–31.

Lawler, E. E. (1971). *Pay and Organizational Effectiveness*. New York: McGraw-Hill.

Lawler, E. E. and O'Gara, P. W. (1976). Effects of inequity produced by underpayment on work output, work quality and attitudes towards work. *Journal of Applied Psychology*, **51**, 403–410.

Locke, E. A. (1965). The relationship of task success to task liking and satisfaction. *Journal of Applied Psychology*, **49**, 379–385.

Locke, E. A. (1976). The nature and causes of job satisfaction. In: M. D. Dunnette (Ed.) *Handbook of Industrial and Organizational Psychology*. Chicago, Illinois: Rand McNally.

Locke, E. A., Feren, D. B., McCaleb, U. M., Shaw, K. N. and Derny, A. T. (1980). The relative effectiveness of four methods of motivating employee performance. In: K. D. Duncan, M. M. Gruneberg and D. Wallis (Eds.) *Changes in Working Life*. Chichester: Wiley.

Lupton, T. and Tanner, I. (1980). Work design in Europe. In: K. D. Duncan, M. M. Gruneberg and D. Wallis (Eds.) *Changes in Working Life*. Chichester: Wiley.

Maslow, A. H. (1943). A theory of human motivation. *Psychological Review*, **50**, 370–396.

Oborne, D. J. (1980). *Ergonomics at Work*. Chichester: Wiley.

Opsahl, R. L. and Dunnette, M. D. (1966). The role of financial compensation in industrial motivation. *Psychological Bulletin*, **66**, 94–118.

Pritchard, R. D., Dunnette, M. D. and Jorgenson, D. O. (1972). Effects of perceptions of equity and inequity on worker performance and satisfaction. *Journal of Applied Psychology*, **56**, 75–94.

Roethlesberger, F. J. and Dickson, W. J. (1939). *Management and the Worker*. Cambridge, Massachusettes: Harvard University Press.

Smith, P. C., Kendall, L. M. and Hulin, C. L. (1969). *The Measurement of Satisfaction in Work and Retirement*. Chicago, Illinois: Rand McNally.

Taylor, F. W. (1911). *The Principles of Scientific Management*. New York: Harper.

Trist, E. L. and Bamforth, K. W. (1951). Some social and psychological consequences of the longwall method of coalgetting. *Human Relations*, **4**, 1–38.

Van Zelst, R. H. (1952). Validation of a sociometric regrouping procedure. *Journal of Abnormal and Social Psychology*, **47**, 299–301.

Walker, C. R. and Guest, R. (1952). The men on the assembly line. *Harvard Business Review*, **30**, 71–83.

Wall, T. O. and Stephenson, G. M. (1970). Herzberg's two-factor theory of job attitudes: A critical evaluation and some fresh evidence. *Industrial Relations Journal*, **1**, 41–65.

Warr, P. B. and Wall, T. D. (1975). *Work and Well-being*. Harmondsworth: Penguin.

Psychology and Social Problems
Edited by A. Gale and A. J. Chapman
© 1984 John Wiley & Sons Ltd.

CHAPTER 7

MANAGEMENT AND INDUSTRIAL RELATIONS

Charles J. Cox and **Cary L. Cooper**

1.—THE EXTENT OF THE PROBLEM

Management can be defined as the achieving of a task or objective through the organization and co-ordination of a range of resources. In most organizations, one of the more important resources is people. Hence, to be effective a manager needs both a knowledge and understanding of human behaviour and a high degree of social skill. Psychology and psychologists have a clear role to play in helping managers achieve these skills. There is also a number of specialist areas, such as personnel selection, training and organizational development, where the psychologist can contribute as a specialist consultant, helping to improve the effectiveness of an organization, although not having a managerial role. Both these aspects of psychology in management, the general knowledge of psychology which a manager needs and the specialist adviser role, are considered in this chapter.

Stress in management and organizations has become a growing problem over the last decade. Stress related illnesses are second and third in the table of those reasons for short-term sickness absence which are on the increase in Britain. Between the early 1950s and the 1970s, 'nervousness, debility and headaches' accounted for an increase of 189% of days off work for men and 122% for women; 'psychoneurosis and psychosis' for an increase of 153% for men and 302% for women (Office of Health Economics, 1971). Still using 'time off work' as our unit of measurement, we find that stress costs the economy substantially more than industrial injury and more than strikes (Marshall and Cooper, 1979).

There are five main areas where psychologists can make a major contribution to management. One of the primary areas of concern for a manager is *selection*—ensuring that the best qualified staff are recruited. Expertise in psychological testing and interview techniques is of value here. Having recruited employees, *training* may be necessary. Knowledge of learning theory and specialist techniques of training is the psychologist's contribution. The third area could rather loosely be called *motivation*. Once in the organization and trained, how does the individual give his or her best performance? This is a very complex issue. The main contribution of the psychologist is in developing, in the manager, a wide range of knowledge and skills concerned with working with people, particularly such skills as communication, leadership and joint decision making. The belief is that effective performance is mainly governed by interactions between members of the organization at the point where work is done. Such interactions will be both between peers and between manager and subordinates. Specialist advisers can also offer techniques for dealing with specific problems. The final two areas are rather more specialized. *Industrial relations* is concerned with the interface between management and unions or 'shop floor' workers. Here again, the social scientist has a dual role—as a trainer to develop appropriate skills in the manager (for example, in negotiating) and as a specialist adviser. *Organizational development* is of relatively recent origin. Organizations, rather like individuals, can rarely remain static for long. There are many pressures for change—changes in the market or technology, development of new products, growth in numbers employed. The organizational development specialist has a range of knowledge and skills to help members of the organization adapt and cope with such changes. Problems such as resolving inter-departmental conflict and developing teamwork are a particularly frequent source of concern.

II.–CONCEPTS OF THE PERSON AND MODELS OF HUMAN BEHAVIOUR

Hugo Munsterberg is usually credited with being the founder of industrial psychology with the publication of his *Psychology and Industrial Efficiency* in 1913. He was concerned to establish a scientific study of behaviour in industrial organizations and concentrated on such topics as learning, and the effect of physical conditions and fatigue on work. He was also one of the first to apply psychological tests in industry. This approach, with a heavy emphasis on scientific method, has had a strong influence on subsequent approaches. But the best framework for understanding the development of psychological thinking in relation to managerial behaviour is that provided by Schein (1972). He outlines the types of assumptions which managers (and psychologists) have made about the nature of man.

Rational/Economic Man   Many of the earlier workers in the field made the assumption that man is essentially rational in his approach to work and that his motives are entirely economic. The best example of this approach is the work of F. W. Taylor, published as the *Principles of Scientific Management* as late as 1947, although based on a lifetime of work from the turn of the century. For Taylor, the essence of good man management is to select employees with the appropriate skills, provide well-designed tools and the correct working environment and offer financial incentives for high output. In this rather mechanistic way would maximum efficiency be obtained. This is a way of thinking which still has much influence in modern management as exemplified by the widespread use of financial incentives and bonus schemes, despite the evidence that they have very little effect, except in rather special circumstances. Also, much of personnel selection is based on the assumption that it is possible to find a perfect match between the skill requirements of a job and the character of an individual. It arises from the heavy emphasis on *scientific method*, with a consequent desire to measure, predict and control. So early theorists and researchers tended to ignore or overlook important factors in work, like feelings, beliefs and social influences, which are not so susceptible to measurement. This raises the question as to whether the early 'scientific' approach was quite so scientific after all, if it failed to measure such important variables.

Social Man   The work of Elton Mayo in the *Hawthorne Experiments* (Roethlesberger and Dickson, 1939) drew attention to the effects of social factors, such as group norms, on work performance. This influenced the development of a view of man as a *social* being, involving the belief that the important factors in work performance are the social influences of peers and leaders. It gave rise to the so-called *Human Relations School*, operating on the belief that the key to productivity is job satisfaction based on good social relationships on the job. The influence of this school can still be seen in some aspects of management thinking which place an emphasis on good communications—it is important for people to understand what they are doing and why—based on openness and trust.

Self-actualizing Man   In the 1950s and early 1960s came a group of theorists strongly influenced by Maslow's (1954) 'hierarchy of needs'. Most influential amongst these were Herzberg (1966) and McGregor (1960). Herzberg's hygiene/motivator theory of motivation placed strong emphasis on the notion that job performance depends on intrinsic factors in the job, such as interest, responsibility and the worthwhile nature of the work. McGregor's concepts of *Theory X* and *Theory Y* fostered a belief in participation and involvement in decision making as a way of increasing commitment and performance. Briefly, and perhaps rather oversimplifying, *Theory X* is the assumption that man is naturally lazy and must, therefore, either be *coerced* into work by punishment (for example, withdrawal of pay) if he does not perform adequately, or be *seduced* into work by rewards such as piece rates or bonuses.

Theory Y is the belief that man is naturally active and co-operative and derives pleasure from work and achievement.

The fundamental assumption underlying all these theories, and stemming from Maslow's *hierarchy of needs*, is that man is a growing and developing individual who, if given the opportunity, will develop rapidly away from a fixation on lower-order needs, such as the physiological needs and safety (Rational Economic Assumption), through social needs to growth and development needs. The true nature of man is, thus, to be *self-actualizing*. There is, of course, still a strong belief in organizations in the value of participation and involvement as a means of increasing effectiveness. (There is further discussion of the Human Relations School, and the work of Herzberg in Chapter 6 by Gruneberg.)

Complex Man   The final stage (so far) of the development of assumptions about man could be designated as that of *complex man*. There are many strands which lead to this. It is partly a realization that there is some truth in all the earlier assumptions, but that no one of them explains the totality of human behaviour in organizations. Man is partly rational and does have economic motives, as well as others, such as social and self-actualizing needs.

Another strong influence is, however, from systems theories. These theories take the view that an organization can be viewed as an *open system*. All living things, all organizations, even countries or indeed the world as a whole can be seen in this way. All open systems have characteristics in common. These include, inputs from the environment, outputs to the environment, conversion processes within the system, and feedback and control mechanisms. The work of people such as Woodward (1965), Miller and Rice (1967) and Burns and Stalker (1961), all draw attention to the complex interaction between technology, the system of organization and individual behaviour. Other writers, for example Likert (1961) and Fiedler (1967), have drawn attention to the relationship between managerial and leadership style and the performance of work groups. Modern thinking is, then, that effectiveness in organizations is a result of a complex interaction between many factors, some inherent in the individual and some conditions within the environment, both technological and social.

III.—INDIVIDUAL ASSESSMENT

The assessment of individuals is largely dealt with below under problems of selection and training.

IV.—THE IMMEDIATE SOCIAL AND EMOTIONAL ENVIRONMENT

The effects of the immediate social environment on satisfaction at work have been dealt with by Gruneberg in Chapter 6.

V.—THE WIDER SOCIAL AND ORGANIZATIONAL ENVIRONMENT

The social and organizational environment has caused enormous stress on managers. One of the most serious of these sources is the increasing feeling among managers that their jobs are less secure than they have ever been. The fear of redundancy and job insecurity is not 'pie-in-the-sky'; the facts indicate that managerial redundancy is at the highest level it has ever been in recent times. The Professional and Executive Recruitment service (PER), the section of the British Employment Services Agency which deals with unemployed managers, has indicated that their number of registrations increased from 29,000 in 1981/2 to 42,000 in 1982/3, an increase of some 44 per cent (all managers who collect unemployment benefits have to register with the PER). In addition, this figure is likely to be an underestimate of the actual number of managers losing their jobs, since some are given long notice during which to find alternative employment and others (probably the more senior ones) do not claim the benefit and attempt to find jobs on their own.

The fear of being made redundant is a particularly stressful one for managers, since until recent times managers were reasonably assured of job security. In fact, a report by the British Institute of Management on managerial mobility found that the average number of job changes for managers across all industries was about 2.7 in a career. This fear is particularly heightened by the fact that managers seem to view 'being made redundant' as a negative evaluation of *themselves* and their job competence and are thus likely to suffer from loss of self-esteem and self-confidence. Redundancy for them becomes a 'personal rejection' rather than a 'cost reduction' act. In addition, managers as a group are highly committed financially (with mortgages, a higher proportion of their children being privately educated, and so on) and they may find unemployment the apocalypse of their particular life style.

Another source of stress to managers in the current economic situation stems from an important aspect of their role in the organization, namely their responsibility for the well-being of their subordinates. With industry facing increasing cutbacks in production and sales, many shop floor workers and first-line managers are facing shorter working hours, reduced overtime, and redundancy. It is one of the responsibilities of management to introduce measures to reduce costs and keep over-manning to a minimum. This situation acts as a source of pressure on the manager in at least two respects. First, the manager feels extreme role conflict. On the one hand, top management expects operating costs to be kept down and, on the other, the manager is expected to look after subordinates' interests, to provide them with a sense of job security and stability. Second, the role of 'hatchet man' must inevitably weaken personal relationships with subordinates and their trust of both the manager and the organization.

Suspicion and mistrust lead to lack of effective communications within the organization and, in many cases, to lack of future consultation. The whole process becomes a cyclical one, where a regression down Maslow's hierarchy of needs to the security level stimulates the individual's primitive self-protective instincts. This cyclic development does not encourage an organizational climate of trust, a 'we-ness', or a shared identity among workers that encourages a substantial common sense of direction by all. The removal of trust can lead to people concealing attitudes and information from one another by communicating in ways that are evasive, aggressive, and misleading, with the ultimate consequence of bad decision-making, increased job dissatisfaction, and so on.

With the restriction of budgets, the cutting back of staff and the attempts to reduce operating costs to a minimum, organizations are also likely to limit promotions, which must inevitably have the effect of increasing the level of competition between colleagues for the scarcer senior posts. This, together with the restricted job opportunities in the wider industrial community (the flow of managerial vacancies was reported by the PER to be down by 30 per cent in 1983 as compared with 1982), must have the consequences of thwarting individual ambition and achievement, of leaving many managers in the position of feeling 'trapped'. The greater the lack of opportunity for mobility, the greater the frustration and consequent displacement. This displaced frustration may be directed toward the organization or authority within it or, if that is too threatening, toward subordinates and/or the family.

In addition to feeling trapped by organizational constraints, managers also feel trapped by the current industrial relations climate. Anyone working in industry in the capacity of an industrial psychologist, consultant, or personnel/industrial relations officer cannot help but notice the deterioration in the industrial atmosphere, the growing rigidity in management and worker roles, the lack of mutual understanding and communication, the concern with winning battles, and the absence of genuine efforts at the long-term resolution of problems. These conditions have led to 'frozen' attitudes on the part of management and trade unions, attitudes which over time have become part of the role expectations of managers and shop stewards alike. These industrial relations 'roles' can be a source of severe stress for the manager, particularly in an inflationary economy based on a wage/price spiral, since they restrict freedom of action and flexibility in negotiating situations and in the communication process itself. These kinds of pressures are in evidence particularly in the small industrial organizations where works managers carry the responsibility for industrial relations in their plant, and in large organizations with autonomous working units which have little, if any, centralized 'management services' (for example, industrial relations specialists). In addition, these confrontations can only adversely affect the organizational climate, reducing the level of trust and encouraging the workers and managers to view one another as the symbolic culprit of their deteriorating standard of living.

Another indirect source of stress on managers in the current economic climate is work overload. Although in many cases the level of production has decreased in industry, there are at least two forces acting on the individual manager to work harder and to take on more work than he can cope with. First, redundancies among both shop floor workers and 'colleague' managers may have the effect of increasing the individual's workload, as one of the remaining organizers. And, second, in a company where there have been managerial redundancies, the individual manager may feel the need to 'be seen' to be working harder, which indicates both psychological and physiological stress as a result of work overload. For example, French and Caplan (1973) made some observations at work on 22 white collar workers for two to three hours a day for three days. Two observers recorded data on events occurring in the job environment and heart rate responses to these events. The heart rate responses were obtained by using a pocket-sized telemetry device which did not interfere with the workers as they were working. Blood samples were also taken at regular intervals to determine cholesterol levels. All the workers filled out a questionnaire on the extent of their work load over the three days, and observers recorded the number of visitors and phone calls received for each during the same period. They found (a) that those people who admitted to feeling under work pressure—work overload—were observed to suffer more interruptions from phone calls and visitors; and (b) they suffered significantly more physiological strain through higher heart rates and higher cholesterol levels.

Further danger arising from economic depression is the effect that work pressures (such as fear of redundancy, blocked ambition, work overload, and so on) can have on the families of managers. At the very best of times young managers face the inevitable conflict between organizational and family demands during the early build up to their careers. But during a crisis of the sort we are currently experiencing, the problems increase in geometrical proportions as managers strive to cope with their basic economic and personal security needs. As Pahl and Pahl (1971) suggest in their book 'Managers and Their Wives', most managers under normal circumstances find home a refuge from the competitive and demanding environment of work, a place where they can get support and comfort. However, when there is a career crisis (or stress from job insecurity as many managers arc now facing), the tensions the managers bring with them into the family affect the wife and home environment in a way that may not meet their 'sanctuary' expectations. It may be very difficult indeed for a spouse to provide the kind of supportive domestic scene their partner requires at a time when they also are beginning to feel insecure, and worried about the family's economic, educational and social future.

VI.—TYPES OF INTERVENTION

As stated above, there are five main areas in which psychological interventions are made in organizations. Each of these are considered in turn.

Personnel Selection

There are two essential questions to answer in the process of personnel selection: (a) what sort of person am I looking for; that is, what personality, skills, abilities and background should he or she have; and (b) how will I recognize the person if I find them; that is, what sort of measures and tests should be applied? There is also another subsidiary question which comes between these two, concerned with 'where should I look for this individual?'; that is, where to advertise.

Job Specification   The answer to the first question is provided by a *job specification*, which is actually a specification of the characteristics of the person who will be most likely to perform effectively in the job in question. There is no precise scientific way to derive this, but it should be done as systematically as possible. First, a thorough *job analysis* must be carried out to determine the requirements of the job. Information can be obtained from a number of sources; for example, direct observation of the job, interviewing existing staff, and from personnel and workstudy records. It is now possible to specify the characteristics required by the person to do the job. Usually some sort of checklist is used to ensure that all aspects of the person are considered. There are many such systems, but one of the most widely used is the *Seven-point Plan* originally devised by Rodger (1952) and described by Wallis in Chapter 5 (see page 108). It is assumed that if a description of the required characteristics is given under each heading, a reasonably full description of the desired person will be obtained. Obviously, the outline can be modified to suit the situation for which it is being used.

The Selection Process   Answering the second question above—'how do we recognize the individual?'—is a much more complex and technical process. Essentially it is a matter of collecting data about the applicants for a job, from which can be built up a picture of characteristics under the same headings as were used for the job specification.

There are many methods, but the most common ones are as follows. An *Application Form* usually provides the initial information from which a 'short-list' may be produced. In some cases, usually where a large number of people are required without any very specific qualities, sufficient information may be provided to make the final selection. The form should be designed to provide information relevant to the job specification, but as it is impossible to control too closely what information is obtained, it is mainly used only for preliminary classification. It is worth noting, however, that a well designed application form provides better control of the data given, than a simple letter of application, since by asking specific questions similar information is collected from *all* applicants, thus making sure that the data obtained are standard and as complete as possible. If a mere letter of application is used, candidates will give only information they consider relevant and will suppress data they consider negative. The *Interview* is a face-to-face discussion with the objective of obtaining data about the candidate's background, experience and personality from which, again, information relevant to the job specification can be obtained. The interviewer should stick to factual matters concerning the interviewee's past performance and activities, and avoid speculative questions. The philosophy of the interview is that an individual's past performance is the best guide to that person's future behaviour. There is, inevitably, some subjectivity in any interview, but a well-trained interviewer can achieve quite high levels of validity. Training is, however, essential to ensure the avoidance of a number of potential pitfalls. A good discussion of the interview process is provided by Sidney and Brown (1961) and by Wicks (1981). From the days of Munsterberg, *Psychological Tests* have been widely used in selection. Information under many of the headings on the Seven-Point Plan can best be obtained from tests. Intelligence, aptitudes and attainments come into this category. Tests may also be useful for assessing some aspects of personality. Data on social and communication skills, leadership and influence can be obtained from observation of the candidate in *Discussion Groups*. There is some doubt as to how much reliance can be placed on such observations, as a person's behaviour could be different in different groups (i.e, the situation is not well controlled). Training of the observer is essential to ensure that only relevant behaviours are recorded. Sometimes useful data can be obtained by asking the candidate to work at a *Simulation* of the actual job. *In-basket exercises* are an example of this. The candidate is asked to work through an 'in-tray' of memos, as if he were a new manager who has just found these on his desk. How he responds can be a useful indicator of his approach to various aspects of his job. Increasingly, selection is being carried out by inviting candidates to take part in a one-, two- or even three-day assessment process using a mixture of any, or all, the above techniques carried out at *Assessment Centres*. In this way a wealth of information can be collected very quickly.

Training

The traditional approach to training has much in common with that of selection, in that it is rather mechanistic and follows clearly defined steps. There is a rapidly developing, more organismic approach, which is discussed later. The first step in the traditional approach is to define precisely the objectives of the training; this is called *Objective Setting*. Ideally, objectives should be in the form of a specific description of the actual behaviour the trainee is expected to acquire on the programme. In order to arrive at a definition of these behaviours, it is necessary to carry out a task analysis, which is a detailed study of the job in question, from which it should theoretically be possible to determine precisely: (a) the activities and actions to be carried out; (b) how the individual knows what action to take at any point in time; (c) how they know when the action has been completed; and, (d) how they know what to do next.

From this information, it is possible to determine what knowledge, skills and procedures the trainee has to be taught (the objectives), and what abilities and aptitudes are needed as a pre-requisite of training (the entry qualifications). Obviously this approach is very difficult to apply in practice. Probably the skills for a basic machine operator or assembly job can be defined in this way, but anything more complex is almost impossible to analyse into such basic components. The job of a manager, for example, cannot be reduced to simple elements. Some other method of defining objectives must, therefore, be found. Very often this simply has to be a matter of judgement on the part of someone very familiar with the job. Objective setting can be made more systematic, if a framework such as that outlined in Table 7.1 is used to check that all levels of objectives have been considered.

TABLE 7.1

A CHECKLIST OF TRAINING OBJECTIVES

A.   **Cognitive (Knowledge) Objectives**
  1) What facts and information are needed?
  2) How is this applied to real-life situations?
  3) How much is it necessary to understand theories and underlying relationships in the information?
  4) Is it necessary to be able to develop new theories for new situations?

B.   **Affective (Attitudes and Feeling) Objectives**
  1) How much involvement is required?
      —passive acceptance,
      —active response.
  2) What attitudes and values are involved?

C.   **Social Skill Objectives**
  1) How much understanding of oneself
      —own characteristics and feelings.
  2) What interpersonal and group skills?
      —listening, influencing, leadership, etc.
  3) What organizational skills?
      —negotiating, consulting, use of authority, etc.

The Training Programme   Having established the objectives of the training, the next step is to design the actual programme. There are many things to take into account here. The first consideration is to decide the *sequence* of the items, so that fundamental skills and knowledge are acquired early, and can be built on with more complex material later in the programme. Design should also be in accordance with the general principles of learning. Another decision to be made concerns the actual training techniques to be used. There is a great number of possible methods, techniques and media which can be used in training, and most readers will be familiar with at least some of these. They include, for example, *books and readings*—a quick and efficient way to transfer material in the cognitive domain, which is possibly insufficiently used in industrial and management training. Again, *films* are mainly of value in relation to cognitive objectives; they have advantages over printed material, providing better and more dramatic examples and illustrations. *Programmed Instruction* is based on the work of Skinner (1954) and Pressey (1959). Material is presented, either in book form or via a visual display unit, in a carefully designed sequence to build up the knowledge or behaviour required. Frequent tests to check understanding are built in, and additional explanations provided for the learner who has not understood. In theory, programmed instruction is an ideal learning medium where each individual can work at their own pace, reaching maximum proficiency in optimum time. As the learner works alone, they are not held back by slower members of a group, or discouraged by seeing others working at a faster pace. An enormous amount of research has confirmed that programmed learning is very efficient. Learning time, the standard of proficiency reached and long-term retention are often all superior to more conventional methods. However, many students find the system very uninvolving, and drop-out rates can be high. After something of a boom in the 1960s, the approach is no longer widely used, although there are specific situations where it has value. *Lectures* are the oldest and still, probably, the most widely used system of instruction. The lecture has the advantage of greater flexibility and ability to respond to learner needs than the methods discussed above. It is possible to adapt rapidly to feedback, and provided the group is not too large, there can be a great deal of interaction between teacher and taught. The main disadvantage, as every student knows, is that effectiveness is heavily dependent on the skill, motivation and knowledge of the lecturer. *Case Studies* originated from medical training but were developed, primarily at the Harvard Business School, as a technique for management training. The trainee is presented, usually in written form, with the details of a situation or problem (the case). The key requirement is to analyse the background and suggest solutions or ways of dealing with the situation. These solutions are then discussed and evaluated with other trainees and/or a tutor. The trainee thus develops insight into a method for dealing with a wide range of situations. Usually, learning is still very much at a cognitive level, but can also meet affective objectives (i.e., those concerned with changing attitudes and feelings). *Simulations* have long been used to gain experience, where experimenting with the 'real' thing would be expensive or dangerous. The best known example of simulations in training is probably in training pilots, where a simulation of the controls and flight deck of an aircraft, which responds exactly as would a real aircraft, is used to enable the trainee pilot to practise all the necessary aspects of flying, take-off, landing etc. Controls can also be set to simulate extreme conditions like ice or high winds. Thus, much of the early training can be given in complete safety, without risking the lives of pilot and instructor, and the cost of an aircraft. Many other such simulations exist for skills as complex as driving a train, to more simple situations such as paint spraying. Simulations are also used for similar reasons to the above for training managers. There can be complex computer based business games where the simulation is of the economic environment, activity of competitors and the production system, or group exercises simulating boardroom discussions or decision-making committees. Simulations are much more concerned with developing skills, either psychomotor or social, than with cognitive objectives. *Role Play* is really a special type of simulation, which may also have some aspects of a case study. The trainee is presented with a situation, and after discussion and consideration of how to respond, actually plays out the role with others taking the parts of key figures in the situation. For example, the trainee may play the part of a manager carrying out a disciplinary interview, or an industrial relations manager carrying out a negotiation with a shop steward. Further analysis and discussion can take place after the role play. Possibly two or three different ways of handling the situation can be tried out, to see which might be most effective and in what circumstances. Learning is mainly at the social skill level.

Seminars and Discussion Groups   constitute a wide group of activities ranged along a continuum, with the traditional formal lecture at one extreme end. Teaching at this end of the scale is usually totally controlled by the lecturer and is non-participative. It can be argued that a good seminar or discussion group is totally at the opposite end of the scale—completely participative and non-directive. In practice, they range along the entire continuum with the group leader or tutor exercising varying degrees of control and encouraging differing amounts of participation. The exact position on the scale is determined by a number of factors, such as the preference of the leader, or the group, and the subject of the discussion. Objectives are again mainly cognitive and affective. *Group Training Techniques* encompass an enormous range of variations in form and structure, but all have a number of central principles in common. In essence, a group of people meet in a group for a period of time—usually a week, but it can be longer or shorter. The objective is to learn about their own behaviour and responses and to develop social skills, learning from their own 'here and now' behaviour. Discussion and learning centres entirely on what is happening *here* in the group *now*. The focus of learning can vary from each individual gaining insight and understanding of their own feelings, responses and reactions, to an emphasis on group or even total organizational dynamics. Other variations are in the degree of control exercised by the trainer, the conceptual system used for analysis, and the degree of structure in the programme.

There are a number of dimensions on which the above techniques differ, but two important ones are: (a) the degree of *learner control* in the situation (directive-non-directive), and (b) the amount of *participation* or activity required from the learner (participative: non-participative). These two scales overlap, but are not identical. The techniques listed above are in roughly increasing order of participation and decreasing directiveness. Books and films are directive and relatively passive on the part of the learner. Group training is, in general, non-directive and active. There is not a total correspondence in the scales. Case studies are high on participation, but also quite high on direction. Some group discussions (seminars) can be active, but tightly controlled.

An obvious question is how does a trainer decide which out of the many techniques available is likely to be appropriate in any given context. There is a number of factors which will determine the degree of participation and direction appropriate in a training situation and thus indicate the appropriate technique to use. The main ones of these are as follows: (a) *The type of objectives*: Table 7.2 indicates the relationship between the various techniques and objectives. (b) *Time available*: participation takes time, the more directive methods can be more effectively used in short time spans. (c) *Participants' expectations*: it can cause confusion and inhibit learning if these are violated. (d) *Trainers' preferences and skills*. (e) *Face validity*: some techniques are not accepted by trainees if they do not seem to be relevant. (f) *Tolerance of ambiguity*: for both trainer and trainees, the more non-directive and participative the situation, the less predictable and hence ambiguous it is. (g) *Dependency needs of participants*: non-directive participative techniques require trainees to take more responsibility for their own learning. (h) *Organizational climate*: techniques will, in general, need to be reasonably consistent with the style of management of the organization.

Evaluation of Training   The final stage in setting up a training programme is evaluation. There are two important aspects to this. (a) Has the trainee learnt what was intended in the programme; that is, have the objectives been achieved? For this, some test of proficiency in the relevant knowledge or skills is required. (b) Are these skills relevant to the job in question; that is,

TABLE 7.2
RELATIONSHIP BETWEEN TRAINING TECHNIQUES AND OBJECTIVES

	Books and Readings	Films	Programmed Instruction	Lectures	Case Studies	Simulations	Role Play	Seminars and Discussion Groups	Group Training Techniques
Cognitive Objectives Knowledge and Information	●	●	●	●	●	◑	○	◑	
Affective Objectives Feelings, Attitudes and Values	○	○	○	○	○	◑	●	●	●
Social Skill Objectives Interactive Skills					○	◑	◑	◑	●

● – indicates very relevant technique
◑ – fairly relevant technique
○ – marginally relevant
Blanks – no relevance

has job performance improved? To verify this, a criterion of job performance
is required.

Motivation and Job Satisfaction

The third form of intervention relates to motivation and job satisfaction.
Psychological involvement in this important aspect of work has a long history.
The topic is considered of such significance that a whole chapter of this book
has been devoted to it. The reader should refer to Chapter 6 by Gruneberg.

Industrial Relations

Strangely enough, it is only relatively recently that psychologists have become
involved in industrial relations and even now their attention is mainly concentrated on the negotiation process, although more and more attention is being
given to the problem of how to maintain good relations, focusing on issues
like good communication and participation. There is, however, a number of
contributions the psychologist can make to good industrial relations. These
are mainly through training managers in the necessary skills and by acting
as *process consultants*.

Industrial Relations Skills There is a number of skills which a manager requires for maintaining good working relationships. Many acquire such skills through their work experience (unfortunately, also many do not), but all of them can be developed through training. They are mainly in the social area and consist essentially of interpersonal, group and intergroup skills. The main ones are in the following areas. *Good Communications*. Many failures of industrial relations can be attributed to poor communication; people not hearing or misinterpreting situations due to preconceived ideas and prejudices. To overcome these problems, a manager needs good communication skills, which include the ability to *listen actively* and thus to understand the full meaning of what is communicated by others and to be able to *express clearly* one's own communications. Chartier (1974) suggests that in addition to these, good communication depends also on having a clear *self-concept*, ability to cope with feelings and *self-disclosure*. *Participation*. Many writers on organizations, stress the need for participation, so that information and feelings from all levels can be incorporated into organizational decisions. Many methods have been tried. For example, placing worker representatives on company boards or setting up 'consultation groups', drawn from different levels of the organization. It seems probable, however, that the most effective form of participation is for managers, when making a decision, to involve as far as possible, all members of the organization who have relevant information or who have an interest in the outcome. The manager thus needs to have a wide range of skills in communication and group decision making. *Conflict Resolution*. Conflict is probably an unavoidable part of organizational life, and, strangely enough, the more open and participative the organization becomes, the more conflict is likely to occur. This is because the underlying conflicts, concerning differences between individual and organizational goals and even differences of opinion between people, which are hidden and suppressed in authoritarian organizations can surface, and have to be resolved. The manager who wishes to maintain good relations in an open participative organization will, therefore, need good conflict resolution skills. *Negotiation*. There will inevitably be issues which have to be negotiated, particularly with trade unions. The manager will, therefore, need negotiation skills. These will include most of the skills mentioned above, but will also involve the ability to plan a negotiating strategy, decide issues for bargaining, assess the opposing negotiators' skills and strategy and the amount of their support. A good introduction to psychological aspects of bargaining and negotiation is provided by Morley (1982).

Process Consultation The other role of the psychologist in maintaining good organizational relationships is as a *process consultant*. Unlike an *expert consultant* who comes into an organization to diagnose a particular problem and then offer an expert solution (for example, accountants, marketing specialists, and so on) the *process consultant* sits with the members of an organization while they carry on their normal work, and helps them review the way they interact and work together. The way individuals interact when working is known as the *process* (as opposed to the *task*, which is the job they have come together to do). Process can, obviously, have an important effect on the quality of the task and on how people feel about the organization. The role of the psychologist as process consultant is to help individuals understand the effect of their behaviour on others and *vice versa*, so that they can become more effective in their interactions.

Organizational Development

There is a tendency, particularly in larger organizations, to take the structure and form of the organization for granted, seeing it as stable and unchanging. In fact, most organizations are evolving and developing, rather like a living organism; and, if they are not, they are probably dying. Many organizations are not developing quickly enough or in the right way to meet changes in their environment—changes in technology, markets or economics, for example. In response to this a new form of specialist has appeared in the last two decades—the *organizational development* (OD) *consultant* or *change agent*.

Three Stages of Organizational Development   It is possible to visualize organizations as potentially developing through three stages, although not all organizations start at the first stage, nor do they necessarily have to develop to later stages. Many, in fact, start and finish within stage two. It is also possible that an organization can have characteristics of all three stages at any one time. The three stages are as follows. *Stage 1. Pioneer Organizations.* Many organizations are started by one individual, who having identified a product or service, sets up a small organization to supply it. Such an organization is often characterized by tight central control by the 'pioneer', who is in close contact with all organization members. This is what Handy (1976), following Harrison (1972), calls a *power culture*, since control is by the power of the pioneer, delegated where necessary to immediate subordinates. Pioneer organizations are very cohesive, flexible and adaptable, and can react rapidly to changes in the environment. Why then should there be need to change this organization structure? There are many reasons; for example, growth in numbers, increasing need for specialists, take over, or the demise of the pioneer. All these pressures tend to push the organization towards *differentiation*. This process has often been hastened by traditional expert consultants, who in diagnosing and prescribing for organizational problems, have often recommended the setting up of *specialist sections* and departments. *Stage 2. Differentiated Organizations.* This is undoubtedly one of the commonest forms of organization at the present time. Such organizations are characterized by separation into sections or departments. These departments may be based on function, product or location. There is usually a complex tree organization chart and control is by authority, delegated from the top. Handy (1976) calls this a *role culture*, as it is one's role in the organization which is important. Differentiated organizations are the product of the thinking of traditional specialists and writers on organizations, using *mechanistic* assumptions, the ideal being to have an organization which runs like a well-oiled machine. Unfortunately organizations, being composed of people, are not like machines and this type of organization rarely runs smoothly. There is often a lack of communication between sections and departments and dysfunctional conflict and rivalries. It is usually difficult for the organization to react swiftly to change and individuals feel alienated and under-utilized. As a response to these symptoms the skills of *OD consultants* and *change agents* have been developed. The traditional expert consultant, it has already been noted, works very much on a 'medical' model. He diagnoses and prescribes a cure. The OD consultant or change agent works much more on a 'psycho therapeutic' model. Here it is not possible to diagnose or prescribe cures. The patient or client must solve their own problems, because there is no way anyone else can do this for them. The role of the therapist is to help them do this. The change agent works with the members of an organization in the same way. Only they can define what their objectives are and what type of organization will best suit their particular situation. The change agent helps them bring this about, often also working as a process consultant, helping them to understand how they relate to each other and the implications of such relationships. Sometimes the change agent will be concerned with organization-wide change, more often with a particular section or department, frequently joining up with a small team who usually work together, helping them become more effective. Usually the aim of these consultants is to move organizations towards greater integration. *Stage 3. Integrated Organizations.* It is not possible to describe precisely what an integrated organization looks like, since, by definition, each will be different. However, it should have certain general characteristics, such as an organismic, flexible structure, adaptable styles of management, and an emphasis on teamwork and participation and decentralization of decision making. Many integrated organizations tend to use *task forces* for problem solving. This is a group of people drawn from all parts of the organization, because of their special skills and knowledge to deal with a specific problem or situation. Another commonly found system is *matrix* organization, where people are grouped in teams according to their skills and the task on which they are working and hierarchical position in the organization becomes unimportant.

VII.—IS PSYCHOLOGICAL INTERVENTION SUCCESSFUL?

In a chapter such as this it is impossible to review all the considerable literature validating psychological interventions in organizations. In general, the two 'traditional' areas of selection and training have been well researched and there is much evidence to support the view that effectiveness is significantly increased by a systematic approach. There are many technical problems involved in validating the selection process. Since it is essentially a process of prediction, the principal one of these is establishing the validity of the techniques used. There are two main aspects of this problem. One concerns the reliability or consistency of the technique. Techniques like interviewing, with a relatively high subjective content, tend to have lower reliability but provide information over a wide range of characteristics. Psychological tests are more reliable, but also narrower in their application. The second aspect is the difficulty of finding a suitable criterion against which to measure validity of a technique (the so-called *criterion problem*). In order to establish the validity of a technique, some criterion of job performance must be available against which to match performance on the selection technique. In many jobs, it is virtually impossible to get a measure of performance which is not contaminated by other variables. Another problem is that no data are available on the candidates not appointed, some of whom might have done better than those selected. Similar criterion problems also exist in attempting to evaluate training, and there is the added complexity of attempting to measure skill levels before training, since without a measure of proficiency before training commences, there is no way of knowing how much the individual has improved as a result of the training programme. Evaluation of other types of intervention is almost impossible; in the case of OD or industrial relations, for example, there is no way of knowing what would have happened without the psychologist. Evaluation is often simply a matter of the 'client' feels better, or improvement can be defined and even measured, but it can only be *assumed* that it was due to the intervention. Discussion of these and associated problems is given by Gruneberg in Chapter 6.

VIII.—METHODOLOGICAL AND PRACTICAL PROBLEMS

One of the central methodological issues in organizational intervention concerns the mechanistic/organismic distinction. For example, the whole area of personnel selection, as practised, is very *mechanistic* in approach, more in keeping with the earlier 'rational/economic' assumptions of man rather than the later 'complex man' assumptions. The traditional approach of selection is to identify the characteristics of a particular job and then find someone to fit them: the square peg in the square hole approach. Thus a static view of organizations and people is taken. If, however, organizations and people are seen as flexible and adaptable, all the careful matching is really unnecessary. Given the motivation, almost anyone could learn to do almost any job. Some evidence for this view is given by the fact that individuals selected for one position are not unknown to move on, in quite a short time period, to another job with a quite different specification. A similar dichotomy exists in the field of training. In the mechanistic traditional view, described above, the trainer or training manager decides the objectives, designs the programme and controls the learning. Trainees are essentially passive and learn what they are directed to learn within a framework provided for them. In opposition to this, as a result of the thinking of people such as Carl Rogers, there is a rapidly developing view that the trainee should be responsible for setting personal objectives and deciding how to achieve them. Rogers (1967, p. 276) says, for example:

> It seems to me that anything which can be taught to another is relatively inconsequential, and has little or no significant influence on behaviour . . . I have come to feel that the only learning which significantly influences behaviour is self-discovered, self-appropriated learning. Such self-discovered learning, truth that has been personally appropriated and assimilated in experience, cannot be directly communicated to another.

This view implies that directive training programmes are dealing essentially in trivia and have little effect on behaviour. Cooper (1979) provides evidence in support of the above view.

How then can learning and change be brought about? Somehow the individual must become responsible for directing their own development. The Training Officer will become a consultant, helping them to define their personal needs and counselling them on how best to fulfil them. Development will be by gaining appropriate experience. There will be less attendance at courses. Courses will be available to develop *specific* skills or knowledge and will be designed on the principles outlined above, but will only be attended by individuals who have for themselves defined their need to attend. One way in which the appropriate experience can be gained is by enabling individuals to undertake projects away from their normal work environment, which provide challenges to extend and develop their skills. *Action Learning* is based on this principle. This is a system developed originally by Revans (1971; 1980), where managers are exchanged between organizations to work on such projects. An important feature is that the project should be 'real', that is, concerned with important problems, and the participant should have full responsibility for dealing with it, in order to generate high involvement and motivation.

A central issue in motivation in organizations concerns the question: Is motivation simply a matter of the manipulation of external factors, principally working conditions and money (Herzberg's hygiene factors)? This is the traditional mechanistic approach, and it is based on a 'rational-economic man' assumption. It involves attempting to reward individuals by paying them according to their output. There are many problems with this assumption. (a) It must be possible to measure the output. Often it is not possible on even basic, unskilled jobs. On more complex jobs, like management for example, it is never possible. (b) Quality of the work and difficulty of the job must be taken into account. Attempts are made to allow for this when fixing rates, but great complexities arise. (c) Close monitoring and measurement of performance are required, which can lead to resentment and attempts to manipulate the measurements. (d) Money is not by any means a universal motivator. The extent to which it motivates depends upon the individual's *need* for money and other personal needs. Workers will often restrict output and reduce earnings in order not to be isolated from the group (social need fulfilment).

In view of the above considerations, it is strange how widely financial incentive schemes are still used. This is possibly because of their simplicity. It is almost as if managers *want to believe* in a world where people are motivated by money and perhaps a few other extrinsic factors, because it would be easier to control. Perhaps the alternative is too complex to handle. However, man is complex and it seems much more probable that people are motivated by a complicated set of factors, as suggested by Herzberg and others. That is, that motivation really comes from intrinsic interest and involvement in the job, within a good environment, both physical and psychological. To accept this, however, would involve a radical re-thinking of the way jobs are structured and the philosophy of management in many organizations.

Another major problem in organizational interventions (particularly training and OD) is concerned with *resistance to change*. Individuals in the organization may not wish to see the changes that the intervention is aimed to bring about. There is a widely held view, probably false, that most people dislike change and will resist anything which upsets the familiar. Most people will only resist change that threatens them in some way, because they do not understand it, perhaps, or because it will require them to adapt in some way for which they do not have the skill. For a few people, all change may fall into this category, but for most, change which is seen as improving life, is welcomed. Much has been written on overcoming resistance to change, but in essence, if change is to be accepted, those concerned must be consulted and involved in the change process. Linked to this is the problem of conflict in organizations. Is it possible to have an effective organization in which all is harmonious? As suggested above, the answer is 'probably not'. Certainly many trade unionists consider that conflict between management and unions is 'built into the system' and it seems a safe assumption that if you have people working together, conflicts are going to arise, from differences in perceptions, beliefs and objectives. What is important is to resolve these conflicts creatively so that new solutions emerge to which all parties can be committed. In this way, the organization is strengthened rather than weakened.

A final issue for this section concerns the training and skills required by an organization consultant or change agent. Ideally, the individual should have a thorough knowledge of human behaviour and organizational theory. He or she should be sensitive and highly skilled in social interaction and aware of the effects of his/her own behaviour. There is, at the moment in Britain, no recognized training or qualifications in this area. A variety of training courses do exist, from those run by consultancy organizations to postgraduate programmes in universities, but these display a wide variation in content and approach. Most practitioners (but by no means all of them) have a background in the social sciences, have been on a variety of skill development programmes and have learned from experience. Perhaps, the most important qualification is the ability to do the latter, but it could be argued that there is a need for some more generally recognized training and qualification.

IX.—PROBLEMS OF ETHICS AND CONFIDENTIALITY

There are three main ethical issues faced by the psychologist working in industry. The first is concerned with selection and, particularly, the use of tests, where it may be that the individual is disclosing information about himself of which he is unaware. Also, the person disclosing the information may not understand how the information is going to be used. The second issue is related, and concerns the keeping of records. In many organizations records are kept of employees' performance and appraisals, the details of which may not be known to the individuals concerned. There is growing support for the view that each person should have access to his or her own record to enable them to check the information for accuracy. The third issue concerns training. Since training is concerned with change and particularly where attitudes and personal behaviour are concerned, it can be argued that no-one has the right to try and impose change on others. This is exactly what directive systems attempt to do. If training is seen as self-development, this issue does not arise.

X.—THE ROLE OF OTHER DISCIPLINES AND PROFESSIONS

It is not common for the industrial or managerial psychologist to work with members of other professions. He or she will frequently work as a member of a team with other psychologists. In some areas, such as OD, the psychologist may work with people trained in other academic disciplines (for example, industrial sociologists) but since there is no recognized formal training for an OD practitioner, people are employed on the basis of their skills and experience; hence there is no differentiation in the role of the psychologist as against any other specialist. In most areas, the role of the psychologist is as a professional adviser to management.

XI.—FUTURE PROSPECTS

There seems to be a growing interest in what organizations do to people, both the managers and the managed. One aspect of this is the interest in organizational stress, leading to the development of methods of stress management. Psychologists (and others) are going to become increasingly involved in helping people to cope with organizational life. One way in which this will be done is by developing counselling services in organizations. Psychologists will also become more involved with developing company personnel policies. Here, the emphasis will also be more on the individual. Each person will have more responsibility for his or her own career planning and personal development. Another very important change is the shortening of the working week due to changing technology. A three-day working week is a real possibility in the not too distant future. A significant part of an individual's career planning will be concerned with keeping up with change and on how to make appropriate use of leisure time. Specialist advisers will be needed to help people with the consequences of all these developments.

XII.—ANNOTATED READINGS

Handy, C. B. (1976). *Understanding Organizations*. Harmondsworth: Penguin.

Good introductory text on organizational psychology; see especially the sections on motivation, leadership power and cultures in organizations.

Cooper, C. L. (Ed.), (1981). *Psychology and Management: A Text for Managers and Trade Unionists*. London: The British Psychological Society and Macmillan Press.

Smith, M., Beck, J., Cooper, C. L., Cox, C., Ottaway, R. and Talbot, R. (1982). *Introducing Organizational Behaviour*. London: Macmillan Press.

The above two books are general textbooks on organizational psychology.

Gibson, T. L., Ivanecevich, J. M. and Donnerly, J. H. (Eds.), (1979). *Readings in Organizations*. Third Edition, Dallas, Texas: Business Publications.

A useful set of readings.

McCormick, E. J. and Ilgen, D. R. (1981). *Industrial Psychology*. Seventh Edition. London: Allen and Unwin.

A basic textbook dealing with the more traditional end of industrial psychology.

XIII.—REFERENCES

Burns, T. and Stalker, G. M. (1961). *The Management of Innovation*. London: Tavistock.

Chartier, M. R. (1974). Five components contributing to effective interpersonal communication In: W. J. Pfieffer and J. E. Jones (Eds.) *Annual Handbook for Group Facilitators*, La Jolla, California: University Associates.

Cooper, C. L. (1979). *Learning from Others in Groups*. London: Associated Business Press.

Fiedler, F. E. (1967). *A Theory of Leadership Effectiveness*. New York: McGraw-Hill.

French, J. R. P. and Caplan, R. D. (1973). Organizational stress and individual strain. In: A. Marrow (Ed.) *The Failure of Success*. New York: AMACOM.

Handy, C. B. (1976). *Understanding Organizations*. Harmondsworth: Penguin.

Harrison, R. (1972). How to describe your organization. *Harvard Business Review*, 50, 3, 119–128.

Herzberg, F. (1966). *Work and the Nature of Man*. Cleveland, Ohio: World Publishing.

Likert, R. (1961). *New Patterns of Management*. New York: McGraw-Hill.

Marshall, J. and Cooper, C. L. (1979). *Executives Under Pressure*. London: Macmillan Press.

Maslow, A. H. (1954). *Motivation and Personality*. New York: Harper and Row.

McGregor, D. (1960). *The Human Side of Enterprise*. New York: McGraw-Hill.

Miller, E. J. and Rice, A. K. (1967). *Systems of Organization*. London: Tavistock.

Morley, I. E. (1982). Bargaining and negotiation. In: A. J. Chapman and A. Gale (Eds.): *Psychology and People: A Tutorial Text*. London: The British Psychological Society and Macmillan Press.

Munsterberg, H. (1913). *Psychology and Industrial Efficiency*. Boston, Massachusetts: Houghton Mifflin.

Office of Health Economics (1971). *Off Sick*. London: Her Majesty's Stationery Office. Pamphlet No. 36.

Pahl, J. M. and Pahl, R. E. (1971). *Managers and Their Wives*, London: Allan Lane.

Pressey, S. L. (1959). Development and appraisal of devices providing immediate automatic scoring of objective tests and concomitant self instruction. *Journal of Psychology*, 29, 417–447.

Revans, R. W. (1971). *Developing Effective Managers: A New Approach to Business Education*. London: Longman.

Revans, R. W. (1980). *Action Learning*. London: Blond and Briggs.

Rodger, A. (1952). *The Seven Point Plan*. London: NIIP Paper No. 1. National Institute of Industrial Psychology.

Roethlesberger, R. J. and Dickson, W. J. (1939). *Management and the Worker*. Cambridge, Massachusetts: Harvard University Press.

Rogers, C. (1967). *On Becoming a Person*. London: Constable.

Schein, E. H. (1972). *Organizational Psychology*. Englewood Cliffs, N.J.: Prentice Hall.

Sidney, E. and Brown, M. (1961). *The Skills of Interviewing*. London: Tavistock.

Skinner, B. F. (1954). The Science of Learning and the Art of Teaching. *Harvard Educational Review*, 24, 86–97.

Taylor, F. W. (1947). *Principles of Scientific Management*. New York: Harper and Row.

Wicks, R. P. (1981). Interviewing. In: C. L. Cooper (Ed.) *Psychology and Manage-*

ment: A Text for Managers and Trade Unionists. London: The British Psychological Society and Macmillan Press.

Woodward, J. (1965). *Industrial Organization: Theory and Practice*. Oxford: Oxford University Press.

Psychology and Social Problems
Edited by A. Gale and A. J. Chapman
© 1984 John Wiley & Sons Ltd.

CHAPTER 8

ACCIDENTS AND SAFETY

Noel P. Sheehy and Antony J. Chapman

I.—THE EXTENT OF THE PROBLEM

Official British statistics are an index of the staggering amount of human suffering caused by accidents. In the late nineteen-seventies approximately 16,000 people per year died of injuries accidentally inflicted, and over a third of these deaths were a consequence of traffic accidents: about one-third of a million people are involved in traffic accidents every year. In home accidents, the corresponding fatality rate is of the order of 5,000 per year, and there are considerably fewer fatal accidents in the workplace: for example, 711 in 1979. The British statistics are broadly similar in patterns and dimensions to those of other industrialized nations, and they suggest that accidents are a health problem of epidemic proportions. In EEC member countries, for example, 1,610,537 road users were involved in fatal and serious traffic accidents during 1979.

More precise estimates of the consequences and costs of accidents are difficult to obtain, but estimates as to the financial burden of British road accidents are published by the Department of Transport. Table 8.1 reproduces the estimates of the cost of road accidents in 1980. The average costs of accidents may conceal a wide range of cost elements, possibly from a large number of minor costs to a small number of large and potentially chronic costs. Estimates such as these must be treated cautiously. It is impossible, for example, to place an absolute or relative monetary value on the acute trauma caused by pain, grief and suffering.

Interpretation of accident statistics is problematic in other ways too. For example, it is not always certain what constitutes an accident, and hence international comparisons are difficult. Most member states of the EEC define a fatal traffic accident as one resulting in death within a 30-day period; but the period is 7 days in Italy, 6 days in France, and 3 days in Greece. Our view of the extent of accident problems is inevitably influenced by such

TABLE 8.1
THE AVERAGE COST OF A ROAD ACCIDENT BY SEVERITY AND COST
ELEMENT, GREAT BRITAIN 1980
(Department of Transport, 1981)

	SEVERITY OF ACCIDENT		
	Fatal	Serious	Slight
Element	£	£	£
Lost output	93,830	1,290	20
Police and insurance administration	220	170	130
Medical and ambulance	440	780	40
Damage to property	1,230	1,000	690
Pain, grief and suffering	36,980	3,840	80
TOTAL	132,700	7,080	960

variations in the standards used to determine whether or not a fatal injury has been accidentally inflicted.

It is useful to view accident recording systems as active surveillance systems rather than just passive reporting systems. An accident surveillance system is designed to detect and quantify the incidence of accidents in the environment. Many factors influence its operation. For example, road users in Britain are legally obliged to report only those accidents which result in physical injury to a person. Presumably, therefore, many accidents which result in no personal injury are not reported: no 'correction factors' are suggested for official statistics, many of which should therefore be regarded merely as estimates of true rates, and then always under- rather than over-estimates. The seriousness of an accident may itself influence the probability of that accident being registered. No doubt fatal and very serious accidents are almost always detected, but accidents which result in minor injuries are probably under-reported. Legal and public consequences also affect the probability of an accident being detected. Fear of prosecution may make a road user try to conceal an accident; and a factory worker may not report an accident for fear of being found negligent or incompetent. The availability of medical assistance can also be an important factor: for instance, geographical isolation may force inhabitants of rural areas to cope with accidental injuries for which urban dwellers would seek professional medical advice.

An effective way of reducing accidents is to limit exposure to situations in which accidents are known to occur. Hence, for example, pedestrian accidents could be eliminated by total segregation of pedestrian from vehicular traffic. The concept of exposure is an important one when interpreting accident statistics, yet such statistics do not normally include a measure of the frequency with which individuals are exposed to the situation. The likelihood of being involved in an accident increases as exposure to the particular situation increases, but knowledge of the ratio of accidents to exposure is necessary to determine the dangerousness of the activity. While exposure statistics make accident statistics easier to interpret, they do not explain *why* accidents occur: they merely indicate that accidents occur when they have an opportunity to occur. These points should be borne in mind when considering the extent and causes of accidents. Accident statistics on their own do not explain anything: there is a need for a set of alternative causal models if statistics are to be interpreted and put to use.

II.—CONCEPTS OF THE PERSON AND MODELS OF HUMAN BEHAVIOUR

Accidents have a conspicuous behavioural element, and within psychology there is a number of theoretical approaches to human error. Ideally any theory of human error should have general applicability and be equally relevant to an understanding of accidents in the home, in the street and at work. Historically there have been three important theoretical approaches to accidents and safety—*proneness theory*, *skills theory* and *information theory*.

Accounts of 'accident repeaters' and 'accident-prone' people are not uncommon in everyday conversation. The concept of accident proneness was first introduced to describe some of the characteristics of the distribution of accidents in a workforce. The majority of people in the population have no accidents while a few have a large number, and hence there is usually a skewed distribution of recorded accidents. There is disagreement about the way accident proneness should be measured and whether it is a useful concept. Because of the infrequency of accidents, statistical differences between high and low accident groups tend to be exaggerated, but these differences are reduced as the frequency of accidents increases. Smith and Howarth (1982) have developed a method for comparing accident proneness in different groups which is not affected by differences in the absolute numbers of recorded accidents. They have re-analysed data from earlier studies of accident proneness and shown that accident proneness exists but that its effect as a causal factor is relatively small. Such small effects could be due to self-fulfilling prophecies or expectations people have about themselves or 'prone' colleagues.

Evidence of repeated accidents is usually taken as evidence for accident proneness. The practice of comparing high-accident with low-accident groups is a common one, for example, in road safety research: this practice again assumes a direct relationship between accident proneness and accident occurrence. However accident prone people might not necessarily be the people who have the most accidents: to be repeatedly involved in accidents they would have to be exposed regularly to the kinds of situations in which their liability to accidents would be realized. The observed distribution of accidents in a population may itself be an aggregation of many smaller distributions of

accidents for sub-groups within the population with different accident liabili-
ties. Eysenck (1965) has argued that a psychological approach to accident
proneness must go beyond statistical analysis. The statistical approach tends
to be primarily descriptive while the psychological approach generates specific
testable hypotheses with regard to the personality of accident repeaters. For
example, 'impulsive' persons might be expected to feature more frequently
in certain types of accident.

Theories which deal with the role of skill in accident aetiology emphasize
the organization of behaviour. Kay (1971) has described a two-stage model
of error in relation to the acquisition of skill. An environmentally controlled
mode of operation comes first. This is a stimulus-response stage in which an
individual's responses are guided entirely by events in the environment.
The second stage involves a pre-programmed mode of operation. Routines
become organized serially so that the performance of a particular routine
action triggers further action; thus skill emerges in the habitual performance
of serially organized action. The environmentally controlled mode of operation is a slow one. Emphasis is placed on the role of environmental feedback
which assures successful performance from the novice. Few accidents are
likely to occur while the individual is responding carefully to events in the
environment. Nor are accidents likely to occur while the individual is responding in the pre-programmed mode of operation, because skill consists in
anticipating events in the environment and regulating behaviour accordingly.

Mourant and Rockwell (1972) studied eye-movements and fixations of
novices and experienced drivers. Novices, being in the environmental stage,
tended to respond to traffic on a moment-to-moment basis and to concentrate
on events occurring within the immediate vicinity of the car. Experienced
drivers, being at the pre-programmed stage, spent more time identifying
features in the environment some distance ahead and predicting future conditions in the environment. As the novice develops expertise and moves from
stage one to stage two, accident liability increases. At this time there is
vacillation between the two response modes. Individuals can fail to monitor
such vacillations and then neglect to anticipate potential hazards, assuming
that they are operating in one mode while actually operating in the other.
When events occur which were not anticipated, an individual may be unable
to revert to the environmentally controlled mode of operation swiftly enough,
and during the switching period accidents happen. Accident statistics show
that drivers are particularly vulnerable to accidents during the first three
years after they have passed the driving test. Presumably this is an important
period where skills are being re-organized and where the driver is consequently most vulnerable.

The information-processing model of accident causation views the individual as a system with limited processing capabilities. Normally the individual
has an amount of spare processing capacity which is not needed for satisfac-

tory performance. This extra mental capacity is brought into play during emergencies or when the system becomes fatigued. New drivers, or indeed novices on any task, are likely to have less of this spare capacity because more of their information-processing capabilities are dedicated to managing the task. Consequently the demands of potentially hazardous situations are more likely to disrupt the activity of the novice than the experienced person.

Brown and Holloway (1974) attempted to measure the spare mental capacity of drivers by having them perform a secondary task (e.g., a short-term memory task) while engaging in routine driving. Good levels of perform-ance on the secondary task are indicative of the level of spare capacity remaining after the primary, driving task. In a sample of thirteen trainee bus drivers the level of spare mental capacity appeared to increase with training. One would expect that drivers with greater spare mental capacity should be in a better position to cope with potentially hazardous situations than drivers with less. It transpired that seven of the bus drivers were subsequently involved in traffic accidents and six were not. In the prior training, the six accident-free drivers had demonstrated increased spare mental capacity by the end of the training whereas the others had not.

Accident investigators and safety practitioners often comment on the apparent gap between psychological theory and practical application. Many safety recommendations do not require sophisticated psychological theory to substantiate their validity; for instance, a recommendation that domestic products should conform to rigid design safety standards hardly requires a sophisticated psychological justification. However, the gap between theory and application is symptomatic of the weak predictive validity of most psycho-logical theories. Psychological theory can predict accidents in a general way, by describing situations in which accidents are likely to occur, but they have a very limited role in predicting exactly when and where such situations are likely to arise. So psychology has developed a band of theory-driven research and a band of task-driven research. The former is concerned with developing and testing psychological theories of error and the latter with identifying and implementing real solutions to specific problems. Both help to identify the psychological variables which matter and therefore both can help to reduce their potentially damaging effects. For example, safety standards for domestic appliances can only be truly effective if we know which products people use and how they perceive product-related hazards. The psychologist is qualified to provide and interpret this sort of knowledge.

III.—INDIVIDUAL ASSESSMENT

Freudian psychoanalytic theory is an obvious starting point from which to examine the role of individual factors in accidents, and it falls within a general theory of error. Its central concept is *fehlleistung*, which literally translated means 'faulty function', but the technical term *parapraxis* has usually been used to define its core features. What supposedly happens is that an impulse to self-injury, which is constantly on the watch and normally finds expression in self-reproach, takes advantage of environmental circumstances with the object of producing an unconsciously desired injurious effect. By engaging the person's defensive forces environmental elements provide an opportunity for the unexpressed desire to free itself from repressive pressure. Parry (1968) has taken up this explanation and applied it to traffic accidents. He argues that the most compelling evidence for psychoanalytic theory is probably the equanimity with which Society accepts high levels of accidents and public indifference to safety programmes designed to change that situation.

Because accidents are such a major cause of death and injury, several psychologists see accidents as 'diseases' whose causes can be identified and eliminated. This ties in with psychoanalytic theory which views accidents as symptomatic of other latent variables. The psychological concept of accident proneness, mentioned above, has been a useful one. There is no single concept of accident proneness but several concepts linked by the hypothesis that some individuals bring to a situation sets of skills, expectations and predispositions which make it probable that they will choose to act in a way likely to increase their liability to accidents.

Eysenck (1964) suggested that monotonous environments set up *reactive inhibition* which is dissipated during involuntary rest pauses and he has developed questionnaires or inventories which measure the individual's degree of extraversion. Extraverted people tend to develop inhibition more rapidly and more strongly than introverted people. Consequently, extraverts take more involuntary rest pauses and increase their liability to accidents in monotonous and repetitive environments. Powell, Hale, Martin and Simon (1971) found that extraversion correlates with recorded shop-floor accidents. They also found that 'chatty' workers had more accidents and it appeared that their 'chattiness' was the variable linking extraversion with recorded accidents. McGuire (1976) has reviewed the literature dealing with personality factors in traffic accidents. He suggests that individuals who have accidents tend to be emotionally immature, less responsible, more asocial and not as well adjusted as other members of the driving population. However, many of these characteristics are age-related and tend to change with maturity. Also the underlying concepts are vague, ill-defined and value-laden.

Manheimer and Mellinger (1967) have examined the accident records of 8,874 four- to eighteen-year-olds. They found that children rated 'high' on a composite measure of accident liability were more likely to be described as daring, active and extraverted by their mothers. Perhaps this is not surprising, being a form of *post hoc* explanation on the part of the mothers; but these characteristics are all ones which might increase the child's exposure to potentially hazardous situations while simultaneously rendering the child less capable of coping with the hazards. Mellinger and Manheimer (1967) have also reported that children with pronounced personality maladjustments have a high level of accident involvement. This they attributed to high risk taking which was a feature of the children's recalcitrance. According to Krall (1964) accident-repeating children are less socialized and more aggressive as a consequence of frustration experienced in an authoritarian family setting. She interviewed 64 five- to eight-year-olds, half of whom had medical records of accidental injury received during the four-year period preceding the study. Krall requested the children to play with some dolls and reported that children with accident histories made more frequent commands and threats. They also displayed more affection-giving and affection-seeking. Krall interpreted these findings as indicative of greater family disorganization among her group of accident children. However, this conclusion may not be warranted. Affection-giving and affection-seeking might just as readily be interpreted as demonstrative of family cohesion; also they may be a direct function of the child's personality.

The utility of personality-based approaches to understanding accidents is partly limited by difficulties involved in describing how such approaches can improve the effectiveness of safety countermeasures. The value of identifying individuals who are 'at risk' by clinical diagnosis and intervention, depends on the availability of measures for modifying risk taking, or selectively restricting access to environments in which the individual is particularly vulnerable. There is also a temptation to focus so much on personality variables that important social variables are neglected.

IV.—THE IMMEDIATE SOCIAL AND EMOTIONAL ENVIRONMENT

The family is an important socializing agent throughout life. It introduces the child to social norms and facilitates the development of a wide range of skills in a socially guided setting. For the adult the roles of father and mother have traditionally represented a significant personal commitment. For the elderly the family provides a vital means of social support. In view of the prominence of the family in individual growth and development, psychologists have sought to understand and explain individual behaviour in terms of the relationship between the individual and the family. Marcus, Wilson, Kraft, Swander, Southerland and Schulhopfer (1964) have suggested that childhood accidents are a consequence of emotional trauma within the family. They compared 23 six- to fourteen-year-olds who had been involved in one or more accidents requiring medical attention with control groups of 23 'non-accident' children and 23 enuretic children. They reported that both the accident group and the enuretic group manifested more emotional problems than children in the non-accident group. Parents of the accident group were more insecure, anxious and non-assertive than parents of other children.

This suggests that childhood accidents may be associated with emotional problems arising from defective parental rearing practices. Backett and Johnston (1959) studied 101 families in which an otherwise healthy child had been involved in a road accident, and compared them with 101 matched families. They found a greater incidence of general illness and more serious illness in their 'accident' families. They also noted that mothers of their group of 'accident' children tended more than the other mothers, to be preoccupied with pregnancy and with employment outside the home. Preoccupation with family and personal crises might increase the vulnerability of adults to accidents, but there is no clear evidence to this effect.

While the relative importance of various contributory factors to accidents is debatable there is no doubting the acute trauma which can undermine interpersonal relationships following accidental injury. The term 'accident victims' covers the family and friends who are affected by the repercussions of an accident, as well as those who are physically involved in the first place. The frequency of two broadly defined states increases after severe trauma: intrusive experiences of a somatic and psychosomatic kind, and a period of denial and numbing. Little is known about the course of post-accident recovery, but emotional reactions to physical disfigurement resemble the grief reactions of bereaved individuals. Recuperation will be partly determined by the quality of responses from the family and peer groups. For instance, the severity of personal crises caused by the accident will be affected by the process of role re-definition in which the victim's part in the community is re-evaluated. The otherwise independent elderly person who has been incapacitated by a domestic accident may suddenly become housebound and dependent on assistance from immediate family and friends. Characteristics of infirmity and illness can easily be attributed to the victim, who is discouraged from resuming a normal life-style. We should be cautious about theories of accident causation among the elderly which stereotype the elderly as partially crippled and senile. Margulec, Librach and Schodel (1970) have studied the distribution of accidents among residents of homes for the elderly and revealed that accident liability increases with *improved* functional capacity and is not a product of poor coordination and diminished competence as such.

Medical and economic indicators of the severity and cost of accidents do not provide good measures of social and psychological variables. The Consumers' Association (1980) has examined the consequences of traffic accidents on victims and their families. Ninety-two per cent of those who had received injuries during the four-year period preceding the study and who were in employment at the time of their accident were absent from work for more than six weeks. This has important implications for the victim and the victim's family, particularly where the accident victim is the breadwinner and where re-definitions of roles and re-distributions of responsibilities within the family have to be negotiated within a brief period of time.

V.—THE WIDER SOCIAL AND ORGANIZATIONAL ENVIRONMENT

People strive to make sense of events in their lives and this search for meaning is particularly intense when accounting for accidents. Accidents often strike us as absurd incidents and we try to make their absurdity meaningful by seeking explanations for their occurrence. Popular models of accident causation have tended to reflect deep-rooted superstitions and beliefs about the hidden meaning of catastrophic events in our lives. These popular models have a similar history to folk theories of disease aetiology. Both were originally viewed as manifestations of evil and have only been subject to more rational analysis in recent times. One popular belief about accidents is that they are events which happen because they *have* to happen. Alternatively they may be regarded as a consequence of the unavoidable coincidental combination of circumstances. Both of these views reflect a belief in the inevitability of accidents although they imply different models of accident aetiology and prevention. The first attitude reflects a belief in the intrinsic significance and hidden purpose of important life events. The second reflects a belief in the importance which luck plays in fashioning our lives. Both attitudes imply a fatalistic view of accident prevention and safety.

People use the term 'accident' to describe events in their lives in a very arbitrary fashion. Accidents are associated with unexpected, chance incidents, having important consequences for the victim. However, serious injury arising from coronary thrombosis and brain haemorrhage may be equally violent and unexpected yet would not be considered accidental. Diseases are usually seen as eradicable and explicable while accidents have qualities of being unavoidable and inexplicable. Society views accidents differently from other causes of death and injury. In Britain this is reflected in the coroner's role. The coroner is expected to conduct investigations into deaths which are violent, sudden or unusual in other respects. The coroner's court provides a quasi-judicial explanation when an appropriate medical explanation cannot be readily identified. Due process in the completion of death certificates does not readily accommodate the possibility that death may not have resulted from a protracted illness: that is, death certificates in Britain may only be issued by the medical practitioner who was in attendance during the deceased's terminal illness.

There is a further attitude towards accidents which many readers will have experienced; it is reflected in the phrase 'accidents never happen—they are caused'. This contrasts with more fatalistic attitudes by emphasizing the rational and explicable aspects. In many respects accident investigators adopt this approach as a working model of accident causation, with the caveat that accidents have many causes which are inter-related in complex ways. A related attitude maintains that human accidents can be explained rationally but not necessarily in causal terms. Causal explanations imply a mechanistic and deterministic model of the person and in doing so concentrate on overt behaviour. Purposive or reason-based explanations concentrate on analysing the covert reasons and purposes of behaviour through which the meaning of a person's actions is disclosed. Both causal and purposive explanations construe accidents as rational consequences of certain forms of conduct and are therefore more optimistic than deterministic attitudes which argue for the inevitability of accidents.

Systematic features in the distribution of accidents according to variables of age, sex and region point to sociological and wider organizational dimensions, and they indicate that accidents have a macro-social dimension. Society has institutionalized certain kinds of behaviour as 'safe', and disparities may be construed as deviant. Porterfield (1960) compared the rank order of metropolitan areas in the USA on indices of suicide, homicide, crime and traffic accidents, and concluded that social forces determine fatalities in all four categories. Preston (1972) examined the distribution of child pedestrian accidents in Manchester and Salford and found a significant positive correlation between the injury rate, an index of crowding and an index of social class. She argued that overcrowded housing conditions tend to force many children into the street. Read, Bradley, Morison, Lewall and Clarke (1963) have also found that children involved in accidents are more likely to come from families living in multi-dwelling housing in densely populated city centre districts. Haddon, Valien, McCarroll and Umberger (1964) have reported more adult pedestrian fatalities within low socio-economic groups. Such studies emphasize the significance of macro-social variables in accident statistics, but the statistics can be explained in any number of equally plausible ways.

Although sociological research provides important information for the co-ordination of safety policy it must be treated cautiously. Usually this kind of information cannot be used to select populations for 'treatment' since the size of the problem is often determined by the size and structure of the sampling frame one chooses to adopt. For this reason safety countermeasures designed to identify and treat 'problem areas' cannot guarantee the effective and efficient use of available resources. In fact such approaches may encourage erroneous beliefs about the ecological concentration of accident problems in society.

VI.—TYPES OF INTERVENTION

Psychological interventions can be remedial or prophylactic. Remedial measures are designed to minimize the severity of the debilitating consequences of accidents and help to plan the course of rehabilitation. Prophylactic measures normally assume the form of safety programmes designed to minimize the likelihood of accidents in the first instance. Safety programmes which aim to change behaviour have an important educational dimension: the biggest problem facing them is actually changing behaviour, rather than just changing knowledge and attitudes. Changes in knowledge and attitudes can easily be misinterpreted as indicating underlying changes in behaviour. Sandels (1975) has shown how Swedish road safety educational programmes have improved the road safety knowledge and attitudes of boys more than they have girls, yet young male pedestrians are still twice as vulnerable as their female peers.

In formulating a safety programme there is a number of points to be borne in mind: for example, the theme of the programme, the treatment of the subject matter, the wording of the message and the affective tone of the programme must all be considered. It is generally recognized that road safety countermeasures propose specific changes in behaviour (e.g., 'Use your seat belt') rather than general ones (e.g., 'Drive safely'). General recommendations tend to be vague and uninformative. 'Treatment of the subject matter' refers to the form in which the information is imparted; for example, whether it is numerical, literal or pictorial. Numerical data, such as statistical facts, contain large amounts of relevant information in a form which is bland and almost impossible to integrate into one's behaviour in a direct way. The wording of a programme can prove particularly difficult: terms and concepts which are clear to programme designers may not be interpreted in the same way by the target population. For instance, Sandels (1975) tested young children's comprehension of words commonly used in road safety texts and teaching materials. She found that children experienced difficulty in understanding words (e.g., 'hazardous'), particularly adjectives and adverbs, when adults had no problems.

The affective tone of the message is also an important variable. The public image of safety is not a good one, and responses to safety programmes are generally poor. This is partly because of difficulties in specifying criteria for safe conduct. Safety is usually characterized negatively, by itemizing things which should not be done. It is difficult for campaigners to do differently and be positive without resorting to vague criteria. Proposing specific positive action can prove hazardous since no act is inherently safe but depends on the attitudes of the individual and the context in which it is executed.

It is difficult to structure objective screening tests during training and selection programmes. Task and skills analyses provide a potentially powerful base from which to design, implement and evaluate accident countermeasures. They facilitate systematic analysis of specific tasks and propose specific alternatives. However, in task analysis and task taxonomy there is a danger of reducing complex action sequences to arbitrary components. When complex tasks and skills are fractured they tend to lose their meaning and their elements resemble nonsense sub-tasks with minimal relevance to what happens in larger purposive activity.

In a study of pedestrian skills Page, Iwata and Neeg (1976) attempted to reduce the vulnerability of a group of mentally retarded men. Training was conducted in simulations of traffic, and results were encouraging: the men were observed to apply their newly acquired skills spontaneously in city traffic, and performance was facilitated on other skills not formally trained. Acquiring skills as integrated wholes rather than piecemeal, is likely to be particularly effective because learning is then undertaken in terms of broad task demands. Given the highly subjective nature of skills testing programmes one may ask whether or not they are successful as a selection process, screening out bad performers. Hoinville, Berthoud and Mackie (1972) have shown that drivers who passed the Institute of Advanced Motorists driving test had 25% fewer accidents over the three-year period after the test had been taken than those who had failed. This testing by subjective methods is a useful preventative measure in that it can aid in the identification of groups of drivers which are likely to have more accidents. The success of subjective tests such as the advanced driving test is probably due to the fact that performance is tested in the environment in which the individual will routinely act. Subjective tests of performance outside that environment would probably not prove so successful.

VII.—IS PSYCHOLOGICAL INTERVENTION SUCCESSFUL?

It is often difficult to cite operational criteria against which the effectiveness of safety countermeasures can be evaluated. If one takes as a criterion for effectiveness the size of the reduction in the accident statistics one would have to wait a long time before a sufficient number of accidents took place. During this time a range of intervening variables might collectively contribute to a reduction in the accident statistics, or alternatively nullify the benefits of countermeasures, thereby confounding the methodology of the evaluation study. For instance, in Britain there was a marked reduction in the number of child pedestrian casualties between 1972 and 1975, and this followed the introduction of the *Green Cross Code* publicity campaign in 1971 and 1972. One might infer that the reduction points to the effectiveness of the *Green Cross Code*. But 1973 and 1974 were years of energy crises, petrol shortages and large price increases. There was a reduction in the national speed limit to 50 mph, and a large-scale pedestrian safety campaign was also launched during this period. It is probable that the reduction in child pedestrian accidents was due to a combination of several factors and not solely to the effects of the *Green Cross Code*.

Where a decision is taken to extend the range of relevant events to include 'near misses' (see Section VIII) it is important that 'near miss studies' should be conducted prior to and after the introduction of a safety countermeasure. Without established baseline information it is impossible to determine the effectiveness of any countermeasure. It should also be an objective of good evaluative research that the expected level of accident reduction should be specified before the intervention is made. If this is not done one may be tempted to treat any reduction in accidents or near misses as acceptable in the belief that any change is better than no change at all. Small changes in accidents or near misses might be ephemeral, and so there is also a need to ensure that a representative range of incidents is sampled over a sufficiently long period of time and over a variety of environmental conditions etc. Very often the effects of countermeasures extend beyond their target audiences. Legislation on drinking and driving has been observed to generalize to vehicle passengers and pedal cyclists, although its effects have not extended to pedestrians (Codling and Samson, 1974).

Bain, Faegre and Wyly (1964) examined the behaviour of young children under circumstances resembling entrapment in refrigerators. The problem was a particularly serious one at the time the research was undertaken and there were few guidelines available for designers to improve the safety of the locking mechanism. Bain et al constructed a small chamber into which they enticed children and then locked the door. Children's attempts to escape were recorded using infra-red cameras. Although the research led to practical and effective improvements in the design of the refrigerator locking mechanism, this kind of research raises serious ethical issues (see Section IX).

Psychological intervention may not always prove effective. Östberg (1980) examined foresters' perceptions of risk and found that the fellers had an accurate and consistent knowledge of risks in typical felling conditions. Certain kinds and levels of risks had become acceptable and it is doubtful whether the accident rate could have been substantially reduced by further training programmes. Most safety countermeasures are not exclusively psychological in their mechanism of operation although many have conspicuous psychological dimensions. For instance, the challenge of making people aware of and interested in the content of safety and training programmes itself presents psychological problems. Because of the complexity of accidents, interventions which are exclusively psychological are unlikely to prove particularly valuable. Effective accident countermeasures require a co-ordinated multi-disciplinary response and there must be a variety of effective measures. The need for a strategic response to the problem of accidents is taken up in Section XI.

VIII.—METHODOLOGICAL AND PRACTICAL PROBLEMS

Behavioural data are essential to an understanding of the nature and role of individual factors in accident aetiology. Accident surveillance systems are not normally designed by psychologists and tend not to foster detailed behavioural data. They usually incorporate accurate measures of readily observable features of an accident. For instance, in the case of traffic accidents in Britain most of the information collected for an accident report (i.e., on the 'STATS 19' form) relates to the spatial and physical context of the accident rather than to the recollections, reasons and explanations offered by victims and witnesses. There is a danger that when psychologists investigate accidents their enquiries may be directed and constrained by information which is readily available within the accident surveillance system and not guided by issues which are psychologically significant but not recorded. Mackie (1972) has shown that follow-up interviews with drivers who were involved in an accident can provide a vital source of psychological data not available in official accident records. A better understanding of drivers' accidents and their theories about the causes of those accidents should assist in the formulation of more effective training and safety propaganda.

Accident investigators are unlikely to witness first-hand more than a few accidents during the course of their enquiries. This limits available opportunities to describe important behavioural elements in accident causation. Since accidents cannot usually be planned or studied in a laboratory setting researchers have attempted to extend their understanding of accidents by examining 'near accidents', otherwise known as 'near misses'). The advantage of extending the range of sampled events in this way is that it increases the number of situations the psychologist can observe. Thus, where a strong correlation holds between the characteristics preceding real accidents and characteristics of near misses, one may be justified in treating the near misses as if they were real accidents with serious consequences. However, if there is indeed a strong correlation, why is it that the near misses do not result in accidents? The fact that many researchers have witnessed many near accidents but none has witnessed many actual accidents suggests that accidents and near accidents may be different on a number of important but poorly understood dimensions. Moreover, investigations of near accidents must be concerned to explain how near misses arise in the routine flow of activity.

Discussion of near accidents raises a further methodological problem for the evaluation of accident countermeasures. Safety programmes have a wide range of consequences, and one must beware not to undervalue them simply because they have no effect on recorded accidents. They may nonetheless contribute to a general improvement in safety: specifically, there may be a significant reduction in near accidents. Thus the study of near accidents may be of value in understanding broader dimensions to the concept of safety, even if it does not lead to a full understanding of accident aetiology.

IX.—PROBLEMS OF ETHICS AND CONFIDENTIALITY

A perennial problem in accident investigation is that it is usually impossible to examine accidents in controlled settings. It would normally be considered morally reprehensible to expose people to danger in order to observe their actions. Where it is possible to model accidents it is questionable whether subjects should be deceived in order to satisfy the need for methodological rigour. In this regard the research of Bain *et al* (1964), above, raises questions about the social and moral responsibilities of psychological science. Professional ethics committees act to ensure that serious breaches of ethical conduct do not occur, but in many cases moral questions do not have clear-cut answers and much is left to the integrity and discretion of the individual researcher or practitioner.

Both legal and moral questions arise in regard to the confidentiality of eye-witnesses' and victims' accounts of an accident. Eye-witnesses find themselves in situations where their confidence and integrity are put to the test and where they are motivated to be correct and avoid looking incompetent. Accounts of an accident are often elicited in an atmosphere in which the individual is concerned not to admit culpability. This is particularly true of traffic accidents where victims may be invited to offer self-incriminating evidence. The victim may be willing to offer a frank account to an independent psychological investigator but where serious discrepancies emerge between accounts elicited by the police and by the psychologist the principle of confidentiality may seem to conflict with the principle of informed and fair justice. Moreover it is possible that the psychologist might be compelled to disclose confidential material to the court, either in a professional or civil capacity.

It was argued in Section V that the apparent absurdity of accidents demands an explanation. The search for an explanation may often be associated with emotive enquiries designed to apportion blame. Edwards (1981) has examined the structure and operation of accident surveillance systems in two companies. He concluded that the model of accident causation implicit in both systems was one based on culpable error and characterized by a concept of safety as an optional extra. This emphasizes that psychological matters do not exist in a moral vacuum, and the accident investigator needs to be conscientious in ensuring that he or she is not working with partisan assumptions about the causes of accidents.

X.—THE ROLE OF OTHER DISCIPLINES AND PROFESSIONS

Often psychological factors are not recognized as the most salient in accident investigation. Environmental features are particularly salient. The contribution of engineering is two-fold. First, engineering innovations can help prevent accidents by structuring the environment so as to isolate individuals from potentially hazardous situations: as intimated earlier, pedestrian accidents would be nil if pedestrians and vehicles were totally segregated. This may be an unnecessarily expensive and inefficient policy, however: effective reductions may be achieved without recourse to radical economic and social changes. Less radical examples of engineering improvements include those to do with the design of chemical containers and household architecture. Engineering can also reduce the severity of the *consequences* of accidents: for instance, good vehicle design (e.g., with respect to bumper construction and height) can reduce the likelihood of fatal injury to pedestrians. Measures of this kind may tend to shift the distribution of injuries from one category to another (e.g., from fatal to serious), rather than eradicate them. This kind of countermeasure forces us to re-examine the broader context in which accidents occur. Reducing the number of fatal injuries may mean an increase in the number of serious injuries, which implies greater demands on medical and social services. The evaluation of any countermeasure must explicitly acknowledge the wider consequences for other aspects of the system.

One cannot take account of the role of engineering without considering the interface between the individual and the environment. The concept of *interface* is complex and poorly defined. At one extreme the environment may be structured so as to permit the individual broad discretion in interpreting and dealing with the information presented. At the other extreme the environment may be rigidly structured and standardized producing extensive task automation. The inflexibility of the interface may conflict with the versatility of the human operator. Winsemius (1965) found that a group of machinists preferred a dangerous movement to a safer one because the safer one involved more complicated movements which interrupted the flow of activity. This was so even though the movement was recognized by the machinists as contributing directly to accidents involving the machinery in question. The opportunities for safer behaviour may be facilitated by designing more flexible and not more constrained man-environment interfaces. Legislation plays an important role in this regard in so far as certain practices are outlawed without actually altering the physical environment.

XI.—FUTURE PROSPECTS

Psychological approaches to accidents have emphasized the importance of individual human factors; yet many accidents occur in a context in which social elements are salient. To some extent all accidents are a product of faulty interaction between the individual and the physical environment. Some accidents, notably traffic accidents, involve two or more individuals interacting with one another in a physical situation. Interaction does not merely provide a social context in which individual traits are realized in behaviour, but the interaction actually forms the behaviour. This suggests that psychology ought to develop an approach to accidents based on social as well as individual units of analysis. In proposing a mainly social approach to the problem of accidents we are broadening our perspective on accident prevention. Accidents have many causes and have social, individual, legal, medical, financial and engineering dimensions. A strategic approach to accidents must be inter-disciplinary. Those working in the area of accident prevention have not tended to contemplate such an approach, preferring instead to work within disciplinary boundaries which lead to narrow evaluation and inflated claims about the success of isolated safety programmes. This kind of thinking also helps sustain a climate in which those who are concerned with safety continue to try out various countermeasures in the hope that doing something is better than doing nothing. Such conduct ignores the fact that any countermeasure has repercussions which extend beyond the immediate interests of the professionals responsible for its development and testing.

Howarth and Lightburn (1981) have outlined a strategic approach to child pedestrian safety which attempts to achieve a co-ordinated policy among psychologists, legislators and engineers. Any strategic approach requires a methodology which complements the complexity of the problem. Epidemiology is an approach to the study of diseases which emphasizes the multifactorial nature of the problem it studies, and it is one which is particularly useful in studying accidents (cf. Chapman, Foot, Sheehy and Wade, 1982). The overriding advantage of an epidemiological approach is that it offers a rigorous methodology capable of dealing with multiple dimensions within a unified framework.

More than anything else there is a basic need to examine popular beliefs and attitudes about accident causation. We suggested in Section V that popular beliefs about accidents are fatalistic to varying degrees. We need to know much more about the origins and correlates of these attitudes and beliefs and their consequences for safety policy. It is possible that one of the strongest determinants of the success of psychological countermeasures is the content of the views of the public about the likelihood of success and consequently the perceived need for safety programmes.

XII.—ANNOTATED READINGS

Chapman, A. J., Wade, F. M. and Foot, H. C. (1982). *Pedestrian Accidents*. Chichester: Wiley.

This edited volume offers a multi-disciplinary perspective on the problems of pedestrian accidents and road safety. Behavioural, educational, legal, social and engineering aspects are considered and the need for an integrated multi-disciplinary approach to road safety is a salient theme. An important feature of the book is that it provides an extensive annotated bibliography of published and unpublished material.

Haddon, W., Suchman, E. A. and Klein, D. (1964). *Accident Research: Methods and Approaches*. New York: Harper and Row.

This is an important reference volume. It comprises readings dealing with a range of disciplinary and theoretical perspectives and considers alternative methodologies in detail. Contributors consider problems in the design, implementation and evaluation of countermeasures, giving the book a distinctly applied flavour.

Kay, H. (1971). Accidents: some factors and theories. In: P. B. Warr (Ed.), *Psychology at Work*. Harmondsworth: Penguin.

This chapter examines conceptual and measurement problems from the perspective of an applied psychologist. Kay presents a two-stage model of accident causation based on the organization and execution of serially organized actions known as 'skills'. The model possesses considerable face validity.

Powell, P. I., Hale, M., Martin, J. and Simon, M. (1971). *2000 Accidents*. London: National Institute of Industrial Psychology.

This is a report about the incidence and causes of over 2000 minor and serious injuries which occurred in four types of industrial workshop. The report emphasizes the fact that accidents have multiple and inter-related causes. It also considers methodological and statistical issues in the operation and interpretation of accident surveillance systems. It is one of the most comprehensive and detailed studies of accident causation yet published.

Road Accidents, Great Britain, Annual Reports. Department of Transport. London: Her Majesty's Stationery Office.

The Department of Transport publishes annually a statistical summary of the incidence of transport-related accidents and casualties in Britain. Detailed breakdowns are provided: for example, by age, sex, severity of injury, and class of road user involved. This is a valuable guide to the way accident statistics are collected and reported, and it clearly highlights the need for theory to organize and make sense of the statistical subject matter.

Shaw, L. and Sichel, H. S. (1971). *Accident Proneness*. Oxford: Pergamon.

This book examines the concept of accident proneness in detail. The authors show that a single, unified concept of accident proneness does not exist, but that there is a large number of inter-correlated concepts. The evidence bearing on accident proneness is extensively reviewed, but in reading this book it should be borne in mind that subsequent research has cast still further doubt on the extent of the role of proneness in accident causation.

Miscellaneous

The Department of the Environment, Transport and Road Research Laboratory, Crowthorne, Berkshire, publishes an extensive range of specialized reports relating to traffic accidents. These are available from the Laboratory's library. Also published is a digest of the available reports.

XIII.—REFERENCES

Backett, E. M. and Johnston, A. M. (1959). Social patterns of road accidents to children. *British Medical Journal*, 1, 409–413.

Bain, K., Faegre, M. L. and Wyly, R. J. (1964). Behavior of young children under conditions simulating entrapment in refrigerators. In: W. Haddon, E. A. Suchman and D. Klein (Eds.) *Accident Research: Methods and Approaches*. New York: Harper and Row.

Brown, I. D. and Holloway, C. (1974). Unintentional Behaviour. Unit 15, Block 5, *Problems and Applications*, Course DS261 (Introduction to Psychology). Milton Keynes: Open University Press.

Chapman, A. J., Foot, H. C., Sheehy, N. P. and Wade, F. M. (1982). The social psychology of child pedestrian accidents. In: J. R. Eiser (Ed.): *Social Psychology and Behavioral Medicine*. Chichester: Wiley.

Codling, P. J. and Samson, P. (1974). Blood alcohol in road fatalities before and after the Road Safety Act, 1967. Department of the Environment, Transport and Road Research Laboratory, Supplementary Report 45UC. Crowthorne, Berkshire: TRRL.

Consumers' Association (1980). *Knocked Down: A Study of the Personal and Family Consequences of Road Accidents Involving Pedestrians and Pedal Cyclists*. London: Consumers' Association.

Edwards, M. (1981). The design of an accident investigation procedure. *Applied Ergonomics*, 12, 111–115.

Eysenck, H. J. (1964). *Crime and Personality*. London: Routledge and Kegan Paul.

Eysenck, H. J. (1965). *Fact and Fiction in Psychology*. Harmondsworth: Penguin.

Haddon, W., Valien, P., McCarroll, J. R. and Umberger, C. J. (1964). A controlled investigation of the characteristics of adult pedestrians injured by motor vehicles in Manhattan. In: W. Haddon, E. A. Suchman and D. Klein (Eds.), *Accident Research: Methods and Approaches*. New York: Harper and Row.

Hoinville, G., Berthoud, R. and Mackie, A. M. (1972). A study of accident rates among motorists who passed or failed an advanced driving test. Department of the Environment, Transport and Road Research Laboratory, Laboratory Report 499. Crowthorne, Berkshire: TRRL.

Howarth, C. I. and Lightburn, A. (1981). A strategic approach to child pedestrian safety. In: H. C. Foot, A. J. Chapman and F. M. Wade (Eds.) *Road Safety: Research and Practice*. Eastbourne: Praeger.

Kay, H. (1971). Accidents: some factors and theories. In: P. B. Warr (Ed.) *Psychology at Work*. Harmondsworth: Penguin.

Krall, V. (1964). Personality characteristics of accident repeating children. In: W. Haddon, E. A. Suchman and D. Klein (Eds.) *Accident Research: Methods and Approaches*. New York: Harper and Row.

Mackie, A. M. (1972). Research for a road safety campaign — accident statistics for advertising formulation. Department of the Environment, Transport and Road Research Laboratory, Laboratory Report 432. Crowthorne, Berkshire: TRRL.

Manheimer, D. I. and Mellinger, G. D. (1967). Personality characteristics of the child accident repeater. *Child Development*, 38, 491–513.

Marcus, I. M., Wilson, W., Kraft, I., Swander, D., Southerland, F. and Schulhopfer, E. (1964). An inter-disciplinary approach to accident patterns in children. In: W. Haddon, E. A. Suchman and D. Klein (Eds.) *Accident Research: Methods and Approaches*. New York: Harper and Row.

Margulec, I., Librach, G. and Schodel, M. (1970). Epidemiological study of accidents among residents of homes for the aged. *Journal of Gerontology*, **25**, 342–346.

McGuire, F. L. (1976). Personality factors in highway accidents. *Human Factors*, **18**, 433–442.

Mellinger, G. D. and Manheimer, D. I. (1967). An exposure-coping model of accident liability among children. *Journal of Health and Social Behaviour*, **8**, 96–106.

Mourant, R. R. and Rockwell, T. M. (1972). Strategies of visual search by novice and experienced drivers. *Human Factors*, **14**, 325–335.

Östberg, O. (1980). Risk perception of work behaviour in forestry: implications for accident prevention policy. *Accident Analysis and Prevention*, **12**, 189–200.

Page, T. J., Iwata, B. A. and Neef, N. A. (1976). Teaching pedestrian skills to retarded persons: generalization from the classroom to the natural environment. *Journal of Applied Behaviour Analysis*, **9**, 433–444.

Parry, M. H. (1968). *Aggression on the Road*. London: Tavistock.

Porterfield, A. L. (1960). Traffic fatalities, suicide and homicide. *American Sociological Review*, **25**, 897–901.

Powell, P. I., Hale, H., Martin, S. and Simon, M. (1971). *2000 Accidents*. London: National Institute of Industrial Psychology.

Preston, B. (1972). Statistical analysis of child pedestrian accidents in Manchester and Salford. *Accident Analysis and Prevention*, **4**, 323–332.

Read, J. H., Bradley, E. S., Morison, J. D., Lewall, D. and Clarke, D. A. (1963). The epidemiology and prevention of traffic accidents involving child pedestrians. *Canadian Medical Association Journal*, **89**, 687–701.

Sandels, S. (1975). *Children in Traffic*. London: Elek.

Smith, H. T. and Howarth, C. I. (1981). Accidents: the consequences of human error? In: C. I. Howarth and W. E. C. Gillham (Eds.) *The Structure of Psychology: An Introductory Text*. London: George, Allen and Unwin.

Winsemius, W. (1965). Some ergonomic aspects of safety. *Ergonomics*, **8**, 151–162.

Psychology and Social Problems
Edited by A. Gale and A. J. Chapman
© 1984 John Wiley & Sons Ltd.

CHAPTER 9

ANXIETY AND DEPRESSION

Tony Carr

I.—THE EXTENT OF THE PROBLEM

Anxiety and depression are the most common psychological disorders in the general population. This is reflected in the finding that the neuroses—a traditional term for the group of disorders that, are in the main, anxiety-based and which includes neurotic depression—account for almost two thirds of the primary psychological disorders seen by general medical practitioners (Shepherd, Cooper, Brown and Kalton, 1981). Furthermore, this high prevalence of primary anxiety and depressive disorders in the community does not include those psychosomatic illnesses and behaviour problems in which these emotions play a significant aetiological role and which cause so much suffering; for example, essential hypertension, headaches, duodenal ulcers, sexual dysfunction, insomnia, obesity, alcoholism etc. Additionally, anxiety is clearly important in many other clinical situations such as patients' recovery from surgery (Janis, 1969) and their ability to cope following a heart attack (Byrne 1979), and depression is a frequent reaction to chronic illnesses and/ or their treatment; for example, multiple sclerosis and cancer. One cannot help but conclude that the problem of anxiety and depression is of enormous proportions in terms of human distress and the consequent demand upon health and social services.

The terms 'disorder' and 'problem' have already been used frequently in association with anxiety and depression. This underlines that fact that these states, particularly anxiety, are not *always* abnormal and do not always constitute disorder. Disorder exists when the person's life is disrupted to an extent that the sufferer finds unacceptable (Carr, 1978). It is normal to feel anxious about events or activities which have potential outcomes that, from one's own perspective are painful or harmful; for example, leaving home, sitting examinations, visiting the dentist, speaking in public etc. It is normal to feel 'down', 'blue', lacking in energy and hopeless following a range of common life events which are characterized by disappointment or loss; for example, failing examinations, interpersonal rejection, redundancy etc. Also, the intense depressive reactions that are consequent upon major losses such as bereavement, abortion and amputation are so frequent and usually of finite duration that they are normal responses to these events. The essential normality of anxiety is also emphasized by its adaptive nature, in that it motivates us to behave in a manner that is designed to avert the anticipated harm; for example, parents of young children are ever mindful of the safety of their offspring and students prepare more thoroughly for examinations.

How then do we recognize or diagnose anxiety and depressive disorders? Are they simply disruptive and extreme instances of experiences, behaviour and cognitions that are otherwise normal? Clearly, there is some communality between normality and disorder but, in both anxiety and depression, there is a discontinuity. The severely anxious person is aware of changes in bodily functions, experience, cognition and behaviour of such dramatic proportions and apparent inexplicability that, frequently, he or she is forced to find radical 'explanations' to account for what is happening. For example, agoraphobic sufferers often make such interpretations of their experience as 'I am dying' or 'I am having a heart attack', and in obsessional disorders people commonly confess that 'I think I am going mad'. In depression of clinical proportions the person is not simply very 'down' or 'blue' but holds so firmly to negative views of himself, his past and his future that they assume a delusional quality (Beck, 1967; Rowe, 1978); for example, 'I am a totally useless and worthless person' or even 'my internal organs are rotting'. In general there are few difficulties in recognizing or diagnosing anxiety and depressive disorders although many patients will have been subjected to a variety of medical investigations to exclude physical causes for their complaints, before they are seen by a clinical psychologist.

Anxiety is usually manifested in a characteristic pattern of subjective experience, psychological changes and behaviour: feelings of apprehension and tension, tachycardia, breathlessness, perspiration, restlessness, gastric disturbances, urinary frequency, and distractibility. In extreme instances or panics these changes are magnified and are accompanied by such experiences as dizziness, of walking on shifting ground, a feeling of imminent fainting, dying or 'losing control'. It is difficult to determine the prevalence of anxiety disorders in the community because people are often very reluctant to disclose their problems for fear of ridicule or admission to mental hospital. Also, people often regard these experiences as signs of weakness in themselves and seek to conceal them, preferring to design their lives around the problem and to contain it. Clearly, these factors affect the accuracy of community surveys as well as estimates based upon cases seen in clinical practice. The commonest specific anxiety disorders are agoraphobia, fears of public and crowded places, with a prevalence of up to 6.3 per 1000 (Agras,

Sylvester and Oliveau, 1969), illness phobias, social phobias and a large group of miscellaneous phobias of animals, heights, thunderstorms etc. There is also a further group, of obsessional disorders, in which the anxiety provokes intrusive thoughts and extensive and ritualized checking or preventive behaviours; for example, fears and thoughts of contamination lead to frequent, ritualized washing that may last for over one hour. The prevalence of obsessional states is about 0.5 per 1000 (Woodruff and Pitts, 1964).

Unipolar depression or depression which does not recur in a cyclical pattern interspersed by periods of elation, is the commonest form of depression. It is traditional, though by no means universally accepted, to divide unipolar depressions into *reactive* and *endogenous* types, the former being seen as a reaction to life events and the latter as arising from some biochemical process within the body. One obvious problem with this disputed dichotomy is the clinician's ability or willingness to perceive a relationship between the depressive state and previous events in the person's life. Whatever the nuances of diagnosis, the basic picture of depression is unmistakeable: apathy, sadness, disturbances of sleep, appetite and concentration, strong feelings of helplessness, hopelessness and personal worthlessness. Often there is psychomotor retardation in the form of slowness in thought and action, although the picture may be confounded by agitation. For the depressed person the world is bleak and the future hopeless. It is not surprising that suicide is one potential, although infrequent, outcome.

To conclude this section we should note that according to figures collated by the Office of Health Economics, in the United Kingdom (excluding Northern Ireland) during 1981 there were 7.5 million prescriptions of antidepressant drugs and 21.9 million prescriptions of sedatives and tranquillizers.

II.—CONCEPTS OF THE PERSON AND MODELS OF HUMAN BEHAVIOUR

Concepts of the person, or 'models of man', have exerted two contrasting influences upon attempts to explain the nature and causes of anxiety and depression. It is inevitable that general notions about the nature of man and human behaviour will influence, or even dictate the types of explanations that are proposed to account for abnormalities of human functioning. Early physicalist concepts of man prompted compatible explanations of disorders. Thus Hippocrates believed that depression resulted from an accumulation of black bile in the brain and as late as the turn of the nineteenth century Kraepelin, who laid the basis of contemporary psychiatric classification, argued that all psychiatric disorders had an organic aetiology. Similarly, the only all-encompassing psychological model of man, psychoanalytic theory, used its own concepts and principles to explain psychological dysfunction. It has been the failure of such macro-theories to provide explanations that have survived experimental investigation that has led to the current emphasis upon mini-theories, upon models of *specific* types of human functioning. Accordingly, contemporary theories of anxiety and depression share a number of common features: (a) they are relatively circumscribed in application; (b) they use variables that lend themselves to empirical investigation, although sometimes with difficulty; (c) they are multifactorial, in recognition of the diverse influences upon human functioning and the range of human processes involved in their aetiology and symptomatology; and (d) they have a recent history of development and refinement in response to improvements in measurement and in techniques of data analysis. Recent reviews and syntheses of theories of anxiety and depressive disorders are illustrative of these points (Akiskal and McKinney, 1975; Carr, 1978).

The predominant contemporary psychological approach to depression combines in varying degrees a number of originally disparate areas of work, theorizing and description: *viz. cognitive theory* (Beck, 1974), *learning theory* (Lewinsohn, 1974), *learned helplessness* (Seligman, 1974) and *attribution theory* (Abramson, Seligman and Teasdale, 1978). The core of this approach is the phenomenon of learned helplessness in which, as a result of uncontrollable aversive experiences, the person believes that events beyond those involved in the original learning are outside their control. The affective, cognitive, motivational and somatic concomitants of depression are seen as a consequence of this belief in the noncontingency of behaviour and outcomes. The elucidation of procedures that induce learned helplessness provided an experimental paradigm that has been used extensively to investigate depression and which has revitalized work in this field. Inevitably, explanations of learned helplessness effects and their correspondence with clinical depression were found wanting in some respects and other theoretical developments were adduced in order to remedy these defects. For example, there have always been some subjects in empirical studies who have been relatively, or completely, insensitive to helplessness-inducing procedures. A reformulation of the helplessness model incorporating individuals' *attributional* styles and the factors that influence attributional processes was developed to account for this and other inconsistencies (Abramson, Seligman and Teasdale, 1978; Abramson, Garber and Seligman, 1980).

In brief, the current position is that the helplessness or depressive reaction develops when individuals believe that they cannot control their environment *and* when they attribute this helplessness to themselves rather than to environmental conditions (internal attribution) *and* if this attribution is made in all circumstances and not just to the circumstance that engendered the helplessness (global attribution). So, it is proposed that depression results from an exaggerated tendency to make *internal*, *stable* and *global* attributions for *negative* outcomes and *external*, *unstable* and *specific* attributions for *positive* outcomes. Although there is now a good deal of evidence in support of the attributional/learned helplessness approach to depression, the advance in theory has generated its own, new problems; for example, it does not yet explain why only *some* people make internal, stable and global attributions for uncontrollable or aversive events.

Just as the learned helplessness paradigm has stimulated theoretical developments in the field of depression so another experimental paradigm, classical conditioning, has facilitated our understanding of the origins of anxiety. In the form of the *two-factor theory* of fear and avoidance (Mowrer, 1939) it has dominated research into anxiety disorders and their treatment by psychological means and it was not until the turn of the last decade (Carr, 1978; Rachman, 1977) that the weight of conflicting data prompted recognition of its inadequacies and elaboration of possible alternatives and refinements.

There is substantial evidence, both experimental and observational, that anxiety disorders can develop through the process of classical conditioning. The likelihood that this will happen depends upon a number of factors such as physiological and emotional attributes of the person, the number of pairings of CS and UCS, the confinement of the person during the pairings and the intensity of the UCS. The conditioned fear generalizes to similar stimuli and motivates fear reducing behaviours, such as avoidance, these behaviours being reinforced by the fear reduction achieved.

Although the model has been refined in various ways, it is now recognized that it is an inadequate account of anxiety development and that anxiety may be acquired by processes which cannot be encompassed by the conditioning paradigm. Rachman (1977) points out that anxiety can be acquired by observing an anxious person (modelling) and by the mere receipt of information about aversive outcomes (information transmission). In order to reconcile the apparently disparate processes of classical conditioning, modelling and information transmission in the acquisition of human fears, it has been proposed that they have in common a cognitive factor, the development of an *anticipation* of harmful outcome when certain stimuli are present (Carr, 1978). It is these stimuli that become phobic objects and anxiety provoking situations, anxiety being evoked by the anticipation of harm in their presence.

Anxiety is an aversive state and people attempt to behave in ways that reduce it. Where physical avoidance is possible, the classical picture of a phobic disorder results; for example, the socially phobic person avoids all social contacts and becomes a social isolate, with panic being the result of exceptional and unforeseen social encounters. When avoidance is not possible other 'solutions' are attempted; for example, people fearful of contamination cannot avoid using toilets and are forced to such lengths as covering the toilet seat to prevent skin contact and prolonged, ritualized washing afterwards. Of course, there are some feared events that do not allow such 'reasonable' anxiety-reducing activity and the person suffers repeated intrusive and aversive thoughts and chronic anxiety regarding death, illness, insoluble conflict etc. It is not difficult to see how the unavailability of 'reasonable' anxiety reducing activities, their failure, or their associated costs in social and familial terms, can create helplessness-inducing experiences and lead to depression.

III.—INDIVIDUAL ASSESSMENT

The objectives of clinical assessment are (i) to determine the nature, extent and severity of the problems; (ii) to construct a satisfactory working model of the development and maintenance of the problem; (iii) to estimate the sufferer's resources and deficits/disadvantages in individual, social and environmental terms; and (iv), in the light of (i) to (iii), to formulate an appropriate response or strategy of intervention.

In view of the diversity and complexity of the information needed to pursue these objectives, it is inevitable that the interview plays a central role in the assessment of the individual. It is important to recognize that the interview serves more functions than the simple acquisition of information by question and answer. It is best regarded as a process in which the psychologist functions as a participant-observer, listening, eliciting information, responding to the patient, observing behaviour, monitoring the interaction and using the information accrued to guide further interaction.

In a well conducted interview, the eliciting of information relevant to objectives (i) and (iii) is combined with the search for information that extends and refines working hypotheses relevant to (ii). In this latter aspect the clinical interview is comparable to an experiment, with hypotheses being developed and information sought that confirms or refutes predictions made on the basis of the hypotheses. In the course of these processes the psychologist observes and notes such features as the patient's dress and appearance, demeanour, motor activity, alertness, eye-contact, speed of understanding, rate and style of speech, speed of recall, and topics the patient avoids discussing. The interview is closed when objectives (i) to (iii) are achieved. In practice, when assessing disorders of anxiety and depression, this is rarely achieved in less than two hours, the time being distributed over a number of sessions to allow other forms of assessment, such as self-rating scales and diary recording, to be interpolated.

Diary recording is a particularly useful tool, especially in the assessment of anxiety disorders. Between interviews, the patient records every incident in which significant anxiety and associated behaviour occurred. A careful analysis of these data usually reveals the specific stimuli to which the person responds with anxiety. This refines the information obtained in interview and may significantly modify the formulation of a therapeutic strategy. For example, it may become apparent that a man's disabling anxiety-response to people in authority is confined to those who make him angry and his anxiety occurs in response to his feelings of anger: he fears 'losing control' rather than any action or attribute of the other person. Such a finer analysis of the problem would orient therapy towards training in the social skills of appropriate self-assertion and expression of feelings rather than, or in addition to, a general anxiety reduction technique. Further detail on the nature of anxiety-provoking events may be obtained by observing the patient behaving in the relevant situation and, if practicable, in a role-play of the situation. Particular attention is paid to the stimuli that precede the person's anxiety reactions and behaviour, and to the consequences of his reactions.

There are many general self-report inventories that can provide limited information on anxiety levels and problems: e.g., the 16 Personality Factor Questionnaire (Cattell, Eber and Tatsuoka, 1970) and the Crown-Crisp Experiential Index (Crown and Crisp, 1979). Of more specific use in assessing anxiety problems are fear survey schedules. The form published by Wolpe and Lang (1964) comprises 108 items commonly found to evoke anxiety and the respondent is asked to indicate the degree of disturbance aroused by each. This provides a valuable assessment of the extent and severity of anxiety problems in the individual case. Another self-report inventory of specific relevance is the State-Trait Anxiety Inventory (Spielberger, Gorsuch and Lushene, 1970). In this instrument, a useful distinction is made between state anxiety—a transitory emotional condition characterized by subjective feelings of tension and apprehension, and trait anxiety—a relatively stable disposition of anxiety-proneness, the individual's tendency to respond to situations perceived as threatening with raised state anxiety. Both forms are brief and easy to complete, the former being particularly useful in assessing subjective feelings of anxiety in response to actual situations.

For a complete and thorough assessment of the anxiety evoked by particular stimuli or situations, one would need to consider physiological changes as well as subjective and behavioural ones. Typically, a parameter such as heart-rate or skin conductance would be monitored during the patient's exposure to the stimuli and these data would be considered together with the behavioural and subjective information.

Generally there are few problems in establishing the presence of depression and the interview is normally sufficient in this respect. Where doubt, or important problems of differential diagnosis exist, the use of a general diagnostic instrument has been the typical procedure for many years, for example the Minnesota Multiphasic Personality Inventory (MMPI). However, depression scales such as the MMPI-D suffer from a number of psychometric weaknesses and are insufficiently sensitive in assessing the *depth* of depression. Consequently, a variety of scales have evolved whose purpose is to assess the severity of depression through an assessment of the intensity or frequency of the subjective, somatic and behavioural aspects of the disorder.

The most popular observer rating scale is the Hamilton Rating Scale for Depression (Hamilton, 1967). When used by two independent raters, a reliable assessment of the severity of depression is obtained. Although subject to the biases of the raters, observer ratings such as this avoid several weaknesses of self-report inventories including uncooperativeness or failure to understand the items.

Several self-report scales of depression are now available of which the most widely used is the Beck Depression Inventory (BDI) (Beck, Ward, Mendelson, Mock and Erbaugh, 1961). It provides a sensitive index of the severity of depression and has yielded acceptable reliability and validity coefficients. The BDI consists of 21 groups of self-evaluative statements, each referring to a common behavioural, cognitive or somatic aspect of depression. The respondents indicate the statement(s) that best describe their experience here and now. In a clinical population some patients need assisting in the completion of the inventory. The BDI is a useful assessment and screening instrument with both clinical and non-clinical populations although distortion will be common with extremely depressed people. This scale and the several other observer and self-report scales are well reviewed by Carroll, Fielding and Blashki, (1973).

IV.—THE IMMEDIATE SOCIAL AND EMOTIONAL ENVIRONMENT

Extreme anxiety and depression each result in such marked changes in the person's behaviour, attitudes, motivation and cognition that there are inevitable consequences for the people with whom they interact. Within the interdependent relationships of family and marriage such consequences may be profound, as they will be in work environments where the person's performance deteriorates in a function that is integral to a corporate activity. Specific anxiety disorders, such as phobic and obsessional states, and depressive disorders are so totally encompassing and invasive that they frequently dominate the life of the family as well as that of the sufferer.

Typically, the agoraphobic sufferer is a woman living with her family (Marks, 1969); as she becomes more restricted her family inevitably becomes involved. She may require the assurance of constant companionship, even at home. Young children may be kept at home and prevented from going to school on the slightest pretext, or the husband may lose time from work. Travelling, except by car, and shopping become impossible. Eventually, all external and many home-based activities are abandoned, the woman being supported by a family who fulfill her former functions, so that the husband does the shopping, older children meet younger ones from school and so on. It is not uncommon to find a teenage girl struggling with schoolwork after a day burdened by shopping, cooking and cleaning for her agoraphobic mother.

In obsessional states, such as those centred on fears of contamination, the person may create strict procedures of cleanliness and decontamination for the whole family; for example, all clothes must be changed immediately upon entering the house and conveyed to the washing machine with rubber gloves, the porch or hall being washed down and disinfected. The house is regularly scrubbed and kept orderly and spotless. Visitors are banned and holidays or outings are avoided. Where the sufferer is a wife and mother she may be unable to prepare food for fear of contaminating it and poisoning her family. At work the obsessional becomes inefficient and inflexible. Concentration on checking or rituals makes people slow and rigid in their approach to tasks: this is as disruptive of manufacturing and assembly tasks as it is of teaching, or office work.

The depressed person usually affects those around them by virtue of inactivity and negativism, rather than by deviant or disruptive activity. The negative views of the past, present and future, the feelings of hopelessness and worthlessness, the lack of interest and motivation and the slowing of thought and behaviour, which are central to many depressive reactions, mean that the person can no longer fulfil previously active roles. Where these roles are important to the functioning of the family, work or social group, severe disruption results with the unfulfilled tasks falling to other people. Also, in the family setting it is difficult to prevent the profoundly negative emotional tone of the depressed person pervading the atmosphere of the home with obvious deleterious consequences.

Inevitably, it is the most intense functional and emotional relationships that are most severely affected by anxiety and depression. Frequently, it is the marital relationship that comes under most strain and this may be exacerbated by the sexual dysfunction that is common in agoraphobia, obsessional states and depression. Of course, where the emotional and behavioural consequences of a depressed spouse satisfy the *needs of the partner*, for example, to support and provide for the spouse or to manage the children, the disorder may paradoxically *strengthen* their relationship. This development can create obstacles and ethical problems for therapeutic intervention. Also, we must remember that children learn much by word of mouth and by imitation or modelling (Bandura, 1976) and an anxious or depressed parent can provide a powerful model. For example, Solyom, Beck, Solyom and Hugel (1974), in their study of 47 phobic individuals and their families, observed the verbal and non-verbal transmission of fears from parents to children.

Overall, it is clear that the characteristics of anxiety and depressive states will lead to severe disruptions and distortions of family life in many instances. The magnitude of the problem of anxiety and depression is significantly increased by these interactive effects in both the short and longer terms.

V. — THE WIDER SOCIAL AND ORGANIZATIONAL ENVIRONMENT

Although there are many difficulties in demonstrating the processes through which social factors may exert a causative influence in anxiety and depression, it is likely that the social network within which a person lives and works serves as an index of that person's vulnerability to these reactions (Zubin, 1979). In general terms the more fully a person is integrated into a supportive social network the less vulnerable they will be to the life stresses that provoke anxiety and depressive reactions. The effect is that of reducing the likelihood of severe adverse reactions rather than of reducing the number of provoking events.

The strength of the effect of social network appears to be greater for depression than for anxiety disorders and although some of the data merely reveal associations with such crude variables as social class, finer analyses delineate specific aspects of social class membership that index vulnerability. Also, at this finer level of description it is possible to envisage the processes through which vulnerability, or protection, may arise.

The pioneering study by Brown and Harris (1978) of a sample of women in a London borough revealed that depression was four times more prevalent among working-class women than middle-class. This striking difference was not due to differences in the frequency of provoking events, for the effect remained when such differences as existed were controlled for. Detailed analysis indicated that vulnerability to depression following a provoking event is indexed by such factors as the lack of a confiding relationship, having three or more children under 14 living at home and lacking employment away from home. The identification of these factors helps to explain the association between vulnerability and social class. Also, their specificity allows consideration of the processes through which vulnerability factors may exert their effect.

Earlier we discussed the role of helplessness-inducing experiences, the experience of uncontrollable aversive events in the aetiology of depression, and the anticipation of harm in the aetiology of anxiety. In considering the relationship between anxiety and the wider social environment, there is a substantial body of experimental work that reveals the importance of the unpredictability and uncontrollability of aversive events in the causation of anxiety (Weiss, 1970). Overall, the less predictable and controllable a noxious event is, the more stress and anxiety it will elicit in anticipation. These two variables each contribute to the intensity of anxiety so that, for example, an uncontrollable noxious event elicits less anticipatory anxiety when it can be predicted than when its timing is unknown and an unpredictable event elicits less anxiety when control is possible despite ignorance of its timing.

When one considers the living environment and the organizational structure of society experienced by many people today, it is clear that these have characteristics that are potentially stressful, anxiety provoking and depressiogenic. There are many things that are moderately or extremely aversive to some people: noise, crowding, poor housing, litter, road building and other city developments that detract from the environment. Conditions and events such as these are not only aversive but they are experienced by most people as *uncontrollable*. Whatever the theoretical possibilities of moving house, influencing the decisions of local government, public enquiries etc., the common experience is one of helplessness in the face of economic and political realities.

There are other aspects of contemporary experience that go beyond aversiveness in being a perceived threat to life, health, welfare of children, and self-esteem. Youth unemployment, redundancy, nuclear war or accident, inadequate schooling, lead in the atmosphere and in tap water, cancer and so on, are characterized not only by their potential harmfulness but also by varying degrees of uncontrollability and unpredictability. It is hardly surprising that carcinophobia is the commonest illness phobia and fears of nuclear war, with avoidance of newspapers, radio and television news broadcasts, are increasingly common in clinical practice.

This listing of potential stressors and sources of threat may seem unremittingly bleak and dangerous but it is the reality of experience for many who are anxious or depressed. However, most people are neither excessively anxious nor depressed. This underlines the central role of individual differences, for whatever the nature of the wider environment, all variables interact with the characteristics of the individual and it is the outcome of this interaction that determines whether or not anxiety or depression will develop.

VI.—TYPES OF INTERVENTION

There are many intervention techniques with potential applicability to anxiety or depressive disorders. Apart from the specific content of each problem and the unique attributes of each patient, this is due to the multifarious 'routes' through which the disorders may develop. For example: a totally disabling travel phobia could develop from a traumatic incident while travelling (although this would be rare). Despite generalization to other forms of transport than that originally involved, the phobia could be treated by a straightforward fear-reduction technique such as desensitization, flooding or graduated *in vivo* exposure. Alternatively, the phobia could be secondary to another anxiety only coincidentally related to travelling. Changes at work could create unavoidable, daily anxiety-provoking situations resulting, primarily, from the person's inability to assert himself appropriately in interpersonal encounters. Anxiety in anticipation of these encounters occurs every day while travelling to work and the phobia develops through conditioning and generalization. In this case, in addition to treatment of the travel fears, the social skill deficit would require assertiveness training with modelling and, possibly, anxiety management training. In time, and without help, depression might ensue, necessitating an approach such as Beck's (1976) cognitive therapy. Clearly, in practice, an intervention strategy is a carefully constructed amalgam of techniques, whose content and combination are specific to the patient and which are implemented synergistically by a skilful therapist.

The choice of a contemporary treatment for anxiety is determined primarily by practicability and relevance in the specific case. Considerations of likely efficacy are paramount in view of the consensus that fears are acquired through processes of associative learning.

Training in deep muscular relaxation (DMR) is a component of several approaches to anxiety problems. The patient learns to achieve a state of deep relaxation through focused relaxation of most major voluntary muscle groups in the body. This skill is then used to inhibit or control anxiety during exposure to the feared stimuli in desensitization, anxiety management and *in vivo* exposure. Generally, anxiety management is the most prophylactic of the three in stressing the patient's ability to control anxiety in the future, irrespective of the stimuli responsible. In contrast to these methods which involve imaginal and/or actual exposure to an ordered hierarchy of fear stimuli, flooding utilizes neither DMR nor graduated exposure. Flooding requires the client to undergo extended, non-hierarchical exposure to the highly anxiety provoking stimuli that might actually be encountered. The stress of flooding and the risk of counter-therapeutic effects tend to restrict its use to cases where other more gradual approaches have failed, or where time is a critical factor.

Modelling involves the patient's copying the therapist's performance of the feared activity and may be combined with anxiety management training to facilitate this process. It has obvious applicability to activities that arouse anxiety, rather than to focal fear stimuli, and it is of particular relevance in the treatment of obsessional behaviours in conjunction with response prevention. The latter is the voluntary or imposed embargo upon perform-ance of the obsessional behaviour.

Treatments for depression are either predominantly cognitive with associ-ated behavioural assignments (e.g. Beck, Rush, Shaw and Emery, 1979) or concentrate on social skills training and other techniques designed to increase the number of positive reinforcements received by the patient (e.g., Lewin-sohn, 1975). With respect to earlier discussions of the aetiology of depression it should be noted that both approaches involve the patient in experiences of mastery and efficacy. Cognitive therapy stresses the patient's learning to identify and to correct maladaptive cognitions and attributions. Activity schedules are used to provide success experiences and the therapist gives feedback and reinforcement for appropriate behavioural and cognitive change.

VII.—IS PSYCHOLOGICAL INTERVENTION SUCCESSFUL?

The question posed above is more appropriately phrased as '*how* successful is psychological intervention?'. Even when rephrased, the question has no simple answer. Despite the large number of relevant publications each year, the question needs qualifying in the light of such further questions as: *which* therapy?; for *which* problems?; compared to *what* alternative strategies?; and by *what* criteria is success to be judged? With such qualifications, the answer may be more precise but remains relative. For example, if it were known that social skills training eliminates all relevant anxiety and avoidance behaviours in 80% of social phobias of recent onset, how successful is it if *two-thirds* of neurotic disorders remit spontaneously (without intervention) within two years and if 20% of effectively treated clients experience frustration of new employment aspirations in the face of a depressed economy?

Studies of the effectiveness of psychological therapies are becoming increasingly sophisticated through attention to problems such as those mentioned above. The accumulation of data indicating the general effectiveness of psychological intervention has focused attention upon the relative power of different approaches and identification of the active components of effective interventions. An example will clarify some of the main points.

McLean and Hakstian (1979) randomly allocated almost two hundred depressed outpatients to either a behavioural therapy, a psychotherapy, a drug therapy, or an attention-placebo condition. The patients were between 20 and 60 years old; had been depressed for at least the previous 2 months and for almost 11 years on average; were diagnosed as suffering with primary depression on the basis of a clinical interview; and scored at or beyond the moderate level on standardized measures of depression such as the Beck Depression Inventory (BDI). All fourteen therapists were experienced in the treatment they conducted and level of experience was examined as an independent variable. Treatment comprised eight to twelve weekly sessions and audio recordings were used to confirm that the treatments used by the therapists were discriminably different from each other. Treatment outcome was assessed with a variety of measures including the BDI and assessments of mood, social functioning, somatic changes, cognitive activity and coping. Patients who dropped out were replaced by additional patients to reduce the effects of a differential attrition rate between the treatments.

Assessment at post-treatment showed that behaviour therapy was significantly superior to all other treatments on three measures including mood, and significantly superior to psychotherapy on six of the ten main measures including mood, BDI scores and social functioning. At this stage 50% of the behaviour therapy patients scored within the normal range on the BDI compared to 25% of each of the psychotherapy and drug therapy groups and 28% of the attention placebo group. Follow-up at 3 months indicated fewer significant differences, with behaviour therapy superior to all other treatments in terms of social functioning and superior to psychotherapy on the mood measure. There was no effect for therapist experience and the drop-out rates were behaviour therapy 5%, drug therapy 36%, psychotherapy 30%, and attention placebo 26%.

This study is exemplary in several respects such as the use of a large number of subjects who were clinically depressed, random assignment to treatments, clear specification of treatment procedures in advance, the use of experienced and qualified therapists, investigation of therapist experience in relation to treatment outcome, the use of recordings showing that the treatments were indeed different from each other, independent documentation that patients receiving the drug treatment were following the prescribed regimen, the use of an attention placebo procedure to control for non-specific effects of treatment and multiple assessments of outcome including a test (BDI) of known reliability and validity.

On the debit side, 10 weeks is hardly sufficient for an insight-based psychotherapy to produce optimal results. Although subsequent follow-ups are planned, a follow-up period of 3 months is rather short in view of the decrease in differences between treatment outcomes over this time. All outcome data were obtained through self-report inventories returned in the post and one of these inventories was of unknown validity.

The study of McLean and Hakstian is fairly typical of contemporary outcome research and it can be readily seen that it allows a positive, if relative and qualified, answer to the question posed in this section. Although this example was concerned with depression, a similar but more positive picture is revealed by outcome studies of therapies for anxiety disorders which are well reviewed by Rachman and Wilson (1980).

VIII.—METHODOLOGICAL AND PRACTICAL PROBLEMS

Effective measurement, particularly of anxiety, is probably the greatest single practical problem with important consequences for research, theory and treatment. The problem arises from the tri-dimensionality of anxiety in comprising subjective, behavioural and physiological elements and from the knowledge that these three components are only loosely coupled (Morrow and Labrum, 1978). The poor correlation between changes in these systems is known as desynchrony (Rachman and Hodgson, 1974) and the practical implication is that we need to assess each component system, rather than only one, if we are to obtain an accurate and detailed picture of the state of the research subject or patient in treatment.

In practice this requires self-report of subjective experience, observation of behaviour in relevant situations and measurement of an autonomic parameter such as skin conductance during exposure to the anxiety-provoking stimuli. The techniques for such comprehensive assessments are currently available, in varying degrees of sophistication, but the time and effort required in their application are inevitable obstacles to their routine use. Consider the few criticisms made of the McLean and Hakstian (1979) study in the previous section. It was pointed out that 3 months was too short a follow-up interval, particularly in view of the reduction in differences between treatment outcomes that was apparent over this period. The authors were aware of this weakness and planned further follow-ups at regular intervals over two years. The work, time and cost that would have been involved in direct observation of the patients' behaviour, psychomotor speed and other measures, on these successive occasions, were undoubtedly responsible for the use of self-report inventories returned by post in the acquisition of follow-up data.

However, the resources invested in detailed measurement will bring significant returns in terms of more rapid reconciliation and development of theoretical models and the refinement of more effective treatments. For example, it is likely that treatments with different emphases will differentially affect the several aspects of anxiety and depression: behavioural therapies may effect changes in behaviour earlier, or more powerfully, than verbally based cognitive therapies, and the latter may have a specific relevance to such factors as attributional style. It is only by reliable and valid measurement of the several aspects of anxiety and depression that the momentum of contemporary theoretical and treatment developments will be maintained.

IX.—PROBLEMS OF ETHICS AND CONFIDENTIALITY

It is unavoidable that in the course of psychological research and intervention, psychologists obtain information of a very personal and often sensitive nature about research participants and clients. The problem is that of protecting the confidentiality of the information and the person's right to privacy. It is hardly surprising that this issue has been the focus of a number of recent official reports in the UK and receives specific attention in the American Psychological Association's Ethical Standards of Psychologists and in the Guidelines for the Professional Practice of Clinical Psychology prepared by the Clinical Division of The British Psychological Society.

It is relatively easy, with care and attention, to develop a personal habit of confidentiality. However, this does not obviate the difficulties that can arise in particular circumstances such as working in multidisciplinary teams, conducting therapeutic work with couples and families and when the client discloses information with serious societal implications. Problems such as these have, of course, been the concern of professions such as medicine for many years. They have become concerns for psychology, particularly clinical psychology, as it has evolved from its early technical role of psychological testing under the direction of psychiatrists, to its contemporary role as an independent profession carrying day-to-day responsibility for clinical intervention and research in a wide variety of human problems across a range of health-care and social settings.

In addition to issues of confidentiality that may arise in specific circumstances, most of which can be resolved satisfactorily, problems of confidentiality exist in connection with the notes and records kept by clinical psychologists who work in the National Health Service (NHS). Within the NHS, patients' case-notes are the property of the employer and, *in extremis*, the psychologist is unable to prevent his employer gaining access to his records, however sensitive the information they might contain. Accordingly, clinical psychologists employed within the British NHS consider carefully the nature of information about patients that they commit to permanent record.

Given that strategies of intervention are concerned with helping people change the ways in which they behave, feel, think and relate to other people, the psychologist is constantly faced with ethical decisions in the course of clinical practice. In this context, the guiding principle is the use of the client's 'informed consent' to the intended strategies. This term refers to the client's consent in full knowledge of the procedures involved, their cost in personal and familial terms and their likely consequences. In most instances of anxiety and depressive disorders a full and detailed explanation by the psychologist, which is itself often a component of therapy, is usually sufficient to ensure that the patient's consent is appropriately 'informed'. However, there is a significant minority of cases, particularly in profound depression or extreme distress and anxiety, where serious doubt must remain about the extent of the patient's understanding and appreciation. A generally useful strategy is to review the patient's consent at several stages throughout the course of the intervention. For example, a severely depressed and agoraphobic housewife may wish to discontinue therapy in the light of increasing marital discord as her depression and phobic symptoms are resolved, particularly if her husband declines to participate in future therapeutic sessions. It is only by regularly reviewing consent that the client has an unambiguous opportunity to withdraw that consent.

Clinical research shares with other psychological research the ethical concerns of research with human subjects. Additionally, there are problems that are specific to such activities as therapeutic outcome research. Consider the use of no-treatment control groups which are necessary if the effects of a therapy are to be properly evaluated. In the McLean and Hakstian study discussed earlier, this group received a dummy treatment to control for the effects of therapist attention. Clearly, such procedures present a unique ethical dilemma in balancing the likely general beneficial effects of such research against the possible cost to individuals who are assigned to control groups from which active treatment is witheld. Existing guidelines and ethical codes contain recommended procedures that minimize the risk of unacceptable consequences to control subjects, but the ethical problem of this cost-benefit equation remains.

X.—THE ROLE OF OTHER DISCIPLINES AND PROFESSIONS

In treating disorders of anxiety and depression the psychologist is one of a number of professionals who might be involved in the care of the patient, either concurrently or in succession. The role played by the psychologist is highly dependent upon the health-care setting within which the service is provided. Until the early years of the last decade, most British clinical psychologists worked within the confines of the large psychiatric hospitals, receiving referrals from psychiatrists who retained overall control of the care of the patient. However, subsequent to the organization of psychology departments that enabled psychological services to be provided across the whole of a Health Authority and following the publication of the Trethowan Report (1977), in which the independent professional status of psychology was recognized, the number of settings within which psychologists work and the range of other professions with which they collaborate has increased dramatically.

Psychological services continue to be provided to psychiatric hospitals where problems of anxiety and depression are seen usually at the request of psychiatrists. The psychologist works in collaboration with the psychiatrist, psychiatric nurse and social worker, among others. The psychiatrist, by virtue of medical training and subsequent in-service training in psychiatry, is uniquely equipped to deal with organic disorders and to administer physical treatments such as electroconvulsive therapy for depression and pharmacological treatments for both anxiety and depression. The social worker is the link between the inpatient, the patient's family, and work, and can provide vital information about the patient's social and familial background, support the family both directly and through detailed knowledge of the welfare system, and play a key role during and after the patient's return to the community. The nurse plays a vital role in providing information about the patient and in the patient's general management, for it is the nurse who has the most extensive contact with the patient. In this setting, whether or not physical treatments are central to therapy, the psychiatrist usually assumes the role of manager, involving other professions and coordinating their activities according to personal judgement. However, in a good multidisciplinary team the overall care of the patient rests with the *team* and the professionals involved assume 'keyworker' status as and when their particular skills are called upon by team decisions and become preeminent in the therapeutic effort.

Although psychologists may see anxious or depressed patients in a range of medical settings such as surgical wards, intensive care units and dialysis units, where the role of the physician is comparable to that of the psychiatrist above, most people with anxiety and depressive disorders are seen as outpatients. The physical setting may be the psychology department, a district general hospital or, increasingly, community health centres. Referrals may come from any source or the patients may self-refer. Apart from the all-too-rare presence of a nurse therapist, who is trained in the use of behaviour therapies, and the professionals already mentioned, the general medical practitioner is the other professional who is frequently involved in the care of outpatients. The general practitioner will often seek the psychologist's advice in the management of a patient and, usually, will act upon this advice. Alternatively, a request may be made for the psychologist's intervention. In this case, providing there is no physical disorder, the general practitioner will usually cease active involvement until the psychologist terminates the intervention. However, pharmacological treatments started before the psychologist's involvement may continue by repeat prescription until withdrawn at the psychologist's request. When working with outpatients the psychologist normally carries day-to-day responsibility for the treatment of psychological problems, and treatment decisions are taken together with the patient.

Clearly, the medical profession continues to play an important role in the treatment of anxious and depressed patients. The reasons for this are predominantly historical and have little to do with the relevance of medical skills to the problems involved. It is hardly surprising that there is an increasing trend for clinical psychologists to work in the community and persistent calls for the demedicalization of the treatment of neurotic and behaviour disorders (e.g., Rachman and Wilson, 1980). This would include psychologists providing psychological interventions from *centres* rather than from *clinics*, for *clients* rather than *patients*, and working towards amelioration of *problems* rather than *cures*.

XI.—FUTURE PROSPECTS

Clinical psychology is an expanding and developing profession. There are many factors, some quite critical, that will influence its future development but it is likely to continue to expand although less rapidly than in the recent past, at least in the immediate future. In the UK much depends upon (i) the availability of funding for training clinical psychologists and for the establishment of new service posts; (ii) the extent to which psychologists adhere to the existing scientist-practitioner model of the profession, or move further towards a predominantly therapeutic role that limits unduly their unique contribution of clinically-informed research expertise; and (iii) the effects of some form of legal registration of psychologists.

The range, sophistication and effectiveness of therapeutic approaches to psychological problems continues to increase. In response to the ever increasing demand upon resources, psychologists will spend more time in a consultancy role, advising other professionals on psychological aspects of the problems with which they deal. Similarly, more time will be devoted to the transmission of intervention skills to other appropriate professionals who are more numerous than psychologists. The move into the community will continue, with more work in community centres and health centres and more advisory and innovative activities with community self-help groups, such as those that currently exist for people with phobic disorders. To some extent this community emphasis will be balanced by an increased psychological contribution in a range of clinical, but not psychiatric, settings including pain clinics and renal dialysis units.

In the longer term, and more radically, there may be a trend towards more preventive work. The sheer scale of the problems of anxiety and depression in the community, quite apart from the prevalence of other psychological problems, suggests that resources will never be adequate to meet the demand. If some of the skills and knowledge that adults acquire in the course of psychological intervention could be acquired at an earlier age, before the majority of psychological problems develop, it is reasonable to suppose that significantly fewer adult problems would occur. Equipping young people with more adequate skills to cope more appropriately with the life-stresses they are likely to meet is an enterprise that would need research, development and resources like any other; but there is little doubt that it is practicable. It is no more sinister than teaching children to clean their teeth or to wash their hands before eating, but it does require that psychological well-being is given as much emphasis in our culture as personal hygiene and physical health. To the extent that such an enterprise improves the quality of life for people and reduces the demand upon health-care provision, the necessary allocation of resources would be a provident investment.

XII.—ANNOTATED READINGS

Coles, E. M. (1982). *Clinical Psychopathology*. London: Routledge and Kegan Paul.

This is a recent general text written by a psychologist. It provides wide coverage of clinical topics, including anxiety and depression, with useful discussions of diagnosis, aetiology, treatments and problems of therapeutic outcome research.

Bellack, A. S. and Hersen, M. (1977). *Behavior Modification, An Introductory Textbook*. Baltimore, Maryland: Williams and Wilkins.

This volume is useful for a clear exposition of therapeutic techniques and, despite the title, includes cognitive approaches. Chapters one to five are most relevant.

Rachman, S. J. and Wilson, G. T. (1980). *The Effects of Psychological Therapy.* Oxford: Pergamon.

This book provides a comprehensive and sophisticated review of studies of therapeutic outcome and useful discussions of the problems involved in research of this kind.

Sluckin, W. (Ed.) (1978). *Fear in Animals and Man.* London: Van Nostrand.

This is a fairly advanced book that will enable the student to obtain a fuller understanding of the nature, development and aetiology of normal and pathological fears.

Phares, E. J. (1979). *Clinical Psychology: Concepts, Methods and Profession.* Homewood: Dorsey.

This book is most valuable for its examination of the development of clinical psychology as a profession, its role and its future. There are also useful sections on therapeutic and other clinical techniques. The UK reader must bear in mind the USA's lack of anything comparable to the British National Health Service.

Abramson, L. Y., Seligman, M. E. P. and Teasdale, J. (1978). Learned helplessness in humans: critique and reformulation. *Journal of Abnormal Psychology*, **87**, 49–74.

This paper is included as a good example of theory development relevant to depression. Students who wish to pursue the topic further will find sufficient leads in the reference section.

XIII.—REFERENCES

Abramson, L. Y., Seligman, M. E. P. and Teasdale, J. (1978). Learned helplessness in humans: critique and reformulation. *Journal of abnormal psychology*, **87**, 49–74.
Abramson, L. Y., Garber, J. and Seligman, M. E. P. (1980). Learned helplessness: an attributional analysis. In: J. Garber and M. E. P. Seligman (Eds.), *Human Helplessness: Theory and Application.* New York: Academic Press.
Akiskal, H. S. and McKinney, W. T. (1975). Overview of recent research in depression: integration of ten conceptual models into a comprehensive clinical frame. *Archives of General Psychiatry*, **32**, 285–305.
Agras, S., Sylvester, D. and Oliveau, D. (1969). The epidemiology of common fears and phobias. *Comprehensive Psychiatry*, **10**, 151–156.
Bandura, A. (1976). *Social Learning Theory.* New York: Prentice Hall.
Beck, A. T. (1967). *Depression: Clinical, Experimental and Theoretical Aspects.* New York: Harper and Row.
Beck, A. T. (1974). The development of depression: A cognitive model. In: R. J. Friedman and M. M. Katz (Eds.) *The Psychology of Depression: Contemporary Theory and Research.* Washington, DC: Winston.
Beck, A. T. (1976). *Cognitive Therapy and the Emotional Disorders.* New York: Hoeber.
Beck, A. T., Rush, A. J., Shaw, B. F., and Emery, G. (1979). *Cognitive Therapy of Depression.* New York: Guilford.
Beck, A. T., Ward, C. H., Mendelson, J. E., Mock, J. E. and Erbaugh, J. K. (1961). An inventory for measuring depression. *Archives of General Psychiatry*, **4**, 561–571.
Brown, G. W., and Harris, T. (1978). *Social Origins of Depression.* London: Tavistock.

Byrne, D. G. (1979). Anxiety as state and trait following survived myocardial infarction. *British Journal of Social and Clinical Psychology*, **18**, 417–425.

Carr, A. T. (1978). The psychopathology of fear. In: W. Sluckin (Ed.) *Fear in Animals and Man*. London: Van Nostrand.

Carroll, B. J., Fielding, C. H. and Blashki, T. G. (1973). Depression rating scales, *Archives of General Psychiatry*, **28**, 361–366.

Cattell, R. B., Eber, H. W. and Tatsuoka, M. M. (1970). *Handbook for the Sixteen Personality Factor Questionnaire*. Champaign, Illinois: IPAT.

Crown, S. and Crisp, A. H. (1979). *Manual of the Crown-Crisp Experiential Index*. London: Hodder and Stoughton.

Hamilton, M. (1967). Development of a rating scale for primary depressive illness. *British Journal of Social and Clinical Psychology*, **6**, 276–296.

Janis, I. L. (1969). Some implications of recent research on the dynamics of fear and stress tolerance. In *Social Psychiatry. Proceedings of the Association*. Baltimore, Maryland: Williams and Wilkins.

Lewinsohn, P. M. (1974). A behavioral approach to depression. In R. J. Friedman and M. M. Katz (Eds.) *The Psychology of Depression: Contemporary theory and research*. New York: Wiley.

Lewinsohn, P. M. (1975). The behavioral study and treatment of depression. In: M. Hersen, R. M. Eisler, and P. M. Miller (Eds.) *Progress in Behavior Modification: Volume 1*. New York: Academic Press.

Marks, I. M. (1969). *Fears and Phobias*. London: Heinemann.

McLean, P. D. and Hakstian, A. R. (1979). Clinical Depression: Comparative efficacy of outpatient treatments. *Journal of Consulting and Clinical Psychology*, **47**, 818–836.

Morrow, G. R. and Labrum, A. H. (1978). Psychological and physiological measures of anxiety. *Psychological Medicine*, **8**, 95–101.

Mowrer, O. H. (1939). A stimulus-response analysis of anxiety and its role as a reinforcing agent. *Psychological Review*, **46**, 553–564.

Rachman, S. J. (1977). The conditioning theory of fear-acquisition: a critical examination. *Behaviour Research and Therapy*, **15**, 375–387.

Rachman, S. J. and Hodgson, R. (1974). Synchrony and desynchrony in fear and avoidance. *Behaviour Research and Therapy*, **12**, 311–318.

Rachman, S. J. and Wilson, G. T. (1980). *The Effects of Psychological Therapy*. Oxford: Pergamon.

Rowe, D. (1978). *The Experience of Depression*. Chichester: Wiley.

Seligman, M. E. P. (1974). Depression and learned helplessness. In: R. J. Friedman and M. M. Katz (Eds.). *The Psychology of Depression: Contemporary Theory and Research*. Washington, DC: Winston.

Shepherd, M., Cooper, B., Brown, A. C. and Kalton, G. (1978). *Psychiatric Illness in General Practice*. Oxford: Oxford University Press.

Solyom, L., Beck, P., Solyom, C. and Hugel, R. (1974). Some etiological factors in phobic neuroses. *Canadian Psychiatric Association Journal*, **19**, 69–78.

Spielberger, C. D., Gorsuch, R. L. and Lushene, R. E. (1970). *STAI Manual for the State-Trait Anxiety Inventory*. Palo Alto, California: Consulting Psychologists Press.

Trethowan Report. (1977). *The Role of Psychologists in the Health Services. Report of the Sub-Committee*. London: Her Majesty's Stationery Office.

Weiss, J. M. (1970). Somatic effects of predictable and unpredictable shock. *Psychosomatic medicine*, **32**, 397–409.

Wolpe, J. and Lang, P. J. (1964). A fear survey schedule for use in behavior therapy. *Behaviour Research and Therapy*, **2**, 27–30.
Woodruff, R. and Pitts, F. N. (1964). Monozygotic twins with obsessional neurosis. *American Journal of Psychiatry*, **120**, 1075–1080.
Zubin, J., (1979). Discussion, part IV and overview. In: J. E. Barrett (Ed.) *Stress and Mental Disorder*. New York: Raven Press.

Psychology and Social Problems
Edited by A. Gale and A. J. Chapman
© 1984 John Wiley & Sons Ltd.

CHAPTER 10

SEXUAL DIFFICULTIES

Derek Jehu

I.—THE EXTENT OF THE PROBLEM

The difficulties discussed in this chapter are sexual dysfunctions rather than sexual deviations or gender dysphorias. Sexual dysfunction refers to some inadequacy of sexual response, while sexual deviation involves a preference for unusual forms of sexual stimulation or activity, and in the gender dysphorias the individual is dissatisfied with his or her identity or role as a male or female.

Sexual dysfunction may involve some inadequacy of motivation, performance, or satisfaction. Both men and women may present with a lack of motivation for sexual activity. Some of these individuals experience such activity as neutral or even pleasurable, while for others it evokes strong aversive reactions.

Male sexual performance may be impaired by erectile dysfunction, premature ejaculation, retarded ejaculation, or retrograde ejaculation. In erectile dysfunction the man suffers from a persistent inability to obtain a sufficiently firm erection, or to maintain this during intromission and intercourse. Premature ejaculation means that the individual reaches climax involuntarily, when he would prefer to prolong his control for a longer period of time. In contrast, retarded ejaculation comprises a persistent delay or failure in reaching climax, despite a full erection and intense stimulation for unusually lengthy periods. It is important to note that both orgasm and ejaculation are retarded or absent in this dysfunction, for it needs to be distinguished from retrograde ejaculation which consists of the involuntary discharge of semen backwards into the bladder rather than forwards through the urethra, so that the man still has erections and orgasms but there is no visible ejaculate.

Sexual performance in women may be adversely affected by vasocongestive dysfunction, orgastic dysfunction, or vaginismus. In vasocongestive dysfunction, the lubrication and swelling of the vagina, and the other physiological changes that are characteristic of sexual arousal, do not occur normally. Thus, vasocongestive dysfunction in the female is analogous to erectile dysfunction in the male. Women suffering from orgastic dysfunction experience difficulty in releasing the reflex contractions of the vaginal and pelvic musculature that constitute an orgasm, making this problem analogous to retarded ejaculation in the male. Finally, vaginismus can be defined as a spastic contraction of the muscles at the outer third of the vagina and the perineum, which occurs as an involuntary reflex response to the threat of vaginal penetration. Consequently, intromission is either completely prevented or only possible with great difficulty and pain.

Some men and women complain of sexual dissatisfaction despite the fact that the physical aspects of arousal and climax are unimpaired. These individuals may say that they 'feel nothing' during sex, or that this is insufficiently pleasurable. For example, a man may obtain and maintain a full erection, but experience little sensation or excitement from penile stimulation, or a woman may have orgastic contractions without the usual accompanying feeling of pleasure.

The condition of dyspareunia, or painful intercourse, also occurs in both sexes. In men, the discomfort may be experienced during erection, insertion, thrusting or ejaculation, and intromission or penile thrusting may be painful for women.

It will be apparent that these definitions of the various dysfunctions involve subjective judgements of inadequacy by the individuals concerned. There are no absolute or prescribed standards of sexual motivation, performance, or satisfaction, and the consequent variability in the criteria used influences all estimates of the incidence of sexual dysfunction in the general population.

One of the few such estimates available is based on 100 predominantly white, well educated, middle class, and happily married couples in the USA. (Frank, Anderson and Rubinstein, 1978). Current erectile or ejaculatory dysfunctions were reported by 40% of the men, and 63% of the women were currently experiencing an impairment of their arousal or ability to reach orgasm. Despite these problems, however, 80% of the couples considered their sexual relations to be satisfying. Thus, impairments of sexual performance appeared to be widespread even in this well favoured and happily married group, but the couples concerned did not necessarily judge these impairments to be detrimental to their sexual relationship. Some of the factors that influence such personal judgements are discussed in Sections IV and V.

II.—CONCEPTS OF THE PERSON AND MODELS OF HUMAN BEHAVIOUR

Historically, sexual dysfunctions have generally been viewed as symptoms of unconscious intrapsychic conflicts in the psychoanalytic approach, or as arising exclusively from interpersonal conflict in the marital therapy literature. More recently, many psychologists have preferred a behavioural model in which the causes of sexual dysfunction are conceptualized in the general categories of organic factors, previous learning experiences, and contemporary conditions, operating singly or in combination in particular cases. There are probably several reasons for this preference. In Britain, most clinical psychologists are trained and experienced in a behavioural rather than any other clinical approach. Two major characteristics of behaviour therapy are its empirical stance and its utilization of theories, principles, and findings from the general body of psychological knowledge. Both of these features tend to appeal to scientifically trained psychologists. Similarly, the substantive evidence on the effectiveness of the methods of treatment for sexual dysfunction which are associated with the behavioural model is stronger than that for either psychoanalytic or marital therapy. The following discussion in this section is restricted to the application of a behavioural model to the causation of sexual dysfunction. In later sections the same model is adopted as a basis for assessing and treating these problems. It incorporates organic factors, previous learning experiences, and contemporary conditions.

In a behavioural model, the relevant organic factors include certain disease conditions, together with the side effects of some types of medication or surgery. For example about 50% of male diabetics suffer from erectile dysfunction. A similar proportion of male patients taking a major tranquillizer called thioridazine (Mellaril) experience retrograde ejaculation. This dysfunction is also extremely common among men who have undergone a surgical excision of the whole or part of the prostate gland. Incidentally these examples reflect the much greater knowledge available at present about the effects of organic factors on male compared to female sexual functioning.

The category of previous learning experiences includes both the learning conditions to which an individual has been exposed, and the learning processes through which these conditions exercise their influence on later behaviour. Certain conditions of a traumatic, restrictive, or familial nature may adversely affect a person's later responses to sexual stimulation. Such traumatic experiences include incest or rape, which are followed by a wide range of sexual dysfunctions in some victims. An excessively restrictive moral or religious upbringing may result in a young adult who is grossly lacking in accurate sexual knowledge and deeply imbued with negative sexual attitudes. Relevant familial experiences include demanding, perfectionistic, or seductive parents, and early exposure to parental death, discord, or stressful separation, any of which may undermine or distort later sexual relationships. It should be noted that while some people who were exposed to traumatic, restrictive, or distressing familial experiences are adversely affected, others do not appear to be impaired, and the sources of these individual differences are not yet known. Similarly, while an assumption is made in the behavioural approach that the learning processes involved in the acquisition of sexual dysfunction are essentially the same as those involved in the acquisition of any other kind of behaviour, the specific contributions of these processes to sexual dysfunction remain to be investigated empirically.

Although sexually dysfunctional responses may have been acquired during previous learning experiences, these responses are initiated and maintained by certain contemporary conditions. For example, a sexual assault in the past may have led to the irrational belief that intercourse is certain to be a painful and unpleasant experience; consequently the current prospect of sex initiates anxiety and avoidance reactions. Likewise, if an incident of sexual dysfunction is followed by a humiliating, critical or angry reaction from the partner, then this is likely to increase performance anxiety and to maintain the dysfunction in future encounters. Among the contemporary conditions that may initiate and maintain inadequate sexual responses in this way are psychological stress, psychiatric disorder, deficient or false information, deficient or inappropriate stimulation, and discord between the partners, which is discussed in Section IV.

Many forms of psychological stress may contribute to sexual dysfunction. Certain aspects of sexual anatomy or activity may be stressful for some individuals; for example, the threat of penile penetration for a woman suffering from vaginismus. Some patients anticipate that sex will harm them in some way, such as the postcoronary patient and partner who fear that a relapse or death may occur during intercourse. Others anticipate failure in sexual encounters, including the possibility of ejaculating prematurely or of not reaching orgasm. There are also stressful situations arising from contraventions of an individual's moral or religious standards. Thus, people whose standards include a complete prohibition on intercourse before marriage, may be sexually unresponsive if they attempt to engage in it. Moreover, it is important to recognize, that stresses of a non-sexual nature can also impair sexual functioning. A person who is worried about loss of a job or a sick relative may experience some repercussions in the area of sexual relationships.

Any of these stresses may evoke reactions that impair sexual responses. Among these reactions are negative emotions such as anxiety, depression, and anger. For instance, it is commonly held that sexual arousal is especially vulnerable to disruption by anxiety concerning sexual performance. The physical avoidance of stressful sexual events is another common reaction, so that sexual encounters tend to be progressively reduced by couples for whom they have become distressing. Cognitive avoidance may also occur, so that erotic thoughts and feelings that are disturbing are excluded from the person's awareness. Another cognitive reaction to stress is the monitoring or 'spectatoring' of sexual performance. For instance, a man who anticipates erectile failure is prone to observe himself to see if he is getting an erection, how full it is becoming, and whether or not he is losing it. This puts him in the role of a spectator rather than a participant in his sexual encounters, and this detachment, together with the distraction of the cognitive monitoring process, results in his being cut off from effective sexual stimulation.

The psychiatric disorder that is most commonly accompanied by sexual dysfunction is depression, and this is particularly likely to lead to lack of sexual motivation.

Any deficiency or inaccuracy in the sexual information possessed by an individual may contribute to sexual dysfunction. For example, ignorance of the location of the clitoris or of the importance of its stimulation in triggering orgasm in many women.

One instance of deficient or inappropriate stimulation is the continued use of a type or site of stimulation which is no longer effective for a spinal cord injured patient, although other types and sites may have become new or enhanced sources of erotic sensation and excitement since the injury.

III.—INDIVIDUAL ASSESSMENT

This comprises the gathering of information about the nature and possible causes of the dysfunction as indicated in previous sections, together with an appraisal of the patient and professional resources that are available for its treatment.

The methods of assessment used include interviews, questionnaires, self-monitoring, physiological techniques, and medical examination. Each of these has certain strengths and weaknesses. Therefore, in order to achieve a balanced and comprehensive assessment it is customary to implement a multimodal scheme comprising a suitable combination of methods.

Interviews are the most frequently used methods of assessment in the field of sexual dysfunction. They have the advantage of not infringing the privacy traditionally afforded to sexual activities in our society, which usually precludes the use of direct observation on both ethical and therapeutic grounds. Another strength of the interview is its flexibility and breadth. The therapist can ask, for example, about the patient's responses in a wide range of situations, and can follow up any promising leads with more detailed questioning. There is, however, the problem of the uncertain validity of patient self-reports as accurate accounts of events as they actually occurred. Specimen interview protocols are available in some of the annotated readings listed below.

The completion of written questionnaires by patients shares the validity problem of self-reports, but it is a method of collecting comprehensive information with relatively little expenditure of time by the therapist. Moreover, the use of questionnaires with acceptable levels of reliability does yield comparable data across occasions, clients and therapists. Therefore such instruments can be used to monitor the therapeutic progress of individual patients as well as in research studies involving groups of patients or therapists. Some of the most commonly used questionnaires are reviewed elsewhere (Jehu, 1979).

Turning now to self-monitoring, in this method of assessment the patient is asked to observe and record specific aspects of his or her own sexual behaviour and its surrounding circumstances, in a systematic manner, either in a diary or on a suitable form. These records can provide a baseline of dysfunctional behaviour before treatment commences, and they are a valuable means of evaluating progress during therapy. The records also yield information about those circumstances that immediately precede and follow the dysfunctional behaviour and which may be initiating and maintaining it. When patients are asked in interviews or in questionnaires to describe events retrospectively, they are often unable to do so with sufficient accuracy and precision, and the compilation of systematic and specific records on an ongoing basis may go some way towards remedying these limitations. Self-monitoring is also a valuable means of systematically observing sexual activity that would not normally be open to observation by others, because of the therapeutic and ethical objections this would entail. Similarly, only the patient can observe his or her own thoughts and feelings in sexual situations.

Currently, the major use of physiological techniques in the assessment of sexually dysfunctional patients is to measure directly the physical aspects of their sexual arousal, by means of penile or vaginal plethysmography. A common type of penile plethysmograph comprises a thin, metal ring, open at the side with one or more strain gauges at the base. This device is fitted round the penis, and as erection occurs the open side becomes wider which causes a slight bending of the strain gauge and produces a measurable increase in electrical output. An interesting application of this technique is in the differential diagnosis between organic and psychogenic erectile dysfunction. In the course of an average night's sleep, people have four or five periods of dreaming during which they exhibit rapid eye-movement (REM). Among sexually unimpaired males and those suffering from psychogenic impotence, these periods of REM sleep are typically accompanied by erections, while this is not so in cases of organic impotence. Thus, the technique of nocturnal penile tumescence monitoring can assist in making this distinction, with its important implications for treatment. The device used in the technique of vaginal plethysmography consists essentially of a vaginal probe with a light source at one end, and a photo-detector cell on the side. This measures the amount of light reflected from the walls of the vagina, which varies with the degree of vasocongestion occurring during sexual arousal.

Finally, it is important not to omit a suitable medical examination from the comprehensive assessment of sexual dysfunction. As indicated above, dysfunction is sometimes caused by disease, drugs, or surgery, and it is essential to identify any such organic factors so that appropriate medical treatment can be provided when indicated.

IV.—THE IMMEDIATE SOCIAL AND EMOTIONAL ENVIRONMENT

The component of the immediate environment that most typically contributes to sexual dysfunction is the relationship between the patient and his or her partner. There are certain patterns of discord that seem to be quite commonly implicated. One of these is the rejection of a partner who is perceived as unattractive or disliked, and whose sexual approaches therefore tend to be insufficiently stimulating, and annoying rather than arousing.

Another pattern is competition between the partners to dominate the relationship, so that power struggles occur which sometimes impair sexual functioning in specific ways. For example, a wife may not respond or reach orgasm because this would represent submission to her husband, or a man may ejaculate before intromission to avoid compliance with his wife's demands for intercourse.

Any insecurity arising from a threat of criticism or desertion by the partner can also impair sexual functioning. Performance anxiety is likely to be compounded if failure is expected to be met with criticism or desertion rather than understanding, and individuals who fear such consequences may be so concerned to ensure their partner's sexual pleasure that they completely subordinate their own satisfaction.

Finally, any friction or hostility between partners, from whatever cause, may well disrupt their sexual relationship. It is difficult for individuals to respond sexually with a partner towards whom they are experiencing considerable feelings of anger, and hostility may be expressed not only by verbal abuse and physical assault, but also in quite subtle ways that damage the sexual relationship. When lovemaking is anticipated, it may be prevented or spoiled by one of the partners provoking a quarrel. Sexual approaches may be made only at times when intercourse is impracticable or not desired by the other partner, alternatively a hostile recipient may respond consistently with apathy, complaints of fatigue or illness, or outright refusal. Some individuals persist in presenting themselves in a physically unattractive manner, or in behaving in annoying ways, so that it is difficult for their partner to respond sexually to them. For instance, a wife may not become aroused if her husband is unwashed, smells of alcohol, or uses foul language. Finally, during sexual encounters, one partner may withhold pleasurable and effective stimulation from the other, and dysfunctions such as premature ejaculation can serve to frustrate a spouse's satisfaction.

In a previous section it was noted that many couples do not judge an impairment of sexual performance to be detrimental to their sexual relationship. One factor that influences such judgements is the quality of the overall interaction between the partners. Thus, in the study cited above (Frank et al., 1978), the researchers concluded that it was not the absolute level of sexual functioning but the 'affective tone' of the marriage which determined a couple's degree of sexual satisfaction. In another study (Chesney, Blakeney, Cole and Chan, 1981) a group of couples who had attended a sex therapy clinic, was compared with a demographically similar group of couples who had not sought therapy. While the latter couples had experienced some of the same sexual problems as those who had attended for treatment, they were able to communicate effectively and to solve these problems constructively, whereas the treatment couples could not handle their sexual problems on their own. Thus, the most important factor in determining sexual satisfaction appeared to be not the occurrence of sexual problems, but how a couple perceived and reacted to these problems.

V. – THE WIDER SOCIAL AND ORGANIZATIONAL ENVIRONMENT

Sexual behaviour may also be judged inadequate according to the extent to which it deviates from what the individuals concerned perceive as the normative standards for such behaviour in the wider social group to which they belong.

These perceived normative standards reflect the beliefs and values concerning sexual behaviour that are current at a particular time. One possible illustration of this is the fact that premature ejaculation was not really recognized as a problem in the 19th century medical literature, perhaps because sex was then regarded as primarily a source of pleasure for the male, who need not try to exercise ejaculatory control in the interests of his partner. In contrast, nocturnal emissions were considered to be a problem at that time, whereas this would not be so today. More recently, it is possible that the so-called 'sexual revolution' during the last two decades or so, has raised the expected standards of performance and gratification during lovemaking. I do not know of any systematic evidence for recent change in this respect, but the popular literature and clinical impression would certainly suggest that men are expected to be able to 'give' a woman an orgasm, and that she is expected to be able to reach climax at least once during intercourse, and preferably to have multiple orgasms.

Individuals who fall short of such perceived normative standards may be liable to regard themselves as sexually dysfunctional and to seek therapeutic help. For instance, in a paper entitled 'The New Impotence', Ginsberg, French and Shapiro (1972) claim that complaints of impotence are more frequent than they used to be, although the authors do not present any supporting evidence for this assertion. They go on to suggest that this alleged increased incidence may reflect a change from the earlier view that sex is primarily a source of pleasure for the male, to a current expectation of orgastic release for the female which she actively seeks from her partner. Some vulnerable men are unable to cope with this enhanced demand for effective performance, or with the loss of the complete control that they formerly exercised over sexual activity, and complaints of impotence may result.

The therapeutic implication of these achievement oriented and genitally focused perceptions of normative sexual behaviour is that the patients concerned need help to relinquish such standards, and instead to regard sex as an opportunity for mutual enjoyment and the expression of love between partners, rather than a challenge to succeed; as involving many forms of sensual and sexual pleasure, rather than being a predominantly genital activity; and as being properly guided by individual sexual preferences, rather than by conformity to perceived normative standards of sexual behaviour.

VI.—TYPES OF INTERVENTION

Many of the interventions used in treatment of sexual dysfunction are listed in Table 10.1 under sub-headings indicating the major, though not the exclusive, purpose of each type. From the range of available interventions, a unique treatment programme is individually tailored to suit each patient.

VII.—IS PSYCHOLOGICAL INTERVENTION SUCCESSFUL?

The specific nature of the treatment programmes and the variation in outcome for different dysfunctions precludes a short summary in this section (see Jehu, 1979, for a more extensive review). Instead, one intervention is selected to illustrate the nature of the treatment approach and its effectiveness.

There is much evidence to support the efficacy of masturbation training in the treatment of women who have never reached orgasm by any physical means. The initial therapeutic goal with many such totally inorgastic patients is to help them to achieve their first climax. This resolves any doubts they may have about their capacity to do so, and begins to alleviate any fears of being harmed, losing self-control or suffering any other adverse effect as a consequence of orgasm. The first experience of climaxing also provides the patient with information about the nature of the stimulation and reactions that preceded it, which she can then communicate to her partner for incorporation in their lovemaking.

Given the initial goal of a first orgasm, there are reasons for thinking that this is most likely to be achieved by the woman stimulating her own genitals. It has been found that more women can reach orgasm through masturbation

TABLE 10.1
TYPES OF INTERVENTION FOR SEXUAL DYSFUNCTION

General Therapeutic Conditions

Therapeutic relationship
Causal explanation
Prognostic expectancy

Sexual Assignments

General pleasuring
Genital stimulation
Sexual intercourse

Specific Procedures

Provision of information
  Verbal
  Bibliographical
  Audio-visual
Modification of attitudes and beliefs
  Sanctioning
  Self-disclosure
  Role-playing
  Cognitive restructuring
Reduction of stress
  Relaxation training
  Desensitization
  Flooding
  Guided imagery
  Thought stopping
  Modelling
  Vaginal dilatation
Sexual enhancement
  Classical conditioning
  Biofeedback
  Hypnosis
  Exposure to erotic material
  Pelvic muscle exercises
  Drugs/hormones
  Prosthetic/mechanical aids
Relationship enhancement
  Increasing positive exchanges
  Communication training
  Problem solving training
  Assertiveness training
  Heterosocial skills training

than by any other means, including sexual intercourse. Moreover, there is other evidence that masturbation produces orgasms which are more intense, both subjectively and physiologically, than those resulting from intercourse or manual stimulation by the partner.

The apparent superiority of masturbation as a means of achieving climax may arise from the intensity of the stimulation it provides as well as the accompanying freedom from certain possible sources of stress. Although sexual intercourse is a highly gratifying psychological experience, at a mechanical level it is not a particularly effective way of providing the clitoral stimulation that seems to be important in triggering the orgastic reflex in women. During intercourse such stimulation occurs only indirectly, through traction on the clitoral hood from penile thrusting, and from pressure on the clitoral area by the pubic bone, whereas genital manipulation of the clitoris during masturbation constitutes a more direct and intense form of stimulation. Furthermore, when a woman stimulates herself in private she is not subject to certain possible stresses, such as the observation and monitoring of her performance by her partner; any time pressures his presence may impose upon the duration of the self-stimulation and speed of her response to it; or the relinquishment of responsibility for stimulation to him when the woman fears that she may be overwhelmed and lose her self-control if this is too intense. However, although a husband may not be directly involved in the early masturbatory assignments being undertaken by his inorgastic wife, it is important for him to understand the rationale for them, so that she is reassured by his acceptance and support. Indeed, in order to facilitate this, as well as to provide sexual release for the husband if the couple are abstaining from intercourse, it is sometimes specifically arranged that he will engage in parallel masturbatory activities.

Lo Piccolo and Lobitz (1972) have proposed a nine-step series of masturbatory assignments for totally inorgastic women. The general outline of their programme can be summarized as follows, but they stress that it requires modification to suit individual patients 1) In order to increase her self-awareness the patient is asked to examine her nude body and appreciate its attractive features. A hand mirror is to be used to examine her genitals and she is to identify the various parts of these with the aid of diagrams. 2) The patient is asked to explore her genitals tactually as well as visually, and to prevent performance anxiety she is not given any expectation of arousal at this point. Instead, the aim of the first two steps is to reduce the stressfulness of seeing and touching the genitals and to accustom the patient to the idea of masturbation. 3) Tactile and visual exploration of the genitals is to be continued with the object of locating sensitive areas that are pleasurable to touch. 4) These sensitive areas are now to be manually stimulated, and the therapist discusses ways of doing this, including the use of a lubricant to heighten pleasure and prevent discomfort. 5) If the patient has not reached climax during the previous step, she is asked to increase the intensity and duration of the genital stimulation. It is important for her to realize that she may have to continue stimulation for a prolonged period, of perhaps 30 minutes to an hour, to give herself sufficient opportunity of reaching orgasm. During this assignment, patients are encouraged to use erotic fantasies, literature and pictures, in order to heighten arousal and to distract themselves from any performance anxiety or spectatoring. 6) If step 5 does not result in orgasm, the patient is asked to repeat it using a vibrator to stimulate herself. In cases of patients who fear loss of self-control during orgasm, it may be helpful if they role-play their conception of the orgastic response in an exaggerated manner. The simulation of anticipated reactions such as involuntary screaming or gross musclar movements, may alleviate their stressfulness and sometimes results in the occurrence of a real orgasm during the role-play. 7) Once a woman has reached orgasm on her own, she may be asked to stimulate herself while her partner is watching. The object of this step is to reduce the stressfulness to the woman of exhibiting arousal and orgasm in the presence of her partner, and to provide him with information about the kind of stimulation that she prefers. 8) This step consists of the partner stimulating the woman in the way she has demonstrated to him. It is important that he follow her guidance concerning her preferences and that he continue to stimulate her for a sufficiently lengthy period without interruption. Otherwise she will have insufficient opportunity to become aroused and reach orgasm, or this process will be disrupted and her arousal level will drop. 9) Once the woman reaches orgasm during step 8, then the couple is asked to engage in intercourse while the man concurrently stimulates the woman's genitals, either manually or with a vibrator.

There are several sources of evidence on the efficacy of this approach, but a recent controlled trial by Riley and Riley (1978) is chosen as an example here. Their patients were all primarily inorgastic, and the treatment was administered on a couple basis. For one group this consisted of pleasuring assignments and supportive psychotherapy, while for a second group it comprised these components with the addition of masturbation assignments for the female partner. The investigators stress that these assignments are only adjunctive to the communication training and sex education provided by the other essential components of the programme.

At the end of treatment, 18 (90%) of the 20 patients in the masturbation group were able to attain orgasm by some means, compared to only 8 (53%) of 15 patients in the pleasuring plus supportive psychotherapy group. Similarly, 17 (85%) of the masturbation group could attain orgasm during intercourse by any means on at least 75% of occasions, compared to only 7 (47%) of the patients in the other group. These improvements were maintained over a one-year follow up period. Thus, the addition of the masturbation assignments appears to have been markedly beneficial.

VIII.—METHODOLOGICAL AND PRACTICAL PROBLEMS

Several methodological problems are mentioned above, including the paucity of information about incidence rates for sexual dysfunction in general populations, the inadequate understanding of why similar events are followed by such varied sexual consequences in different individuals, and the many limitations in the data available on the outcome of interventions. Only the last topic is considered further in this section.

Not a great deal of progress has been made in identifying the personal characteristics of patients that influence the outcome of treatment. The variable that has received the most attention is the nature of the presenting problem, and it seems clear that some dysfunctions such as premature ejaculation and vaginismus, have been more successfully treated than others such as primary erectile dysfunction. There is also some evidence to suggest that the primary or secondary nature of the problem may be of prognostic significance. For instance, the outcome for primary orgastic dysfunction is generally better than in cases where the woman has experienced climax at some time. Finally, a severe degree of discord between the partners has been shown to be accompanied by a poorer outcome in several studies. Other patient variables that require further investigation to ascertain their influence on outcome include level of motivation, religious and moral beliefs, organic and psychiatric conditions, co-existing sexual deviations, the availability of a regular partner, and the presence of sexual dysfunction in both partners.

Very little information is available about the influence of specific treatment variables on outcome. In one of the few studies that has been conducted, Mathews et al. (1976) found some evidence for a superior outcome from a combination of sexual assignments and therapeutic interviews, when compared to the outcomes from the delivery of each of these components separately. Another finding in this study concerned the provision of treatment through a dual sex co-therapy team or an individual therapist, the former having some slight superiority in the combined assignment and interview programme. This inadequate state of knowledge about the influence of certain components of treatment on its outcome, clearly requires supplementation through further investigation. Equally obvious is the need for inquiry into the influence of many other treatment variables, including the characteristics of the therapists, the nature of the treatment setting, and the timing of therapy.

It would be advantageous if the same criteria of outcome with identical definitions were more widely adopted in future studies, in order to facilitate comparison between them. Attention also needs to be paid to the *clinical* significance of these criteria; for while a statistically significant improvement may occur in some aspect of sexual functioning, this may still leave a residual problem of considerable clinical significance because of the distress it continues to cause to the patient and his or her partner.

The methods of data collection used in many outcome studies are lacking in information about their validity and reliability, and the comparison of results would be facilitated if some of the better instruments and techniques were more widely adopted in future studies.

The scarcity of adequately controlled investigations is a very significant impediment to the evaluation of outcome, making it difficult or impossible to distinguish the influence of many patient and treatment variables. For example, although Masters and Johnson (1970) reported high success rates with the largest series of sexually dysfunctional patients ever studied, we do not know how well these patients would have fared if they had received certain other forms of treatment or no systematic treatment at all. Nor do we know the extent to which the various components in this programme contributed to its outcome, and only slightly more information is available about some of the characteristics of the patients which influenced their response to treatment.

Turning now to some practical problems, these include a lack of effective methods of treatment for certain dysfunctions, such as inadequate sexual motivation and primary erectile dysfunction, together with the many obstacles or resistances that may interfere with the process and progress of therapy (Munjack and Oziel, 1978).

A patient simply may not understand a therapeutic recommendation and therefore be unable to comply with it correctly. Alternatively the recommendation may be understood, but the patient may not have the skills required to implement it. For example, a person may be deficient in the social skills needed to communicate sexual preferences to a partner in a non-threatening manner. Some patients are insufficiently motivated towards therapeutic change, or they do not expect treatment to be successful. The possible rewards may not seem worth the effort, or the risk of failure is avoided by not trying. Resistances may also be manifested when feelings of anxiety or guilt are evoked in therapy. Thus, talking about certain topics, such as an incestuous experience, may be very disturbing, or certain assignments, such as those involving masturbation, may be quite repugnant for some patients. Consequently, such topics or assignments are avoided and the therapeutic process is blocked. This may also happen because the sexual dysfunction is in some way rewarding to the patient. Examples of such secondary gains include the control of the sexual relationship by the patient, and the frustration of a partner towards whom the patient feels resentment or anger.

IX.—PROBLEMS OF ETHICS AND CONFIDENTIALITY

All therapists are confronted by ethical issues arising from the selection of goals and interventions, the consent of the patient to the proposed programme, the accountability of the therapist for its progress and outcome, and the handling of confidential information concerning patients.

The goals of treatment for sexual dysfunction are not derived from any norm or standard for sexual performance, rather they are chosen by the patient and partner in accordance with their own wishes and values, although in consultation with the therapist. His or her role in this task is to help the couple to explore alternatives and their consequences before deciding on the goals to be pursued. Inevitably, the therapist's own opinions and values will influence this process, and it is incumbent on him or her to disclose these views to the couple so that they can take them into account when deciding between goals. Sometimes this will lead the patient to wish to seek treatment from someone else, in which case the therapist will assist in making a suitable referral.

The therapist plays a larger part in the selection of intervention procedures, although certainly not to the exclusion of the patient. These procedures must be personally and ethically acceptable to both therapist and patient. For instance, a patient's genuine belief that masturbation is sinful would preclude its prescription for therapeutic purposes. The protection of patients' rights in such matters is ensured by the need to obtain their informed consent to the proposed programme. Informed consent is usually held to require knowledge, voluntariness, and competency. Patients have the right to adequate knowledge about what is involved in the programme, including its goals and the procedures to be used, as well as its potential risks and benefits. Alternative programmes should be discussed and their relative merits and demerits fairly evaluated. It should be made clear to patients that they are free to refuse consent or to revoke it at any time. This consent should be given voluntarily and in the absence of any coercion or duress. It also requires competency, in that the patient can understand the information given and is able to make a reasoned judgement.

The therapist is accountable for the satisfactory progress of treatment. This requires that its effects are systematically monitored and evaluated, so that appropriate changes can be made in the programme when necessary. The data collected should certainly be made available to the patient, and perhaps also to other professionals and the organization employing the therapist.

The disclosure of this or any other information to persons other than the patient is done only with his or her explicit consent, and in conformity with the ethical code for the profession to which the therapist belongs. A particular issue concerning confidentiality sometimes arises when one partner discloses information in an individual interview that he or she has not revealed to the other partner, perhaps about an extra-marital affair or an incestuous or homosexual experience. Both partners are told beforehand that any such confidences will be respected and not passed on to the other partner, although the therapist may encourage disclosure to the partner if this is indicated on therapeutic grounds, and in some circumstances a refusal to do so may mean that treatment is not a viable proposition.

X.—THE ROLE OF OTHER DISCIPLINES AND PROFESSIONS

It is clear from the literature and from personal knowledge, that the treatment of sexual dysfunction has been undertaken by therapists from a wide variety of professions and specialities, including counsellors, family doctors, gynaeco-logists, nurses, physicians, psychiatrists, psychologists, social workers and urologists. At present, there is no systematic evidence to indicate the relative superiority of any of these groups in conducting such treatment, although *prima facie* arguments have been advanced in favour of each of them, usually by members of the profession or speciality concerned. It is of course essential to have the particular expertise of each group available when it is required; for example, a suitably qualified medical practitioner to undertake the neces-sary screening for any relevant organic conditions, or a psychologist trained in behaviour therapy to implement specific procedures such as desensitization. Psychologists may also have a special contribution to make with their exper-tise in research methodology, for example, in controlled studies of outcome.

Probably more important than the particular professional discipline of the therapist, are the attitudes, knowledge and skills that he or she brings to the treatment of sexual dysfunction. These attributes are fundamentally similar to those acquired and exercised in the profession to which the therapist belongs, but they may well require some extension and refinement for this particular therapeutic task. While again, there is no systematic evidence available about the respective influences of certain attitudes, knowledge and skills on the process and outcome of the treatment of sexual dysfunction, it seems highly probable that a therapist will need to understand and accept his or her own sexuality, to exhibit positive attitudes towards sex, and to be tolerant of a wide range of sexual behaviour, if communications and relationships with dysfunctional patients are not to be inhibited or distorted. Clearly, he or she will need to be generally well informed about the whole sphere of sexual behaviour, and more especially knowledgeable about the causation, assessment and treatment of sexual dysfunctions, as well as possessing the clinical skills to undertake these assessment and treatment tasks.

XI.—FUTURE PROSPECTS

It is difficult to speculate specifically on possible future developments in the understanding and treatment of sexual dysfunction. All one can say is that the methodological and practical problems outlined in a previous section are being tackled at the present time, and their resolution is an important chal-lenge for the future. At a theoretical level, more satisfactory accounts are needed of the psychological processes involved in the acquisition and performance of all forms of sexual behaviour, as well as the processes that mediate the therapeutic interventions for sexual dysfunction.

Fortunately, the behavioural approach on which this chapter is based does hold out some promise for the successful pursuit of these objectives. It represents an attempt to apply principles and findings from many areas of psychology and related disciplines to the explanation, assessment, and treatment of psychological problems. Thus, a large and growing body of psychological knowledge may be brought to bear on these problems just as anatomy, physiology, and biochemistry contribute to physical medicine. Moreover, another major characteristic of the approach is a commitment to empiricism and scientific method. Strong emphasis is placed on the operationalization of concepts and the collection of data by valid and reliable techniques. Therapeutic procedures are described with precision so that they can be measured and replicated. Treatment interventions are experimentally evaluated using research designs that are as rigorous as the clinical conditions permit. This self-corrective mechanism promises cumulative improvement in the help available to sexually dysfunctional patients and perhaps constitutes the greatest hope for the long-term viability and efficacy of this particular approach to their treatment.

XII.—ANNOTATED READINGS

Belliveau, F. and Richter, L. (1971). *Understanding Human Inadequacy*. London: Hodder.

An authorized, clearly written, summary of the classic, Masters, W. H. and Johnson, V. E. (1970). *Human Sexual Inadequacy*, New York: Bantam.

Heiman, J., Lo Piccolo, L. and Lo Piccolo, J. (1976). *Becoming Orgasmic: A Sexual Growth Program for Women*. Englewood Cliffs, N.J.: Prentice-Hall.

A valuable guide to the understanding and treatment of arousal and orgastic dysfunctions in women, for patients as well as professionals.

Jehu, D. (1979). *Sexual Dysfunction: A Behavioural Approach to Causation, Assessment, and Treatment*. Chichester: Wiley.

Offers more extensive discussion and documentation of the topics outlined in this chapter.

Kaplan, H. S. (1974). *The New Sex Therapy: Active Treatment of Sexual Dysfunctions*. New York: Brunner/Mazel.

A rich source of clinically relevant material on the nature, causes, and treatment of sexual dysfunction.

Kaplan, H. S. (1979). *Disorders of Sexual Desire: and Other New Concepts and Techniques in Sex Therapy*. New York: Brunner/Mazel.

The only available book on the important problems of low sexual motivation.

Kolodny, R. C., Masters, W. H. and Johnson, V. E. (1979). *Textbook of Sexual Medicine*. Boston: Little, Brown.

A comprehensive and authoritative text on the implications of disease, medication and surgery for sexual functionings.

Zilbergeld, B. (1978). *Male Sexuality: A Guide to Sexual Fulfillment*. New York: Bantam.

An excellent guide to male sexual functioning and its problems, for both patients and professionals.

XIII. – REFERENCES

Chesney, A. P., Blakeney, P. E., Cole, C. M. and Chan, F. A. (1981). A comparison of couples who have sought sex therapy with couples who have not. *Journal of Sex and Marital Therapy*, 7, 131–140.

Frank, E., Anderson, C. and Rubenstein, D. (1978). Frequency of sexual dysfunction in 'normal' couples. *New England Journal of Medicine*, 299, 111–115.

Ginsberg, G. L., French, W. A. and Shapiro, T. (1972). The new impotence. *Archives of General Psychiatry*, 26, 218–220.

Jehu, D. (1979). *Sexual Dysfunction: A Behavioural Approach to Causation, Assessment, and Treatment*. Chichester: Wiley.

Lo Piccolo, J. and Lobitz, W. C., (1972). The role of masturbation in the treatment of orgasmic dysfunction. *Archives of Sexual Behaviour*, 2, 163–171.

Masters, W. H. and Johnson, V. E. (1970). *Human Sexual Inadequacy*. New York: Bantom.

Mathews, A., Bancroft, J., Whitehead, A., Hackman, A., Julier, D., Bancroft, J., Gath., D. and Shaw, P. (1976). The behavioural treatment of sexual inadequacy: a comparative study. *Behaviour Research and Therapy*, 14, 427–436.

Munjack, D. J. and Oziel, L. J. (1978). Resistance in the behavioral treatment of sexual dysfunctions. *Journal of Sex and Marital Therapy*, 4, 122–138.

Riley, A. J. and Riley, E. J. (1978). A controlled study to evaluate directed masturbation in the management of primary orgasmic failure in women. *British Journal of Psychiatry*, 133, 404–409.

Psychology and Social Problems
Edited by A. Gale and A. J. Chapman
© 1984 John Wiley & Sons Ltd.

CHAPTER 11

DRUG AND ALCOHOL DEPENDENCE

Michael Gossop

I.—THE EXTENT OF THE PROBLEM

Horses sweat and men perspire but ladies only glow. Translated into the world of drug and alcohol abuse this might read, I drink socially, you drink too much, he's a drunk.

Before we can determine the extent of a problem, it is necessary to define the problem itself. Presumably the alcoholic who drinks a bottle of whisky every day, whose social world is collapsing and whose liver is burning up, constitutes some sort of problem. But there would be no such agreement as to whether the drinker who became drunk every Friday and Saturday night was abusing alcohol. With illicit drugs, the definition of abuse is even further confused. People who take heroin are seen as part of the drug abuse problem even though their use might be non-dependent and present no social, medical or psychological difficulties. Social problems are socially defined. From their different perspectives and priorities the police officer, the clinical psychologist, and the physician are likely to define drug and alcohol abuse differently. As a result, arguments about the extent of such problems in our society sometimes resemble the theological dispute over the number of angels that might stand on the head of a pin.

Nevertheless, there can be no doubt as to the serious social, psychological and physical damage that can follow from the unwise use of drugs and alcohol, and it is important to make some estimate (however imperfect) of the extent of such problems. Alcohol presents one of the most serious problems. There are probably about 350,000 alcoholics in Britain's population of 55 million, though some estimates put the number as high as 700,000. Despite the extent of alcoholism, there is remarkable public complacency about alcohol abuse. In marked contrast are the more emotive attitudes towards heroin addiction: yet the number of people who were notified to the Home Office during 1981 as being addicted to opiates (such as heroin, morphine and methadone) was just over 6,000. The pattern in the USA is rather different. It is estimated that there may be around 6 million alcoholics (again, roughly 1 per cent of the population), but the number of opiate addicts, which has been estimated at between 500,000 and 800,000 addicts is, proportionately, much higher than in Britain.

The British Home Office Index is sometimes challenged on the grounds that it seriously under-estimates the actual numbers of opiate addicts in the community. Although several studies found that the majority of addicts in their samples were known to the Home Office, others suggested that there may be at least as many addicts who are not notified. There can be no final answer to the question of whether or not the Home Office Index provides an accurate assessment of the opiate problem, but after a careful review of this issue, Edwards (1981) concluded that, despite its flaws, the Index has been a useful monitoring device. Where no such index exists (as for instance with stimulant drugs), estimates of the size of the problem become still more problematic.

The problem of drug abuse is not confined to illicit drugs. Although it receives little recognition, the abuse of legally available and medically prescribed drugs is considerable. The minor tranquillizers, of which Valium and Librium are the best known, are used and abused on a vast scale; Valium is the most prescribed drug in the world. These drugs are increasingly available as 'street' drugs and there is a steady demand for them on the black market. Sedatives, notably the barbiturates, are also widely abused. One survey suggested that there were between 200,000 and 2,000,000 US citizens who misused or who were addicted to sedative drugs.

Even such apparently innocuous drugs as aspirin are widely abused. Every year the British population swallows about 2,000 tons of analgesics, and there are more than a million people who regularly take such drugs every day. One criterion for identifying analgesic abuse is the consumption of more than 1 kilogram of the drug in a six-month period. On this basis there may be as many as a quarter-of-a-million analgesic abusers in Britain. Heavy use of these drugs can cause gastro-intestinal bleeding, stomach ulcers and kidney damage, and they are one of the commonest causes of accidental death among children.

However, there is no necessary relationship between the extent of a problem and its recognition, nor between the recognition of a problem and any move to modify it. The misuse of drugs such as aspirin is classified as a drug abuse problem only in the most extreme circumstances. Similarly there is a general reluctance to classify the misuse of medically prescribed drugs as a problem. There is even a considerable leeway allowed to the drinker before he or she is thought to have a drink problem. The person whose drug taking is most likely to be identified as abuse is the one who is found to be taking illicit drugs.

II.—CONCEPTS OF THE PERSON AND MODELS OF HUMAN BEHAVIOUR

In practice, the most influential view of drug and alcohol dependence has been the personality disorder model. This has been massively influential in psychiatry and many psychiatrists have difficulty in working with any other explanation of drug or alcohol abuse. The personality disorder model has been stated succinctly by Kohut (1977): in drug dependence, 'the individual suffers from a central weakness, from a weakness in the core of his personality . . . the symptoms . . . arise secondarily as an outgrowth of a defect in the self.'

The greatest obstacle to this view has been the failure to specify what form this disorder might take. Personality research has produced little evidence to support the existence of an 'addictive personality'. The few findings to emerge with any degree of consistency in this area suggest that drug addicts and alcoholics tend to score highly on measures of neuroticism (Barnes, 1979; Gossop, 1978a), and psychopathic deviance or toughmindedness (Gossop and Eysenck, 1980; Miller, 1976). There are some data to suggest that the drug upon which a person becomes dependent is chosen because of its self-medicating effects. Teasdale (1972) suggested that stimulant drugs are frequently used to reduce social anxieties. Similarly, Gossop and Roy (1976) suggested that opiate addicts might be using drugs to cope with the distress associated with hostile and aggressive feelings. As yet, these suggestions have not been followed up in research.

The clinical implications of the personality disorder model, particularly in its general form, can be unhelpful since it offers no clear guidelines about how to modify such non-specific problems. The therapeutic implications that follow from the idea that drug addiction and alcoholism are 'diseases' are somewhat clearer and have had an enormous influence upon the treatment of addicts and alcoholics. The most significant proponent of this view of alcoholism was Jellinek, whose book *The Disease Concept of Alcoholism* (1960) has been a classic contribution in this field. In recent years, however, it has become increasingly apparent that, despite its vast influence, this model of alcoholism has been accepted, defended, taught and reified without any systematic attempt to test its basic premises.

The disease model has also been applied to drug addiction. Dole and Nyswander (1967) suggested that opiates such as heroin cause metabolic changes in users as a result of which they develop a physiological need for their drug in precisely the same way that the diabetic needs insulin. Again, the nature of this metabolic disease was never clearly stated and subsequent research has failed to confirm any such metabolic changes. Nonetheless, as with the disease concept of alcoholism, this view has had a great influence upon the way that drug addicts have been treated. This is especially true in the USA where methadone maintenance has proved such a popular option.

Physiological models of addiction have enjoyed something of a revival in recent years. This is largely due to the discovery of naturally occurring chemicals in the brain (endorphins) with powerful morphine-like effects which act upon specific receptor sites. The discovery of these chemicals represents a major advance in neuroscience. However, their function is not properly understood, and it is unfortunate that many investigators have been tempted into making extravagant claims about them. From the evidence available, it would appear that the interaction of externally administered opiate drugs with these endogenous peptides plays an important role in the development of tolerance and physical dependence to such drugs.

A general problem inherent in biochemical research of this sort is that it leads to a view of addiction which is narrower than the range of problems presented by real drug addicts. Physiological accounts have comparatively little to say, for instance, about such phenomena as psychological dependence, compulsive drug seeking, or the tendency to relapse shown by many addicts even after long periods of drug-free treatment.

The model that would be most familiar to the experimental psychologist also carries some of the most specific implications for treatment. The principles of learning theory have been applied to a wide range of problems in abnormal psychology, notably the neurotic disorders (Gossop, 1981). One of the first attempts to describe drug dependence in conditioning terms was that of Wikler (1948), and during the intervening 35 years this approach has generated an impressive volume of research.

The regular use of most drugs leads to tolerance (i.e., the effects of a given dose gradually decrease), and a number of experiments have pointed to the involvement of a Pavlovian conditioning process in the development of tolerance (Siegel, 1977). Experimental analyses have looked at drug taking in terms of the positive primary reinforcement provided by the drug itself and in terms of the positive secondary reinforcement that is offered by stimuli which have become associated with the use of drugs.

Drug taking can also be a way of escaping from, or avoiding aversive stimuli, and here too the opiate withdrawal syndrome is known to have a substantial conditioned component. O'Brien (1976) has described conditioned withdrawal symptoms as being due to the repeated pairing of environmental cues (CS) with drug withdrawal (US) which leads to abstinence symptoms (UR) such that the environmental cues themselves come to precipitate the withdrawal symptoms. Wikler (1961) suggested that the relapse of many opiate addicts could be attributed to the failure of treatment programmes to deal with conditioned stimuli and their experiential counterpart, craving.

Craving is an especially interesting psychological state, since for both drug addicts and alcoholics it regularly leads to the consumption of their particular drug. The learning theory account of Meyer and Mirin (1981) described craving in terms of the various stimulus properties of addictive drugs (including alcohol); and Hodgson and his colleagues at the Addiction Research Unit in the University of London have also shown how the cognitive and physiological effects of drinking alcohol can become cues which elicit, or at least influence, craving (Hodgson, Rankin and Stockwell, 1978).

One criticism that has been levelled against explanations of drug and alcohol dependence (for instance by Gossop, 1979), is that they have tended to see the problem as an inevitable result of powerful forces which act upon the individual, as a compulsion to use drugs over which the user has no control. It is a considerable advantage of the formulation offered by Hodgson and his colleagues that they are able to avoid this pitfall, and they conclude that 'loss of control is certainly not an inevitable consequence of consuming drink even for the severely dependent alcoholic' (pp. 341–349). Pessimistic views of drug and alcohol dependence that underestimate or deny the individual's capacity to control and direct their own behaviour can have the most unfortunate implications for treatment.

III.—INDIVIDUAL ASSESSMENT

Drug and alcohol dependence are not specific, unitary disorders. There are many routes which lead to these destinations, and the social and psychological characteristics of people with drug or alcohol problems vary enormously.

The assessment of such problems covers a correspondingly wide area. It must deal with the medical and physical problems associated with drug or alcohol abuse, with those psychological problems that may be regarded as a result of drug taking, and with the psychological characteristics and social circumstances of the user.

The first of these, the assessment of physical complications, is perhaps the least immediately relevant to the psychologist, though the psychological implications of physical damage should not be underestimated. Alcohol causes cirrhosis of the liver and is clearly implicated in pancreatitis. There are also various neurological disorders that can be induced by alcohol: alcohol can cause damage to virtually any part of the nervous system. Symptoms may include epileptiform fits, ataxia, muscular weakness, amnesia, psychotic confusion and dementia. There may be similar problems associated with drug abuse. The general health of drug addicts is often poor and, because of the ways in which they use drugs, a large proportion may suffer from serious ill health. The injection of drugs carries a risk of such problems as hepatitis, abscesses and septicemia. Solvent abuse, the most common form of which is glue sniffing, has been said to cause neurological damage, though the evidence on this question is unclear. For most other drugs of abuse, the evidence of drug-induced neurological damage is even less convincing despite the confident assertions of certain authors.

The assessment of psychological problems that are (in some sense) a direct consequence of drug taking, presents a separate issue. High dose amphetamine abuse, for instance, may cause persecutory delusions and visual, auditory and olfactory hallucinations. Amphetamine psychosis is sufficiently similar to paranoid schizophrenia to create a real danger of the former being falsely diagnosed as a schizophrenic illness. This may have seriously misleading implications with regard to the treatment and management of the patient since the symptoms of amphetamine psychosis may occur in otherwise normal individuals and will disappear when the person is drug-free.

Other drugs can also occasionally produce catastrophic reactions. The effects of both the hallucinogens (of which LSD is the best known and the most widely used) and cannabis are largely dependent upon psychological and social factors, and some inexperienced drug users have been very disturbed by the altered states of consciousness that they have experienced after taking these drugs. Anxiety, panic, confusion, depression, delusions and full-blown hallucinations have all been reported as adverse effects of these drugs, though to regard them as directly drug-related in the same sense as amphetamine psychosis is misleading.

> The individual, under the influence of a strange drug, loosened from his traditional moorings, heavily sensitive to and influenced by his equally naive companions, comes to look upon his own behaviour and experiences not merely as eccentric but as an unquestionable sign of actual insanity . . . and his conviction of his own insanity, the novelty of the sensations he is experiencing, the interpretations of his friends, his negative feelings about letting go or losing control, all conspire to push him in the direction of an actual psychotic outbreak. (Goode, 1972; pp. 111–112).

However, for those who are primarily interested in helping someone with a drug or alcohol problem, the most imperative problems of assessment concern the psychological characteristics and the social circumstances of the individual user. It is important, for instance, to know whether users take their particular drug mainly in social settings or when they are alone. There are various social rewards associated with drug taking. Peer pressure can have a powerful influence upon the development of problem drinking among adolescents, and alcoholics and drug addicts often report considerable difficulty in remaining abstinent when they are in certain social settings. Anyone who has tried not to drink alcohol at a party or in a pub will know something of the pressures that might be involved.

Drugs are also powerful tools for altering the subjective state of the user and it is clear that many people run into difficulties because of the way in which their drug taking reduces feelings of psychological discomfort. The distress associated with anxiety, anger and depression can be reduced by many commonly abused drugs. Where this sort of self-medication occurs, it is usually necessary to set up an appropriate programme directed towards treating the underlying problem and several studies have reported some success in the treatment of alcoholics and drug addicts through the use of systematic desensitization (Hodgson and Rankin, 1976; Kraft, 1969).

A full assessment should also look at the resources (or, more often, the lack of resources) which are available to the individual who is trying to avoid further problems. These may vary from such psychological characteristics as general intelligence or sociability, through social skills, occupational and educational skills, to specific features of the environment, such as whether the person has somewhere decent to live or any family or friends to provide encouragement and support.

IV.—THE IMMEDIATE SOCIAL AND EMOTIONAL ENVIRONMENT

The way in which someone responds to a drug is only partly determined by pharmacological factors. There are numerous illustrations of this point, the best known of which is the series of experiments by Schachter and Singer (1962). Their ingenious work showed that in the absence of information about how a drug would affect them, their subjects reacted in the same way as an experimental stooge with whom they had to share a room. Despite the fact that they had only received an injection of adrenaline (which produces no consistent psychological effects), they displayed either euphoria or anger, according to the example of the stooge.

This effect is no less important outside the laboratory. In what has established itself as a classic study of cannabis smokers, Becker (1953) showed that many of the effects of cannabis are shaped by social learning processes. These processes seem to apply to all the psychoactive drugs, including alcohol and heroin. Indeed, because social and cognitive factors play such an important part in determining how people respond to drugs it is possible for them to react as if they had taken a drug even when no drug has been used. This is the placebo effect.

It is hazardous and misleading to discuss the use and abuse of drugs and alcohol without taking full account of the social environment in which they are taken, and the meaning that they have for the user. There can be few more dramatic illustrations of the importance of the immediate social environment in the abuse of drugs than the behaviour of American troops during the Vietnam War. The use of all kinds of drugs was widespread among American soldiers in Vietnam. Cannabis was used by the majority of troops, and amphetamines and barbiturates were also widely used. Perhaps the most alarming findings were that 85 per cent of the men reported being offered heroin during their tour; 35 per cent of Army enlisted men tried heroin and 19 per cent became addicted to it (Robins, Helzer, Hesselbrook and Wish, 1980). This caused a good deal of concern both in terms of its implication for the effectiveness of the army as a fighting force, and in terms of the prospect of thousands of experienced combat troops returning to the streets of the USA with an addiction to heroin.

A follow-up study of the soldiers who had been addicted in Vietnam after their return home presented a surprising but extremely interesting finding. More than half of the men who used opiates in Vietnam did not use them at all within three years of their return to America, and *more than 90 per cent who were addicted to opiates in Vietnam never became re-addicted, even temporarily*. This marked contrast between the patterns of drug taking in the USA and in Vietnam challenges several widely accepted myths about the irreversibility of addiction, and points to the important influence that the social environment can have.

While serving in Vietnam, the US soldier was exposed to a powerful combination of social factors facilitating drug use. The experience of suddenly being removed from a safe, familiar environment to a strange, foreign and extremely threatening one, increases the pressure upon the individual to take drugs. Drugs are a useful means of coping with the mixture of fear, physical tiredness and boredom that is such a familiar feature of military life during a war. Also, the tour of duty in Vietnam was characterized by a removal of many of the usual social and moral restraints that reduce the likelihood of drug taking. The soldiers themselves were inclined to regard their tour of duty as something separated from 'real life' and there were various social pressures to take drugs simply because so many others were using them. Last but not least, there was the physical availability of all kinds of drugs. It is difficult to imagine conditions more likely to promote their widespread use (Gossop, 1982).

There are other, less dramatic illustrations of the way people can be put at risk because of their close contact with drugs or drink. In a study of Austrian brewery workers who received a free daily allowance of four litres of beer, clinical and biochemical tests showed that they were three times more likely to have some form of liver damage than another group of workers from a nearby factory. Other occupations said to be at risk in this respect include barmen, merchant seamen, members of the armed forces and journalists. There have also been many well-publicized casualties of drug addiction and alcoholism among professional musicians.

The prevalence of drug addiction among socially disadvantaged groups is very high in the USA where Blacks, Puerto Ricans and other ethnic minorities from deprived inner-city areas are over-represented among the addict population. A more precise statement of the social conditions associated with drug addiction pointed to high concentrations of under-privileged minority groups, poverty and low economic status, low educational attainment, disrupted family life, crowded housing conditions and high proportions of teenage males (Chein, Gerrard, Lee and Rosenfeld, 1964). The position in Britain, however, is quite different, and there is little evidence that poverty or social disadvantage *per se* lead to or are correlated with increased levels of addiction. Indeed, it is a curious and unexplained observation that West Indians and Asians living in Britain seem to be less at risk of being addicted to drugs despite their economic and social disadvantages (Gossop, 1979).

V.—THE WIDER SOCIAL AND ORGANIZATIONAL ENVIRONMENT

It is not sufficient merely to concentrate on the individual drinker or drug taker if one is trying to understand, prevent or alleviate such problems. The social factors that influence the ways in which a person uses or abuses drugs or alcohol extend from specific details of social interaction to the broadest cultural influences.

In France, alcohol plays an important role in everyday life. The consumption of alcohol is generally encouraged and there are few proscriptive norms to restrict drinking. Indeed, intoxication appears to be socially acceptable. A survey of public opinion in France asked what quantity of wine a working man could consume every day without harm, and obtained the remarkable estimate of 1.6 litres; 38 per cent of respondents felt that two litres of wine would not be harmful. One consequence of this is that the prevalence of alcohol-related pathology (such as cirrhosis of the liver) and of other alcohol-related problems (such as public drunkenness) is extremely high in France. Current thinking about alcoholism relies heavily upon the proposition that as national *per capita* levels of alcohol consumption increase, then the number of people in that society who damage themselves by drinking will also increase: the converse is also held to be true, namely that as *per capita* levels of consumption decrease so there will be fewer people damaged by drinking. This view should not, however, be treated as if it were a scientific law. There are exceptions. Over certain periods the trends in the UK have not been consistent with this view.

One of the best known examples of the way that cultural factors can have a protective effect concerns the use of alcohol by the Jews. Practically all Jews drink alcohol, yet very few become alcoholics. In contrast to orthodox Jews in America, the incidence of alcoholism among Irish-Americans is extremely high. Keller (1970) attributed this to the fact that the Irish style of drinking is convivial and the desired effect is achieved through the pharmacological action of alcohol; in Jewish life, the pharmacological effects of alcohol are said to be secondary to the social meanings that surround drinking. Both Keller (1970) and Snyder (1958) have argued that the Jewish drinker gains considerable protection from alcohol problems because of the social rituals that regulate the manner in which the Jew uses alcohol. Weil

(1972) used a similar argument in his discussion of the way hallucinatory drugs are used in a controlled manner by South American Indians.

The social factors that influence drug taking are themselves subject to change. In most cultures men have traditionally been more likely to drink alcohol and to develop a drinking problem than women. With the changes in sex roles that have taken place during the past few decades, there has been a steady rise in the number of women who are running into difficulties with alcohol. The Royal College of Psychiatrists' (1979) report on drinking suggested that one of the prices to be paid for a more equal place for women in society may be their more equal rate of alcoholism. (The same point has been made about the incidence of smoking among men and women and the respective rates of lung cancer and respiratory diseases).

It is also usual to find a greater proportion of men than women presenting at drug dependence clinics. In the UK, men generally outnumber women by about three to one. However, this may be partly due to different social responses to different social patterns of drug use. More men than women use illicit heroin but more women receive medically-sanctioned supplies of tranquillizers and sedative drugs. Since drug dependence in medical practice is less readily identified than illicit drug abuse, these sorts of social factors may give a distorted impression of the relative numbers of men and women with drug problems.

Some sociologists have taken the view that deviant behaviour (including many of the so-called mental illnesses) is better seen in terms of ascribed social roles. Societal reactance, or *labelling theory*, asserts that there need be little relationship between the personality or psychological characteristics of the individual and the deviant behaviour identified as their problem (Lemert, 1967). However, it is now clear that there are areas of abnormal psychology in which this perspective is of only limited value (Gossop, 1981) and labelling theory has not always benefitted from the excessive enthusiasm of some of its proponents. Nonetheless, it has a certain relevance to the problems associated with the abuse of drugs and alcohol.

Erickson (1981) looked at the effects on a group of young Canadians, of being convicted of possession of cannabis. Their sentence had little, if any effect upon subsequent cannabis use (only eight per cent had not used it since their court appearance), but the users felt 'more criminal' and were less satisfactorily employed. In some case, the social consequences of being publicly identified as an illicit drug user can be extremely severe.

Young (1971) has discussed this issue at some length by reference to what he terms the 'deviancy amplification spiral'. In Young's analysis, the enforcement of anti-drugs laws may increase feelings of group cohesiveness among drug takers in reaction to what they feel to be harsh and unsympathetic treatment. It may lead drug takers to adopt a more isolated position in society in which their world becomes increasingly centred around drugs;

and as the drug taker evolves deviant forms of behaviour, this makes it more difficult to re-enter the wider society. As part of this process, drug taking regularly assumes an exaggerated value to the isolated group as a symbol of its difference from, and defiance to society; intoxication and the abuse of drugs become positively valued and sought after. The sense of alienation from society that is felt so acutely by many addicts, presents a substantial obstacle to any attempt to change their pattern of drug taking.

VI.−TYPES OF INTERVENTION

Almost every conceivable form of psychological, behavioural and physical treatment has, at one time or another, been used with drug addicts and alcoholics. In one sense, this diversity could be seen as laudable insofar as it reflects the diverse range of problems and needs among the people who develop such difficulties, and it would be reassuring to report that the chosen treatments were primarily geared to the needs of the individual.

Unfortunately one is left with an uneasy suspicion that the choice of treatment often owes as much to the theoretical orientation and implicit beliefs of the therapist about the problem, as to the circumstances and characteristics of the patient. In some cases, this rather erratic process can lead to the use of highly problematic treatment interventions which may be inappropriate or even damaging to the patient. Psychosurgery stands as an example of this. Miller and Hester (1980) cite a study in which surgery was performed on the hypothalamus of two alcoholics, one of whom relapsed immediately after recovery from the operation. Brain surgery has also been performed on drug addicts with neither theoretical justification nor empirical success. In one instance, a 19-year-old man addicted to heroin was given a leucotomy: it made no difference to either his chaotic life-style or his use of drugs. Fortunately, such extreme interventions are rare.

Various drugs have been used in the treatment of alcoholics. Disulfiram (Antabuse) produces headache, nausea, vomiting, dizziness and weakness when combined with alcohol. The reaction is highly aversive. Disulfiram has been given to alcoholics to help them keep to a decision to abstain from alcohol. The use of narcotic antagonist drugs represents a similar sort of approach to opiate addiction. Narcotic antagonists block the euphoric effects of opiates, apparently by occupying opiate receptor sites in the brain. Most addicts who use antagonists are said to feel little urge to use drugs while on an antagonist blockade; there has, however, been some difficulty in persuading addicts to take such antagonists. In one American study, of the 735 addicts who volunteered to participate in a trial with one of these drugs, 543 (74 per cent) dropped out before even receiving the first dose (O'Brien and Greenstein, 1981). Such medical approaches to treatment seem to be suited only to those addicts who are strongly and consistently motivated to stop using opiates.

The most immediate problem of treatment usually involves withdrawing the drugs from the person. Sometimes this can be done abruptly (as with amphetamines). With other drugs, in order to minimize the dangers of inducing epileptiform fits or other serious withdrawal symptoms, it is better to use gradually reducing doses of the drug (as with barbiturates, Valium and heroin), or to use some other form of drug 'cover' during this period (as with alcohol). In all cases, however, the withdrawal phase of treatment is comparatively easy to manage (in an in-patient setting), and it is of little significance for the long-term prospects of the user. The problems of treatment lie not in getting people off drugs but in helping them to avoid relapse after withdrawal.

One of the most influential of the physical treatments of opiate addiction has been methadone maintenance. The pioneers of methadone maintenance were Dole and Nyswander, whose model of treatment proposed that heroin addiction could be treated by methadone in the same way that diabetes is treated with insulin (Dole and Nyswander, 1967). Whether because it offered a more humane alternative to the punitive approaches to heroin addiction that were so often used in the USA, or for other reasons (for example, its promise of a medical cure for drug addiction), methadone maintenance has been extremely popular in the USA. In its first four years, one programme in New York admitted more than 38,000 individuals, and the annual budget for another New York programme had grown to 20 million dollars within a few years of its inception. Although the provision of legally prescribed drugs for those addicts who are unable or unwilling to stop taking drugs may have some advantages, it now seems clear that the initial enthusiasm and the claims made for methadone maintenance were naive and excessively optimistic (Gossop, 1978b).

In a more general sense, methadone maintenance belongs to that tradition which has looked for a drug to cure drug addiction. This tradition encompasses a catalogue of errors. It is worth noting that morphine was once used as a treatment for cocaine addiction, cocaine as a treatment for morphine addiction, and most astonishingly of all, heroin was once seen as a safe and non-addictive alternative to morphine. The important aspects of drug maintenance are not matters of pharmacology, but simply follow from the fact that drugs are available legally and within a controlled and therapeutic setting.

It is in the realm of the more purely 'psychological' interventions that the range of treatment options is so bewildering. Aversion therapy, covert sensitization, relaxation therapy, systematic desensitization, hypnosis, cognitive therapy, group psychotherapy, therapeutic communities, interpretative individual psychotherapy, family therapy, social skills training and many other approaches have all been tried both on their own and in various combinations (cf. Miller, 1980).

A commitment to the classical conditioning model of addiction is likely to lead to a taste for extinction-based treatments. Aversion therapy is an example of this type of approach. Drinking and drug taking have been paired with both electrical and chemically aversive stimuli. Covert sensitization, in which verbally guided imagery of drinking or drug taking is associated with unpleasant sensations, has also been used in treatment. The rationale behind aversion therapy and covert sensitization is similar, in that both are usually aimed at establishing a conditioned abstinence.

Many addicts and alcoholics have problems with anxiety, and the relief of anxiety through drink or drugs may provide a substantial degree of reinforcement for their addiction. Among the treatments that have aimed at reducing the underlying anxiety are relaxation training and systematic desensitization. Relaxation techniques have generally been based on the progressive deep muscle relaxation developed by Jacobson, and they have been used to reduce levels of anxiety and arousal and to reduce craving for drink and drugs. In systematic desensitization, relaxation is paired with specific stimuli that usually make a person feel tense or anxious. The stimuli are presented in a hierarchy starting with the least stressful, and the person is encouraged to relax before moving on to the next item in the hierarchy.

Of all the group-based approaches, Alcoholics Anonymous is perhaps the best known. This carries an ideological position of its own which members are required to accept: in particular they are expected to admit their inability to control their drinking, to identify drinking as a form of disease, to admit personal defects and make reparation for harm done in the past, and entirely to give up alcohol for an abstinent life. There is also a number of therapeutic communities for addicts, among them, Phoenix House and Narcotics Anonymous. The original therapeutic community for addicts was Synanon. This was founded in 1958 and was modelled directly upon Alcoholics Anonymous. Most therapeutic communities make extensive use of group methods. Another feature which is less easy to describe is their quasi-religious and evangelical style. Those addicts who do well in these communities often appear to have undergone some sort of 'conversion' experience.

Group psychotherapies of one sort or another have been widely used and 'group psychotherapy' is said to be one of the most common of all the techniques used in the hospital treatment of patients with addiction problems. Unfortunately, the actual procedures and interventions used in group psychotherapy are seldom specified and despite a general consensus about the value of group approaches, the actual operation of groups remains shrouded in mystery.

Until quite recently the possibility that moderate drinking could be a goal of treatment for alcoholics was virtually ignored. Indeed, most models of alcoholism refused on *a priori* grounds to accept that this was possible. When, in 1962, Davies published a paper showing that some alcoholics were able to drink moderately, this aroused a good deal of angry feeling and was condemned by many as irresponsible. Within the past decade, there has accumulated enough evidence to confirm Davies' observations. However, those who seem likely to achieve this have been found to be consuming smaller amounts of alcohol, to show less severe symptoms of alcoholism and to have a briefer history of alcohol problems. Moderate drinking may, therefore, only be a realistic goal for the less severely dependent problem drinkers. The question of whether drug addicts could learn to moderate their drug taking has received virtually no attention, and abstinence seems to be universally accepted as the ultimate goal of treatment.

VII.—IS PSYCHOLOGICAL INTERVENTION SUCCESSFUL?

How successfully can you treat drug or alcohol dependence? Few questions are asked more often and few are more difficult to answer. 'Addiction', like 'mental illness', does not refer to any unitary process or disorder. It is just as meaningless to ask which is the best treatment for people addicted to drugs or alcohol as it is to ask how best to treat people suffering from mental illness. The addiction therapist must match the treatment to the *specific* circumstances, needs and problems of the individual. It is futile to look for a single treatment intervention which can be used to treat all addicts or all alcoholics.

There are also problems surrounding the criteria by which success should be measured. This issue is by no means as clear as might be supposed. It is tempting to assume that the single goal of treatment should be abstinence. For the therapist, however, other social and psychological difficulties of the patient may seem equally deserving of attention, and such goals as improved social functioning, anxiety reduction, reduced criminal activity, obtaining and maintaining regular employment, and improved physical health have all been used by different studies as indicators of treatment success. The choice of treatment *goals* may need to be as individually based as the choice of treatment methods. Because different criteria have been used in different studies it is often difficult to make any direct comparison of results.

The choice of controlled drinking as a goal in the treatment of alcoholics brings together a number of these issues. Several patient characteristics appear to increase the chances of regaining control over drinking. These include being younger, having a shorter history of drinking problems, having run into fewer social difficulties as a result of drinking, and having a lower level of pre-treatment alcohol consumption. In general terms, it seems that controlled drinking is most likely to be attained by people with less severe drinking problems. In their recent review of the subject, Heather and

Robertson (1981) pointed out the advantages of using controlled drinking rather than abstinence as a treatment goal. Among these are the fact that the adoption of total abstinence constitutes a deviant role in contemporary industrialized society which may itself attract problems of psychosocial adjustment, that the 'abstinent alcoholic' may be subject to periodic episodes of depression, and that there is little relationship between the attainment of abstinence and overall improvement in social functioning. Heather and Robertson suggest that abstinence may not be an appropriate goal for problem drinkers (as distinct from long-term alcohol addicts.)

A baseline measure which has sometimes been used as a reference point in discussions of treatment effectiveness is 'spontaneous recovery'. This refers to the chances of improvement or recovery without the benefit of a formal course of treatment. A recent review of nine studies of spontaneous recovery among alcoholics found yearly improvement rates of between 1 per cent and 33 per cent (Smart, 1976). The marked variation in these rates may partly be accounted for by differences in the criteria for improvement used in different studies, but it may also reflect unknown or unreported differences in the subject samples.

One of the best known follow-up studies of British addicts looked at a group of heroin addicts who approached London drug dependence clinics in 1969. After seven years, it was found that 31 per cent were no longer dependent upon opiates (Stimson, Oppenheimer and Thorley, 1978). Most follow-up studies have supported this finding; over a seven-year period, about one-third of any group of addicts will cease to be dependent upon drugs. It is not clear whether this recovery rate should be regarded simply as spontaneous remission, or as an outcome rate averaged across a range of treatments. Over a period of years, most addicts approach a number of treatment agencies and are offered a bewildering variety of medical, behavioural and social interventions.

Despite the immense difficulties involved, there has been a number of attempts to evaluate specific types of treatment intervention. The reader who is interested in a detailed discussion of these is referred to Miller's book *The Addictive Behaviors* (Miller, 1980). For most forms of treatment, there is either not enough controlled research to support any definite conclusion, or the research findings are inconsistent. However, several of the treatments used with alcoholics do receive tentative support from studies (Miller and Hester, 1980). There is some consistency among studies investigating the effectiveness of behavioural self-control training. As used by Miller and his colleagues, this represents an educationally-oriented approach to treatment. It usually involves the setting of specific attainable goals, self-monitoring of behaviour, self-reinforcement training, and training designed to teach alternative coping skills.

The studies of Sobell and Sobell (e.g., 1978) have been widely cited in relation to controlled drinking. These studies show significant and long-lasting improvements, both in drinking and in general adjustment, among alcoholics treated by individualized behaviour therapy programmes which focus upon problem solving skills training, stimulus control training and regulated drinking during treatment. There is also some evidence to support the effectiveness of broad-spectrum approaches including desensitization and social skills training.

Several studies have made claims for the effectiveness of disulfiram, aversion therapies and video-tape self-confrontation, though there is some question as to whether the risk, costs and discomfort of these approaches outweigh their attendant benefits. Of the treatment methods which have fared poorly in evaluative research, Miller and Hester argue that hypnosis, insight-oriented psychotherapy and routine multimodal treatment packages have been shown to be ineffective in the treatment of alcoholics. The position with regard to the treatment of drug addicts is even more confused, though the same tentative conclusions about the effectiveness of specific interventions would seem to apply.

For each of the addictive disorders, any treatment outcome may be regarded as depending upon three factors, the nature and extent of the person's problems, their willingness to engage and co-operate with the treatment offered, and, lastly, the treatment procedure itself. We do not know the relative contribution of each of these factors to the outcome, but it is quite likely that the actual treatment procedure is of only comparatively minor importance among the factors related to recovery from a dependence upon drugs or alcohol. Social factors such as educational and occupational skills, or having a supportive spouse or close friends may well be of more significance. The course of treatment and the chances of recovery may well also be powerfully influenced by the beliefs, attitudes and intentions of the individual, though these cognitive factors have only recently begun to attract any attention (e.g., Gossop, Eiser and Ward, 1982).

VIII.—METHODOLOGICAL AND PRACTICAL PROBLEMS

It should by now be clear that neither drug addiction nor alcoholism is the sort of disorder that attacks its passive victim. To some extent (and usually to a greater rather than a lesser extent), both disorders are a consequence of an active pursuit of intoxication. By the time an addiction is established, the use of drugs or alcohol has become an important part of the user's life, and it is, therefore, correspondingly resistant to modification. The chosen drug is also the focus of various beliefs, attitudes and values, positive as well as negative.

Those who have been involved in the treatment of drug addiction and alcoholism will be aware that most patients are ambivalent about the use of their particular drug; or, at least, they find it difficult to maintain indefinitely a wholehearted commitment to living without their drug. Because of this, a persistent theme underlying the treatment of these disorders concerns the person's motives and intentions.

Drug addiction and alcoholism cannot be treated without the co-operation and commitment of the patient. In this field, treatments cannot be applied mechanically. Indeed, the traditional notion of 'treatment' is rather inappropriate in this context. 'Treatments' are essentially instrumental by nature; they consist of *what is done*. But rather than being an event that *happens to* the addict, treatment in this field is a process in which the patient takes an active role. The actual series of events that make up the treatment intervention are extremely complex. They occur within a confused system of social, psychological, legal and quasi-medical pressures, and despite the concise descriptions given in the research journals, the actual treatment is seldom a precise and delineated procedure, but an uncontrolled and poorly understood series of events. Indeed, when we use the word 'treatment' in this context, we are using the term in a metaphorical as much as a literal sense.

By concentrating upon the treatment itself, and upon the question of the effectiveness of specific interventions, evaluative research has frequently served to obscure the crucial role of individual differences within the addict population. It is not uncommon for treatment evaluative research to leave patient factors uncontrolled and unspecified, and to interpret the results as if they were entirely the product of the intervention itself. Yet with a co-operative, highly motivated sample of individuals which has comparatively few psychological and social problems, even the most feeble treatment procedure might be expected to produce a satisfactory outcome. In contrast, the most powerful procedures could be expected to fail if used with a resistant and highly disturbed sample.

In methodological as well as practical clinical terms, this requires a move away from models which focus exclusively upon treatment procedures. To a limited extent this shift is already taking place in alcoholism research. It can be seen, for instance, in some of the recent work dealing with controlled drinking. Sadly, the same cannot be said of evaluative research in drug addiction where patient factors are seldom acknowledged or incorporated into research designs.

IX.—PROBLEMS OF ETHICS AND CONFIDENTIALITY

This whole area is surrounded by problems of ethics and confidentiality. Consider the following problems:

Person A is an ex-alcoholic who has been attending Alcoholics Anonymous for two years. He has been completely abstinent throughout that time. He has heard from a friend that your clinic teaches alcoholics how to drink in a controlled manner. He asks if you will teach him how to drink normally. Given the present state of knowledge, it cannot be predicted with certainty that this will succeed. He may well relapse into alcoholism if he uses alcohol again. Should the therapist agree to help him?

Person B is an opiate addict and is receiving methadone on prescription from your drug clinic. He works as a bus driver but his employers do not know that he is using opiates. Methadone interferes with his concentration and alertness, and his drug taking constitutes a serious risk to the public in this job. He refuses to inform his employers of his addiction which he believes would cause him to lose his job. What, if anything, should the therapist do? If an accident occurs, what blame would attach itself to the therapist who prescribed the drugs?

From the patient's perspective, the social stigma that attaches itself to the labels 'drug addict' or 'alcoholic' makes it important that the confidentiality of patient information be carefully protected. As a general rule, a therapist may not give information about a patient to a third party without the patient's consent. In the USA, two statutes were passed by Congress during the early 1970's which strictly define the circumstances under which information about addicts or alcoholics may be disclosed. Any breach of these regulations is punishable by a fine of up to $500 for a first offence or up to $5000 for each subsequent offence.

However, the simple directive that information should not be divulged without the patient's consent is often less easily reconciled with the confusions of real life. Consider a third illustrative case:

Person C, a schoolboy, is referred to you by a school-teacher who is worried about his erratic behaviour and poor school performance. The child confesses that he is sniffing glue with a group of friends at school. He says that he finds it difficult not to take part in the glue sniffing because of the social pressures. None of the teachers suspects that drugs are involved. Is there any case for informing them of the situation? What special problems are involved in obtaining consent from a minor? Suppose that it was felt to be essential to the success of any treatment effort to involve the boy's family but that the child refuses to allow them to be told that he was taking drugs?

In practice, the role of therapists in the addictions is defined by several parties, notably the therapist, the patient, the patient's family, commercial interests, professional interests, and by the State. Often the interests of these different parties conflict, and it is at this point that the ethical problems become most acute.

Some of the strongest views on this subject have been voiced by Thomas Szasz (1972) who argues that the whole problem of drug and alcohol abuse is a moral and ethical problem.

Abuse cannot be defined without specifying the proper and improper uses of certain pharmacologically active agents. The regular administration of morphine by a physician to a patient dying of cancer is the paradigm of the proper use of a narcotic: whereas even its occasional self-administration by a physically healthy person for the purpose of 'pharmacological pleasure' is the paradigm of drug abuse. I submit that these judgments have nothing whatever to do with medicine, pharmacology, or psychiatry. They are moral judgments. Indeed, our present views on addiction are astonishingly similar to some of our former views on sex.

Szasz's main worry is that, in its response to the addictions, medicine is increasingly the servant of the State and not of the patient.

The most extraordinary commitment to the primacy of the interests of the State over those of the addict was made by Lesse in a 1972 editorial of the *American Journal of Psychotherapy*. Lesse suggested that 'Chronic heroin addicts with a history of felonious criminal behaviour prior to their becoming addicts should be permanently institutionalized on work farms.' 'Sterilization of narcotics addicts . . . should be considered.' 'The children of heroin addicts should be taken from the parents' (pp. 328–329).

The sociologist Becker used the term 'moral crusaders' to describe those individuals who campaign to eliminate social evils from society. The Women's Christian Temperance Union was successful in its efforts to establish Prohibition (of alcohol) in the USA, and there is no shortage of moral crusaders in the modern war against drugs. Drug taking continues to be surrounded by a miasma of confusion and fallacy. One of the principal causes of this has been the masquerade of moral values as biomedical facts.

X.—THE ROLE OF OTHER DISCIPLINES AND PROFESSIONS

One development of recent years has been an increasing emphasis on the complexity of the addictions, and a correspondingly greater readiness to involve a wide range of professional groups in the assessment and treatment of such problems. At one time or another there may be an important role for nurses, physicians, psychologists, psychiatrists, social workers, occupational therapists and teachers. It is probable that the involvement of workers from so many different professional backgrounds contributes a good deal to the treatment and welfare of people with drug and alcohol problems. However, it also adds further to the complexity of work in this area.

A number of the difficulties that it introduces are general ones and apply to many other areas as well as this. Most inter-disciplinary teams face familiar problems to do with leadership and decision-making. In the absence of a single leader who makes treatment decisions on an executive basis, team discussions have a tendency to take up excessive periods of time while everyone is permitted to make a contribution. This can be minimized by a chairman who keeps the discussion to a specific agenda and directs it towards the decision in hand.

It is less clear how to confine discussion to a reasonable limit on those occasions when members of the team hold contradictory views. A decision imposed upon the team by any one member may reduce morale and commitment to team policy. On the other hand, there may be occasions on which even the most protracted discussion fails to produce any consensus view. Such problems may be especially acute in this area because of the absence of any theoretical structure or of an adequate body of empirical examples to provide clear guidelines towards clinical practice. As a result, discussions on how best to deal with individual cases can resemble an attempt to reach agreement about the true meaning of a Rorschach ink-blot; and often such discussions owe more to the prior assumptions and biases of members of staff than to the characteristics of the patient (Gossop and Connell, 1983).

There are other professional stresses that follow from trying to run an effective clinical team in the absence of clear guidelines to treatment. These can lead to a 'retreat from the patient'. It is some years since Rosenhan commented upon how much time staff in psychiatric hospitals spend in formal and informal staff meetings and how little time is spent actually with the patients (Rosenhan, 1973). This retreat from the patient can be exacerbated by certain types of patient. Psychoanalysts have long been interested in the phenomenon that they term 'transference'. 'Negative counter-transference' refers to the negative attitudes and feelings of the therapist toward the client. Whether or not one wishes to accept the arcane doctrine that goes with these concepts, all therapists should be aware that they work better, or are more comfortable, with certain types of patients than with others. The behaviour of addicts and alcoholics in treatment does not always make them the most rewarding individuals to work with; they can for instance, be uncooperative, hostile and verbally abusive. If a disadvantage of the multi-disciplinary team is that it offers a temptation for the therapist to retreat from the patient into endless staff discussions, the team also offers a corresponding advantage in that it can help to diffuse the negative feelings of individual members of staff against 'difficult' patients.

XI.—FUTURE PROSPECTS

It would be reassuring to be able to predict a steady, continuous increase in our understanding of drug and alcohol dependence, and a corresponding improvement in the techniques available for the treatment of such problems. I sincerely hope both of these things occur. However, there is some room for doubt.

We still have only the most rudimentary understanding of the ways in which drugs are used and abused, and what little understanding we have gained has been more the result of isolated studies than of any systematic, progressive research process. Nor is there any general consensus upon what sort of problems drug and alcohol dependence really are. The view presented in this chapter emphasizes the social and cognitive aspects. This is not the most widely held view. Although less widely accepted than it was fifteen or twenty years ago, the biomedical model continues to be the most influential view of the addictions, and there is no shortage of research into the physiology, pharmacology and biochemistry of drug dependence.

Such research has been comparatively productive in scientific terms. The isolation of the endorphins and the work following their discovery, for instance, has been an important development in this area, and it has unquestionably advanced our understanding of the physiochemical effects of the opiates and other drugs. However, it has not led to any advances in treatment, and it is unfortunate that this sort of research has helped to confirm the supremacy of substance-based views of the addictions.

The massive investment in physiological and pharmaceutical research into drug dependence reflects and confirms this view. There is a vast research effort committed to work developing new drug treatments. In one recent conference, which was convened to present a broad view of research into problems of drug dependence, five new drug treatments were introduced (this does not include the half dozen or so papers which dealt with methadone and naltrexone.) It is interesting to observe in passing that the research presented at this conference was funded by no less than 33 pharmaceutical companies.

A good deal of current interest is focused upon LAAM (Levo-Alpha Acetylmethadol), a derivative of methadone, which offers the prospect of a long-acting oral maintenance drug for opiate addicts. This may or may not turn out to be a fruitful avenue for treatment research. However, one could perhaps be forgiven for a certain scepticism when one looks at the history of the type of research that has sought a drug to cure drug addiction (see page 242).

Although an addiction to heroin may differ in important respects from addictions to alcohol or Valium, there may be psychological features which are common to each. Conversely, an emphasis upon chemical similarities may obscure important social and psychological differences between the people addicted to particular drugs. The needs, values, and social realities of the street heroin addict may be vastly different from those of the practising physician who has become dependent upon opiates. The reasons why a person takes drugs, their beliefs and attitudes towards their drug taking, and the circumstances in which they crave for and use drugs, are important aspects of drug and alcohol dependence. In treatment, such matters are of crucial importance, yet they have received very little research attention.

One of the most pressing research issues in the treatment of the addictive disorders is that of how best to match available treatment programmes and procedures to the needs of the individual patient. Our present understanding of this question is woefully inadequate. Further research could hardly fail to advance both our understanding of the nature of the addictions and our ability to help people with such problems.

XII.–ANNOTATED READINGS

Edwards, G. and Grant, M. (1977). *Alcoholism: New Knowledge and New Responses*. London: Croom Helm.

This is a collection of short chapters, covering most aspects of alcohol abuse.

Gossop, M. R. (1982). *Living with Drugs*. London: Temple Smith.

A book which covers all forms of drug taking, presenting them within a broad social and cultural context.

Miller, W. R. (Ed.), (1980). *The Addictive Behaviors*. New York: Pergamon.

This is directed more towards the clinical aspects. It deals with smoking and obesity; in addition it has chapters on opiate addiction and alcoholism.

Royal College of Psychiatrists. (1979). *Alcohol and Alcoholism*. London: Tavistock.

This is a report produced by a committee and contains much useful information about drinking problems. In some parts, it may be thought to reflect the medical and psychiatric biases of the authors.

XIII.–REFERENCES

Barnes, G. E. (1979). The alcoholic personality: a reanalysis of the literature. *Journal of Studies on Alcohol*, **40**, 571–634.
Becker, H. (1953). Becoming a marihuana user. *American Journal of Sociology*, **59**, 235–242.
Chein, I., Gerrard, D. L., Lee, R. S. and Rosenfeld, E. (1964). *Narcotics, Delinquency and Social Policy, The Road to H*. London: Tavistock.
Davies, D. L. (1962). Normal drinking in recovered alcoholics. *Quarterly Journal of Studies on Alcohol*, **23**, 94–104.
Dole, V. P. and Nyswander, M. E. (1967). Heroin addiction—a metabolic disease. *Archives of Internal Medicine*, **120**, 19–24.
Edwards, G. (1981). The Home Office Index as a basic monitoring system. In: G. Edwards and C. Busch (Eds.) *Drug Problems in Britain*. London: Academic Press.
Edwards, G. and Grant, M. (1977). *Alcoholism: New Knowledge and New Responses*. London: Croom Helm.
Erickson, P. G. (1981). *Cannabis Criminals: The Social Effects of Punishment on Drug Users*. Toronto: A.R.F.
Goode, E. (1972). *Drugs in American Society*. New York: Knopf.
Gossop, M. R. (1978a). A comparative study of oral and intravenous drug dependent patients on three dimensions of personality. *International Journal of the Addictions*, **13**, 135–142.
Gossop, M. R. (1978b). A review of the evidence for methadone maintenance as a treatment for narcotic addiction. *The Lancet*, 812–819.

Gossop, M. R. (1979). Drug dependence: a reappraisal. In: D. J. Oborne, M. M. Gruneberg and J. R. Eiser (Eds.) *Research in Psychology and Medicine. Volume 2.* London: Academic Press.

Gossop, M. R. (1981). *Theories of Neurosis.* Berlin: Springer.

Gossop, M. R. (1982). *Living with Drugs.* London: Temple Smith.

Gossop, M. R. and Connell, P. H. (1983). Drug dependence: who gets treated? *International Journal of the Addictions*, **18**, 99–109.

Gossop, M. R., Eiser, J. R. and Ward, E. (1982). The addict's perceptions of their own drug taking. *Addictive Behaviors*, **7**, 189–194.

Gossop, M. R. and Eysenck, S. B. G. (1980). A further investigation into the personality of drug addicts in treatment. *British Journal of Addiction*, **75**, 305–311.

Gossop, M. R. and Roy, A. (1976). Hostility in drug dependent individuals: its relation to specific drugs, and to oral or intravenous use. *British Journal of Psychiatry*, **128**, 188–193.

Heather, N. and Robertson, I. (1981). *Controlled Drinking.* London: Methuen.

Hodgson, R. J. and Rankin, H. J. (1976). Modification of excessive drinking by cue exposure. *Behaviour Research and Therapy*, **14**, 305–307.

Hodgson, R. J., Rankin, H. J. and Stockwell, T. (1978). Craving and loss of control. In P. E. Nathan, G. A. Marlatt and T. Loberg (Eds.) *Alcoholism, New Directions in Behavioral Research and Treatment.* New York: Plenum.

Jellinek, E. M. (1960). *The Disease Concept of Alcoholism.* New Brunswick, New Jersey: Hillhouse Press.

Keller, M. (1970). The great Jewish drink mystery. *British Journal of Addiction*, **64**, 287–296.

Kohut, H. (1977). Preface to *The Psychodynamics of Drug Dependence.* Washington, DC: U.S. Government Printing Office.

Kraft, T. (1969). Treatment of drinamyl addiction. *International Journal of the Addictions*, **4**, 59–64.

Lemert, E. (1967). *Human Deviance, Social Problems and Social Control.* Englewood Cliffs, New Jersey: Prentice Hall.

Lesse, S. (1972). Narcotics addiction: an overview. (Editorial). *American Journal of Psychotherapy*, **26**, 327–329.

Meyer, R. E. and Mirin, S. M. (1981). A psychology of craving. In: J. H. Lowinson and P. Ruiz (Eds.) *Substance Abuse, Clinical Problems and Perspectives.* Baltimore, Maryland: Williams and Williams.

Miller, W. R. (1976). Alcoholism scales and objective assessment methods: a review. *Psychological Bulletin*, **83**, 649–674.

Miller, W. R. (1980). *The Addictive Behaviors.* New York: Pergamon.

Miller, W. R. and Hester, R. K. (1980) Treating the problem drinker. In: W. R. Miller (Ed.) *The Addictive Behaviors.* New York: Pergamon.

O'Brien, C. P. (1976). Experimental analysis of conditioning factors in human narcotic addiction. *Pharmacological Reviews*, **27**, 533–543.

O'Brien, C. P. and Greenstein, R. A. (1981). Treatment approaches: narcotic antagonists. In: J. H. Lowinson and P. Ruiz, (Eds.) *Substance Abuse, Clinical Problems and Perspectives.* Baltimore, Maryland: Williams and Williams.

Robins, L. N., Helzer, J. F., Hesselbrook, M. and Wish, E. (1980). Vietnam veterans after Vietnam. In: L. Brill and C. Winick (Eds.) *The Yearbook of Substance Use and Abuse. Volume 11.* New York: Human Sciences Press.

Rosenhan, D. (1973). On being sane in insane places. *Science*, **179**, 250–258.

Royal College of Psychiatrists. (1979). *Alcohol and Alcoholism.* London: Tavistock.

Schachter, S. and Singer, J. E. (1962). Cognitive, social and physiological determinants of emotional state. *Psychological Review*, **69**, 379–399.

Siegel, S. (1977). Morphine tolerance acquisition as an associative process. *Journal of Experimental Psychology*, **3**, 1–13.

Smart, R. G. (1976). Spontaneous recovery in alcoholics: a review and analysis of the available research. *Drug and Alcohol Dependence*, **1**, 277–285.

Snyder, C. R. (1958). *Alcohol and the Jews*. New Brunswick, New Jersey: Center of Alcohol Studies Publications.

Sobell, M. B. and Sobell, L. C. (1978). *Behavioral Treatment of Alcohol Problems*. New York: Plenum.

Stimson, G. V., Oppenheimer, E. and Thorley, A. (1978). Seven year follow-up of heroin addicts: drug use and outcome. *British Medical Journal*, **1**, 1190–1192.

Szasz, T. S. (1972). The ethics of addiction. *Harper's Magazine*. April.

Teasdale, J. D. (1972). The perceived effect of heroin on the interpersonal behavior of heroin-dependent patients: a comparison with stimulant-dependent patients. *International Journal of the Addictions*, **7**, 533–548.

Weil, A. (1972). *The Natural Mind*. London: Cape.

Wikler, A. (1948). Recent progress in research on the neurophysiologic basis of morphine addiction. *American Journal of Psychiatry*, **105**, 329–338.

Wikler, A. (1961). On the nature of addiction and habituation. *British Journal of Addiction*, **57**, 73–79.

Young, J. (1971). *The Drugtakers*. London: Paladin.

Psychology and Social Problems
Edited by A. Gale and A. J. Chapman
© 1984 John Wiley & Sons Ltd.

CHAPTER 12
SMOKING

Stephen R. Sutton

I.—THE EXTENT OF THE PROBLEM

Cigarette smoking is the single biggest preventable cause of premature death in the Western world, and as such it is a major social problem. Deaths per annum due to smoking are estimated to number at least 95,000 in the UK and 346,000 in the USA (Surgeon General, 1979; Wald, 1978). The main smoking-related diseases are lung cancer, chronic bronchitis/emphysema and heart disease. It is the combination of the riskiness of smoking and its continued popularity that produces such a high annual death toll. Cigarette smoking is one of the most hazardous of everyday activities. The proportion of men aged 35 who will die before reaching the age of 65 is 40 per cent for heavy smokers (25 or more cigarettes a day) compared with only 15 per cent for nonsmokers (Royal College of Physicians, 1977). Although most of the epidemiological work has been done on men, there is no reason to believe that the situation is any better for women if they smoke to the same extent.

Recent surveys show that about 42 per cent of men and 37 per cent of women in the UK smoke cigarettes (Office of Population Censuses and Surveys, 1981). While the sexes have converged with regard to smoking prevalence, a definite social class gradient has emerged over the last 20 years, particularly among men. Twenty-one per cent of men in professional occupations smoke cigarettes compared with 57 per cent of men in unskilled manual occupations.

The number of cigarettes consumed per smoker per year has actually increased over the same period. It is not clear to what extent this trend is due to (a) smokers increasing their consumption over this period; (b) lighter smokers having a higher rate of giving up than heavier smokers; and/or, (c) new recruits to smoking consuming more cigarettes than established smokers.

The situation in the USA is similar, though the prevalence of cigarette smoking appears to be somewhat lower than in the UK, around 33 to 36 per cent, with women several percentage points behind the men. The decline in prevalence over the last 15 years or so in the USA has been offset by population growth, so that the number of smokers has actually *increased* over this period (Surgeon General, 1979).

Cigarette smoking is a problem of the twentieth century. Before this, tobacco use took the form of pipe and cigar smoking and tobacco chewing. In the last century, many smokers died from diseases like cholera, typhus and influenza before tobacco-related diseases could claim them. Nowadays, with the major infectious diseases largely eliminated, smoking is less often preempted as a cause of death.

II.—CONCEPTS OF THE PERSON AND MODELS OF HUMAN BEHAVIOUR

Many different theoretical approaches have been applied to the problem of why people smoke. Three main approaches are singled out for attention here. It should be stressed from the outset that they are neither exhaustive nor mutually exclusive. They all have implications for the development, maintenance and cessation of cigarette smoking.

The Learning Model

Few psychologists would disagree with the statement that cigarette smoking is a learned behaviour. In learning theory terms, smoking can be regarded as an operant behaviour based initially on a continuous or near-continuous positive reinforcement schedule. The novice smoker is rather like the rat in the Skinner box who quickly learns that a particular response (bar-pressing) is nearly always followed immediately by a reward (food pellet). The probability that the response will be repeated soon approaches unity, and it develops a strong resistance to extinction. The rewards for the smoker are probably largely social at first; for example, the feeling of being one of the gang, the excitement of engaging in an 'adult' activity. However, it is thought that the strong pharmacological rewards provided by the administration of nicotine (see below) quickly take over as the primary reinforcer. With each inhaled puff, a 'shot' of nicotine is delivered to the brain within a few seconds. At ten puffs per cigarette and 20 cigarettes a day, this amounts to about 70,000 distinct reinforcements a year (Russell, 1976b). Thus smoking can be regarded as a highly overlearned habit sustained by an efficiently delivered pharmacological reward.

Smoking may also be *negatively* reinforcing in so far as it alleviates the unpleasant feelings brought about by tobacco deprivation. These unpleasant feelings may or may not depend on actual physical dependence on the drug nicotine; that is, physiological adaptation of the body to repeated administration of the drug. Thus, smoking may develop into an escape/avoidance response to aversive withdrawal effects. For an elaboration of this view see Ternes (1977).

Not every cigarette is rewarding. That cigarette smoking is maintained despite this is perhaps less surprising in view of studies that have shown that animals continue to respond at the same rate when the schedule of reinforcement is changed from continuous to partial (in which only a proportion of responses is rewarded).

Cigarette smoking may also involve other learning processes. For instance, by repeated association with rewards derived from the effects of nicotine, other stimuli (the taste of the tobacco, the act of smoking) may themselves come to have reinforcing properties (Hunt and Matarazzo, 1970). (These stimuli may also be rewarding in themselves and not simply by virtue of their association with the rewarding effects of nicotine.) In addition, social learning theorists like Bandura (1977) would probably emphasize the role of imitation of models (parents, peers) in the acquisition of smoking.

The learning theory analysis of smoking has stimulated the development of a number of different behavioural treatments designed to promote 'unlearning' of the behaviour, for example aversion therapy.

The Nicotine Addiction Model

The nicotine addiction model can be regarded as complementary to the learning theory analysis outlined above. In this view, smoking is regarded first and foremost as a dependence, psychological and/or physical, on the drug nicotine. Nicotine is a powerful drug with a range of pharmacological actions some of which may provide a basis for dependence (Gilbert, 1979). It may stimulate 'pleasure' centres in the brain and, by altering arousal level, it may enhance alertness, concentration and performance. Absence of these rewards may be distressing and this may make it difficult to give up smoking in the same way that it is difficult for some gamblers to give up gambling. This is what is confusingly referred to as 'psychological' dependence—confusing because the desired effects are of course physically mediated. In addition, repeated administration of nicotine may stimulate the nervous system to make a semi-permanent adaptation to the drug, known as 'tolerance'. When nicotine is then withdrawn, the rebound overactivity of the nervous system that ensues is experienced as very unpleasant. This is the 'physical withdrawal syndrome' and indicates physical dependence on the drug. It should be said that it is still not known to what extent dependence on nicotine is physical or psychological or both. Although there is evidence for a fairly consistent pattern of withdrawal effects (e.g., increased tension and anxiety, drop in blood pressure, sleep disturbance), one cannot infer from their physical or psychological nature that their origins lie in physical or psychological dependence respectively. Physical symptoms may have psychological origins and *vice versa*.

The most common version of the nicotine addiction model holds that smokers, or at least the more dependent ones, attempt to maintain a particular level of nicotine in the bloodstream. When the nicotine level drops, as it does very soon after smoking a cigarette, this change is registered internally in some way and the smoker responds by 'topping up' the level with another cigarette, so as to avoid or escape the unpleasant effects of nicotine deprivation. Some support for this view comes from experimental studies which have investigated the effect on smoking pattern of changing the amount of nicotine taken in by the smoker; for example, by smoking through ventilated holders (Sutton, Feyerabend, Cole and Russell, 1978). Such studies suggest that smokers will alter their smoking pattern by increasing puff rate and puff volume so as to compensate, albeit incompletely, for a reduction in nicotine delivery.

Based on this nicotine regulation model, Schachter has proposed an explanation for the observation that smokers smoke more when under stress (Schachter, 1978; Schachter, Silverstein, Kozlowski, Perlick, Herman and Liebling, 1977). He argues that stress has the effect of increasing the acidity of the urine which leads to more rapid excretion of nicotine into the urine and hence a more rapid fall in blood nicotine levels. The smoker then compensates, unwittingly, by smoking more to 'top up' the blood nicotine level. In support of this view, Schachter and his co-workers showed that, when taking tablets that acidified the urine, heavy smokers smoked 17 per cent more cigarettes than when they were taking placebo tablets. Furthermore, in an experiment in which smokers were exposed to either high stress (painful electric shock) or low stress (barely perceptible shock), high stress led to more smoking among those taking placebo tablets but not among those given bicarbonate tablets to stabilize the pH of their urine. In other words, stress only affects smoking when the presumed mediating mechanism (increase in urinary pH) is allowed to operate. Although these results are consistent with Schachter's theory, it should be noted that a recent study by Cherek, Lowe and Friedman (1981) failed to demonstrate changes in smoking behaviour after acidification of the urine.

The Attitude-behaviour Model

A third approach focuses on the smoker's attitudes towards smoking and health. Attitude-behaviour models differ with regard to the emphasis placed on the 'affective' and 'cognitive' components of attitude, and this is reflected in their application to smoking. Thus, smoking can be seen as a behaviour that is dependent on having a favourable attitude (positive affect) towards smoking. People who have such an attitude will tend, as a result, to be smokers; conversely, people who have an unfavourable attitude (negative affect) towards smoking will tend, as a result, to be nonsmokers.

'Cognitive dissonance' theorists, on the other hand, emphasize the link between cognition and behaviour. According to this approach, a smoker who acquires a belief that is inconsistent with his or her smoking will experience a state of mental tension known as cognitive dissonance. For example, the belief that 'Cigarette smoking is damaging my health' is inconsistent with the cognition 'I am a cigarette smoker'. The smoker will seek to reduce this dissonance by any of a number of means; for example, by denying the health risks. Unfortunately, the theory contains no clear rules as to which method of dissonance reduction is likely to be preferred.

More elaborate theoretical approaches incorporate both the affective and the cognitive components of attitude. For example, according to the subjective expected utility (SEU) model of behavioural decision theory (Edwards, 1961), the decision to continue to smoke or to stop smoking is based on an assessment of the possible outcomes of these alternatives in terms of their 'utility' (their value, positive or negative, to the person) and their subjective probability of occurrence. In making a decision, the person is assumed to behave as if he or she has multiplied each utility by its corresponding subjective probability, summed these products for each alternative course of action and then has chosen the course of action that is associated with the largest sum; that is, the largest subjective expected utility. In this way, the person maximizes their outcomes. Mausner and Platt (1971) applied this approach to smoking and found some support for it. In particular, subjects who reported substantial reductions in their smoking five days after taking part in a role-playing experiments had SEU scores that were significantly more in the direction of stopping smoking than subjects who reported a small or no reduction.

The three approaches briefly outlined above should be regarded as complementary rather than competing theories of smoking behaviour. For instance, the attitude-behaviour model addresses smoking at the level of a course of action (continuing *versus* stopping) rather than at the level of smoking a single cigarette. The three approaches have different implications for how one might go about trying to change smoking behaviour. The learning model implies an 'unlearning' strategy; the addiction model implies the use of a nicotine antagonist or a nicotine substitute; and the attitude-behaviour model implies the use of persuasive communications.

III.—INDIVIDUAL ASSESSMENT

A variety of questionnaires has been used to assess different aspects of an individual's smoking. Depending on the interests of the assessor, questionnaires have been designed to measure motives for smoking, situations in which smoking occurs, beliefs about health, type of smoking, and degree of dependence. No one of these has become a standard instrument of assessment. Perhaps the most common kind of questionnaire used in research on smoking has been the smoking typology questionnaire. This is designed to give a smoking profile for an individual across a number of different types of smoking. For example, on the questionnaire developed by Russell, Peto and Patel (1974), the smoker indicates whether each of 34 statements about smoking applies to them 'not at all', 'a little', 'quite a bit', or 'very much so'. The statements consist of reasons for smoking (e.g., 'I smoke in order to keep myself from slowing down') or occasions for smoking (e.g., 'I like smoking while I am busy and working hard'). A factor analysis of the responses of 175 normal smokers to the questionnaire suggested six types of smoking: psychosocial, indulgent, sensorimotor, stimulation, addictive and automatic. Although smokers themselves find the exercise interesting and informative, such questionnaires may prove to be of limited value unless they can be shown to be predictive of, for instance, smoke intake measures, actual situations in which people smoke, and success in stopping smoking.

Personality scales in common use have also been administered to smokers in the hope that they will account for some of the variation in smoking behaviour. For example, many studies have found that on average smokers are more extravert than nonsmokers and that heavy smokers are more extravert than light smokers, but the differences, though statistically significant, are small (e.g., Eysenck, Tarrant, Woolf and England, 1960). Studies of the relationship between smoking and neuroticism have yielded conflicting evidence.

The measure most frequently used in smoking treatment and research is cigarette consumption; that is, the number of cigarettes smoked in a given period of time. This is obtained either by self-report or by getting smokers to monitor and record their smoking. Although there are problems in its measurement (e.g., the tendency for respondents to round off their answers), cigarette consumption has been found to be predictive or important variables like mortality and morbidity, motivation to stop, severity of withdrawal, degree of dependence and probability of stopping smoking.

A welcome development in assessment is the attention being given to biochemical measures of smoke intake. These are important (a) because the health consequences of smoking would be expected to be more closely related to the overall intake of smoke to the lungs than to the number of cigarettes smoked; (b) because a rigorous test of the nicotine addiction model requires measures of how much nicotine is absorbed; (c) because intake measures may prove to be a better indicator of dependence on smoking than cigarette consumption (in terms of predicting the likelihood, severity and longevity of withdrawal symptoms, and treatment outcome); (d) because they provide an accurate way of checking smokers' claims of abstinence; and (e) because feedback concerning a smoker's intake could be used to encourage him or her to stop or to stay off smoking. One of the most widely used of the biochemical intake measures is the concentration of carbon monoxide (CO) in the air expired by the smoker (Jarvis, Russell and Saloojee, 1980). This correlates closely with the concentration of CO in the blood and reflects the smoker's overall intake over the past eight hours or so.

Finally, sophisticated devices for measuring the smoker's puffing pattern (in terms of number of puffs, puff volume, puff duration, puff pressure and interpuff interval) have recently been developed. The usual arrangement is that the smoker smokes a cigarette through a holder connected to transducers which measure the pressure and flow of the smoke through the holder. Puff recorders may supersede the more traditional observational methods but they have two limitations. They may alter, as well as record, the puffing pattern; and, second, they measure only the volume of smoke taken into the mouth, not that which is actually inhaled.

IV.—THE IMMEDIATE SOCIAL AND EMOTIONAL ENVIRONMENT

Social factors are of great importance in cigarette smoking, particularly in its onset. Smoking usually begins in adolescence, and peer pressure is one of the major influences on experimentation with cigarettes and the acquisition of the smoking habit. In a study conducted in the UK, Bynner (1969) found that the most important factor associated with smoking in schoolboys was the number of their friends who smoked. Another important social influence is whether or not the person's immediate family (parents, siblings) smoke. Williams (1971) found the highest prevalence of smoking in those children who lived in a household where both parents and an older sibling smoked, and the lowest where none of the immediate family was a smoker.

Although the effects of parental and sibling smoking habits weaken as the teenage smoker becomes an established adult smoker, peer pressures probably continue to be important. The adult smoker is likely to have many friends who also smoke (McKennell and Thomas, 1967). Smoking habits of spouses or cohabitants are probably the most important single social influence on the maintenance of smoking. An American survey showed that 68 per cent of young women smokers had husbands or boyfriends who were also smokers, compared with only 41 per cent of the nonsmokers (Clark, 1976).

As mentioned in the opening section of the chapter, social class, as measured by occupation, has a strong relationship with smoking, at least among men in the UK. The professional classes have the lowest rates of smoking, unskilled and semi-skilled workers the highest. This is probably due in large part to differences in health beliefs. The social class differences have been created by men in the former group giving up smoking over the last 20 years, presumably for health motives stimulated by the cumulative effect of anti-smoking publicity. In the case of women, the relationship between smoking and socioeconomic status is much weaker, and there is evidence from the USA that smoking is *more* prevalent among white-collar than among blue-collar female workers (Schuman, 1977). Among psychologists, women are more likely to smoke than men (Dicken and Bryson, 1978), a finding which the authors interpret in terms of role conflict experienced by women as a result of the convergence of sex roles.

Social factors are important not only in the onset and maintenance of smoking but also in smoking cessation. A smoker who has a spouse who smokes or friends who mostly smoke is less likely to give up successfully (e.g., Schwartz and Dubitsky, 1968). Eisinger (1971) found that 'the number of former smokers among their 20 best known friends' was related to successful abstinence. Finally, it should be said that, while the role of social factors in smoking has been established, very little is known about exactly how these factors operate. For instance, it is not known how parental smoking influences the likelihood of the child becoming a smoker.

V. — THE WIDER SOCIAL AND ORGANIZATIONAL ENVIRONMENT

This section briefly discusses some of the wider social influences on smoking. These include price, availability, pro- and anti-smoking advertising, and legislation and restrictions on smoking activity.

As with alcohol, the cost and availability of cigarettes have an enormous influence on smoking. The effect of price changes on cigarette sales has been demonstrated in a number of studies (see, for example, Peto, 1974). There is little doubt that a massive price increase would lead to a drastic and lasting fall in cigarette sales. Although tax on cigarettes is regularly increased, the increases have not been large enough to affect consumption significantly, with the possible exception of 1981 when the tobacco industry claimed a 15 per cent fall in sales in the UK. In spite of tax increases, in real terms cigarettes are cheaper now than they were 20 years ago. Not only are they cheap, cigarettes are readily available at newsagents, tobacconists, supermarkets, kiosks, petrol stations, cafes, bars, places of entertainment, vending machines and so on. As with alcohol, restrictions on availability would be likely to have a significant effect on sales.

As well as cost and availability, the design of the cigarette itself is important. In particular, the yields of tar and nicotine may determine consumer choice of cigarettes, number of cigarettes smoked and smoke intake. In both the UK and the USA, the yields of tar and nicotine (weighted by cigarette sales) have decreased substantially. Cigarettes today are much milder than they were 20 years ago. The biggest contribution to this reduction came with the switch from plain to filter-tipped cigarettes which contain less tobacco. (Incidentally, the financial benefits to the tobacco companies of this change are frequently overlooked. Cellulose acetate filters are much cheaper than the same volume of duty-paid tobacco). In recent years, the reduction in the average sales-weighted nicotine yield seems to have flattened out at around 1.3 milligrams. This has been interpreted as reflecting an 'acceptability barrier' below which it becomes unacceptably difficult or even impossible to maintain one's intake of nicotine. 'Low tar' brands (which have relatively low yields of nicotine as well as tar) are not popular; only about 1 in 5 smokers smoke them. These reductions in cigarette yields, which have also been accompanied by a reduction in the carcinogenicity of the tar, may have contributed to the recent fall in lung cancer rates.

Although cigarette advertising on television was banned in the UK in 1965 and in the USA in 1971, there are still many ways open to the tobacco companies to advertise and market their products. In particular, the money that was previously spent on television advertisements now goes into sponsorship of sporting and cultural events. There are also signs that the tobacco companies may try to take advantage of the rapidly expanding home video market. One company has already announced a deal to add a three-minute commercial to video films.

Since the banning of cigarette advertisements on television there has been no further anti-smoking legislation in the UK. Instead, the government has attempted to control the activities of the tobacco industry by means of voluntary agreements. One tangible result of this strategy has been the printing of health warnings and the tar group of the cigarette on cigarette packets and cigarette advertisements. The smoker who wants to make an informed choice of brand can also draw on the tar-and-nicotine 'league tables' which have been regularly published by the Department of Health since 1973.

In recent years, many restrictions on smoking have been introduced by non-governmental bodies. These include the provision of nonsmoking areas in many cinemas and on public transport. Segregation of smokers and nonsmokers is increasing in many sectors of public life.

In the UK, the government, through the Health Education Council (HEC), is responsible for most of the anti-smoking advertising. However, the communications battle with the tobacco companies is an unequal one. The HEC's annual budget of a million pounds or so is minute in relation to the estimated £100 million or more spent on promoting cigarettes. In addition to the official anti-smoking campaigns, the publication of the Royal College of Physicians' reports in the UK and the Surgeon General's reports in the USA attracted a great deal of media attention, and there is evidence that they produced a temporary decline in smoking prevalence.

Compared with 20 years ago when smoking was regarded by all, even nonsmokers, as a pleasurable pastime, the current climate of opinion is very definitely negative. Most people are aware of the link between smoking and serious illness, and a substantial minority of smokers now believe that tobacco advertising should be banned. The climate of opinion both reflects and influences the various strands of anti-smoking activity outlined above.

Finally, specialist support systems to cope with the smoking problem are few and uncoordinated. In the UK there are approximately 50 smoking clinics, a number that is hopelessly inadequate to deal with the nation's 18 million smokers, most of whom say they would like to stop smoking. The potential of health care professionals such as general practitioners (GPs), other doctors, nurses and health visitors in advising and helping people to stop smoking is virtually untapped.

VI.—TYPES OF INTERVENTION

Many different approaches have been applied to the problem of persuading and helping adult smokers to stop smoking and of dissuading adolescents from starting smoking. The main approaches are described briefly below. All of them can be regarded as 'psychological' in some sense, though not all of them are administered or evaluated by psychologists. Discussion of the effectiveness or otherwise of these approaches is reserved for the following section of the chapter.

Smoking Clinics

Smoking clinics exist in a variety of forms and typically provide some mixture of information, encouragement and support for smokers wishing to stop. Many of these clinics offer variations of the 5-Day Plan originated in the USA by the Church of the Seventh Day Adventists (see McFarland, Gimbel, Donald and Folkenberg, 1964). In addition, there are a number of expensive commercial clinics. Unfortunately, evaluations of the effectiveness of clinics, if attempted at all, are usually inadequate.

Behavioural Approaches

These are usually administered by clinically-trained psychologists in university or hospital settings. The clients are often students from these institutions. Most of the treatment approaches are derived from learning theory explanations of smoking. One of the most popular has been *aversion therapy* in which the idea is to try to form an association between the target behaviour (smoking) and an aversive stimulus (electric shock, noise, or hot smoky air) so that the feeling of discomfort produced by the aversive stimulus becomes a conditioned response to smoking. In *covert sensitization* both the target behaviour and the unpleasant stimulus occur covertly in the smoker's imagination. Images of smoking are paired with vivid images of extreme nausea. In *stimulus control* techniques the aim is to dissociate cigarette smoking from the environmental cues (e.g., meals, cups of coffee, telephone calls) that are thought to act as triggering stimuli. Behavioural approaches are more often evaluated than other approaches, but there are a number of common methodological deficiencies (see Section VIII).

Drug-based Approaches

Several different drugs have been used as the main component in smoking treatment. Tranquillizers and sedatives, sometimes combined with amphetamine, have been used to alleviate the anxiety experienced in withdrawal from cigarettes. Lobeline, which appears to mimic some of the actions of nicotine, has been tried in a number of studies. Recently, the development in Sweden of a chewing-gum containing nicotine has made feasible a treatment based on nicotine substitution (Jarvis, Raw, Russell and Feyerabend, 1982).

Hypnosis, Sensory Deprivation, and Acupuncture

Hypnosis has been used in many smoking treatment studies, often in combination with other methods. However, the term 'hypnosis' covers a wide range of related procedures and there is no consensus as to what it actually is. Although high success rates have been claimed, there have been few controlled trials of hypnosis as a treatment for smoking. Another related approach that has been tried is 'sensory deprivation' (24 hours in a dark, quiet chamber).

Acupuncturists claim to be able to treat smoking along with many other behavioural problems, and, like hypnosis, the technique has much mystical appeal. Again, however, such claims have not been subjected to experimental test.

School Education Programmes

On the assumption that it is better to prevent children from starting smoking than to treat them when the habit has become entrenched, many education campaigns have been mounted in schools. Most often these involve dissemination of information about the health risks of smoking in the form of lectures, leaflets and so on. Sometimes, smoking education is incorporated into the curriculum. One type of approach attempts to exploit peer influence by using older children as the educators.

Other Mass Media Approaches

Numerous anti-smoking campaigns have been conducted since the link between smoking and long-term illness was first discovered. They have used posters, leaflets and television and cinema advertisements with the aim of reaching a large number of people. They tend to be motivational in emphasis; that is, they concentrate more on persuading smokers to stop rather than on helping those who already want to stop. Another type of intervention that can be included in this section is the use of doctors' advice.

Large-scale Intervention Trials

In recent years several ambitious large-scale intervention programmes have been mounted. Perhaps the best known of these is the Stanford Heart Disease Prevention Program (Meyer, Nash, McAlister, Maccoby and Farquhar, 1980). This involved three communities in the USA, one of which was exposed to an extensive two-year mass media campaign on heart disease risk factors including smoking, the second of which received both a mass media campaign and face-to-face instruction for selected high-risk groups, and the third of which served as a control. Two other programmes that should be mentioned are the North Karelia Study in Finland which was based on a televised smoking cessation clinic (McAlister, Puska, Koskela, Pallonen and Maccoby, 1980), and the recently completed Multiple Risk Factor Intervention Trial (MRFIT) in which a large group of men received an intensive group intervention programme for the reduction of heart disease risk factors backed up by extended follow-ups (Multiple Risk Factor Intervention Trial Research Group, 1982).

VII.—IS PSYCHOLOGICAL INTERVENTION SUCCESSFUL?

Of all the efforts that have been made to persuade or help smokers to stop, only a small proportion has been evaluated. Of these evaluations, differences between studies make it extremely difficult to compare the effectiveness of the treatments investigated. There are no standard outcome criteria by which to judge the success of a treatment. For instance, while most studies report results in terms of the percentage of smokers abstinent, the base differs from one study to another. Some studies base their success rate on the number of smokers who start treatment, others on the number who complete treatment. Given the high drop-out rates that frequently occur during treatment, this can make a big difference to the reported results. Operational definitions of 'abstinence' also vary from one study to another. Furthermore, the follow-up period may vary from the end of treatment right up to one or two years after treatment.

Those who have reviewed the smoking intervention literature have reached essentially the same conclusions concerning the effectiveness or otherwise of the different approaches tried (see, for example, Raw, 1978; Surgeon General, 1979):

  (i) Smoking clinics and behavioural methods seem to be more effective than other approaches. The modal success rate of these approaches is around 20 per cent abstinent at one year after treatment.
 (ii) There is little or no evidence, however, for specific treatment effects. When treatments are compared with an 'attention-placebo' condition involving basic support and encouragement by the therapist, they are not found to be consistently more effective. The fact that they produce similar results suggests that all treatments (including attention-placebo) have certain nonspecific elements in common, for example, motivated volunteering, behavioural structuring, and self-monitoring (McFall and Hammen, 1971).
(iii) Some treatment (including attention-placebo) seems to be better than no treatment at all; that is, doing something is better than doing nothing.
 (iv) Most treatment methods seem to produce high short-term success rates. The problem is sustaining the success; that is, preventing relapse, which tends to occur in the first three months following treatment.
  (v) Within any treatment, some smokers stop, others do not. It is important to find out which individual difference variables influence the probability of success. This has not been studied extensively but there is some evidence, for example, that in treatment studies men are more successful than women and that light smokers are more successful than heavy smokers.
 (vi) Taken on a single study basis there is no evidence that school-based education campaigns or mass media campaigns aimed at adults have any measurable effect on smoking. However, national surveys show that smoking prevalence among particular groups (especially professional men) has fallen over the last 20 years, and this may reflect in part the cumulative effect of repeated anti-smoking publicity.

Although this is a generally depressing picture, there are some more hopeful signs. For instance, promising results have emerged from a recent clinical trial of nicotine chewing-gum (Jarvis et al., 1982), and this treatment method certainly deserves further research.

Smoking intervention approaches should not be judged simply on their success in persuading and helping smokers to stop; that is, on the *benefits* of the approach. The *costs* too should be taken into account, in particular, the time spent by the therapist on each client. In cost-benefit terms, one is looking for a treatment intervention that will yield a large number of successful long-term stoppers relative to the time and effort put in. A treatment with a 100 per cent success rate is of no general use if it involves, to take an extreme example, the patient spending six months in a special treatment centre with two highly-paid trained therapists. A recent study suggests that simple advice to stop smoking given routinely by family doctors on a large scale could in a few years make a significant dent in the number of smokers in the population (Russell, Wilson, Taylor and Baker, 1979). This is potentially a cost-effective approach which should be pursued further.

Of the large-scale intervention trials, the Stanford study produced promising results. Three years after the start of the programme, the proportion of smokers had decreased by 3 per cent in the control community, by 8 per cent in the media-only community, and by 24 per cent in the media-plus-instruction community. It has been estimated that the North Karelia Project yielded about 10,000 long-term ex-smokers (abstinent for at least six months), and that about $1 was spent for each success. A first assessment of the results of the MRFIT, on the other hand, would suggest that the cost per abstinent smoker was too high for this to be considered to be a cost-effective approach.

VIII.—METHODOLOGICAL AND PRACTICAL PROBLEMS

One of the most important methodological problems in smoking intervention research concerns the choice of follow-up period. As mentioned earlier, this varies from study to study and can produce large arbitrary differences in reported success rates. By convention, a one-year follow-up period (i.e., one year after treatment) is deemed to be desirable, but most treatment studies fall short of this standard. Since the aim of any smoking intervention is ultimately to reduce the risks to health among the groups involved, then the choice of any given follow-up period, whether it be six months, one year, two years, or five years, is based on the assumption that those smokers who stay off smoking for the period in question will continue to stay off, if not permanently, then at least for a period long enough to reduce their health risks significantly. There is actually little evidence on the question of how many smokers who stay off smoking for a year will still be abstinent 10 or 15 years on. More trials with very long-term follow-ups are needed before any particular period can be accepted as a standard.

A related problem concerns the reliance on smokers' self-reports of abstinence, which may be subject to several kinds of bias. As indicated in the section on assessment, the use of biochemical validation is increasing, and this is a welcome development. Studies in which both kinds of measures are used may show that particular forms of question elicit self-reports that are acceptably valid. The use of biochemical validation introduces its own problems. In particular, as another element in the treatment programme and evaluation, it may interact with the treatment to influence success rate; that is, the treatment may only be effective if followed by biochemical validation. Furthermore, biochemical tests are more expensive and less convenient than self-report measures.

Many smoking intervention studies are flawed by the lack of adequate control groups. The most useful control group is one to which nothing is done at all, since, given random assignment, this allows one to answer the question 'How good is this particular treatment, X, compared with what would have happened anyway?' In practice, no-treatment control conditions are difficult to create, since subjects are usually aware that other people are receiving treatment. 'Waiting-list' control groups are one solution to the problem. The subjects are told that they have been accepted on the treatment course, but that there will be quite a long wait before treatment can start because of the number of people wanting treatment. More detailed information about 'spontaneous' cessation rates in the particular population groups would also be helpful in assessing treatment effectiveness. When it can be shown that a given treatment is consistently more effective than no treatment, then this can become an additional standard for comparison. 'Attention-placebo' seems to have achieved this status, though this term covers wide variation in amount, frequency and type of support given.

A final point concerns the need for large samples. It is likely that some treatments are somewhat more effective than others, but this difference may not be detectable if small samples are used. Larger samples would increase the probability of achieving statistically significant differences in treatment effectiveness and would thus allow more confident conclusions to be drawn.

IX.—PROBLEMS OF ETHICS AND CONFIDENTIALITY

There are no ethical issues peculiar to the field of smoking treatment and research. Research into any kind of intervention that may be beneficial to individuals or to society cannot avoid the ethical questions posed by the need to evaluate the effectiveness of the intervention. For example, is it ethically defensible to deprive a group of subjects (the control group) of a treatment which may be effective? Is it defensible to deceive or mislead them about the fact that other groups are getting something that they are not getting? There are no easy answers to these questions, but it is clear that designs involving control groups are necessary if interventions are to be properly evaluated.

Confidentiality is not really a problem in smoking treatment because there is little social stigma attached to being a cigarette smoker compared with, for instance, being an alcoholic or a heroin user. In the latter cases, the patient is likely to want and expect any information given to the therapist to be treated in strict confidence. While confidentiality would normally be respected in the same way in smoking treatment, the patient is less likely to be concerned about other people (e.g., the police or employer) finding out that he or she is a smoker. It is also relevant that, unlike heroin use for instance, there are no legal restrictions on the use of cigarettes by the individual. (The Children's Act of 1908 made it illegal in the UK to *sell* tobacco to children under 16 years of age, but this act has never been strictly enforced.)

A wider moral question that has come to the fore in recent years concerns the rights of nonsmokers. Fuelled by reports of the harmful effects of 'passive smoking', nonsmokers have become more vociferous in defending their right to eat, travel and work in a smoke-free atmosphere. The practical solution to the conflict between smokers and nonsmokers has been segregation of the two groups in enclosed public situations like cinemas and railway carriages. An interesting counter-development to the nonsmokers' rights movement has been the emergence in the UK of a society of smokers called FOREST (Freedom Organisation for the Right to Enjoy Smoking Tobacco) dedicated to defending and asserting their right to smoke.

X.—THE ROLE OF OTHER DISCIPLINES AND PROFESSIONS

Smoking is above all a health problem, and it is not surprising that health professionals, more than other professional groups, have been involved in smoking intervention. For example, smoking clinics in the UK are mostly run by Health Education Officers, though general practitioners or other doctors are often involved as advisers. Overall, however, the extent of involvement of the medical profession and other health workers in smoking intervention is still minimal and is not commensurate with the seriousness of smoking as a health problem. This partly reflects the general emphasis in the health services on curative rather than preventive medicine. Of the health professionals, general practitioners are potentially the most important group for effective action in the area of smoking because collectively they have access to the bulk of the population.

Psychologists, particularly those with clinical training, have been involved in developing and testing behavioural techniques for smoking cessation. Much of this work has been done in the USA at universities and medical schools. If psychologists are to make an important contribution to reducing the smoking problem, they need to devote more of their time to the development and evaluation of techniques that can be applied on a mass scale at a relatively low cost.

XI.—FUTURE PROSPECTS

The smoking problem will no doubt still be with us at the end of the century. Smoking prevalence will probably continue to decline slowly and steadily in

Western industrialized countries, though this is likely to be offset to some extent by the increase in population, so that the numbers of smokers may fall more slowly. It is tragic that cigarette smoking in underdeveloped and developing countries is likely to increase massively in this period. The tobacco companies, worried by the static market in the West are already looking to the potentially vast market in the Third World to ensure future profits. Sadly, these countries, with their desire to emulate the West, are unlikely to learn by our mistakes and a smoking epidemic there seems inevitable.

The situation in the West is more hopeful. Although reducing the smoking prevalence in the population is a slow and painful process, alternative goals may offer more promise. One alternative is the development of a 'safer' cigarette. If cigarettes could be developed which were no less acceptable than those currently on the market but which by virtue of their design would be smoked in such a way as to lead to a much lower intake of the harmful combustion products, then this would be a major contribution to solving the smoking problem. The development of safer cigarettes depends on learning much more about (a) which constituents of tobacco smoke are necessary or sufficient for satisfaction, and (b) which constituents are responsible for the increased risk of lung cancer, chronic bronchitis/emphysema, and heart disease. At present, we know more about the second question that the first. The substances that are responsible for lung cancer and for chronic bronchitis and emphysema are known to be in the 'tar' produced by burning tobacco. The role of carbon monoxide and nicotine in the other smoking-related diseases is not yet clear. However, if it were found that nicotine were both relatively safe and a necessary condition for obtaining satisfaction from smoking, then a recipe for a safer cigarette would be one low in tar and carbon monoxide but with a nicotine yield similar to currently popular cigarettes. Such a cigarette would enable the smoker to obtain his/her required dose of nicotine while taking in as little as possible of the harmful tar and carbon monoxide (see Russell, 1976a). If one accepts that smoking is helpful and enjoyable to millions of people, then a strategy that does not require them to give up smoking altogether makes good sense. After all, it is the health consequences of smoking, not smoking *per se*, that is the problem.

On the same lines, alternative sources of nicotine should be explored. Snuff, for instance, is a tobacco preparation which has been shown to produce nicotine levels in the bloodstream comparable to those obtained from cigarette smoking (Russell, Jarvis and Feyerabend, 1980). As with inhaled cigarette smoking, the absorption of nicotine from snuff is extremely rapid. It is also likely to be much safer than smoking, since there are no combustion products. Perhaps the main drawback of snuff is its messiness, but it may be possible to develop cleaner forms.

This section has discussed two alternative approaches to the smoking problem. To make any impact on smoking mortality and morbidity, they would have to be applied on a large scale. Psychologists have an important role to play in the development and evaluation of these and other approaches to reducing the smoking problem.

Acknowledgements

I would like to thank the Medical Research Council for financial support and current and former members of the Smoking Research Group, Addiction Research Unit, Institute of Psychiatry, for their helpful comments on an earlier draft of this chapter.

XII.—ANNOTATED READINGS

Surgeon General. (1979). *Smoking and Health*. Washington, DC: United States Department of Health, Education and Welfare.

An authoritative report packed with information about smoking. About two-thirds of this formidable volume is devoted to the health consequences of smoking, the remainder to behavioural aspects and education and prevention.

Royal College of Physicians. (1977). *Smoking or Health*. London: Pitman Medical.

The British counterpart of the Surgeon General's report, it is much shorter and can be read at a single sitting.

Ashton, H. and Stepney, R. (1982). *Smoking: Psychology and Pharmacology*. London: Tavistock.

An excellent review of the current state of knowledge about smoking, particularly, as the title suggests, the psychological and pharmacological aspects. Very clearly written.

Raw, M. (1978). The treatment of cigarette dependence. In: Y. Israel, F. B. Glaser, H. Kalant, R. E. Popham, W. Schmidt and R. G. Smart (Eds.) *Research Advances in Alcohol and Drug Problems*. Volume 4. New York: Plenum.

A thorough and detailed review of smoking treatment research. Concludes that there is no evidence for specific treatment effects and that the modal one-year success rate is around 20 per cent.

Schachter, S., Silverstein, B., Kozlowski, L. T., Perlick, D., Herman, C. P. and Liebling, B. (1977). Studies of the interaction of psychological and pharmacological determinants of smoking. *Journal of Experimental Psychology: General*, 106, 3–40.

This set of papers reports a series of elegant studies designed to investigate Schachter's theory that the 'smoker's brain is in the bladder'. Changes in the acidity of the urine, brought about by stress, lead to changes in the rate of nicotine excretion which in turn lead to changes in smoking behaviour. The findings tend to support Schachter's theory, but it should be noted that Cherek et al. (1981) failed to replicate one of the key results.

Russell, M. A. H. (1976). Low-tar medium-nicotine cigarettes: A new approach to safer smoking. *British Medical Journal*, 1, 1430–1433.

A persuasive presentation of the argument for developing 'safer' cigarettes, in particular one with a low tar yield and a medium nicotine yield.

XIII.—REFERENCES

Bandura, A. (1977). *Social Learning Theory*. Englewood Cliffs, New Jersey: Prentice-Hall.

Bynner, J. M. (1969). *The Young Smoker*. Government Social Survey. London: Her Majesty's Stationery Office.

Cherek, D. R., Lowe, W. C. and Friedman, T. T. (1981). Effects of ammonium chloride on urinary pH and cigarette smoking behavior. *Clinical Pharmacology and Therapeutics*, **29**, 762–770.

Clark, R. (1976). Cigarette smoking among teenage girls and young women: Summary of the findings of a survey conducted for the American Cancer Society. In: J. Wakefield (Ed.) *Public Education about Cancer: Recent Research and Current Programmes*. Union Internationale Contre Cancer Technical Report Series, Volume 24, Geneva.

Dicken, C. and Bryson, R. (1978). The smoking of psychology. *American Psychologist*, **33**, 504–507.

Edwards, W. (1961). Behavioral decision theory. *Annual Review of Psychology*, **12**, 473–498.

Eisinger, R. A. (1971). Psychosocial predictors of smoking recidivism. *Journal of Health and Social Behavior*, **12**, 355–362.

Eysenck, H. J., Tarrant, M., Woolf, M. and England, L. (1960). Smoking and Personality. *British Medical Journal*, **1**, 1456–1460.

Gilbert, D. G. (1979). Paradoxical tranquillizing and emotion-reducing effects of nicotine. *Psychological Bulletin*, **86**, 643–661.

Hunt, W. A. and Matarazzo, J. D. (1970). Habit mechanisms in smoking. In: W. A. Hunt (Ed.), *Learning Mechanisms in Smoking*. Chicago, Illinois: Aldine.

Jarvis, M. J., Raw, M., Russell, M. A. H. and Feyerabend, C. (1982). Randomised controlled trial of nicotine chewing gum. *British Medical Journal*, **285**, 537–540.

Jarvis, M. J., Russell, M. A. H. and Saloojee, Y. (1980). Expired air carbon monoxide: A simple breath test of tobacco smoke intake. *British Medical Journal*, **281**, 484–485.

McAlister, A., Puska, P., Koskela, K., Pallonen, U. and Maccoby, N. (1980). Mass communication and community organization for public health education. *American Psychologist*, **35**, 375–379.

McFall, R. M. and Hammen, C. L. (1971). Motivation, structure, and self-monitoring: Role of nonspecific factors in smoking reduction. *Journal of Consulting and Clinical Psychology*, **37**, 80–86.

McFarland, J. W., Gimbel, H. W., Donald, W. A. J. and Folkenberg, E. J. (1964). The Five-Day Program to help individuals stop smoking. *Connecticut Medicine*, **28**, 885–890.

McKennell, A. C. and Thomas, R. K. (1967). *Adults' and Adolescents' Smoking Habits and Attitudes*. Government Social Survey. London: Her Majesty's Stationery Office.

Mausner, B. and Platt, E. S. (1971). *Smoking: A Behavioral Analysis*. New York: Pergamon.

Meyer, A. J., Nash, J. D., McAlister, A. L., Maccoby, N. and Farquhar, J. W. (1980). Skills training in a cardiovascular health education campaign. *Journal of Consulting and Clinical Psychology*, **48**, 129–142.

Multiple Risk Factor Intervention Trial Research Group. (1982). Multiple risk factor intervention trial: Risk factor changes and mortality results. *Journal of the American Medical Association*, **248**, 1465–1477.

Office of Population Censuses and Surveys. (1981). *Cigarette smoking: 1972–1980*. OPCS Monitor GHS 81/2. London: Office of Population Censuses and Surveys.

Peto, J. (1974). Price and consumption of cigarettes: A case for intervention? *British Journal of Preventive and Social Medicine*, **28**, 241–245.

Raw, M. (1978). The treatment of cigarette dependence. In: Y. Israel, F. B. Glaser, H. Kalant, R. E. Popham, W. Schmidt and R. G. Smart (Eds.) *Research Advances in Alcohol and Drug Problems*. Volume 4. New York: Plenum.

Royal College of Physicians. (1977). *Smoking or Health*. London: Pitman Medical.

Russell, M. A. H. (1976a). Low-tar medium-nicotine cigarettes: a new approach to safer smoking. *British Medical Journal*, **1**, 1430–1433.

Russell, M. A. H. (1976b). Tobacco smoking and nicotine dependence. In: R. J. Gibbins, Y. Israel, H. Kalant, R. E. Popham, W. Schmidt and R. G. Smart (Eds.) *Research Advances in Alcohol and Drug Problems*. New York: Wiley.

Russell, M. A. H., Jarvis, M. J. and Feyerabend, C. (1980). A new age for snuff? *Lancet*, **1**, 474–475.

Russell, M. A. H., Peto, J. and Patel, U. A. (1974). The classification of smoking by factorial structure of motives. *Journal of the Royal Statistical Society (A)*, **137**, 313–346.

Russell, M. A. H., Wilson, C., Taylor, C. and Baker, C. D. (1979). Effect of General Practitioners' advice against smoking. *British Medical Journal*, **2**, 231–235.

Schachter, S. (1978). Pharmacological and psychological determinants of smoking. *Annals of Internal Medicine*, **88**, 104–114.

Schachter, S., Silverstein, B., Kozlowski, L. T., Perlick, D., Herman, C. P. and Liebling, B. (1977). Studies of the interaction of psychological and pharmacological determinants of smoking. *Journal of Experimental Psychology: General*, **106**, 3–40.

Schuman, L. M. (1977). Patterns of smoking behavior. In: M. E. Jarvik, J. W. Cullen, E. R. Gritz, T. M. Vogt and L. J. West (Eds.) *Research on Smoking Behavior* (National Institute on Drug Abuse Monograph No. 17). Rockville, Maryland: National Institute on Drug Abuse.

Schwartz, J. L. and Dubitsky, M. (1968). Requisites for success in smoking withdrawal. In: E. F. Borgatta and R. R. Evans (Eds.) *Smoking, Health, and Behavior*. Chicago, Illinois: Aldine.

Surgeon General. (1979). *Smoking and Health*. Washington, DC: United States Department of Health, Education and Welfare.

Sutton, S. R., Feyerabend, C., Cole, P. V. and Russell, M. A. H. (1978). Adjustment of smokers to dilution of tobacco smoke by ventilated cigarette holders. *Clinical Pharmacology and Therapeutics*, **24**, 395–405.

Ternes, J. W. (1977). An opponent-process theory of habitual behavior with special reference to smoking. In: M. E. Jarvik, J. W. Cullen, E. R. Gritz, T. M. Vogt, and L. J. West (Eds.) *Research on Smoking Behavior* (National Institute on Drug Abuse Monograph No. 17). Rockville, Maryland: National Institute on Drug Abuse.

Wald, N. (1978). Smoking as a cause of disease. In: A. E. Bennett (Ed.) *Recent Advances in Community Medicine*. London: Churchill Livingstone.

Williams, T. M. (1971). Summary and Implications of Review of Literature Related to Adolescent Smoking. Washington, DC: United States Department of Health, Education and Welfare.

Psychology and Social Problems
Edited by A. Gale and A. J. Chapman
© 1984 John Wiley & Sons Ltd.

CHAPTER 13

INTERGROUP CONFLICT

Miles Hewstone and **Howard Giles**

I.—THE EXTENT OF THE PROBLEM

The social problems associated with intergroup conflict are immediately evident, far-reaching, and have undeniable consequences. We need only think of the conflict between Catholic and Protestant in Northern Ireland, Jew and Palestinian in the Middle East, and Black and White in Britain. The essence of intergroup conflict was noted by one of the protagonists of the violence in Lebanon: 'When we deal with others individually, we can be civilized . . . But when we deal with each other as groups, we are like savage tribes in the Middle Ages'.[1] These are not problems which will go away, and such conflicts can leap only too quickly from periods of relative quiescence to phases of extreme violence.

In spite of the stark reality of intergroup conflict, it is not easy to provide data on incidence. The scope of this chapter is not limited to collective behaviour, urban riots or crowd psychology. Rather it is about *any* phenomena which reflect the behaviour of one person towards others, or being behaved towards, in terms of *group* membership. We may be sure that many estimates of the magnitude of the problem are *under*estimates. Take for example, racial conflict in Britain; although there were over 1,000 reported cases of racialist attacks in the 18 months ending December 1982, we know that some minority groups lack faith in the police and fear reprisals from their tormentors. Thus we suspect that many incidents go unreported.

Clarification of the nature of intergroup conflict calls for precision in defining our terms. We therefore begin by mapping out some important concepts and making our own theoretical position explicit.

Intergroup behaviour has often been treated as a variant of interpersonal behaviour. Thus, phenomena such as intergroup conflict have been reduced

---

1. The words of Nabih Berri, Lebanon's Shiite Amal militia chief, were quoted in *The Guardian Weekly*, 26th September 1982.

to intra-personal dynamics ('the racist bigot') or seen as the relations between 'persons' who just happen to be members of different groups. This has resulted not only in a relative paucity of empirical research on relations between social *groups*, but also naïve theoretical extrapolations from intra- and inter-individual studies to intergroup relations. Undoubtedly, some notions are transported from interpersonal to intergroup relations, but their nature tends to change in the process. Hence we refer below to notions of *frustration* and *aggression*, but only in relation to relative *inter*group deprivation, *inter*group social comparison, and so on. There will always be certain individuals for whom an intra-personal analysis seems necessary, superior or even complementary to an intergroup one. However, to deal with intergroup conflict in general, these 'personality' approaches are not sufficient, and may even not be necessary.

To convey the differences between inter-individual and intergroup behaviour, Tajfel (1978) proposed a hypothetical continuum, with end-points of pure interpersonal and pure intergroup behaviour. At the pure interpersonal end are relations which are completely determined by interpersonal characteristics of those involved; for example, the friendship between Tom and Harry. At the other pure intergroup extreme, one is concerned with relations which are defined totally in terms of individuals' memberships of social groups or categories, as in the case of Jew and Arab discussing the Palestinian question. Our concern is with this latter end of the continuum.

The importance and originality of Tajfel's analysis is that most social psychological research findings are relevant *only* to individuals at the interpersonal end of the continuum. However, there is growing experimental evidence that our perception of ourselves and others is especially influenced by *group* memberships in some contexts and that people's behaviour in *collective* settings is different. For example, groups are more competitive, aggressive or retaliatory than individuals under the same conditions. More generally all ingroup members in intergroup contexts tend to behave in the same way towards outgroup members and they ignore differences between individual members of the outgroup.

The study of intergroup relations concerns the relations between members of large-scale social categories and our adopted *cognitive* definition of the social group is based not on face-to-face interaction between group members, but on the subjective perceptions and identifications of members of different groups. Two or more people who share a common social identification of themselves or perceive themselves to be members of the same social category are thereby considered 'a group'. *Social identification* can refer to the process of locating another person within a system of social categories (e.g., '*you are Welsh*'), or to defining oneself in terms of a social category (e.g., '*I am English*'). The fundamental criterion for defining intergroup behaviour (Sherif, 1966) is that interaction between individuals is being determined by the interactors' different *group* memberships. Whenever individuals belonging to one group encounter another group or its members, collectively or individually, in terms of their group identification, we have intergroup behaviour.

But what do we mean by intergroup *conflict?* Although many definitions include an emphasis on incompatible goals and limited resources, we do *not* see this aspect as fundamental. Tajfel and Turner (1979) distinguished between *objective/explicit* and *subjective/implicit* conflicts. The former are characterized by institutionalized and realistic competition, as in social, economic and historical conflicts. Subjective/implicit conflicts are inherently social psychological, as in the case where laboratory subjects are placed into groups on the slightest of criteria, yet still discriminate readily. Such conflicts are concerned with non-instrumental discrimination between groups, aimed at defining the ingroup positively in comparison with outgroups.

We adopt a loose and broad interpretation of intergroup conflict, embracing studies on *social* competition (achieved by defining the ingroup positively with respect to outgroups) and *realistic* competition (over scarce resources, such as power, prestige and wealth). We also accept that a wide range of phenomena have been, and should be, subsumed under this umbrella which may involve just two individuals or many. They include acts varying from delivering an electric shock to an individual in a laboratory study, to management-union relations, to racial prejudice and discrimination, and to lynchings and riots (Konecñi, 1979).

II.—CONCEPTS OF THE PERSON AND MODELS OF HUMAN BEHAVIOUR

Theories determine and dominate what becomes the subject matter of interest to any discipline. Thus intra- and inter-personal theories of intergroup conflict relate to phenomena which are very different from those considered by group-based theories. The locus of conflict is seen differently, as well as the method of study and the proposed intervention to reduce conflict. We focus on group approaches to intergroup conflict. Although there are some accounts of this area which are based on intrapersonal (e.g., Adorno, Frenkel-Brunswik, Levinson and Sanford, 1950) and interpersonal (Rokeach, 1960) concepts, we consider these to be limited (Brown and Turner, 1981). We maintain that the isolation of a particular personality factor or individual motivation cannot be a *sufficient* condition for explaining intergroup conflict, nor can one generalize directly from interpersonal to intergroup relations. Such approaches tend to ignore the wider intergroup context and are only likely to be predictive in settings where social factors minimize prejudice and conflict (see Section IV).

The first *group* approach to intergroup conflict is that of *realistic group conflict theory*, which assumes that group conflicts are rational in the sense that groups have incompatible goals and compete for scarce resources (i.e., the source of conflict is 'realistic'). Attitudinal and perceptual biases favouring the ingroup over the outgroup (i.e., 'ethnocentrism') are seen as serving two main functions: preserving ingroup solidarity and justifying the exploitation of outgroups (Brewer, 1979). The Sherifs' work is the best known of this tradition in contemporary social psychology (i.e., Sherif, 1966) and is based on studies using naturalistic groups of boys at summer camps. Through various manipulations, the development of normal friendships among boys at the camp was countered by the division of the boys into groups. Status and role differentiations emerged within groups, along with norms, and organized competitions between the groups led to overt hostility. Such conflict was only reduced when *superordinate* goals were established, requiring both groups to work together in order to overcome particular problems. This perspective sees intergroup conflict as caused by *real* conflict of group interests, or competitive goals, whereas intergroup co-operation is brought about by superordinate goals.

The other major group approach to be dealt with here is that of *social identity theory* (Tajfel and Turner, 1979). A careful reading of Sherif's earlier work reveals that mere knowledge of the *presence* of another group led to negative outgroup reactions. The simple act of *categorizing* individuals into ingroups and outgroups could produce differentiation of attitudes and behaviour towards the two groups. That is, competition between the groups was *not* a necessary precondition for the emergence of intergroup conflict.

According to social identity theory, individuals define themselves to a large extent in terms of their social group memberships and tend to seek a positive social identity (or self-definition in terms of group membership). They achieve this by comparing their own group with other groups to establish a positively valued distinctiveness between the two groups. Claiming that motivational as well as cognitive factors underlie intergroup differentiation, the theory holds that positive comparisons (intergroup differences seen to favour the ingroup) provide a satisfactory social identity, while negative comparisons (differences which favour the outgroup) convey an unsatisfactory identity. For example, Mann's (1963) study in South Africa showed that Hindus compared themselves positively with Whites on 'spiritual' dimensions, rather than negatively on economic dimensions.

Empirical support for this approach was gained initially through studies using the 'minimal group paradigm' (*cf.* Tajfel, 1978), which demonstrated that social categorization alone can be sufficient to engender intergroup discrimination in which the ingroup is favoured over the outgroup (for example, more money is allocated to ingroup members). Laboratory subjects classified into groups on the flimsiest of criteria (the toss of a coin) gave more money to ingroup than outgroup members. They were even content to award a smaller absolute sum to another ingroup member, in order to establish the maximum difference (in favour of the ingroup) between the rewards for the two groups. This maximum differentiation was interpreted as a striving for a positive social identity, and participation in such experiments has also been shown to raise self-esteem.

This theory has been examined in diverse settings and, in spite of some methodological controversies, there has been wide support for the notion that group members seek to view their own group positively. They may do this by giving more favourable ratings to their own group on particular evaluative judgements (for example, 'we' public schoolboys have higher academic ability than 'you' comprehensive schoolboys; see Hewstone, Jaspars and Lalljee, 1982). Studies in the 'real world' also direct our attention to an important difference between the theories of Sherif and Tajfel. Contrary to Sherif's view, ingroup favouritism is by no means a universal response to competition. Studies on minority or low status groups completed in the 1960s (see Turner and Brown, 1978) revealed that some groups actually accept their consensual inferiority; this point is taken up in Section V.

III.—INDIVIDUAL ASSESSMENT

Studies on intergroup relations have often required individual respondents to make ingroup, and/or outgroup, ratings on a variety of perceptual, attitudinal or behavioural dimensions. These have included evaluative judgements of individual group members or groups as a whole on attitudinal scales, allocation of monetary rewards, ratings of the quality of group products, and intended or actual behaviour towards members of either group.

In many studies group members are asked to describe, rate or evaluate members of their own and other groups on bi-polar rating scales. These judgements are thought to reflect the division of the social world into categories. When an individual gives markedly different ratings to representatives of two groups, we can reasonably assume that the social categorization is psychologically meaningful. Analysis of these ratings reveals to what extent an individual treats different members of the same group as equivalent, and treats the two groups as distinct.

The traits ascribed to group members constitute a *stereotype*, and all members of the same group are described and evaluated in the same manner. Some of the perceived differences may be realistic, while others are imagined. Unfortunately, many studies provide subjects with a list of traits which have not been chosen for theoretical reasons. Careful pilot work is needed before a study, to know what judgements to examine and on what dimensions ingroup and outgroup members should be judged. It is particularly important to investigate both positive and negative dimensions and to give each group tested the chance of a positive description in its chosen manner.

One problem with asking respondents to ascribe traits to ingroup and outgroup members is the rather unusual nature of the task. It is also direct, and may *force* responses which would otherwise not have been made. A slightly more unobtrusive approach is to provide subjects with a short description or videotaped sequence of an outcome, and then to ask for an explanation. For example, rather than seeking a stark judgement of Black *versus* White stereotypes, one might provide information about the school record and examination performance of a (Black or White) pupil and request an explanation (or causal attribution) for this achievement. The responses of group members to such material often reveal the working of stereotypes and a search for differentiation. For example, a racist might explain the academic success of a Black pupil in terms of good luck, while seeing a White pupil's success as due to ability and effort. Thus, any positive behaviour of ingroup members may be attributed to their personal characteristics but to 'the situation' when this very same behaviour is now associated with outgroup members. Similarly, negative behaviour may be attributed 'externally' for ingroup members but 'internally' for outgroup members. Such patterns of attribution could help to maintain stereotypes (and thereby sustain conflict) in the absence of real differences in achievement, by 'explaining away' positive events associated with outgroup members (Hewstone, 1983; Pettigrew, 1979).

A limitation of this focus on ratings and judgements is that they may tell us little about intergroup *behaviour*. It is normally assumed that social categorization functions to guide behaviour, but this assumption is not always tested. It is therefore necessary to explore the impact of intergroup perceptions on behaviour. This raises practical problems of eliciting and measuring behaviour (rather than the relatively easy presentation of a questionnaire), but these are not insuperable. Studies have measured the strength of intergroup aggression (e.g., intensity of electric shocks given), duration and content of intergroup communication, and so on. These measures are obviously a vitally important aspect of assessment and must be used as an adjunct to the above measures.

To summarize, we view the assessment of intergroup conflict in terms of tapping the perceptions and behaviour of individuals acting as group members. This approach still allows for considerable variation in data-collection methods and permits sophisticated analysis. It also restricts us to a social psychological analysis—the level of the individual in the social world.

IV.—THE IMMEDIATE SOCIAL AND EMOTIONAL ENVIRONMENT

In a short chapter it is impossible to do justice to this vast set of factors. We acknowledge that a complete treatment should deal with the influence of the family and peers on intergroup attitudes (see discussion of norms in the following section) and with the socialization of young children (Milner, 1975). However, in line with our group emphasis we provide a very short summary of the impact of some intra- and inter-group factors on various aspects of intergroup conflict. Thanks to recent reviews by Brewer (1979) and Turner (1981), the influence of these factors is now considerably clearer than it was and we therefore limit ourselves to the three main conclusions drawn.

First, although social categorization alone can engender intergroup discrimination, *co-operative* intra-group interaction tends to increase ingroup favouritism. Turner emphasizes that, where there is more face-to-face interaction with ingroup than outgroup members, preference for ingroup members should be expected. Thus, manipulations involving an increase in intra-group interaction should augment ingroup favouritism. He sees this as quite reasonably based on *real* differences in contact and information, not bias. It may be that intra-group interaction draws attention to similarities between ingroup members, a factor which has been shown to be associated with an increase in intergroup discrimination. Second, ingroup favouritism is typically found not only under conditions of intergroup competition, but also when there is *co-operation* between groups (or simple interdependence). Third, although *anticipated* or *actual competition* between groups sometimes increases ingroup bias, biases induced by intergroup co-operation may be just as large.

To explain the findings relating to intergroup co-operation and competition Brewer (1979) and Turner (1981) converge on the fundamental importance of the salience of social categorization. Brewer suggests that, as the presence of explicit competition can increase ingroup bias (or even have no effect), it may act by clarifying the distinction between ingroup and outgroups. Studies showing more ingroup bias by manipulating shared group fate would be accounted for in a similar fashion. Turner is more explicit, proposing that intergroup competition *accentuates* the ingroup-outgroup division and co-operative intra-group relations implied by *any* intergroup orientation. It does this by enhancing the salience of *group boundaries*, generating *expectations of intra-group co-operation* and engendering *hostility* towards outgroup members. However, a kind of ceiling effect may operate, such that an ingroup-outgroup distinction which is already strongly salient *cannot* be heightened by intergroup competition. Under such circumstances, differences between intergroup co-operation and competition may disappear.

The research summarized here has important implications for the study of intergroup conflict and practical strategies designed to reduce conflict. Any factors operating to sharpen ingroup-outgroup distinction (whether they act by enhancing ratings of ingroup members or devaluing ratings of outgroup members) may exacerbate intergroup conflict. Of particular importance are co-operative interaction within groups and competition between groups.

V.—THE WIDER SOCIAL AND ORGANIZATIONAL ENVIRONMENT

This section considers how broader social variables act through individuals to assume psychological significance. Our brief here could be immense: concentration camps and genocide; the effects of poor housing, unemployment and education. Without in any way denying the force of these factors, we must again limit our analyses. We are particularly interested in how such factors *bring about* and *maintain* conflict between groups and how their assessment can be subsumed under a social psychological analysis.

The first factors to be described here lie on the boundary between immediate environmental conditions and wider concerns. These are social *norms*—expectations about how to treat ingroup and outgroup members, how to behave in certain contexts, and so on—and we are interested in how they may encourage conflict or inhibit attempts at its reduction. An early idea, supported by later research, was that emerging attitudes towards American Negroes were not so much moulded by contact with Blacks as by contact with the prevalent attitude towards them (Harding, Proshansky, Kutner and Chein, 1969). Thus individuals may be expected to hold certain attitudes towards other groups and conformity may be enforced by overt or subtle means. Failure to conform in this fashion is often sanctioned (e.g., by withdrawal of status, opprobrium, rejection by other group members, and so on).

Minard's (1952) study of a West Virginian coal-mining community illustrates the way in which socio-cultural norms may dominate individual dispositions in favour of or against prejudice. Norms in this community segregated Blacks and Whites in social life 'above ground' and preserved inequality. Down the mine, however, social intégration was the norm and there was equality based on similarity of work and shared danger. Safety may well have been a superordinate goal for both groups of Black and White miners. Similar results were obtained by Harding and Hogrefe (1952) in their study of White department store employees towards Black co-workers. In South Africa and the Southern USA, where there are powerful norms and traditions of anti-Black prejudice, racial attitudes have been shown to be more related to conformity with social norms than to personality factors such as authoritarianism (Pettigrew, 1958).

Milner (1981) has stressed that a social psychological perspective is necessary, but not sufficient, especially when conflict involves social groups distinguished by definite physical and cultural characteristics, with a history of realistic conflict based on economic and political factors; in such cases intergroup discrimination is 'over-determined'. This is obviously the case for the Jews, *vis à vis* the Nazis. They constituted a different religious and cultural group, but they were also the victims of intergroup conflict created and exacerbated for political and nationalistic reasons.

But, despite these wider determinants, the social psychological approach can still make a valuable contribution by examining ingroups' and outgroups' cognitive representations of socio-structural forces and by taking account of the relationship between individual discrimination and institutionalized conflict. Thus, Milner argues for the analysis of racial prejudice in Britain against the back-drop of discriminatory immigration laws, while Allport (1954) has underlined the role of segregation in fuelling hostile racial stereotypes. One way in which the effect of broader 'macro' variables on intergroup conflict has been considered is in terms of the implied *status* accorded to various social groups in a society, the social psychological correlates of which are usually studied in terms of the attitudes and behaviours shared by members of relatively high or low status groups.

Social identity theory has begun to pay attention to the effects of status on intergroup relations, starting from the view that a *completely* secure identity is seen as highly unlikely. Rather, positive social identity is something that some groups must toil to achieve and others must strive to maintain, with status differences intensifying or reducing antagonism and conflict. When the social identity of a low status group is insecure, its members will perceive some alternatives to the present social system. Under these conditions, they will challenge the high status group, and the perception of the system's *stability* and *legitimacy* are particularly important in this respect (Turner and Brown, 1978). When low status groups come to see the position of high status groups as illegitimate, and/or unstable, they acknowledge that comparisons between the groups *can* be made on various dimensions and hence they challenge the dominant group. This accounts for the finding that group membership and intergroup comparisons may be more relevant to members of *low status* groups (Brewer, 1979). The identity of the high status group may also be insecure or threatened, in which case its members may engage in social or realistic competition with the low status outgroup. Where position of the high status group is secure, however, and where distinctiveness is under no threat, they may 'play down' intergroup differences with the conscious aim of maintaining the *status quo*. Strategies used to achieve a positive social identity can take various forms (for example individual mobility, social creativity and competition) some of which are discussed in Tajfel and Turner (1979).

Conflict between real groups is nearly always intimately bound up with status differentials. This section has indicated how such variables are incorporated, by considering individuals' cognitive representations of social status characteristics. It has also underlined the functioning of social norms in the community, often acting to maintain and inflame conflict. We see in the following section that such factors may have an unwelcome effect on attempts to reduce intergroup conflict.

VI.—TYPES OF INTERVENTION

In their source book of research on intergroup relations Austin and Worchel (1979) make the valid point that understanding the factors that initiate conflict does not mean that we can eliminate conflict by removing those factors. Once again there are many potentially important factors. There may be psychological consequences issuing from a whole variety of non-psychological interventions (such as improvements in welfare, housing, jobs, etc.) but such data are often indirect and uncontrolled. In this section we concentrate instead on specifically social psychological types of intervention.

One should start with the long held view (Allport, 1954), that *contact* between individual members of different groups will improve relations between them. The assumption is that contact will give participants a more accurate picture of members of the relevant outgroup if opportunities arise to perceive intergroup *similarities*. It has, furthermore, been the basis of many social policy decisions advocating racial integration in schools, housing, education and sport (Amir, 1969). However, Allport was fully aware of the potential positive *and* negative outcomes associated with contact, and therefore emphasized the *type* of contact.

Equal status contact (i.e., similarity of socio-economic standing) may work beneficially at the intergroup level by drawing attention to common category memberships of individuals drawn from a similar sub-stratum of society, and by implying similarity of values which would facilitate interpersonal attraction. However, while similarity may lead to attraction on the inter-individual level, the assumption that similar groups will enjoy more co-operative relations than different groups is unproven. On the contrary, it appears that groups which converge too far towards similarity may *precipitate* intergroup discrimination when their distinctiveness is threatened. Despite the faith placed in contact by some researchers, Sherif acknowledged that contact alone was not enough. Boys in one study (albeit still in the competitive stage of the research) utilized contact to exchange invectives, blame the outgroup for existing tensions and pelt each other with food (Sherif and Sherif, 1965)! He therefore maintained that contact would only be effective in the context of *superordinate* goals, rendering contact and associated communication positive, not negative.

Superordinate goals are intrinsically a special form of co-operation and several researchers have addressed the effectiveness of co-operative manipulations in reducing conflict. Worchel (1979) reports that in several applied settings co-operation has increased intergroup attraction and communication, reduced tension, led to greater trust, and increased satisfaction with group production. Explanations for the workings of co-operation are complex and varied. As Worchel's (1979) review makes clear, several perspectives can explain *some*, but not all, of the results. It is particularly problematic to explain, for example, why co-operation which results in task *failure* does not reduce conflict. Worchel's answer is that this outcome leads to scapegoating or blaming the outgroup, a development which heightens intergroup differences. He then concludes that co-operative interaction only decreases conflict when it attenuates the salience of ingroup-outgroup differences. For this reason, variables which may strengthen group boundaries—such as distinctive physical differences, failure and status inequalities between the groups (see also Section IV)—tend to inhibit the positive effects of co-operation.

One major problem still exists: how can conflictual groups be persuaded to co-operate, given their mutual hostility, suspiciousness and distrust? Worchel discusses a variety of solutions but accepts that no single method will work in all contexts. He therefore advocates simultaneous *reduction* of *threat potential*, provision of *open communication* and *exchange of information*, in the presence of *superordinate* goals. Cooper and Fazio (1979) suggest that *forced compliance* be used to break the vicious circle of distorted evidence and negative expectancies. The idea is that individuals may be motivated to change their attitudes to outgroup members by being obliged to behave in a manner which is inconsistent with their original attitudes. Thus, if individuals may be brought to co-operate with outgroup members (and, most important, be made to feel that they *freely chose* such behaviour) they will reduce the tension associated with this inconsistent behaviour by adopting a more positive attitude towards the outgroup. Cooper and Fazio stress that attitudes changed in this manner tend to be persistent, confidently held, resistant to influence and related to behaviour. But the problem now becomes how to make individuals feel that they have *chosen* to meet and co-operate with the outgroup (Austin and Worchel, 1979). One possibility may be to take a 'secret ballot' of what group members think should be done, thus giving the illusion of free choice, but to manipulate the outcome in favour of intergroup co-operation.

Although contact, superordinate goals and intergroup co-operation have been three of the major approaches to the reduction of conflict, rather different proposals emerge from social identity theory and its emphasis on social comparison. As Brewer (1979) spells out, individuals will tend to *maximize* differences between ingroup and outgroup on dimensions where the ingroup's position is *more favourable*. For example, after many years of success in international competition, Welshmen almost certainly prefer to compare themselves with Englishmen in relation to rugby, rather than football. Such intergroup differentiation is most likely minimized when the ingroup's position is less favourable. Only in their more optimistic moments would Englishmen seek to compare themselves with the Welsh in terms of rugby. The fact that attenuation occurs on *some* dimensions does not imply any reduction of accentuation on other dimensions. The upshot of this perspective, then, is that research might usefully concentrate on establishing *mutually positive* intergroup differentiation rather than swimming against the tide and attempting to reduce intergroup conflict *per se*.

There is evidence that perceived threat to individual and group distinctiveness may be resolved by making comparisons on *new or different* dimensions and that low status groups may perceive differences between themselves and high status groups on particular sets of traits. Groups which are inferior in terms of objective social relationships cannot contribute to an individual's positive social identity unless differences are accentuated on other dimensions on which the ingroup is superior. An illustration is Mann's (1963) finding, already mentioned, that Hindus in South Africa accept their inferiority in relation to Whites in scientific and economic fields, but claim superiority in spiritual, social and practical fields. Turner (1981) contends that this type of co-operative interdependence should not be seen as incompatible with positive distinctiveness. He suggests, in fact, that the realization of superordinate goals may often call for a division of labour between groups which are to co-operate, and where their activities are differentiated and co-ordinated into separate but complementary work-roles. Mutual recognition of superiorities and inferiorities would be the product of this combination of contact, co-operation *and* superordinate goals, with members of each group valuing their own group and holding positive stereotypes of the outgroup, consistent with the group's stereotype of itself.

We see therefore that the problem of conflict reduction may be more realistically handled by working towards mutual intergroup differentiation, rather than seeking to reduce intergroup relations to interpersonal functioning and to cleave the individual from the group.

VII.–IS PSYCHOLOGICAL INTERVENTION SUCCESSFUL?

The reported effects of *contact* have been inconsistent. Amir (1969) failed to find reduction of prejudice or conflict by inter-racial contact between individuals of equal social or occupational status, while some studies reported by Riordan (1978) are more positive. Following Riordan we should, however, be very cautious of interpreting any results as the *direct* consequence of equal status contact; he suggests that some of the effects attributed to this variable have been due to intimacy, institutional support and other factors.

Intimate contact has often been conceived in terms of racial integration in housing and some results are quite positive. White people who live in public housing projects in close contact with Blacks of the same general economic standing tend to have more favourable attitudes towards Blacks than White people who live in segregated accommodation. Thus, integrated housing seems to create the conditions for friendly contacts and accurate social perception. However, the problem with such findings is that of generalizability. Will such positive attitudes generalize to other Black people in different contexts? The same problem dogs results from studies investigating contact in the form of shared combat conditions, similarity of work experience, and so on. As we saw in Section IV, racist norms in the wider society may prevail, and restrict such positive outcomes to limited forms of encounter.

The success of contact in reducing intergroup conflict is, then, questionable. Frequent contacts with members of outgroups *can* increase the salience of ingroup-outgroup distinctions and play some role in the formation, rather than destruction, of negative outgroup images. *Equal status* contact, the best hope, is extremely difficult to achieve and complex manipulations may be required just to achieve equal status *within*, let alone outside, the contact situation.

The introduction of *superordinate goals* can produce a marked decrease in hostility and an increase in friendly contacts with members of the outgroup (Sherif and Sherif, 1965). In Sherif's studies, this method was more successful than contact alone and other interventions, but we still have some reservations. This success appears to have been achieved by fusing together the two conflictual groups and thereby the situation is arguably no longer an intergroup one at all. We should also recall that the groups used in Sherif's research were *ad hoc*, formed at a summer camp for a short period of time. Results may therefore be of limited relevance to more enduring conflicts between natural groups. Bringing Blacks and Whites together for the purposes of joint problem-solving may have dramatic short-term effects, but the acid test remains whether this harmony endures in the future and outside the setting of the intervention.

The same sort of criticism can be applied to work on *intergroup co-operation*. For example, Worchel, Andreoli and Fulger (1977) found that intergroup co-operation which results in failure led to an increase in attraction to the outgroup *only* where the groups had not previously competed. Where they had previously competed, co-operative failure was associated with a decrease in attraction to the outgroup (co-operative success always increased attraction). The interpretation offered for these results was that groups which had previously co-operated (or had been interdependent) reacted to their outcome *as if they were one group*, while previously competitive groups maintained their distinctiveness. Thus, Worchel *et al.* emphasize that co-operation will not necessarily improve intergroup attitudes unless the ingroup-outgroup division is eliminated. Theoretically and methodologically, there can be no disagreement with such studies. However, the proposal that co-operation increases intergroup attraction to the extent that it reduces the salience of group boundaries gives us little faith in this method of conflict reduction. Such an approach can surely have little effect on groups which will never merge, whose distinctions are insurmountable and whose daily lives are lived out in contexts which strengthen intergroup distinctions.

Thus the findings of some outcome studies are rather disappointing.

Contact, superordinate goals and intergroup co-operation have all been used in many cases, but with dubious long-term effects. Contact may often worsen intergroup relations and appears to have been too narrowly conceived. The other two approaches both aim to break down group boundaries and form a large common social group. Positive changes reported by these studies may not, however, reflect any meaningful changes in *private* intergroup attitudes and conflict may blow up once again, as soon as the immediate goal has been achieved (Turner, 1981). Future research should therefore take more account of the historical, economic and political aspects of life outside the laboratory. Short-term co-operative goals in a project to improve Arab-Israeli relations would surely pale in comparison with the psychological impact of an event such as the 1982 Israeli assault on Lebanon; Protestants and Catholics must be aware of the low economic status of Catholics in Northern Ireland. Against the background of such factors, social psychological attempts to change intergroup attitudes and reduce conflict are presented with the task of Sisyphus. As indicated in the previous section, we have high hopes of approaches which accept intergroup distinctions and work towards the acceptance of mutual positive social identities. Studies in this vein may yield more encouraging results, when they come to be completed, but we cannot overestimate the enormous difficulties of such research.

VIII.—METHODOLOGICAL AND PRACTICAL PROBLEMS

A pertinent practical problem is where to conduct studies of intergroup conflict. There are arguments in favour of, and against, laboratory and field studies with the former often heralded as having higher 'internal' validity (i.e., they allow for confident conclusions about the effects of various manipulated factors on the dependent measures), while the latter possess more 'external' validity (i.e., their findings may be generalized across times, settings and persons). Given the very real, often dire, consequences of intergroup conflict, it is appropriate to question the relevance of findings in experimental situations for problems of real life; thus, field studies have sometimes been used (for example, the work of the Sherifs). However, field studies have disadvantages too; theoretically relevant variables are rarely found in any pure form in realistic settings and there may be unavoidable confounds or impractical controls. For example, collecting data in youth clubs has the advantage of making respondents more relaxed, but one cannot control against distractions and interruptions, as one can do in the laboratory. Recently, some scholars have questioned whether the findings, rather than the theories should be generalized, and have cautioned that irrelevant theories are not made any more relevant simply because they are tested in the field, rather than in the laboratory.

We suggest therefore that social psychology should continually move back and forth between the laboratory and the real world. The former will be particularly suited for some studies (such as teasing apart the direct determinants of intergroup co-operation) but the real world must be considered too. Thus we have laid stress on the problems of generalizing from research with *ad hoc* groups (whether in the laboratory or field) to realistic situations where groups must continue to exist outside the experimental context, submerged by long-existing discrepancies in power, status, and so on. To be sure, where realistic groups are used, detailed pre-testing will be necessary (e.g., Hewstone *et al.*, 1982) and experimenters should specify those variables which have not been manipulated, but could affect the results (Sherif and Sherif, 1965). Moreover, a shortcoming of much work in this domain is that it is stranded in time. As Sherif and Sherif (1965) argued, the solution to the complexity of intergroup research has been largely sought in cross-sectional multivariate designs, rather than longitudinal research. Of course, when attempting psychological intervention researchers have examined the reduction of conflict over time, but often the elapsed time between test and re-test has been a matter of hours, not even days. The measurement of change is always a complex matter and the nature of change is especially complex when considered alongside economic and social changes which accompany a study over time. In this case, it may be difficult to partition variance due to psychological and non-psychological factors, and great care must be taken in the choice of psychological measures.

In addition to all these problems, there are some standard methodological points that the reader should check in any study. In an area such as intergroup conflict, it is useful to think not of a true or unbiased judgement of an ingroup or outgroup member but of a labile decision which may be affected by a variety of situational factors (Milner, 1981). For example, where the social group membership of the experimenter or interviewer is different from that of the respondent, the hostility and extremity of actual attitudes may be attenuated. Close attention should also be paid to the judgement demanded of respondents. Ratings of ingroup and outgroup members on descriptive scales should be based on pre-testing to ascertain how groups view themselves and other groups, not on an arbitrary choice of traits. Where different types of measure are used, inter-relations between them should be considered and every attempt should be made to control for evaluative and descriptive aspects of the language used in questionnaires and instructions.

Finally, when intergroup conflict is examined against the backdrop of societal forces (for example, anti-discrimination legislation), researchers may need to explore covert measures of prejudice and discrimination to tap true responses (Milner, 1981). In turn, any of these expressed views must be related, eventually, to actual behaviour. The strength of this relationship will depend on a host of wider social factors, thus further emphasizing the continual interplay between the psychological and non-psychological factors of relevance to intergroup conflict.

IX.—PROBLEMS OF ETHICS AND CONFIDENTIALITY

Ethical considerations affect what we can actually do in the form of research. Thus Milner (1981) discusses how racial attitudes and stereotyped images may be taught to children through comics, but accepts that ethical issues would prevent a systematic study of the causal link between images of Blacks in children's comics and such attitudes. A subsequent problem is that of reporting the results of research in this sometimes volatile area and Sherif and Sherif (1965) admit that publication of mutual stereotypes of nations and groups can be harmful. Such concerns are important, although it might be argued that conflict itself is of sufficient gravity to justify doing and reporting the research, despite problems of this nature. However, researchers should anticipate and discuss such questions rather than publish and be damned.

A more compelling issue is that of the ideological bias of conflict research. We must ask ourselves whether the aim of the scientific community is to support or to criticize the social order. The main issue is whether social stability should be seen as natural and social change as conflictual. In fact, the constructive side of conflict is accepted by most researchers, with its positive effects on intra- and inter-group learning, morale and production of 'healthy' social change. However, there still appear to be large differences between researchers as to how far conflict should be taken, especially with regard to challenges to the *status quo* from a wide variety of minority groups and social movements.

Problems of this nature are most telling in relation to conflict reduction, and, as Turner and Giles (1981) argue, we should be careful not to overplay the need for *reducing* social conflict, thereby implying that it is dysfunctional. Riordan (1978) is fairly typical in reporting favourable results as decreases in prejudice and discrimination against racial and ethnic groups, or as increases in tolerance and acceptance. But is it desirable to show that a minority has accepted and internalized an inferior or oppressed position?

We conclude this brief section with the assertion that ideology is not something than can easily be left out of such discussions. The values of the social scientist are inextricably tied up with the key concepts of whichever analysis is adopted and whatever theories are put forward tend to be contaminated by contemporary social values. These are not points of mere semantics, but reflections of the moral positions which underlie such research. They cannot be ignored.

X.—THE ROLE OF OTHER DISCIPLINES AND PROFESSIONS

While social psychology has made its own unique contribution, the study of intergroup conflict has also been pursued in other related disciplines, such as sociology and political science. As Austin and Worchel (1979) have argued, the study of group phenomena lies at a 'crucial analytical junction', occupying the middle ground between individualistic approaches and more macro, structural approaches. It is for this reason that lip-service is often paid to multi- and inter-disciplinary co-operation.

However, there are dangers inherent in this well-intentioned eclecticism which justify our own specifically social psychological perspective. In particular, non-psychological variables may account for *more* of the variance observed than do psychological variables, thus making *psychological* interventions apparently trivial. Attempts to encompass the full range of political, economic, historical and social determinants of intergroup conflict may drive the researcher into an impasse, where the complex of determining factors may induce a feeling of impotence and discourage intervention (Milner, 1981). Thus, while wider influences should be considered, our attempts to study and reduce conflict should limit themselves to a social psychological level of analysis if, as psychologists, we are to have any impact. Results of our studies should, of course, be considered in the light of findings from other disciplines; in this way we protect ourselves from the pursuit of trivial, irrelevant and invalid results.

XI.—FUTURE PROSPECTS

Our examination of research on intergroup conflict leads us to the conclusion that intergroup conflict is easy to engender, but difficult to eradicate. We know that minimal manipulations of social categorization can trigger intergroup discrimination, but that the reduction of conflict through increasing intergroup attraction has been difficult to achieve. We must agree with Tajfel's (1982) prescription that, for the field of intergroup behaviour, the future must be longer than the past. This short conclusion advances some of our personal views as to the nature of that future.

First, more research is needed on the conditions under which social identity becomes *salient*, as several authors have noted. We know that group membership seems to assume salience in confrontations and conflicts with the outgroup, is affected by a group's distinctiveness in the social environment and may depend on the number of group members present (Brown and Turner, 1981), but a more complete theory of group salience is required. Second, the paucity of research dealing with conflict *over time* has also been mentioned and this too must be a priority for the future. We have a fairly good idea of how groups come to view each other negatively and elaborate stereotypes, but we know little of how conflict is maintained over time. Third, in view of the problems encountered in the *reduction* of conflict, this must be a major focus of future research. Some of the ameliorative factors have been identified, but Worchel (1979) is correct to argue for more multivariate research aimed at identifying their most effective combinations. Fourth, given that our societies are not in a state of constant conflict, research might look at what societal characteristics help to *contain* conflict. A vivid illustration is provided by Rappaport's (1967) account of an elaborate and ritual pig-killing cycle observed by the *Tsembaga Maring* of New Guinea. This cycle fulfils a variety of homeostatic functions including control of the severity and frequency of intergroup fighting. Examples need not be so esoteric, for it is an ancient idea that sports and warfare might serve as alternatives to each other, or that intergroup problems could be resolved on the playing field rather than on the battlefield (Sipes, 1973). However, Sipes' research provides evidence to the contrary, showing that sports may be complementary to warfare. In societies where warlike behaviour was found (e.g., the USA) so too combative sports were typically found (e.g., American Football). Such a finding runs counter to hydraulic models of aggression which claim that violent sport acts as a substitute or outlet. We have given only two examples, both drawn from anthropology, but it does seem important to further our understanding of how conflict is contained as well as when it is excited.

Finally, whilst not wishing to devalue laboratory research, we should like to see more researchers grappling with the problems of intergroup conflict between realistic groups, whose relations outside the laboratory are determined by historical, economic and other forces. In particular, the reduction of conflict between such groups poses seemingly intractable problems which have been avoided by too much of the existing research. We have no illusions about the difficulty of undertaking such research, but argue that success in this sphere must be the litmus test of our discipline's achievements. We acknowledge that laboratory artificiality promotes theoretical progress, but we also see studies relating to wider, burning issues in the real world, as crucial for the growth to maturity of our theories. John Stuart Mill said: 'As often as a study is cultivated by narrow minds, they will draw from it narrow conclusions.'

Acknowledgements

Miles Hewstone gratefully acknowledges the financial support of The Leverhulme Trust during the time at which this chapter was prepared. Both authors thank Michael Bond for his careful reading of an earlier version and Robert Munroe for his helpful comments.

XII.—ANNOTATED READINGS

Amir, Y. (1969). Contact hypothesis in ethnic relations. *Psychological Bulletin*, **71**, 319–342.

A complete review of one of the most well-tried methods of reducing intergroup conflict, bringing groups into contact with each other.

Austin, W. G. and Worchel, S. (1979). *The Social Psychology of Intergroup Relations*. Monterey, California: Brooks/Cole.

Beautifully produced and highly readable sourcebook of research in this field. Major sections on theory, development, maintenance and reduction of intergroup conflict are particularly useful (see Chapters 1, 3, 6, 9, 16, 17).

Brewer, M. B. (1979). In-group bias in the minimal intergroup situation: A cognitive-motivational analysis. *Psychological Bulletin*, **86**, 307–234.

Extremely clear. Deals with the sources of variation in ingroup bias, salience of social categorization, selection of dimensions for intergroup differentiation and the components of ingroup favouritism.

Tajfel, H. (1979). *Differentiation Between Groups*, London: Academic Press.

More difficult but valuable collection of chapters on social identity theory. Major concepts are dealt with (Chapters 1–4), as well as studies in laboratory (Chapter 9) and other settings (Chapters 8, 16).

Tajfel, H. (1982). Social psychology of intergroup relations. *Annual Review of Psychology*, **33**, 1–39.

A compendium of research in the area. Selective rather than exhaustive, but a concise overview.

Turner, J. C. and Giles, H. (1981). *Intergroup Behaviour*. Oxford: Blackwell.

A companion to, rather than competitor of, the Austin and Worchel book. The introductory chapter (1) is most useful, supported by discussions of interpersonal and intergroup behaviour (Chapter 2), experimental intergroup research (Chapter 3) and racial prejudice (Chapter 4), as well as other important related areas, all firmly in the social identity theory mould. Available in paperback.

XIII.—REFERENCES

Adorno, T. W., Frenkel-Brunswik, E., Levinson, D. J. and Sanford, R. N. (1950). *The Authoritarian Personality*, New York: Harper.

Allport, G. W. (1954). *The Nature of Prejudice*. Reading, Massachusettes: Addison-Wesley (paperback edition, 1979).

Amir, Y. (1969). 'Contact hypothesis in ethnic relations. *Psychological Bulletin*, **71**, 319–342.

Austin, W. G. and Worchel, S. (Eds.) (1979). *The Social Psychology of Intergroup Relations*. Monterey, California: Brooks/Cole.

Brewer, M. B. (1979). In-group bias in the minimal intergroup situation: A cognitive-motivational analysis. *Psychological Bulletin*, **86**, 307–324.

Brown, R. J. and Turner, J. C. (1981). Interpersonal and intergroup behaviour. In: J. C. Turner and H. Giles (Eds.) *Intergroup Behaviour*, Oxford: Blackwell.
Cooper, J. and Fazio, R. H. (1979). The formation and persistence of attitudes that support intergroup conflict. In: W. G. Austin and S. Worchel (Eds.) *The Social Psychology of Intergroup Relations*. Monterey, California.
Harding, J. and Hogrefe, R. (1952). Attitudes of white department store employees towards negro co-workers. *Journal of Social Issues*, **8**, 18–28.
Harding, J., Proshansky, H., Kutner, B. and Chein, I. (1969). Prejudice and ethnic relations. In: G. Lindzey and E. Aronson (Eds.) *The Handbook of Social Psychology*. Volume 5. Reading, Massachassettes: Addison-Wesley.
Hewstone, M., (1983). *Attribution Theory: Social and Functional Extensions*. Oxford: Blackwell.
Hewstone, M. and Jaspars, J. M. F. (1982). Intergroup relations and attribution processes. In: H. Tajfel (Ed.) *Social Identity and Intergroup Relations*. Cambridge/ Paris: Cambridge University Press, Maison des Sciences de l'Homme.
Hewstone, M., Jaspars, J. and Lalljee, M. (1982). Social representations, social attributions and social identity: the intergroup images of 'public' and 'comprehensive' schoolboys. *European Journal of Social Psychology*, **12**, 241–269.
Konecňi, V. J. (1979). The role of aversive events in the development of intergroup conflict. In: W. G. Austin and S. Worchel (Eds.) *The Social Psychology of Intergroup Relations*. Monterey, California: Brooks/Cole.
Mann, J. W. (1963). Rivals of different rank. *Journal of Social Psychology*, **61**, 11–28.
Milner, D. (1975). *Children and Race*. Harmondsworth, Penguin.
Milner, D. (1981). 'Racial prejudice. In: J. C. Turner and H. Giles (Eds.) *Intergroup Behaviour*. Oxford: Blackwell.
Minard, R. D. (1952). Race relationships in the Pocahoutas coal fields. *Journal of Social Issues*, **25**, 29–44.
Pettigrew, T. F. (1958). Personality and socio-cultural factors in inter-group attitudes: a cross-national comparison. *Journal of Conflict Resolution*, **2**, 29–42.
Pettigrew, T. F. (1979). The ultimate attribution error: extending Allport's cognitive analysis of prejudice. *Personality and Social Psychology Bulletin*, **5**, 461–476.
Rappaport, R. A. (1967). *Pigs for the Ancestors: Ritual in the Ecology of a New Guinea People*. New Haven, Connecticut: Yale University Press.
Riordan, C. (1978). Equal-status inter-racial contact: A review and revision of the concept. *International Journal of Inter-Cultural Relations*, **2**, 161–185.
Rokeach, M. (1960). *The Open and Closed Mind*. New York: Basic Books.
Sherif, M. (1966). *Group Conflict and Co-operation: Their Social Psychology*, London: Routledge and Kegan Paul.
Sherif, M. and Sherif, C. W. (1965). Research on intergroup relations. In: O. Klineberg and R. Christie (Eds.) *Perspectives in Social Psychology*. New York: Holt, Rinehart and Winston.
Sipes, R. (1973). War, sports and aggression: An empirical test of two rival theories. *American Anthropologist*, **75**, 64–86.
Tajfel, H. (Ed.) (1978). *Differentiation Between Social Groups: Studies in the Social Psychology of Intergroup Relations*. London: Academic Press.
Tajfel, H. (1982). Social psychology of intergroup relations. *Annual Review of Psychology*, **33**, 1–39.
Tajfel, H. and Turner, J. C. (1979). An integrative theory of ingroup conflict. In: W. G. Austin and S. Worchel (Eds.). *The Social Psychology of Intergroup Relations.*, Monterey, California: Brooks/Cole.

Turner, J. C. (1981). The experimental social psychology of intergroup behaviour. In: J. C. Turner and H. Giles (Eds.) *Intergroup Behaviour*, Oxford: Blackwell.

Turner, J. C. and Brown, R. J. (1978). Social status, cognitive alternatives and intergroup relations. In: II. Tajfel (Ed.) *Differentiation Between Social Groups*. London: Academic Press.

Turner, J. C. and Giles, H. (1981). *Intergroup Behaviour*. Oxford: Blackwell.

Worchel, S. (1979). Co-operation and the reduction of intergroup conflict: Some determining factors. In: W. G. Austin and S. Worchel (Eds.) *The Social Psychology of Intergroup Relations*. Monterey, California: Brooks/Cole.

Worchel, S., Andreoli, V. A. and Fulger, R. (1977). Intergroup co-operation and intergroup attraction: The effect of previous interaction and outcome of combined effort. *Journal of Experimental Social Psychology*, **13**, 131–140.

Psychology and Social Problems
Edited by A. Gale and A. J. Chapman
© 1984 John Wiley & Sons Ltd.

CHAPTER 14

BLINDNESS AND DEAFNESS

C. I. Howarth and D. D. Clark-Carter

I.—THE EXTENT OF THE PROBLEM

It may seem strange to write about the problems of the blind and of the deaf in one short chapter. There are so many difficulties which are specific to the form of handicap, and so many of the aids available are equally specific. A hearing aid is of little use to a blind person unless that person also happens to be deaf. But both the deaf and the blind, in somewhat similar ways, may find it difficult to survive in the world of the hearing and the sighted, and they evoke similar responses in care givers.

Both the deaf and the blind tend to become dependent on others (this is particularly the case for the blind) and to form a restricted subculture with others similarly handicapped (this is especially the case for those who become severely deaf before they learn to speak). For people with either sensory handicap, it may be difficult to become an independent member of normal society, and attempts to help them may accentuate this problem rather than alleviate it.

It is difficult to produce precise figures for the number of people afflicted by deafness or blindness because of some uncertainty about the precise degree of sensory handicap which qualifies one to be called either 'blind' or 'deaf', and because there is always a degree of under-reporting of the handicap by people who overcome it more successfully than others, or by people who wish to avoid the stigma of being labelled.

Local authorities maintain registers of the handicapped in their area, but the accuracy of these varies. Inclusion on a register for the visually handicapped depends on an assessment by an ophthalmologist, while no medical examination is necessary to get on to a register of the hearing impaired. Part of the reason for this is that the registered blind qualify for some financial benefits, while the registered deaf do not. Despite this Cullinan (1977) has estimated that 34% of those eligible are not on the blind register, while 20% of the partially sighted also fail to register.

The majority of those on the blind register can see more than the mere presence of light. The official classification states that even those with visual acuity of 6/60 can be classified as blind if their visual field is 'markedly' contracted. Equally, 'deaf' does not necessarily mean unable to hear at all. 'Profound deafness' refers to a hearing loss in the speech frequencies of greater than 95 dB in the better ear, while a loss of 35 dB is generally accepted as the minimum to qualify as hearing impaired (Haggard, Gatehouse and Davis, 1981).

For both the blind and the deaf the lesser degree of impairment tends to be labelled in a way which accentuates the remaining capacity: in the case of visual impairment the term is 'partial sight', and for hearing impairment, it is 'partial hearing'. It is often difficult to decide just where to place the boundary between the more and less severe form of the impairment, and equally difficult to place the boundary between mild impairment and 'normality'. Because of the poor quality of the definitions and the possibly misleading nature of the labels used, there have been attempts to produce less ambiguous and internationally accepted terminology (World Health Organization, 1980).

Table 14.1 shows the prevalence and incidence of visual and hearing impairment in the United Kingdom. Such statistics should be treated cautiously for the reasons already given. Perhaps the most striking feature of these statistics is the age distribution. Seventy per cent of the partially sighted and 75% of the blind are over retirement age, and this is a growing trend. Of new registrations 79% of the partially sighted, and 83% of the blind were above retiring age (Department of Health and Social Security, 1980). A similar age distribution is found for deafness. Davis (1983) has found that 50% of people of the age of 75 years or older experience difficulty with conversations in the presence of background noise, while only 15% of the 15–24 age groups show this mild degree of deafness. As in the case of blindness, there is a tendency for the deaf population to be increasingly elderly. This is because there are more old people in the population, and because the causes of sensory impairment in the young are more amenable to medical intervention.

The main causes of blindness among children are congenital anomalies, optic nerve atrophy and cataracts, though retrolental fibro-plasia is still a significant cause. Among adults the main causes vary with age; optic nerve atrophy for the 16–49 age group; retinal conditions, such as diabetic retinopathy for the 50–64 group; and macular lesions for those over 65. Cataracts and congenital anomalies are the chief causes of partial sight under 4 years of age. Nystagmus, congenital anomalies, cataracts and optic nerve degeneration are the commonest causes of partial sight between 5 and 15. From 16–24 retinal conditions, choroidal atrophy and optic nerve atrophy are the main causes. Over the age of 65, macular lesions, glaucoma and cataracts

TABLE 14.1
PREVALENCE AND INCIDENCE STATISTICS FOR SENSORY
IMPAIRMENT IN THE UNITED KINGDOM
(i.e., total and new registrations)

VISUAL IMPAIRMENT				
Category	Total Registrations		New Registrations in One Year	
	Total	Rate†	Total	Rate†
Registered Blind	122,426	2.2*	14,330	0.26
0–4 Years	—	—	75*	—
Partial Sight	58,422	1.0*	9,413	0.17*
0–4 Years	—	—	61	—
Blind and Deaf	2,181	0.04*	****	****
Blind and Partial Hearing	4,214	0.08*	****	****

HEARING IMPAIRMENT		
Category	Total Estimated	
	Total	Rate†
Profoundly Deaf (>95 dB)	89,510	1.6**
35 dB − 95 dB	5,504,890	98.4**
1 year age cohort (at 8 years)	919	1.0***
Of whom with visual impairment	61	0.07***

† per 1,000
Data extrapolated from
* Department of Health and Social Security, 1980
** Haggard et al., 1981
*** Commission of the European Community, 1979
**** Unavailable from any source

account for the majority of cases (Department of Health and Social Security, 1979).

The main causes of deafness among adults are presbyacusis, industrial noise, or amplified sound, and Ménière's disease (Department of Health and Social Security, 1973). Among children the commonest causes are maternal rubella (German measles), genetic problems, meningitis, jaundice and anoxia (Commission of the European Communities, 1979).

Some of these conditions should be preventable. Retrolental fibroplasia was identified in 1954 as being caused by the administration of too much oxygen to premature babies. By 1964, reduction of the amount of oxygen had resulted in the virtual disappearance of the condition. Rubella, contracted by the mother in the early weeks of pregnancy, can be prevented by routine immunization of girls. Noise induced hearing loss is predictable and avoidable by the use of ear defenders or by a reduction in the noise level by other means.

Sensory impairment can interfere with many aspects of normal life. Deafness in children has a dramatic effect on their education. For example,

Conrad (1979) has shown that the average reading performance of profoundly congenitally deaf school leavers is equivalent to that of hearing children aged about 8 years. Webster, Wood and Griffiths (1981) have shown that even this horrifying statistic is misleading, because deaf children achieve that score in a quite different way from hearing children. Their vocabulary may be better, but their understanding of syntax is much worse. For mathematics the picture is a little brighter. Wood, Wood and Howarth (1983) have shown that the mathematical performance of congenitally deaf 16-year-olds is equivalent to that of 12½-year-old hearing children. Moreover their errors and difficulties are essentially the same as those of the younger hearing children.

The main problem in the education of young blind children is also connected with reading. Blind children have a much better understanding of language than deaf children, but Braille is difficult to learn, and even the best blind readers read at only half the speed of sighted children. The partially sighted can often read large print almost as fast as the sighted can read normal print. However, visual field defects, particularly when central vision is poor, can be very disruptive.

A peculiar effect of congenital blindness is that it seems to prevent the development of a normal sense of space and of the individual's orientation within space. Dodds, Howarth and Clark-Carter (1982) have shown that congenitally blind children cannot, when turning a corner, appreciate the effect that this has on the direction of a fixed point relative to their bodies. Nor can they draw any sensible representation of a route they have just walked. Blindfolded, sighted children, and children who have gone blind a few years after birth have far less difficulty with either of these tasks.

Those who go blind in adult life also have difficulty in learning to read Braille and suffer a dramatic loss of independent mobility (Clark-Carter, Howarth, Heyes, Dodds and Armstrong, 1982; and Todd, 1967). Blind people may also have difficulty in social situations because of their inability to detect facial expressions and gestures. Those who go deaf in adult life may learn to lip read, and so be able to communicate fairly normally with hearing people. If, however, deafness does interfere with normal social conversation, then the adult deaf are much more likely to become clinically depressed (Thomas and Gilhome-Herbst, 1980).

II.—CONCEPTS OF THE PERSON AND MODELS OF HUMAN BEHAVIOUR

One important factor affecting a person's self-esteem is how others view them. Many perceive the blind to be helpless and incompetent, and the deaf to be stupid. By a less extreme version of the same attitudes, those who deal with the handicapped person may be tempted to patronize them and over-protect them. Both these attitudes accentuate the difficulty which the blind and the deaf experience in an area where self-esteem is involved – in seeking employment (Quigley and Kretschmer, 1982). But the difficulty may also be due to a lower level of aspiration in the handicapped person. A further consequence of unemployment or under-employment is lack of financial independence. This may be particularly distressing for the newly disabled.

There are two basic ways in which the handicapped can deal with their problem: they can minimize its detrimental effects and demand to be treated on equal terms with the non-handicapped, or they can call for special treatment. Each strategy has an extreme version: denial that any problem exists, and resentment against such terms as 'impairment', 'disability' and 'handicap', or a desire for segregation from the general population, thus removing the need to compete, and so to risk failure. Each can be seen as a way of maintaining a positive self image.

Acquired deafness or blindness both seem to be potentially more emotionally disturbing than the congenital forms of the impairment (Cooper, 1976; Kirtley, 1975). This may be because those with the acquired handicap are fully aware of what they are missing. They also bring to the handicap the prejudices which they had before losing their vision or their hearing However, the depression which often accompanies acquired handicap has also been reported when vision has been restored after removal of a congenital cataract (Gregory and Wallace, 1963).

Rehabilitation programmes can markedly improve the attitudes of the handicapped. De L'Aune, Lewis, Needham and Nelson (1977) found that the emotional and behavioural adjustment of blind people, as measured by the Minnesota Multiphasic Personality Inventory, were related to the blind person acquiring skills in reading and in mobility. Delafield (1974) demonstrated most clearly the increased self-esteem of blind people following systematic training in mobility skills. Those who come to terms with the handicap and cease to hope for miracle cures show greater adjustment (Kirtley, 1975). Greater adjustment, in turn, lessens the degree to which the handicapped person feels disadvantaged in comparison with the non-handicapped.

III.—INDIVIDUAL ASSESSMENT

Visual impairment, if there is any vision remaining, is usually measured in two ways: visual acuity and visual fields. Visual acuity is measured by reading letters of different sizes, or by detecting the orientation of gratings of progressively narrower spacing. The results of such tests are expressed in terms of the distance at which the individual can read a letter compared with the norm for that size of letter. Thus 6/60 means that the person can see at 6 feet letters which can normally be distinguished at 60 feet. Children do not reach 6/6 vision until about the age of 4. It is difficult to use eye charts with very young children, but gross visual disability can sometimes be detected in the newborn by observing pupillary reflexes, and later by observing binocular converging and following reflexes.

Visual fields are measured by using a perimeter. In one version the client fixates a central light and is asked to report when another light appears or disappears in peripheral vision. Normal vision can extend as much as 100° on either side of a fixated point (but with much reduced acuity). People can be surprisingly unaware of scotomata and other deficiencies of peripheral vision, but defects of central vision are much more handicapping because the greatest acuity is normally in the centre of the visual field.

Adult hearing is usually tested by audiometry. The most common of these is pure tone audiometry, which measures the lowest intensity at which the client can hear pure tones of various frequencies. Usually measurement is restricted to those audible frequencies which are important in hearing normal speech (between 125 Hz and 4,000 Hz). The client wears headphones through which the tones are played, to one ear at a time, and reports when the tone begins to be or ceases to be audible. Since deafness may also lead to confusion of different frequencies as well as lower sensitivity to pure tones, more sophisticated audiometric techniques may attempt to measure this. Speech audiometry is an attempt to get a measure which relates specifically to the person's difficulty in hearing speech.

Until recently early diagnosis of hearing impairment in children has been rather difficult, and in 60% of cases there has been a delay of 6 months or more between parental suspicion and confirmation of hearing loss (Commission of the European Communities, 1979). New techniques are improving this situation. It is now possible to test the hearing of neonates by detecting startle reflexes, head jerks, changes in respiration, and bodily activity in response to sounds. A special cot which detects any of these changes has been developed and linked to a microprocessor which correlates such physical signs with the presence or absence of auditory stimuli (Bennett, 1979). Other techniques known as Evoked Potential Audiometry (EPA) have been attempted involving the external recording of brain waves. However, they have necessitated children below about 18 months being anaesthetized, and early versions have shown poor accuracy for children below about 2 years of age. Nonetheless this approach has still not been abandoned at the time of writing.

To test the intelligence of the sensorily impaired presents special problems. Tests which have been separately standardized on an impaired population, as in the case of the Williams' test for children with defective vision, and the Snijders-Oomen Non-verbal Intelligence Test for the Deaf and Hearing Subjects (Snijders and Snijders-Oomen, 1970), make it possible to rank the sensorily impaired, but avoid the question of whether the handicap affects normal intellectual development. As one would expect, deaf children do relatively poorly on the verbal scales of conventional intelligence tests, and relatively well on most spatial and other non-verbal tests (Meadow, 1980). Blind children cannot of course even be tested on some forms of non-verbal intelligence, but Dodds *et al.* (1982) have shown that they can have severe deficiencies in spatial understanding.

IV.—THE IMMEDIATE SOCIAL ENVIRONMENT

The different forms of social adaptation available to the adult sensorily impaired have already been described. These are facilitated by various organizations and pressure groups such as in the UK, The Royal National Institute for the Blind, and the Royal National Institute for the Deaf. American equivalents are the American Foundation for the Blind, and the National Association of the Deaf. All of these in their various ways seek to help the sensorily impaired, either by providing specific aids such as talking books or rehabilitation programmes, or by acting as a focus for self help and 'consciousness raising'. All of these organizations attempt to increase the awareness and sensitivity of the normal population to the needs of the handicapped.

Sensorily handicapped children present a special problem. They are often treated in a different way by their parents. Mothers of deaf pre-school children are less permissive, less creative and flexible, more intrusive and didactic, and show less approval (Meadow, 1980). The specific adaptations which adults make to the problems of deaf children may themselves increase rather than reduce the disability, but once these effects are understood they may be relatively easy to overcome (Wood and Wood, in press). The effect on parents of having a handicapped child may take a number of forms, ranging from realistic acceptance to rejection, denial or guilt (Kirtley, 1975). The rearing of a handicapped child can become a fulltime occupation, not only because of the extra help the child is felt to need, but also because parents tend to become involved in handicap organizations, and in fund raising.

Siblings of the handicapped child are likely to be jealous of the special attention the child receives. They may find they gain more parental approval by joining in the care process. The effect on them can be more important when the handicap involves a language difficulty, and the parents become so channelled into non-verbal methods of communication that the language development of subsequent children suffers (Kew, 1975).

In addition to their mobility problems, the blind have difficulty in social situations because of their inability to detect the non-verbal cues, facial expressions or eye contact, which provide the context for normal speech. These non-verbal cues are known to determine the moment at which it is appropriate for speakers to take turns in conversation, and may also modify the significance of the spoken word. Lacking these cues the blind may appear socially clumsy or even tactless.

V. — THE WIDER SOCIAL AND ORGANIZATIONAL ENVIRONMENT

Legislation has been passed in an attempt to improve the lot of the handicapped in relation to education, housing and welfare, mobility and access to buildings, and employment.

In the UK, The Chronically Sick and Disabled Persons Act (1970) has helped to change attitudes to the disabled, but has not achieved the full practical benefits which were expected. Despite the requirement on local government authorities to identify those in need of special help, no time limit was set and therefore many authorities have not complied with this requirement. There are also 'let-out' clauses for those who wish to comply with the letter rather than the spirit of the Act. For example, before any alteration is made to an existing building to make it more accessible or less dangerous, that alteration must be deemed practical and reasonable. The interpretation of this latter phase has been very varied, and it is often left to the disabled themselves, their friends and pressure groups to press for a more generous implementation of the Act (Greaves, 1981).

The Disabled Persons (Employment) Act (1944) has had a similar level of success. It states that for employers of twenty or more persons at least 3% of the work force should be taken from registers of the disabled. But this obligation can be avoided if no disabled person is qualified or available for the job. If firms undertake to consider all disabled applicants from a Job Centre they can receive a permit to employ non-registered people, even when they have not fulfilled their 'quota'. Many firms do not even bother to apply for such permits, but few prosecutions are ever sought under the Act (Darnbrough and Kinrade, 1981).

Whether the disabled will fare any better from legislation related to education remains to be seen. The Education Act (1981) states that the handicapped should, as far as is practical, be integrated into normal schools. It also requires the special needs of such children to be assessed and education provided appropriate to those needs. It appears to give some powers to parents to insist on appropriate treatment of their children. But again there is a number of provisos, all of which are perfectly reasonable, which may allow the intentions of the Act to be circumvented.

The 1981 Act was inspired by the Warnock Report (1978) which recommended integration as far as possible, and when special schooling was unavoidable, that much closer liaison should be set up between the special schools and their ordinary counterparts, so that their expertise can be shared. In many authorities this has led to the setting up of special units within ordinary schools and the closing of many special schools.

Legislators and educators can have far reaching effects on the lives of the sensorily handicapped. Sometimes their decisions are based on no more than unsubstantiated and controversial opinions. The arguments about the use of signing in the education of deaf children is an example of this. Outside the educational system the early profoundly deaf are most likely to communicate with each other in sign language. Yet in the United Kingdom approximately 77% of deaf children are not taught and do not use a sign language in school of the kind they are likely to use as adults (Commission of the European Community, 1979).

The reasons for not exposing children to manual communication during the course of their education can be summarized as follows. If the deaf are not to be cut off from communicating with the rest of us, they must learn to understand and speak our language. If as children they are taught and allowed to use manual communication, then this may lessen the incentive, or even interfere with the ability to learn our language. Most sign languages, except those which have been devised by educators, are more ideographic than spoken language; that is, they are based, like ancient Egyptian hierogly-phics on pictures. As such, it is argued, they are less precise, subtle and flexible than spoken language. Since language may be a medium for thought, some theorists have argued that users of sign language will not be able to think as clearly as those who use spoken language.

Most of these arguments have their opponents. Short of the rest of us learning sign language, it is impossible to refute the idea that those who do not learn spoken language will be isolated. However, two reports have shown that only a very small proportion of children leaving deaf schools have intelligible speech and good lip reading ability (Conrad, 1979; Department of Education and Science, 1968). If children without intelligible speech and useful lip reading are not taught sign language, they may be virtually without language (Furth, 1973), and it is not surprising that many of them pick up signing while still at school, and improve their ability as signers after leaving school.

Bellugi and Fischer (1972) claim that sign language can be just as efficient as spoken language for expressing ideas, although there are some studies which seem to show the opposite (e.g., Hoemann, 1972). Freeman (1976) has claimed that the use of sign language can actually enhance the acquisition of spoken language, but Quigley and Kretschmer (1982) point out that this is dependent on the type of sign language employed, and that early intensive oral education may be as effective. The results of research do not justify the excessively partisan stances taken by the opponents in this debate. The greatest need is to devise new and better methods for introducing deaf children to language, taking inspiration from the undoubted successes which have been achieved by both oral and manual methods.

VI.—TYPES OF INTERVENTION

Attempts to help the blind or the deaf may concentrate upon their special difficulties and on developing specific remedies, prostheses or training programmes. Or they may concentrate on making it easier for the sensorily deprived to become integrated into normal society, and on the relatively non-specific problems which afflict any handicapped or dependent group. These two approaches are not alternatives. They are of course complementary, and any effective rehabilitation programme will make use of both in appropriate combination. In this chapter, it is argued that the most appropriate way of integrating the specific and non-specific approaches is within a flexible problem-solving framework aimed at minimizing the differences between the abilities and performance of the handicapped group and those of the normal population.

Specific Aids for the Blind

The specific difficulties of the blind are due to their inability to know and to make sense of their physical surroundings. They can only detect objects at a distance if those objects create a characteristic sound. They may detect a near object by touch, but may be unable to recognize it. They have difficulty orienting themselves in space and in understanding the spatial relationships between different parts of their environment. This latter difficulty is particularly marked for the congenitally blind (Dodds et al., 1982). All of these deficiencies reduce the capacity of the blind to be independently mobile.

Specific remedies for the blind are aimed at improving their ability to detect objects at a distance. For example, the sonic torch (Kay, 1964) was designed to enable the blind to sense the presence of many objects in their environment simultaneously, by making use of the time delay between the emission of an ultrasonic pulse, and the detection of its reflection by the device. An alternative approach is to extend the range of touch detection by the use of a long cane, supplemented by training programmes to prepare blind people to make the maximum use of their hearing and other aids to mobility (Hoover, 1950). Other devices, such as tactile maps and route instructions on audio-tape, can be used to help the blind to navigate by reference to the landmarks which they can detect.

The most heroic visual prostheses are those devices which feed signals directly to the visual cortex through electrodes permanently implanted in the brain (e.g., Brindley and Lewin, 1968). Although some blind patients have, in this way, been able to 'see' signals derived from a television camera mounted on their heads, the images they receive are limited to what can be achieved with up to 50 separately stimulated points. Perception of large symbols is possible, but no useful object perception has yet been achieved.

Despite the claims for the '6 million dollar man', we do not yet have the technology.

Specific Aids for the Deaf

The specific problems of the deaf are concentrated on their inability to hear and understand speech. They have other difficulties of course, in detecting warning signals, car horns, door bells, alarm clocks and music. But in comparison with the consequences of failing to understand speech, these problems are relatively minor. People who have difficulty hearing and understanding normal conversation are three times more likely to suffer from clinical depression as are those who are less severely deaf. The most profoundly deaf are no more likely to be depressed than are those whose deafness is only just severe enough to interfere with normal social conversation. The ability to talk freely with others seems to be the critical factor preventing the deaf from becoming depressed (Thomas and Gilhome-Herbst, 1980).

The commonest specific remedy for deafness is the hearing aid which amplifies sound and feeds it directly into the ear. Modern electronics have made it possible to achieve amplifications of up to 50 dB for ear level aids (i.e., where the receiver is behind the ear), and of up to 80 dB for chest mounted aids. The difference is due to the fact that ear level receivers pick up the output from their own amplifiers more easily than do chest mounted aids, and are therefore more liable to feedback. The improvement in hearing achieved with hearing aids is usually much less than one would expect. This is because the commonest form of deafness (sensori-neural deafness or 'nerve' deafness) produces a reduction in the range of useful hearing as well as raising the threshold for detection of sound. For this reason, a sound only slightly more intense than that required to reach the threshold of hearing, may seem unbearably loud and even painful.

Direct stimulation of sensory surfaces in the inner ear or of the auditory nerve has been attempted. These operations are a little more useful than their visual equivalents for a very small proportion of deaf people (Berliner, 1982).

As in the case of blindness, attempts have been made to supply information normally available to the deficient sense, through an alternative sensory channel. The most familiar of these methods is the use of sign language and lip reading. People who go deaf slowly learn to lip read so effectively that they may not be fully aware of the degree of their deafness. People who go deaf suddenly can be taught to lip read.

However, if a child goes deaf before learning to speak, then it is very difficult to acquire speech through the medium of lip reading (Conrad, 1979). We have already referred to the belief that language is better taught to deaf children through the use of manual communication. There are many varieties of sign language. Some have developed as a living language in the rather restricted culture of the pre-lingually deaf. Examples of these are American Sign Language (ASL) and British Sign Language (BSL). These 'natural' languages tend to have rather different grammars from spoken English and this may create difficulties for the development of literacy. To counteract this apparent deficiency of 'natural' sign languages, various artificial languages have been constructed to mirror the syntax and structure of spoken and written language. Examples of such constructed languages are Signed English and the Paget Gorman Sign Language. Among the educated deaf, sign language is always supplemented by finger spelling which enables them to convey words for which no conventional sign exists (Quigley and Kretschmer, 1982).

Non-specific Difficulties of the Sensorily Handicapped

All handicaps tend to induce dependence, but sensory handicaps, which interfere with normal communication cause particular difficulties. For example, there is a radio programme in Britain for handicapped people which is called 'Does he take sugar?' because that question is often asked of a relative, friend or care giver in the presence of the handicapped person, and it is particularly infuriating, because it implies that such a person cannot be relied upon to give an appropriate answer. The deaf complain of similar treatment, and frequently insist that they are 'deaf not daft'.

What some deaf and blind people are complaining about is an unfortunate side effect of our caring attitudes. We tend to do too much for them; to do things which they could do for themselves; to take responsibilities away from them which they need in order to maintain their self-respect and competence. This is not an easy problem to solve because the handicapped complain equally bitterly if they get less than the help they need. It is not easy to steer the thin line between providing too little or too much help, between giving them responsibilities which they cannot meet or insulting them by giving them too little responsibility.

This difficulty is one which is also met in other contexts. For example, Wood has shown that instruction is more efficient if it provides the pupil with the minimal amount of help required to perform the task being taught. Either too much help or too little help is less efficient. The best strategy he found was a 'contingent' one in which, when the child successfully followed an instruction, the next instruction provided a little less help, and thus gave a little more responsibility to the child, and when the child was unsuccessful, the next instruction was a little more helpful, a little more controlling (Wood, Wood and Middleton, 1978). This effect is not a small one. Wood has repeatedly found correlations of about 0.9 between the proportion of instructions which follow his contingency rule and the amount learned by the child, as measured by a test immediately after the instruction was completed. He is therefore prepared to speculate that the contingency can account for 80% of the variance in the normal range of teaching, and that it may be the major difference between good and bad teaching.

It seems likely that something similar to Wood's contingent strategy could be used by care givers dealing with the sensorily handicapped. Wood and Howarth (1979) and Wood, Wood, Griffiths, Howarth and Howarth (1982) have presented evidence that teachers of the deaf use far more controlling language when speaking to deaf children than do teachers of hearing children. In particular, teachers of the deaf ask a large number of questions requiring no more than 'yes' or 'no' for an answer, and may even, in attempting to correct the children's speech try to achieve absolute control over the child's next utterance.

For example

Teacher	What did you do yesterday?
Child	TV
Teacher	Did you watch TV in the evening?
Child	Yes
Teacher	What did you see?
Child	Football
Teacher	Did you watch football?
Child	Yes
Teacher	Say: I watched football on the television
Child	Football TV
Teacher	No, say: I watched football on the television

Wood and his associates have now shown that by exerting less control over the deaf child's speech, one can ensure that the child produces more words, that the words are more varied and informative, and that the child begins to take greater control of the conversation by, for example, asking questions of the teacher (Wood and Wood, in press). These issues and ideas can be applied equally to oral and manual methods. It is possible that greater improvements in the education of deaf children could be made by the application of these general principles than by any specific technique such as the use of sign language or various kinds of speech therapy. Some of the most successful educators of deaf children already seem to be working in this way, but the reason for their undoubted success may be concealed by their unnecessary involvement in controversies about oralism *versus* signing.

Another approach to the problem of dependence in handicapped people, is behaviour modification. The proponents of this approach argue that dependent behaviour in the handicapped is rewarded by giving help and attention, whereas independent behaviour is punished because it is seen as unremarkable and may be ignored (see, for example, Ullman and Krasner, 1976). In this way care-giving can induce and increase dependence in the handicapped. The principles of behaviour modification suggest that the contingencies should simply be reversed, and that competent independent behaviour should be consistently remarked upon and rewarded, while incompetent and dependent behaviour should be ignored. The effectiveness of this strategy has been demonstrated many times with all manner of handicapped and disturbed people. Despite this, the behavioural approach has not been universally adopted by care givers. Indeed, many care givers regard this approach as morally dubious, requiring a cold-blooded manipulative approach when tender loving care would seem more appropriate.

It should, however, be possible to devise care-giving strategies which are a combination of Wood's contingent approach to the provision of appropriate levels of help and the behaviour modification approach to the equally contingent provision of rewards. The commonsense and ethical objections to behaviour modification are surely not to the rewarding of appropriate and successful behaviour, but to the ignoring of inappropriate and unsuccessful behaviour when the latter demonstrate very clearly a need for help?

The combined approach would require the formulation in advance of actions and statements representing different levels of help. For this purpose Wood described five levels of instruction which are relatively easy to recognize and almost equally easy to produce when appropriate, and a similar set of descriptions can be produced for both the verbal and practical help which may be offered to handicapped people. These are set out in Figure 14.1. It is assumed that help is offered in relation to some task which can be analysed into constituent elements by some form of task analysis. It is further assumed that each unit of verbal or practical help will refer to one element in the task and that the care giver will pause after each intervention to give the helped person an opportunity to complete the element in the task, but offering one degree less of help than was given in relation to the successfully completed element. When the handicapped person fails to complete an element, then a helper needs to intervene and offer one degree more of help.

When moving up the scale in response to successful performance, it would be appropriate to reward the success in some way. When moving down the scale in response to failure, then little praise may be appropriate. However, when the contingent strategy is being used, it is unlikely that the handicapped person will fail to get any aspect of a task element correct. Consequently, although it will be necessary to correct errors, it may also be possible to give praise in relation to those aspects of the task element which he or she performed correctly. Hence, in Figure 14.1, correction is shown as being accompanied by limited praise rather than by no praise at all.

This adaptation of the techniques of behaviour modification avoids the dilemma of doing nothing when the handicapped person fails. It can be

FIGURE 14.1
A STRATEGY FOR REDUCING DEPENDENCE BY SUPPLYING HELP AND REWARD CONTINGENTLY

In relation to any element of a task, help can be either verbal or practical, and may be more or less controlling, ranging from vague encouragement to complete verbal or practical control. Following Wood *et al.* (1978) one can describe *five* levels of control. A contingent strategy would require the helper to offer more or less control depending upon the success of the handicapped person in responding to any help which has been offered. If he or she copes successfully and completes one element of the task, then the appropriate praise should be followed by slightly less controlling help in relation to the next element of the task. If he or she fails, then further help should be given of a slightly more controlling kind. This is inevitably what happens when correcting an error. The danger is that any failure on the part of the handicapped person may produce overly controlling help at Level 5. If any aspect of the task element has been done correctly then that should be noted and limited praise given before attempting to correct errors or failures.

Five levels of help can be distinguished fairly easily.

Verbal Help	Practical Help	Contingency Rules
1. General encouragement	1. Benign observation	Correct performance of task element leads to praise followed by lowering of control. Incorrect performance or failure leads to limited praise followed by correction i.e. by greater control.
2. General instruction, suggesting nature of what needs to be done.	2. Indication of task area by pointing, etc.	
3. Partial instruction, suggesting some details of what needs to be done.	3. Indicating aspects of what needs to be done by pointing or starting some details.	
4. Specific instructions, suggesting most of what needs to be done.	4. Partial help, doing part of task element.	
5. Total instruction, specifying explicitly all that needs to be done.	5. Total help, doing whole of task element.	

The effect of operating a scheme of this kind should be to encourage independence because increasing independence gets the greatest reward. But incompetent or dependent behaviour is not ignored, instead it leads to a minimal increase in the help given.

regarded as a modification of the 'shaping' procedure used by animal trainers, but taking account of human ability to follow verbal instructions and to understand the structure of any task. Before attempting to provide the detailed help for which a contingent strategy would be appropriate, it may be necessary to make sure the handicapped person understands the structure of a new or unfamiliar task either by giving a verbal description of it, or by a practical demonstration, both of which are, in effect, at Level 5, before attempting to provide contingent help.

It will also be necessary to take special measures when complete lack of success leads to repeated Level 5 interventions. It may then be appropriate to alternate Level 5 verbal instructions and Level 5 demonstrations. It may even be necessary to undo the element of the task which has just been demonstrated, to give the handicapped person an opportunity to imitate completely what has been demonstrated. If neither of these strategies is successful in lifting the client above Level 5, then it must be recognized that the task is too difficult or has been inappropriately structured or analysed.

A Problem-solving Approach to the Care of the Sensorily Handicapped

Remedies for the specific and non-specific problems of the handicapped are of course complementary. To be most effective one must achieve an optimal integration of all possible measures. This is most likely to be achieved within a systematic problem-solving framework, and the approach has been described many times, by people working on many types of problem and starting from many different theoretical positions. In a previous paper, Howarth (1980) has argued that the problem-solving framework is an underlying and under-appreciated framework for the whole of psychology, pure and applied (see Chapter 1). Here we shall merely illustrate the application of the problem-solving approach when seeking to help the sensorily handicapped.

For this purpose, five stages can be distinguished:
  (i) *Formulate and clarify the purposes, aims or expectations which define the problem*. Unless one is clear about the nature of the problem and what would constitute a solution to it, then one cannot even begin.
 (ii) *Survey, seek out, invent, appropriate resources which may be helpful in achieving the purposes*. These include the resources available to the clients or to potential caregivers. They may be pieces of equipment or skills, or organizational procedures, or simply the goodwill of the people concerned.
(iii) *Devise a strategy whereby the resources may be deployed to meet the expressed purposes*. This process may require the goodwill and coopera-tion of many people and their ideas should be consulted in formulating the strategy. Strategies can be described in many ways. One of these is in terms of a task analysis describing the sequencing of and relationships between different elements in the strategy. Such an analysis is essential, for example, if one is to offer contingent help as described in Figure 14.1.
 (iv) *Implement the strategy*. This will be done initially in a tentative and pilot form with the intention of improving and refining it in the light of experience. The cooperation of many people may be needed and many practical difficulties will be met which must be overcome to give the strategy a fair chance of succeeding.
  (v) *Evaluate the strategy objectively*. So often any new programme will be

welcomed, simply as a gesture of goodwill. This 'Hawthorne' effect (see Chapters 6 and 7) must not be confused with proper evaluation. Objective measures must be attempted, methodological rigour insisted upon, and evaluation continued for a reasonable length of time.

This sequence is not simply linear. Ideally it is a loop which should continue to operate, and hence continually improve the services offered to handicapped people. Among other things, it should allow a progressive escalation of the expectations of the handicapped, and of the people who care for them. This has already occurred in the world of the deaf as a result of improvements in hearing aids, and in the world of the blind as a result of the availability of mobility training and vocational training.

There are however many reasons why the ideal problem-solving approach cannot be achieved. One of these, to which we have already referred, is that the purposes of the care givers may not be consistent with the ambitions of the handicapped. The care givers may find it easier to keep the handicapped in a dependent role, and may like the sense of moral wellbeing which they get from 'looking after' handicapped people. The expectations of the handicapped may be unrealistically low because of their limited experience. There may be financial constraints, but in the long run money may be saved if the amount of financial or salaried help required by the handicapped can be reduced.

Another source of inefficiency is that it is rare for any one person or cooperating group of people to be responsible for all five stages of the problem-solving process. This is a deficiency in the organization of many aspects of our society, but nowhere is this more apparent than in the world of the sensorily handicapped. Pressure groups of various kinds may restrict themselves to Stage (i) and seem unrealistic and strident in their demands for help. Inventors, designers and others may produce new resources which take a very long time to be made available, or may be ill-adapted to the aspirations and needs of the handicapped. Parliament or charities may provide new resources without any systematic investigation of what is needed or how successful it may be. Care givers are stuck with everyday problems and have little free energy to try new solutions. Academics and bureaucrats may attempt to evaluate the services which are provided, but the ethos of our society often prevents this from being done systematically and effectively (see, for example, Howarth and Gunn, 1984).

But, despite all these difficulties, it must be said that the lot of the sensorily handicapped in industrially developed nations has improved since the Second World War as a result of a more caring attitude, increased wealth, and the dedication of many individuals. The main point of this chapter is to argue that even more could be achieved if the systematic problem-solving approach adopted by a small number of individuals could become the norm in our attempts to improve the lot of the sensorily handicapped. To make this point more concrete, we now illustrate the argument by describing the work for the blind of our late colleague, Alfred Leonard.

In 1962 Leonard had the task of evaluating a recently invented sonic torch for the blind. He devised a test route and found that users of the aid (both blind and blindfolded) could negotiate it successfully. Instead of simply reporting this finding and making recommendations for training, he decided to look further into the question of the mobility of blind people. He wondered how many blind people could benefit from the use of the sonic aid, what type of tasks they would be helped with, and how such aids compared with existing alternatives. To begin answering these questions he read widely, visited schools and organizations for the visually handicapped, and he persuaded the UK Office of Population Censuses and Surveys to carry out a survey of the mobility needs of the visually handicapped.

Leonard found that there was a sufficiently large group whose visual handicap seemed to be the only factor which reduced their mobility, and in turn their employment prospects. He then made himself acquainted with all the information about existing mobility aids, training and rehabilitation. In doing so he was impressed by the long cane technique developed by Hoover (1950) to help blinded war veterans in the USA, and after a visit to the USA he judged the long cane to be a rival to the sonic torch.

In association with a blind man, Walter Thornton, he persuaded the Nuffield Foundation to set up a training school for mobility instructors. He evaluated the American training method, and produced a briefer version of it which was implemented at the school. From then until his death, he and his co-workers researched further ways of improving the mobility of the visually handicapped. For example, they have produced a simplified version of the sonic aid, The Nottingham Obstacle Detector (Heyes, 1981), and a kit for producing simple tactile versions of visual maps (James, 1982).

The point of this story is that Alfred Leonard took it upon himself to engage in all five stages of the problem-solving process described above. He participated in the formulation of objectives by interacting with organizations and pressure groups of and for the blind, and by instigating a survey of their needs. He investigated the resources available by studying the mobility performance of blind people, and by looking at devices and training schemes in the UK and other countries. He concluded that mobility instruction in the use of the long cane provided the best available aid for active blind people, and he took steps to make it available. He continued to monitor the achievements of the new services, and to suggest ways of improving them.

It is extremely rare for one man or one team to be involved in all five stages of the problem-solving process, and it was not always easy for Leonard to be so. There is a general assumption that research workers will devise new schemes which will be administered by other people, presumably because different skills are required. There is a similar assumption that those who originate or administer a new scheme shall not evaluate it, presumably because they cannot be trusted to be dispassionate. There is some justification for these assumptions, but there is an equally strong justification for allowing a dedicated and honest scientist to attempt to push through all five stages of the problem-solving process, since that person will have a better idea of the inter-dependence of the five stages than anyone who works in only one or two stages of the process.

VII.—IS PSYCHOLOGICAL INTERVENTION SUCCESSFUL?

In the previous section, the rather large claim is made that psychological intervention is most likely to be successful if the psychologist operates at all five levels of the problem-solving approach, and is willing to engage in the political activity necessary to ensure that proposed remedies are widely adopted. Evaluation should, of course, occur at every stage in this process from the laboratory studies through the pilot interventions to the final wide-spread implementation of any new measures. Success may occur at any of these levels, but sometimes effective technical ideas are not found to be socially acceptable, while at other times effective social movements may have no scientific justification. Ideally, one would like one's ideas to be evaluated successfully at all levels from the scientific to the political, but it must be admitted that this is very rare.

It must also be admitted that our grandiose claims about the problem-solving approach have not themselves been evaluated. They are based on logic and on descriptions of a relatively small number of successful interventions such as those of Hoover, Leonard and Wood.

However, there is no shortage of more limited types of evidence for the success of psychological interventions. For example, laboratory trials showed that the Nottingham Obstacle Detector (Heyes, 1981) is very easy to use and that the musical scale used is a better indicator of distance than a number of alternative codes. The NOD was then subjected to a limited field trial by being given to a selected group of blind people (Dodds, Armstrong and Shingledecker, 1981). This provided clear evidence that the device is of value to some blind people in their everyday lives. It is not yet commercially available, so that its success on a wider scale cannot yet be evaluated.

Similarly the type of intervention recommended by Wood has been evaluated in a limited number of pilot studies (e.g., Wood and Wood, in press), but it is still too soon to estimate the likelihood that these ideas will be taken up, or what impact they will have on the education of the deaf.

To look for evidence of success on a wider scale one must look at interventions with a longer history. The work of Hoover in the USA which was taken over and amplified by Leonard in Britain is one of the few examples of an intervention which can be evaluated at all levels. In many respects it has been extremely successful. Individual blind people, particularly active young blind people, have, as a result of the work of Hoover and Leonard, been able to achieve a level of independent mobility which would have been inconceivable to earlier generations. However, one should perhaps modify one's rapture by remembering that most blind people are elderly, that many of them have other handicaps, and that the majority of such people benefit little from mobility training at present, even if it is offered to them.

It is extremely difficult to estimate the cost effectiveness of different programmes. But in some cases intervention can produce beneficial effects without any additional cost (for example, by changing the teaching methods used in classrooms). There is little doubt that future research should be directed at improving the efficiency of existing support systems since that is the approach whose cost effectiveness is most easy to assess.

At the same time relatively expensive technological solutions should not be totally discouraged. There is no doubt that the hearing aid is the most effective single measure of help available to deaf people, and as technologies improve, new sensory aids will no doubt be developed. The various ultrasonic devices being tried out by blind people may, in the near future, lead to a relatively cheap device which will give blind people better information about their surroundings than they currently get from a long cane and unaided hearing.

There is always a difficulty in deciding whose criteria will be used in assessing a rehabilitation programme. These are discussed, with other ethical issues, below.

VIII.—METHODOLOGICAL AND PRACTICAL PROBLEMS

The main methodological and practical problems in work with the sensorily handicapped, as in so many areas of applied psychology, are related to the difficulty one has in negotiating appropriate opportunities to do research, to study the effects of different kinds of intervention and to evaluate existing provisions for the handicapped.

If one is carrying out research with the deaf or the blind, then it may be difficult to get access to subjects. If children are to be used there is the advantage that a number can be found in one place: the school. But teachers, not surprisingly, may feel they have to protect their pupils from the attentions of too many researchers. One may therefore need to convince teachers that the research will be of direct benefit to their children. In some cases the benefit cannot be guaranteed and that problem should not be fudged.

Having gained access, the experiments must have a degree of face validity, or cooperation may be withdrawn. When completed it is important to report back any findings to the school and its teachers. Similar considerations apply in the institutions which are for handicapped adults. If these things are mishandled, all opportunities for research may be lost.

Those subjects who are easy to get at may not be representative of the rest of the population. For example, rehabilitation centres may have an excess of young newly handicapped people, and very few old or chronically handicapped people.

When a new device or training programme has been developed, it is important to assess the potential market for it. Failure to do so has resulted in commercial firms marketing an aid, and losing money because of over-production. Health services or local authorities may also try to provide services which are not wanted.

In evaluating existing services one is likely to encounter some political opposition, since it would seem that evaluation is always something which should be done to *other people*, and is inappropriate when applied to one's own practices or sacred cows!

IX.—PROBLEMS OF ETHICS AND CONFIDENTIALITY

Some of the ethical problems faced by workers with handicapped people are relatively easy to solve. No research is justified if it will predictably harm the people being studied. Those taking part in any experiment or evaluation should, if possible, be made aware of what is happening and consent to it. If that would prejudice the result, then they must always be 'debriefed'. If anyone has retrospective objections then the investigation has been badly planned and must be abandoned or radically redesigned.

Other ethical problems are more difficult to solve. In particular, it is always difficult to decide who shall set the criteria for deciding the effectiveness or otherwise of a rehabilitation programme. The most obvious people to decide this are the handicapped people themselves. Are they satisfied with the results? Do they agree with the methods used to evaluate the programme? But handicapped people may set impossible criteria, such as being treated as if they had no handicap. Or they may set criteria which are unacceptably demanding on other people either financially or in terms of the time they give to serving the needs of the handicapped.

In these circumstances the decision is often left to the good judgement of responsible caring professionals. Often this is satisfactory, but these same professionals have their own needs which sometimes conflict with the real needs of the handicapped, or of the rest of society. For example, those providing medical care may seek, on humanitarian grounds to acquire for their service a degree of support which starves other equally worthy causes of funds.

It is therefore inevitable that a degree of political control has to be exerted over the activities of organizations of and for the handicapped, and over the professionals who care for them. But political control can itself lead to anomalies and inhumane results. There is no ideal solution to these particular ethical problems. We must just muddle along as best we can.

In the course of research, as with rehabilitation, in order to have a complete picture of the handicapped people with whom one is dealing, it will be necessary to acquire much information of a confidential nature. This will often have been gathered by other professions who will be reluctant to part with it, particularly if they think that the information may go further. A typical example is the information contained on the BD8—a British form completed by ophthalmologists for the visually handicapped—which includes sensitive details such as cause of the handicap, and the prognosis. Members of the medical profession are particularly guarded about allowing access to information which they have gathered. The individual psychologist must obviously treat such information as confidential, if for no other reason than that any breach of confidence would cause the loss of that source for the profession as a whole.

Frequently in research with the handicapped, fewer subjects are used than would be when the non-handicapped act as subjects, and also, even within one type of handicap, there is great heterogeneity. Hence, individual cases are often described. When reporting individual cases in any psychological research it is important that details which could identify specific individuals are not included. When dealing with the handicapped only a few such details may be enough for identification—for example, mention of the particular school attended and the syndrome suffered by a child.

X.—THE ROLE OF OTHER PROFESSIONS

To give an idea of the number of other professionals with whom the psychologist could be involved, it is worth mentioning the disciplines which the Department of Health and Social Security identifies as being concerned with the deaf. Apart from those with an interest in psychology and psychiatry, they include audiologists, audiological technicians, developmental paediatricians, engineers, epidemiologists, health visitors, industrial medical officers, linguists, lip-reading teachers, medical otologists, neuro-anatomists, neurophysiologists, consultant otolaryngologists, pathologists, physicists, social workers, speech therapists and teachers of the deaf (Department of Health and Social Security, 1973). There are an equivalent number who are concerned with the blind, including blind persons' rehabilitation officers, technical officers and mobility officers. Many of them are in more constant and direct contact with the clients than is the psychologist, and they are often the people who will, or will not, implement any of the psychologist's recommendations. As with the question of access to subjects, it is essential, if their cooperation is to be enlisted, that they be kept informed of why the psychologist has come to a given conclusion. They have often been working with the handicapped group for a long time, and will want more than the mere say-so of a psychologist before they change the procedures they have always used, particularly when the advice conflicts with the way they were originally trained. Often there will be allies who already see flaws in the orthodoxy of their profession and are anxious to see an alternative approach. Mention has already been made of the manual *versus* spoken communication debate among teachers of the deaf; an equivalent difference of opinion exists among mobility officers over how much account should be taken of a client's remaining vision.

There are a number of ways of keeping other professionals aware of any findings and of sounding out opinion. Many have their own journals and hold annual conferences. As long as they judge that what is being done is relevant, they will be willing to accept contributions.

The voluntary organizations, which can range between pressure groups who seek radical change and those who provide services, also play an important part, and have to be taken into consideration. Among workers—professional and voluntary—with both types of sensory impairment there are opposing political forces, and the professional has to be wary of alienating one faction, if this will hamper the implementation of new ideas.

XI.—FUTURE PROSPECTS

There is no doubt that the sensorily handicapped can benefit from the interest and attentions of psychologists. There are new ideas emerging in academic psychology, such as a better understanding of the nature of instruction and of language learning, or ideas about the conceptualization of space and the strategic use of limited vision, which have obvious implications in rehabilitation. In addition there are many examples of ideas flowing back into academic psychology as a result of experience gained in helping to solve the real life problems of the blind or deaf. In this field, as in so many others, academic and applied psychology are symbiotic and of mutual benefit one to the other.

However, there are many academic psychologists who think they will best advance their studies by concentrating on laboratory studies of theoretically interesting problems. These are matched by practitioners (including various kinds of applied psychologists) who believe that academic psychology cannot improve on common sense when it comes to solving real life problems. These academics and practitioners need one another because each reinforces the other's prejudices. But these prejudices are the most serious limitation to the development of new and effective rehabilitation. Future prospects will depend on the degree to which these particular prejudices can be overcome.

XII.—ANNOTATED READINGS

Myklebust, H. R. (1964). *The Psychology of Deafness*. Second Edition. New York: Grune and Stratton.

A general introduction to the area, which, although it concentrates on childhood, also covers adulthood. It gives an historical perspective, but needs to be supplemented by Quigley and Kretschmer for more recent research.

Quigley, S. P. and Kretschmer, R. E. (1982). *The Education of Deaf Children: Issues, Theory and Practice*. London: Edward Arnold.

This book gives more up-to-date research findings about deaf children in education. It has descriptions of a number of the manual communication methods.

Woll, B., Kyle, J. and Deuchar, M. (Eds.) (1981). *Perspectives on British Sign Language and Deafness*. London: Croom Helm.

This book is the edited proceedings of a conference and includes a number of contributions from psychologists who work primarily with the pre-lingually deaf. It includes an appendix on the notation used to describe signs from the British Sign Language.

Fraiberg, S. (1977). *Insights from the Blind*. London: Souvenir Press.

An account of the early years of blind children. It covers their development of attachment, language and motor skills, and includes in-depth descriptions of individual children.

Chapman, E. K. (1978). *Visually Handicapped Children and Young People*. London: Routledge and Kegan Paul.

This book deals with the schooling and further education of the visually handicapped, including an account of their recent history. It covers social and personal development, and vocational guidance and placement. Also included is a list of assessment tests and their sources.

Welsh, R. L. and Blasch, B. B. (1980). *Foundations of Orientation and Mobility*. New York: American Foundation for the Blind.

This book covers a very wide range of topics related to the orientation and mobility of the visually handicapped. It includes details on the use of low vision, alternative senses, and aids such as electronic obstacle detectors, and deals with the problems of additional handicaps.

Mittler, P. (1970). *The Psychological Assessment of Mental and Physical Handicaps*. London: Methuen.

This book contains a chapter by W. Lanyon on assessment of children with visual difficulties, and one by M. Reed on assessment of those with hearing difficulties. There is also a section on general assessment which covers such areas as the design of remedial programmes and techniques of testing and is applicable to both types of handicap.

Thomas, D. (1982). *The Experience of Handicap*. London: Methuen.

This book examines the way in which the handicapped see themselves, and how they view the treatment they receive from the non-handicapped. Although not written only from the point of view of the blind or deaf, it gives many examples which are relevant to them.

XIII.—REFERENCES

Bellugi, U. and Fischer, S. (1972). A comparison of sign language and spoken language. *Cognition*, **1**, 173–200.

Bennett, M. J. (1979). Trials with the Auditory Response Cradle: I: neonatal responses to auditory stimuli. *British Journal of Audiology*, **13**, 125–134.

Berliner, K. I. (1982). Risk versus benefit in cochlear implantation. *Annals of Otology, Rhinology and Laryngology*, Supplement 91, Vol. **91**, No. 2, Part 3, 90–98.

Brindley, G. S. and Lewin, W. S. (1968). The sensations produced by electrical stimulation of the visual cortex. *Journal of Physiology*, **196**, 479–493.

Clark-Carter, D. D., Howarth, C. I., Heyes, A. D., Dodds, A. D. and Armstrong, J. D. (1982). The Visually Handicapped in the City of Nottingham 1981: a survey of their disabilities, mobility, employment and daily living skills. Blind Mobility Research Unit Publication, No. 1. Summarized in *New Beacon*, **64**, 141–143.

Commission of the European Communities (1979). *Childhood Deafness in the European Community*. Brussels, Luxembourg: ECSC-EEC-EAEC.

Conrad, R. (1979). *The Deaf School-child: Language and Cognitive Function*. London: Harper and Row.

Cooper, A. F. (1976). Deafness and psychiatric illness. *British Journal of Psychiatry*, **129**, 216–226.

Cullinan, T. R. (1977). The Epidemiology of Visual Disability: Studies of Visually Disabled People in the Community. Health Services Research Unit Report No. 28, University of Kent at Canterbury.

Darnbrough, A. and Kinrade, D. (1981). The disabled person and employment. In: D. Guthrie (Ed.) *Disability: Legislation and Practice*. London: Macmillan Press.

Davis, A. C. (1983). Hearing disorders in the population: first phase findings of the MRC National Study of Hearing. In: M. E. Lutman and M. P. Haggard (Eds.) *Hearing Science and Hearing Disorders*. London: Academic Press.

Delafield, G. L. (1974). Guide Dogs and Self-Esteem in Blind People. Paper given at the British Association for the Advancement of Science Symposium on Aids to the Handicapped—The Visually Handicapped—Problems and Studies, September, 1974.

De L'Aune, W., Lewis, C., Needham, W. and Nelson, L. (1977). Speech compression: personality correlates of successful use. *Journal of Visual Impairment and Blindness*, **71**, 66–70.

Department of Education and Science (1968). *The Education of Deaf Children*. London: Her Majesty's Stationery Office.

Department of Health and Social Security (1973). *Deafness: Report of a Departmental Enquiry into the Promotion of Research*. Reports on Health and Social Subjects, No. 4. London: Her Majesty's Stationery Office.

Department of Health and Social Security (1979). *Blindness and Partial Sight in England 1969–1976*. Reports on Public Health and Medical Subjects, No. 129. London: Her Majesty's Stationery Office.

Department of Health and Social Security (1980). Personal Social Services Local

Authority Statistics A/F80/7: Registered Blind and Partially Sighted Persons. Year ending 31 March, 1980, England.

Dodds, A. G., Armstrong, J. D. and Shingledecker, C. A. (1981). The Nottingham Obstacle Detector: development and evaluation. *Journal of Visual Impairment and Blindness*, **75**, 203–209.

Dodds, A. G., Howarth, C. I. and Clark-Carter, D. (1982). The mental maps of the blind: the role of previous visual experience. *Journal of Visual Impairment and Blindness*, **76**, 5–12.

Freeman, R. D. (1976). The deaf child: controversy over teaching methods. *Journal of Child Psychology and Psychiatry*, **17**, 229–232.

Furth, H. G. (1973). *Deafness and Learning: A Psychosocial Approach*. Monterey, California: Wadsworth.

Gray, P. G. and Todd, J. E. (1967). *Mobility and Reading Habits of the Blind*. Government Social Survey No. SS386. London: Her Majesty's Stationery Office.

Greaves, M. (1981). The disabled person looks at the legislation. In: D. Guthrie, (Ed.) *Disability: Legislation and Practice*. London: Macmillan Press.

Gregory, R. L. and Wallace, J. G. (1963). Recovery from early blindness: a case study. *Experimental Psychological Society Monograph No. 2*, Cambridge.

Haggard, M. P., Gatehouse, S. and Davis, A. (1981). The high prevalence of hearing disorders and its implications for services in the UK. *British Journal of Audiology*, **15**, 241–251.

Heyes, A. D. (1981). The Nottingham Obstacle Detector: a technical description. *Journal of Visual Impairment and Blindness*, **75**, 206–207.

Hoemann, H. W. (1972). The development of communication skills. *Child Development*, **43**, 990–1003.

Hoover, R. E. (1950). The cane as a travel aid. In: P. A. Zahl (Ed.) *Blindness*, 353–365. Princeton, NJ: Princeton University Press.

Howarth, C. I. (1980). The structure of effective psychology. In: A. J. Chapman and D. Jones (Eds.) *Models of Man*. Leicester: The British Psychological Society.

Howarth, C. I. and Gunn, M. J. (1984). Experimental legislation. In: D. J. Müller, D. E. Blackman and A. J. Chapman (Eds.) *Psychology and the Law*. Chichester: Wiley.

James, G. A. (1982). Mobility maps. In: W. Schiff and E. Foulke (Eds.) *Tactual Perception: A Source Book*. Cambridge: Cambridge University Press.

Kay, L. (1964). An ultrasonic sensing probe as a mobility aid for the blind. *Ultrasonics*, **2**, 53–59.

Kew, S. (1975). *Handicap and Family Crisis: A study of the siblings of handicapped children*. London: Pitman.

Kirtley, D. D. (1975). *The Psychology of Blindness*. Chicago, Illinois: Nelson-Hall.

Meadow, K. P. (1980). *Deafness and Child Development*. London: Edward Arnold.

Quigley, S. P. and Kretschmer, R. E. (1982). *The Education of Deaf Children: Issues, Theory and Practice*. London: Edward Arnold.

Snijders, J. T. and Snijders-Oomen, N. (1970). *Non-Verbal Intelligence Tests for Deaf and Hearing Subjects* (Fourth Edition) Nv. Groningen: Wolters-Noordhoff.

Thomas, A. J. and Gilhome-Herbst, K. R. (1980). Social and psychological implications of acquired deafness for adults of employment age. *British Journal of Audiology*, **14**, 78–85.

Ullman, L. P. and Krasner, L. (1976). *A Psychological Approach to Abnormal Behaviour*. Second edn. Englewood Cliffs, NJ: Prentice-Hall.

Warnock, H. M. (1978). *Special Education Needs: Report of the Committee of Enquiry into the Education of Handicapped Children and Young People*. London: Her Majesty's Stationery Office.

Webster, A., Wood, D. J. and Griffiths, A. J. (1981). Reading retardation or linguistic deficit? I: interpreting reading test performances of hearing impaired anolescents. *Journal of Research in Reading*, **4**, 136–147.

Williams Intelligence Test for Children with Defective Vision. Slough: National Foundation for Educational Research.

Wood, D. J. and Howarth, C. I. (1979). The deaf child, his teacher and the psychologist, a 'research triangle'. *Journal of the British Association of Teachers of the Deaf*, **3**, 81–90.

Wood, D. J., Wood, H. A., Griffiths, A. J., Howarth, S. P. and Howarth, C. I. (1982). The structure of conversations with 6–10 year old deaf children. *Journal of Child Psychology and Psychiatry*, **23**, 295–308.

Wood, D. J., Wood, H. A. and Howarth, S. P. (1983). Mathematical abilities in deaf school leavers. *British Journal of Developmental Psychology*, **1**, 67–73.

Wood, D. J., Wood, H. A. and Middleton, D. (1978). An experimental evaluation of four face-to-face teaching strategies. *International Journal of Behaviour Development*, **1**, 131–147.

Wood, H. A. and Wood, D. J. (in press) An experimental evaluation of five styles of teacher conversation on the language of hearing-impaired children. *Journal of Child Psychology and Psychiatry*.

World Health Organization (1980). *International Classification of Impairments, Disabilities, and Handicaps*. Geneva: World Health Organization.

Psychology and Social Problems
Edited by A. Gale and A. J. Chapman
© 1984 John Wiley & Sons Ltd.

CHAPTER 15

MENTAL SUBNORMALITY IN CHILDHOOD AND ADULTHOOD

A. D. B. Clarke and Ann M. Clarke

I.—THE EXTENT OF THE PROBLEM

Mental subnormality (synonyms: mental deficiency, retardation, handicap) is a term describing about 2% of the population with IQs below about 70 points (two standard deviations below the mean of 100) although in practice IQs of 75 or even higher are sometimes used. Although 2% sounds like a very tiny proportion, it represents almost a million persons in England and Wales. As we see below, however, we do not find that anything like this number are labelled as such. Indeed, those so designated are identified because of intellectual limitations associated with educational, social or other problems. The lower the IQ from 70 downwards the more closely are intellectual and social difficulties correlated.

There are two somewhat distinct sub-populations among the mentally subnormal: the severe cases with IQs below 50 who have little or no chance of achieving real independence, and the mild, with IQs above 50, for many of whom a reasonably normal, though limited, life is possible. Approximately 75% of the mentally subnormal exhibit mild retardation and 25% severe, in rough accord with the predictions made by the normal distribution curve. These two sub-populations differ not only in incidence, prevalence and degree of handicap, but in aetiology and social prognosis, although there are of course overlapping problems.

Mental retardation, as we have seen, refers to significantly sub-average intellectual functioning, existing concurrently with deficits in adaptive behaviour, manifested during the developmental period. It is important in this context to recollect that a low IQ score predicts certain kinds of failure but not necessarily others. In our consideration of these groups of people it may be useful to think in terms of an individual's ability to make use *spontaneously* of information coming in from the surrounding environment. Spontaneous learning includes the ability to organize or code incoming stimuli in a variety of ways and to build up schemata appropriately which enable the individual to respond selectively and to embark upon the next stages of learning. It includes the capacity to perceive relationships and make deductions without the intervention of another human agent. It is not argued that even the fairly severely retarded have no spontaneous learning ability, merely that it is very greatly impaired. By contrast, parents and teachers of the gifted are constantly surprised at the amount such children pick up 'untaught'.

Other common characteristics should also be mentioned. The severely retarded develop at a much slower rate than the average child, attaining at best in adolescence an intellectual level similar to a normal seven-year-old. There are commonly deficits in attention and concentration, in short-term memory and verbal development; above all their language skills are greatly impaired. Indeed, a full list would give a gloomy picture. However, provided appropriate training is given, much can be done to develop limited skills. For the mild cases, frequent failure experiences are often associated with emotional problems which also have roots in the adverse backgrounds of so many. There are again limitations on the general intellectual development of such persons and often an awareness in them that they are 'different'. Much can be done for them, however, and anyway in many there appears to be something of a 'self-righting tendency' which moves them towards normality as they get older.

Mentally retarded children and adults who have been given up as hopeless non-learners by parents and teachers have frequently been taught skills, sometimes of a quite complicated nature, by means of special techniques. They had the opportunity to acquire these for themselves by exposure to normal visual, motor and social experiences, but had failed to do so, yet later had shown a capacity for learning, albeit at a slow rate; hence our conclusion that mentally retarded persons show a relative inability to learn spontaneously from ordinary life experience.

As a result they have a limited behavioural repertoire and are often at a disadvantage socially, particularly during the years of schooling when their delayed mental development ensures that they cannot keep abreast of peers of average ability, either in the classroom or in extra-curricular activities. Tasks which average young people find challenging but take in their stride are likely to be overwhelming for the retarded. If nothing succeeds like success, by the same token nothing fails like failure, and it has been shown that individuals who are expected to perform excessively difficult and therefore frustrating tasks do not develop an adequate self-motivating system. In terms of Rotter's theory of locus of control, reinforcement may be viewed as being due to an outside influence (external) or a consequence of the individual's own actions (internal). Normally there is a developmental progression from external locus of control to internal which in the case of the retarded rarely occurs.

Estimates for incidence (new cases arising) and prevalence (numbers in the population at a given time) of these conditions vary greatly with age, but the general pattern in different studies is strikingly similar. Severe cases are identified at birth or very early in life; however, infant mortality is common among them. Mild cases seldom come to notice before age of school entry, after which the prevalence rates increase markedly. But nearly always we deal with administrative rather than true prevalence, and this partly reflects the existence or otherwise of special educational or other provision—it is no good officially labelling children retarded if their chances of entry into a special school or class are small. In 1966, for example, there were about 45,000 children in British schools for the educationally subnormal. The comparable figure in 1979 for the mildly educationally subnormal (ESN[M]) was a little over 60,000, not because the true prevalence had increased but because of extra provision and therefore an increase in administrative prevalence.

Moreover, a society's attitudes to both labelling and provision may change with results which can obscure 'true prevalence'. Thirty years ago a majority of mildly retarded or slow learners were *segregated* in special schools for the Educationally Subnormal; at present there is a strong movement towards *integrating* them into ordinary schools whenever possible.

All prevalence studies show a steady increase towards a peak at the end of the school years of about 0.4% for severe and about 1.5% for mild cases. Thereafter there is a considerable decline in overall numbers. By and large the severe cases remain recognized as problems for society, but the majority of mild cases cease to be so labelled, or never have been identified administratively. There are several reasons for this which are outlined later, but declining prevalence figures as age increases do no more than reflect the point made earlier, that the prospects for a reasonably satisfactory social adjustment in the case of mildly retarded adults are often good.

Concerning aetiology, there are over 200 known causes of the more severe types of subnormality, the majority being rare or exceedingly rare. An exception is Down's syndrome (mongolism) which accounts for about a third of severe cases and is associated with an extra chromosome and usually also with late maternal age. Thus the chances of bearing such a child are about 1/2400 in a 20-year-old, 1/100 for a 40-year-old and 1/46 for a 45-year-old mother. A large proportion of other severe cases results from the action of recessive genes, but infections, toxins, birth problems and post-natal illnesses are also implicated.

For mild cases, perhaps only some 20–30% have associated organic features, but this estimate may vary from one sample to another. The vast majority are either the result of normal polygenic variation or arise from the action of adverse psychosocial circumstances interacting with rather poor biological potential. These are the so-called subcultural. The evidence for a social component in their condition arises from (a) cumulative deficit in ability as age increases, that is a deceleration of development which occurs in extremely adverse circumstances, often reflected in, among other things, a declining IQ; (b) responsiveness to ecological change or prolonged intervention; and (c) the apparent 'self-ameliorating' nature of some of these conditions based on a combination of recovery from the effects of deprivation, together with prolonged social learning (see also Begab, Haywood and Garber, 1981).

Figure 15.1 opposite illustrates the relationship between aetiology, terminology and IQ.

Both biomedical experts and behavioural scientists have, during the last 25 years, made considerable advances in understanding aetiology and hence in the possibilities of prevention. For both social and biomedical reasons a diminishing incidence of severe subnormality is to be expected. Mild subnormality, however, poses a more intractable problem so far as prevention is concerned. In both severe and mild conditions, however, considerable advances have been made in developing methods of amelioration, and these are discussed later.

II.—CONCEPTS OF THE PERSON AND MODELS OF HUMAN BEHAVIOUR

Because of their delayed retardation and impaired learning ability, it is easy to assume that at least the more severely subnormal are non-learners. Their care and education are quite exceptionally demanding of patience and tolerance, which sometimes regrettably degenerates into passive sentimentality. More obnoxious, however, is their dehumanization by busy caretakers who gradually over a period of time, particularly in institutions, come to assume that the subnormal are incapable of normal feelings and thus unworthy of the niceties of civilized living. In this respect they have something in common with the geriatric population. Moreover, a low Mental Age (MA) (and hence IQ) tends to justify the notion that adolescents and adults are forever children, and sometimes termed and treated as such. Clearly, however, an MA of 8 is very different in meaning for a 20-year-old retardate and a normal 8-year-old.

III.—INDIVIDUAL ASSESSMENT

Assessment has four main functions:
(i)   To describe the individual as he or she is at a particular point in time, upon intellectual, social, emotional, educational or other variables with reference to a normative or contrast population.
(ii) To predict the individual's probable status at later points in time.

FIGURE 15.1
THE RELATIONSHIP BETWEEN AETIOLOGY, IQ AND TERMINOLOGY

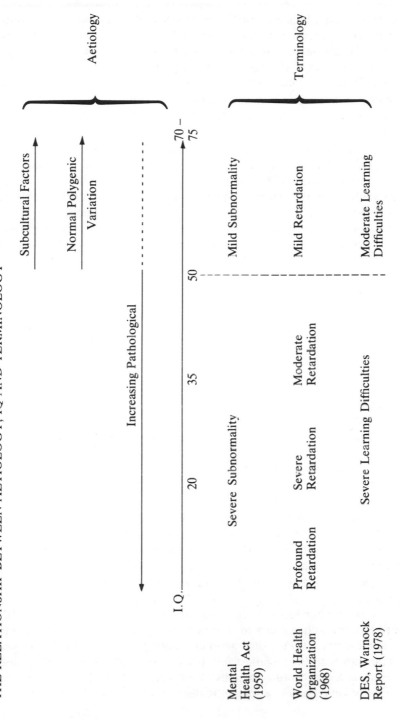

(iii) To provide a behavioural profile of assets and deficits as a starting point for remedial programmes.

(iv) To provide an objective means of checking upon progress or lack of it for an individual or a group—a base-line.

The psychologist will be especially interested in the third and fourth categories indicated above, and should be a sophisticated psychometrician, fully aware of the advantages and limitations of the techniques used. The psychologist will have available the usual range of well-known, appropriate and properly standardized tests as described by Mittler (1973) and by D. F. Clark (1974). Those administering tests should be aware that many subnormals underfunction before intervention and these predictions should be exceedingly cautious. Hence repeated assessments of the variables under study will be far more rewarding than 'single shot' evaluations.

This point is particularly well illustrated by offering data from the minimal training of institutionalized severely subnormal male adults, undertaken many years ago (see Table 15.1).

TABLE 15.1

Task	Initial Range	Final Range	Duration of Training
Guillotine: wire cutting to an exact length	15–40 wires cut per 5 min.	33–57 wires cut per 5 min.	2 × 1 hr. periods
Television plug soldering	4 min.–19 min. per plug	1 min. 42 sec.–3 min. 30 sec. per plug	34 trials
Bicycle pump assembly	4 min. 20 sec.–10 min. 45 sec. per assembly	54 sec.–1 min. 50 sec. per assembly	30 trials

SOME BASIC DATA: Before and After Minimal Training.

On these industrial tasks a 'single shot' assessment would have yielded data suggesting that such work was very unsuitable for a group with an average IQ of only 35. Yet minimal training transformed their abilities, and initial level was no guide to responsiveness to opportunity. The initial assessment on its own would have represented the traditional psychometric approach.

There is another lesson here. The use of *ad hoc* understandardized tests, like those above, has much to commend it, if the problem is to describe the individual's current level of functioning and then track subsequent progress on that same task. Standardized tests may well be essential, but tests especially relevant to programmes of habilitation can also easily be created, and indeed may possess a special realism.

The psychologist should bear in mind the social context of the subnormal person in considering how the problem will be perceived and what action can most appropriately be taken. A school age child with an IQ of 75 is likely to seem much more handicapped if born to highly intelligent and educated parents than if reared in the family of an unskilled worker, where the discrepancy between the child's competence and that of family and neighbours will not be so great. The same point relates to the type of peer group in which the subnormal individual finds themself.

IV.–THE IMMEDIATE SOCIAL AND EMOTIONAL ENVIRONMENT

Estimates suggest a far higher incidence of emotional problems both in severe and mild cases than in the normal population. This is entirely understandable for a variety of reasons. In some instances of brain damage, one of the effects may be to place the individual 'at the mercy of every stimulus' and to exhibit 'short-circuit reactions'. In others, the conditions of social rearing have been very adverse, with effects which may produce an unfortunate feedback on the individual: the 'difficult' subnormal person elicits hostility from people in the immediate environment and this further reinforces any problem behaviour. Yet in others, rearing in a succession of less than adequate institutions may promote emotional difficulties, as will rearing by rejecting parents. Finally, experience of repeated failure is likely to have detrimental consequences.

Provided there has been some change for the better in the individual's circumstances, and provided sympathetic and often directive counselling is offered, many of these problems may be ameliorated. Emotional immaturity concordant with cognitive immaturity is far more a feature of the subnormal individual than a deep-seated neurosis. Psychotherapies which rely upon verbal interchange are unlikely to be rewarding in persons whose most obvious deficit lies in the verbal sphere. Rather, ecological change plus planned success experiences are more likely to be effective. Parents may be considerably helped by informed advice over a long period.

So far as institutions are concerned, it seems probable that size and type of internal organization are particularly important. A number of studies claim that small group homes, run fairly autonomously, are in every way superior to the hierarchical essence of many large institutions. In the former, it is easier for staff to build personal relations, and exhibit more personal and immediate responsibility for their charges.

V.–THE WIDER SOCIAL AND ORGANIZATIONAL ENVIRONMENT

For many years there has been a debate over the extent to which special services are required for the mentally subnormal as opposed to general services, perhaps somewhat modified, which are available to the rest of the population. These issues remain unresolved; indeed the most suitable provisions for the retarded are likely to vary across time and social context as societies change.

Two major reorganizations of services took place in Britain in the early 1970's. As a result of a powerful parental lobby, the care and education of *all* severely subnormal children of school age was taken over from the health services by the Department of Education and Science. These children are now to be found in schools for the Educationally Subnormal (Severe), (ESN[S]), which may be either residential or for daily attendance. Some are located within hospitals.

Reflecting the debate mentioned above, there is a move towards integrating the mildly subnormal within special classes in ordinary schools, termed 'main-streaming' in the USA; however, a substantial number are educated in special schools for the mildly retarded (ESN[M]).

Severely subnormal adults in the community may be placed in Adult Training Centres (sometimes now termed Social Education Centres), which as a result of further reorganization are now administered by the Social Services. Here the educative process should be continued in the context of work experience, often of a simple industrial nature, and with particular attention to the improvement of social skills. Under happier employment conditions than at present, there was a small movement out into sheltered, semi-sheltered or even open employment of a simple nature. There is evidence that the staff of such Centres, as in other organizations, tend to underestimate the potentialities of their charges.

Finally, National Health Service hospitals, under the Mental Health Act, cater for a proportion of the severely retarded who cannot be looked after by their parents or relatives, or who have associated severe physical problems. Such hospitals also care for a much smaller number of difficult, disturbed mildly-handicapped persons, as well as long institutionalized individuals. There has been for many years a move towards community placement of many of these unfortunates, and hostels and small community homes are increasingly being set up, as well as fostering schemes. Many believe that hospitalization is quite inappropriate for the handicapped, except where there are additional severe physical or emotional problems. In the latter connection, Special (Secure) Hospitals exist for these and other persons.

VI.—TYPES OF INTERVENTION

Many important interventions are, of course, neuro-surgical or pharmacological. An example of the former is the treatment of hydrocephaly, while in the latter category phenylketonuria (PKU), a rare recessively transmitted genetic defect, can be treated by early identification and a diet low in phenylalanine. This greatly diminishes the damaging effects to the nervous system. In this section, however, we are concerned with interventions which may be undertaken by psychologists.

Intervention may be defined as any systematic attempt to alter the course of development either from its predicted path or from an established path. In either case it may aim to produce 'desirable' behaviour or prevent the emergence or continuation of 'undesirable' behaviour; it may be short-term or long-term, intensive or sporadic. Psychosocial intervention thus covers a very wide span of approaches, including educational, clinical, occupational and social skills training.

Laboratory experimentation with severely subnormal subjects owes a great deal to the pioneering work of Jack Tizard and his colleagues in the 1950's, who tested various generalizations made by professional personnel about the psychology of these persons: they were said to be unable to concentrate, to be easily distracted, to possess very poor dexterity and so forth. These early experiments confirmed such assessments, but went on to show that initial ability before training bore little relation to later responsiveness, granted the use of sophisticated principles of learning (e.g., the use of appropriate incentives, task analysis, spaced trials and so on). In brief, careful, individual instruction over a few weeks could transform the specific skills of these adults who could learn simple tasks quite well, could retain that learning and transfer it to similar tasks. Others showed that this type of finding could also be elicited in 'real life' industrial tasks, and where the tasks were simple, the main difference in performance between severely subnormal adults and normals lay not in differences of ultimate skill but in the time taken to achieve it.

The evolution of behaviour modification techniques has probably been the single most important source of behavioural intervention for the retarded, particularly the more severely handicapped. This is partly because of the emphasis on planned and systematic training following task analysis and partly due to the use of *positive* reinforcement, except in rare cases. Unfortunately many caretakers without adequate training use these techniques inappropriately; but, at their best, in the hands of intelligent and sensitive therapists, they have been shown to be highly effective in promoting a wide variety of social skills and in diminishing destructive and self-destructive behaviour. In these latter cases there may be a significant reduction in the use of drugs.

For many years a major pre-occupation of psychologists has been with early intervention for children *at risk* for *mild* mental retardation. The philosophy of pre-school education has been well expressed by the directors of the famous Milwaukee project (see p. 341) thus: 'to prevent from occurring those language, problem solving and achievement motivation deficits which are known to be common attributes of mild mental retardation'. The aim was to intervene in such a way that children from seriously disadvantaged families, known to be producing retarded offspring, would enter school with language and cognitive skills at a sufficiently high level to enable them to take full advantage of the school curriculum (see Section XII). The psychological theory buttressing these programmes was one widely prevalent in the 1960's, namely that the first few years of life are of critical importance for later development. This is an appealing idea, considering the immensely rapid maturational changes which normally occur between birth and school entry, when the social stimulation essential to cognitive development is supposed to become at least partly the responsibility of teachers. But, of course, the maturational process continues during the years of schooling, and with a bio-social model of development it might be expected that long-term environmental disadvantages cannot be compensated for by even the most elaborate and enduring pre-school programmes.

VII.—IS PSYCHOLOGICAL INTERVENTION SUCCESSFUL?

Sufficient hard research evidence has now been obtained from the evaluation of several properly designed studies to support the following conclusions. During the intervention period there is a substantial rise in IQ in children randomly allocated to experimental intervention, not observed in children assigned to the non-intervention condition. Structured teaching around language and problem solving skills is more effective at this stage than other methods. On entry into school, control children typically show a small increase in IQ, while gradually over a period of years pre-school educated children decline in cognitive performance and the difference between the groups disappears. Group differences on intelligence tests are, of course, of little importance in themselves whatever the children's age; it is what IQs predict in terms of scholastic and social achievement that matters. A careful analysis of the pooled data from several high quality programmes in which children had been followed up into adolescence showed that regularly children who had received pre-school education were significantly less likely to be allocated to special classes or to repeat a grade. However, with a few exceptions, on standardized achievement tests there was no significant difference in reading and a statistical difference significant beyond the one per cent level only for mathematics. These effects remained when the sex, ethnic background, early IQ, type of programme, length of intervention, number of hours per year of instruction, presence or absence of language goals, degree of parental involvement, location of programme (centre *versus* home), training or nontraining of teachers, were controlled in the analyses. It appears unlikely that these variables were differentially unimportant if the programmes themselves were directly responsible for long-term effects on the children. As the authors point out, it seems probable that noncognitive aspects of development were affected. Of the four areas explored, two yielded strong results: the mothers of preschool children had much higher vocational aspirations than the children had for themselves. Second, the children were much more likely to mention achievement related reasons for feeling proud of themselves. It seems clear that no simple theory can account for the results but rather that there is a complex network of causes and effects involving interactions between children, parents, teachers and peer groups across time.

At present it appears that bio-medical prevention and intervention, to be mentioned later in this chapter, is only partly successful and in consequence there remains a significant number of severely retarded children whose life expectation is prolonged, and who will need the help of psychologists in collaboration with members of other disciplines fully to utilize their limited capacity. Similarly it is clear that early psycho-social intervention with children at risk for mild retardation, while useful, cannot counterbalance the powerful social and probably biological, forces which are present in certain seriously disadvantaged sections of society. Indeed, it is questionable whether any form of remediation can be entirely successful within the context of the circumstances giving rise to its need. There remain substantial numbers of mildly retarded children who require all the support that teachers, psychologists and other caretakers can provide.

There are a few well documented cases of mentally subnormal children who have been rescued from conditions of exceptional adversity (usually including severe malnutrition and almost total lack of sensory/motor stimulation). After removal they have shown a dramatic recovery, gradually over time, with special help and commonly an unusually supportive adoptive family, becoming completely normal—physically, cognitively and emotionally. There are also a very few properly controlled studies of intervention with groups in adolescence, usually again with removal from adverse social conditions, and again with encouraging long-term results. However, this remains an area where further research is much needed, both to shed light on factors affecting the developmental process and also in an endeavour to diminish the negative effects of social disadvantage.

VIII.—METHODOLOGICAL AND PRACTICAL PROBLEMS

Change in human characteristics is normally assessed either by comparison of scores across time, or by studying the rate of declining correlations from base-line to later measures. The first relates to a comparison of levels, and the second to rank order. It is important to realize that these two, applied to the same data may give quite different results. For instance, it would be possible for a moderately high correlation to be found between, for example, IQ measures taken on a group at age 15 and similar measures at age 25. It would also be possible for this same group on average to have improved markedly in level over this period.

In longitudinal studies, sample attrition can have a seriously distorting influence. Sample loss is always selective; the problem is whether it is selective-relevant to the hypothesis or selective-irrelevant. The usual method is to compare the base-line characteristics of the lost with the retained subjects. If there is no difference, then commonly researchers believe that the loss has been irrelevant. However, this is not necessarily so, for not only may there be relevant variables unknown to the researcher, but also the later non-availability, or refusal to co-operate of some subjects, may reflect the development of later and different characteristics from those who remain in the sample. The best precaution is to minimize sample loss! A number of studies show that granted sufficient resources, this can be achieved.

The use of control groups in evaluating change should not need stressing. However, there are sufficient pitfalls in the arrangement of treated and untreated subjects to warrant discussion of the problems. Where social/educational intervention is undertaken with retarded children or infants at risk of becoming retarded, sufficiently large groups are necessary to make it possible to match on a number of relevant variables before *randomly* allocating the subjects to experimental or control conditions. Among the variables often overlooked are those which discriminate *within* groups of disadvantaged families and which may make a critical difference to the background support which a child receives—or for that matter to the child's biological status. Thus, before the randomization of groups can be undertaken, care should be taken to ensure that groups will be matched for parental education and child-rearing attitudes, which necessitates the exclusion of families who demand that their children will be experimentally treated. Some of these points are relevant in the evaluation of later interventions or where comparisons are demanded between two or more types of education.

For laboratory-type experiments, some modification of procedures may be necessary. Commonly, matching takes place on obvious variables, such as sex, age, IQ, length of institutionalization, clinical types and so on. However, to match on the variable under investigation is rarely done, but is of the utmost importance. Thus, to equate two groups on the conventional variables prior to an experiment on the learning of spatial relations is essential. It is also essential to include their initial ability on spatial relations as part of the match.

Another common error with the use of controls is based on the Test/Train/Retest paradigm for members of the Experimental Group, compared with Test/no-intervening-activity/Retest for the Controls. Such a design fails to hold constant the subjects' contact with the experimenter, which may have strongly motivating consequences. It is a perfectly straightforward procedure to insert for the controls an intervening activity which engages their attention and effort, but which is different from the training task.

If change is frequently monitored over time (as in the well-known Milwaukee Project) practice effects in both experimental and control groups are likely to occur. Where a longitudinal study without external controls is undertaken, these effects may be misinterpreted. So, too, with regression towards the mean—an inevitable problem where subjects are selected on the basis of extreme test scores. Low scores are likely on average to improve on retest because either (a) the initial selection of low scorers include some who by chance underfunctioned, or (b) some were included who happened at that point in time to be exhibiting an unusual trough in their developmental paths. The first is one aspect of errors of measurement; it is not difficult to imagine that errors of measurement in a few individual cases might be different and opposite at the (minimally) two points of assessment. A real lack of change in level of the individual might be concealed by 'under-functioning' at first assessment and 'over-functioning' at the second, suggesting an overall improvement.

Enough has been said to indicate that these problems are important in this as in all other fields. Applied psychologists need to develop a considerable methodological sophistication if they are fully to exploit the potential of their fields of work, and to evaluate sensibly the work of others.

Experimental psychologists have tended to concentrate on short-term studies of particular processes in the mentally retarded, outlining the possibilities for and constraints upon change, as well as comparing their subjects with MA or CA matched controls, according to the hypothesis being researched. The more sophisticated of these studies have been of value, especially in indicating whether or not particular processes could be enhanced in the short-term, whether such changes could be retained, and the extent to which newly developed skills transfer to other activities. In cases where positive results occurred, it is a reasonable assumption that longer-term training might have greater and more lasting consequences.

The evaluation of the success of longer-term studies is more complex than it sounds. For example, retaining a first job has been one criterion for adolescent success. Any change of job, redundancy, or sacking is, if one uses this as a single criterion, a sign of 'failure'. But the same declining validity of success over time would apply equally to normal adolescents. These issues have been admirably discussed by Cobb (1972) in the most comprehensive review in the literature.

All follow-up studies, whether or not special help has been given, show on average increasing social adjustment of the retarded as age increases. This is true even of the upper levels of severe subnormality. Hence, writes Cobb, it is more realistic to predict a positive outcome until or unless negative signs appear than, as traditionally, a negative outcome until positive signs are apparent.

There are of course two constraints upon outcome. First, the constitutional limits beyond which individuals cannot pass. Second, the resources or lack of them which form part of the context of the person's development. It is very rare for the latter to be optimal. Even so, it can at least be reiterated that, on average, adult outcome is better for the mildly retarded than one might predict from their adolescent status. One should not, however, ignore the range from which such an average statement is appropriate. At one extreme one finds a minority deeply involved in multiple deprivation from which no escape seems possible. At the other, a minority become fully independent and successful 'ordinary' citizens. Both groups are atypical.

Under economic conditions of full employment, one would expect about 70 per cent of the ESN(M) to be self-supporting by early adulthood. The remainder would include a substantial number who, with further help, ultimately would achieve independence. Others might well remain dependent or semi-dependent all their lives. Among them would be some who more appropriately might be categorized as mentally ill or severely subnormal.

The present economic situation in developed societies may of course alter this hitherto quite hopeful picture. However, even in these circumstances, the retarded person should be encouraged to be a useful citizen, contributing to domestic and neighbourhood societies in a positive way, while hopefully receiving the tolerant support of other members.

IX.—PROBLEMS OF ETHICS AND CONFIDENTIALITY

In the last decade or so, there has fortunately occurred a growing sensitivity to ethical and related problems. Two principles are widely supported in many fields. First, the principle of informed consent; the adult subjects, or their parents or guardians if the subject is a child, must be fully aware of the nature of any experimental intervention, and something of its purpose. Second, no procedure should be potentially harmful or distressing. There have been some abuses of these criteria, both in the biomedical and also the behavioural field.

Confidentiality, however, has been a longer and more universally accepted rule. There are real problems of informed consent especially when one reaches the lower grades of mental subnormality. At what level of retardation can one really say that the subnormal understands what may be involved? Clearly severely subnormal children cannot and, if in hospital, their guardians may be the hospital authorities themselves who may have some vested interest in the research. Parental involvement may help in these matters. There can also be difficulties over the use of distressing procedures, especially among some of the less thoughtful behaviour modifiers in North America.

Aversive techniques may only be justified on a cost-benefit analysis such as in cases of self-mutilative or seriously destructive behaviour.

Fortunately, applied psychologists in this area of work have as their main aim the assistance of the mentally subnormal. Most are involved with attempting to develop limited assets, teaching specific skills or offering supportive counselling. Ethical problems seldom arise here. On the other hand, some experimental psychologists may use the retarded as a convenient captive population for hypothesis testing, and in such circumstances care should be taken to indicate that their experimentation cannot harm the individual, and that at least it has some potential for helping.

The psychologist, as a professional expert, is supposed to decide what is desirable for the mentally handicapped person. In so far as psychologists subscribe to the notion that it is a basic human right for individuals to develop to the highest level of functioning of which they are capable, and in so far as this is the psychologist's aim, there seem to be no great ethical problems here. But sometimes, as in intervention with the disadvantaged, any considerable success with the child may ultimately lead to parent-child alienation if the former is of limited ability and the latter achieves normality.

X.—THE ROLE OF OTHER DISCIPLINES AND PROFESSIONS

In the last two decades the most significant advances in the field of mental retardation have been in the biomedical field, notably in connection with detection of handicapping conditions very early in pregnancy, enabling therapeutic abortions to be undertaken, but also in the area of genetic counselling. Unfortunately, as is so often the case, use of these facilities is unevenly distributed among different sections of the population so that the well educated who are the least numerous members of a community are most likely to seek the appropriate services.

It seems likely that paediatricians and others concerned with preventive medicine and public health will increasingly press for ways of reaching mothers at risk of producing retarded children by virtue of adverse environmental factors before, during and after birth. However, once the child is through the neonatal period, if he remains at risk, the chances are that the psychologist in collaboration with parents, teachers and social workers will be required to assume an increasing responsibility for ensuring that he receives the best possible environment in which to develop.

For historical reasons the hospital and community care of the mentally subnormal was the prime responsibility of psychiatrists, and it was only in the post-war years that psychologists became deeply involved. While psychiatrists certainly have a role, especially where mental illness co-exists with retardation, the main problem in amelioration lies in understanding and using the learning processes. The more progressive psychiatrists recognized this and enabled a small group of clinical psychologists in the 1950's to advance their work. It should be realized that, as a World Health Organization report once put it, no single profession holds the key to problems of mental retardation. Hence collaborative team work is appropriate, and indeed is increasingly used. For some problems, psychiatry will be the prime focus for an individual case; in others, psychology; and in others, teaching or social work. In many, all may be involved.

XI.—FUTURE PROSPECTS

Clearly, prevention of mental subnormality must be of the highest priority. In the USA, the President's Committee on Mental Retardation (1972) stated that, using present knowledge and techniques in the biomedical and behavioural sciences, it is possible to reduce the occurrence of mental retardation by 50 per cent before the end of the century. This might well be true of the more severe cases, where biomedical advances have been considerable. It is manifestly untrue of the majority, the 75 per cent who comprise the mildly subnormal, and indeed the Committee quietly conceded this point a few years later.

It is as yet unclear whether societal improvement might diminish the number of mildly retarded. In so far as some owe their condition, at least partly, to social factors, then this seems possible. If it proved so, then there is absolutely no reason to suppose that individual differences would disappear. In this case it is by no means fanciful to suggest that the dullard of today might be regarded as the mildly subnormal of the future.

So far as amelioration is concerned, psychologists have made major contributions. The subnormal, whether mild or severe, commonly under-function for a variety of reasons. These include social adversity, the effects of many failure experiences, inadequacy of educational or training facilities and the low expectations of many professionals. Much has been learned of techniques which can greatly improve levels of functioning in the vast majority of cases. Sometimes these improvements are only small and really negligible; more often they are considerable and occasionally even startling. The major priority for the immediate future is the application in practice of existing knowledge, initially by means of controlled pilot projects. It is counterproductive to plunge into nation-wide schemes without properly evaluated field trials.

The most hopeful finding of the past has been that all long-term follow-up studies show an average improvement in the retarded as age increases. This results from prolonged but delayed maturation and slow social learning which is common among the subcultural cases, as well as responsiveness to educational or social help. But these latter are commonly of far less than optimal quality, and the implication therefore, is that with greater help, a larger proportion would achieve higher levels of functioning and much earlier in life.

A further conclusion, well supported by empirical data, is that wherever possible, parental involvement in habilitation should be sought. It must be recognized, however, that this may be very difficult to achieve where parents are themselves multiply deprived and crushed by problems over which they may have little control and little capacity to solve.

The Trethowan Committee on *The Role of Clinical Psychologists in the National Health Service* paid tribute to the contribution of psychologists in changing the outlook upon subnormality. Whether clinical, developmental, educational or 'pure', this field, contrary to earlier traditions is a most rewarding one in which to work.

XII.—ANNOTATED READINGS

Begab, M. J., Haywood, H. C. and Garber, H. L. (1981). *Psychosocial Influences on Retarded Performance*, Volume I: *Issues and Theories in Development.* Volume II: *Strategies for Improving Competence.* Baltimore, Maryland: University Park Press.

These two volumes include an up-to-date account of some of the most important ongoing studies. They are cited here for their particular relevance to psychosocial interaction.

Clarke, A. M. and Clarke, A. D. B. (1974). *Mental Deficiency: The Changing Outlook.* Third Edition. London: Methuen.

This textbook covers the whole field up to the early 1970s and is to be found in many libraries. A shorter paperback edition containing twelve key chapters together with a new overview, *Readings from Mental Deficiency: the Changing Outlook* (1978), University Paperback, London: Methuen, is an alternative. A Fourth Edition is in preparation.

Cobb, H. V. (1972). *The Forecast of Fulfilment.* New York: Teachers' College Press, Columbia University.

This book reviews all outcome studies of persons who at some stage have been classed as mentally retarded. The evaluation is reasonably optimistic, even for groups for whom relatively little help has been offered. An alternative source of similar material, by J. Tizard, is to be found in Clarke and Clarke (1974).

Milwaukee Project. This was conducted by Heber and latterly by Garber of the University of Wisconsin. Starting with the discovery that mild retardation was not randomly distributed within a Milwaukee slum, but was primarily to be found in the families of mildly retarded women, a six-year intervention programme for both mothers and their babies was initiated. The development of the children in the experimental group became well above average, with the controls between 20 and 30 IQ points below. Two errors seem to have been made. First, repeated retesting of both groups made the absolute IQ values suspect and, second, the intervention ceased too early, at age six. Both groups have now declined in status, and their educational standards are characteristic of the lowest in inner city schools. A brief account may be found in Begab et al. (1981). Thus the experimental group's average IQs do not predict scholastic achievement.

Mittler, P. (1973) (Ed.), *Assessment for Learning in the Mentally Handicapped*. London and Edinburgh: Churchill Livingstone.

Mittler reports the proceedings of a symposium in this volume. Among other things it emphasizes the inadequacy of the traditional psychometric 'single shot' approach to assessing the potentials of the mentally retarded, and has implications for psychometrics in general. It also includes an important chapter on behaviour modification by Bricker and Bricker.

President's Committee on Mental Retardation (1972). *Entering the Era of Human Ecology*. Washington, DC: DHEW Publication No. (OS) 72–77.

This booklet over-optimistically predicts that the biomedical and behavioural sciences will, if applied, enable a 50 per cent reduction in prevalence to occur before the end of the century. Nevertheless, it emphasizes the need for ecological improvements which few would deny.

Trethowan Committee (1977). *The Role of Clinical Psychologists in the National Health Service*. London: Her Majesty's Stationery Office.

This evaluates the past role of clinical psychologists and makes important proposals for the future. 'The field of mental handicap was one in which psychologists were seen as having a specially important part to play . . . recent fundamental policy changes have occurred in the case of the mentally handicapped in which psychologists were seen as having been the prime movers'.

World Health Organization, (1968). *The Organization of Services for the Mentally Retarded*. WHO Technical Report Series, 392. Geneva: WHO.

This forward-looking monograph relates research findings over the previous two decades to the type of services needed to assist the mentally subnormal.

XIII.—REFERENCES

Begab, M. J., Haywood, H. C. and Garber, H. L. (1981). *Psychosocial Influences on Retarded Performance*. Volume I. *Issues and Theories in Development*. Baltimore, Maryland: University Park Press.

Begab, M. J., Haywood, H. C. and Garber, H. L. (1981). *Psychosocial Influences on Retarded Performance*, Volume II. *Strategies for Improving Competence*. Baltimore, Maryland: University Park Press.

Clark, D. F. (1974) In: A. M. Clarke and A. D. B. Clarke (1974) (Eds.) *Mental Deficiency: the Changing Outlook*. Third Edition. London: Methuen.

Clarke, A. M. and Clarke, A. D. B. (1974). *Mental Deficiency: The Changing Outlook*. Third Edition. London: Methuen.

Cobb, H. V. (1972). *The Forecast of Fulfilment*. New York: Teachers' College Press, Columbia University.

Department of Education and Science (1978). *Report of the Committee of Enquiry into the Education of Handicapped Children and Young People*. (The Warnock Report). London: Her Majesty's Stationery Office.

Mittler, P. (1973). (Ed.) *Assessment for Learning in the Mentally Handicapped.* London and Edinburgh: Churchill Livingstone.

President's Committee on Mental Retardation (1972). *Entering the Era of Human Ecology.* Washington, DC: DHEW Publication No. (OS) 72–77.

Trethowan Committee. (1977). *The Role of the Clinical Psychologists in the National Health Services.* London: Her Majesty's Stationery Office.

World Health Organization (1968). *The Organization of Services for the Mentally Retarded.* WHO Technical Report Series, 392. Geneva: World Health Organization.

Psychology and Social Problems
Edited by A. Gale and A. J. Chapman
© 1984 John Wiley & Sons Ltd.

CHAPTER 16

AGEING

Robert Slater

I.—THE EXTENT OF THE PROBLEM

Growing older can create a variety of difficulties. But one major cause for concern is the very notion that ageing actually *is* a problem. A most pervasive problem facing older people is the attitudes which others have towards them. In response, older people may *themselves* come to hold attitudes about old people. In a paper entitled 'Agism: another form of bigotry' Butler (1969) claims that 'age prejudice' exists. Given such prejudice, we might espouse a plethora of negative and inaccurate beliefs about ageing and older people. Palmore (1977) has devised a short 'Facts on Ageing' twenty-question quiz which taps many such often-held but fallacious beliefs. For example, item 8 is 'Aged drivers have fewer accidents per person than drivers under age 65' (which is true). A person scoring 20 would be entirely accurate in his/her perception of ageing on the test items; in this author's experience first year psychology students sometimes score as low as 3 or 4.

Most advanced industrial societies have an 'ageing' population: that is, the absolute number of older people is increasing, and the proportion of older people in the total population is also increasing. In 1901 in the United Kingdom there were some 200,000 women aged 75 and over; in 2001 the projected figure is five times as large (1.1 million). In 1900 in the United States 4.1% of the population was aged 65 and over; in 1971 9.9%. This increase in the population of older people can produce resource strains because, for example, the 16% of the population of Great Britain who are of pensionable age receive some 48% of the public expenditure on social security, health and welfare.

Three other 'problems' concerning ageing should be mentioned here. The first problem concerns the extent that living at home presents difficulties for people who are becoming increasingly frail. Hunt's (1978) survey of the elderly at home suggests, for example, that the numbers of elderly people

345

(particularly those aged 85 and over) with housing, mobility, health and loneliness problems will increase over the next two decades. Ill health and loneliness seem to be the things most disliked about being old, although suggestions *from* old people for helping older people most often concern improving their financial resources. As a generality (but appreciating there are always many exceptions), the older people are, the less financially well-off they are and the poorer is their accommodation; also they are less able to look after themselves and keep mobile, they have fewer social contacts and they generally show less contentment with their lives.

The second problem facing applied psychologists (and their colleagues in health and social service disciplines) is how to intervene to improve the quality of life of those who comprise that small proportion of retired people (some 5%) living in residential homes for old people or in other forms of institutional accommodation. Many individuals residing in long-stay hospitals display the third of the problems with ageing, *viz.* senile or arteriosclerotic dementia. The incidence of organic psychiatric syndromes is considered to be some 3.1–5.6% of people aged 65 and over who live in the community, and some 5.7–15.4% (depending on the sources) of people of pensionable age may have mild mental impairment (Bergmann, 1978). Clinical psychologists are increasingly becoming involved with older people having psychiatric conditions, whether they are resident in hospitals, old people's homes or in the community, as is evidenced in the formation in the United Kingdom in 1979 of PACE (Psychology Applied to the Care of the Elderly). It is mainly on this psychogeriatric subpopulation that the rest of the chapter is focused.

II.—CONCEPTS OF THE PERSON AND MODELS OF HUMAN BEHAVIOUR

When age is in the wit is out.
Tri-weekly. Try weekly. Try weakly.
The time of life when a man flirts with girls, but can't remember why.
(Anon)

Last scene of all,
That ends this strange eventful history,
Is second childishness and mere oblivion,
Sans teeth, sans eyes, sans taste, sans everything.
(As You Like It)

The model the layperson appears to apply to ageing is one of regression to childhood, epitomized in Shakespeare's vivid description of senile dementia in its last phase. Such powerful images perhaps encourage people to make easy and over-simple comparisons of 'the elderly' with children. Young children, like their aged grandparents, are considered to be sexually inactive, dependent, need looking after, apparently cannot be trusted to make up their own minds sensibly, apparently cannot take responsibilities, apparently have to be protected from themselves and others in their own best interests, are physically and mentally vulnerable, and apparently have to be told what to do. These associations of childhood with old age seem to lead to behaviour being taken decreasingly at its face value and increasingly as illustrative if not symptomatic of a person's age: 'They all say/do that at their age'; 'What do you expect at your age?'. Thus there appears to be an increasing tendency to presume that someone's behaviour may be the product of some form of undisclosed mental deterioration, or, such behaviour is given less credence simply because it emanates from someone who is old.

We are caring and nurturant towards children. We expect adults to be fully responsible for the consequences of their rationally conceived actions. Old people often become placed in a limbo where their behaviour is considered normal if acceptable, and due to their age or mental status if unacceptable. This model of the adult-returning-to-childhood is easily assimilated by many people in the 'caring professions' because they have been professionally trained to 'look after' the bodily needs of patients in hospitals. Further, the fact that residents of homes or hospitals are conceptualized as *patients*, reinforces the infirmity-leads-to-dependency spiral, and is strengthened by the notion that 'those in second childhood' are perforce dependent. The practical consequence of such interpretations of behaviour and such concepts of the person is that dependency producing and inducing behaviour is entrenched in old people and in the staff caring for them—a practical issue to which we return. The conceptualization of old people as asexual in a similar way denies their right to undertake activities considered normal and desirable in adults. An old man is easily seen as a 'dirty old man'. That such notions ultimately and unnecessarily circumscribe the sex lives of older people as self-fulfilling prophecy has been well argued by Puner (1974) in humorous vein.

A model of older people currently endorsed by many gerontologists is, in fact, a general model of man, somewhat akin to that proposed by Howarth (1980), where man is viewed as a problem-solver (see Chapters 1 and 14). This model assumes that successful problem-solving involves: an agreed purpose to be achieved, well-understood resources to be brought to bear in solving the problem, and an effective strategy for making the best use of resources available. Much current work with institutionalized older people and care staff, and with older people and their families in the community, lies in assisting them to set goals, to delineate the range of resources available, and then to use an effective strategy to reach the goal through the use of those available resources.

Part of such effective strategies will often require an analysis of the situation in terms of reinforcement contingencies. All too often, dependency in older institutionalized people is strengthened through the reinforcement of dependency behaviours. This happens because it is quicker, easier and more efficient 'for staff to do it' than it is for staff to let the resident do it for herself. Such an approach also implies a model of man operating on 'the principle of least effort' (Zipf, 1965). It is ultimately less effort for staff to wheel slow but ambulant residents to bed and less effort for residents to be wheeled to bed, but such an apparently reasonable arrangement ultimately leads to a model of residents as 'objects' to be 'serviced', to situations where independence and autonomy are undermined and where social interaction—the mainstay of a humane model of man—is marked by its absence.

III.—INDIVIDUAL ASSESSMENT

The role of the applied psychologist in assessment has largely been to assist in the development of instruments to ascertain the levels of physical and mental functioning of the older resident. There are two broad reasons why such assessments are needed. First, if the actual extent of physical and mental disability on, say, a ward can be established, then this enables staffing ratios to be more exactly matched with demands. Often it is found that staff overestimate the level of disability, probably because it is easy to assume that 'if they don't, they can't'. Assessment batteries attempt to provide as far as it is practically possible an objective appraisal of a resident's abilities. Often, however, such assessment has to be made by care staff, and it is the task of the applied psychologist to produce an instrument that is valid and reliable (and objective) enough to be of practical help in the settings in which it is intended to be used. Plutchik, Conte, Lieberman, Bakur, Grossman and Lehrman (1970), for example, produced a 31-item 'Geriatric Rating Scale' to be used by ward attendants which had an inter-judge reliability based on independent assessment of 0.87. Items covered aspects of the individual's behaviour ranging from eating, toiletting and bathing, walking, sleeping, talking, through assessments of auditory and visual acuity, to items concerning sociability, helpfulness, and disruptiveness. The following examples are not untypical of items to be found in a variety of assessment tools for rating the behaviour and performance of older institutionalized people.

When eating the patient requires:
  no assistance (feeds himself/herself)
  a little assistance (needs encouragement)
  considerable assistance (spoon feeding, etc.)
The patient is incontinent:
  never
  sometimes (once or twice a week)
  often (three times per week or more)

With regard to restless behaviour at night, the patient is:
seldom restless
sometimes restless
often restless
The patient disturbs other patients or staff by shouting or yelling:
never
sometimes
often

Such assessments are not just used in a descriptive fashion nor just to assist in matching staff resources to ward requirements; they also provide baseline data from which attempts to intervene and change behaviour in a directed manner can be assessed. Thus, in order to set goals for patients' behaviour, a realistic knowledge of baseline behaviour is required.

With psychogeriatric patients in mind particularly (i.e., those with senile or arteriosclerotic dementia), applied psychologists have devised assessment protocols to measure 'mental status'. These conventionally comprise a range of *cognitive* tasks, often concerned with the resident's *orientation, memory* and *concentration*. Orientation tests might ask residents their name, age, the time and date, the day of the week, the month, the season, the year, the name of the place they live in, the town and street where they are and to recognize and name people in their environment. Assessment of memory might cover 'personal items' such as their recollection of when they were born, where they were born, which school they attended, what their occupation was, the names of their spouses and siblings, the name of any town where they had worked, and 'impersonal' items such as the dates of the First and Second World Wars, and the names of the monarch and the prime minister. Often a test of short-term memory is given by psychologists telling the residents at the beginning of the session who they (the psychologists) are and where they are from, and asking the residents to recall this information at the end of testing, some five or ten minutes later. Concentration tests may, for example, require residents to recite the months of the year backwards, and count from 1 to 10 forwards and then backwards. Pattie and Gilleard (1979) give an example of such a test as part of several procedures for assessing elderly people, and Schaie and Schaie (1977) provide a comprehensive guide to tests used to assess older individuals.

The remaining area where applied psychologists have produced assessment protocols concerns 'ward environment'. Essentially such protocols give a descriptive assessment of the degree to which the environment has the characteristics of a 'total institution' as described by Goffman (1961). Measures of ward atmosphere often focus on the rigidity of the routine, cleanliness, 'block treatment' of residents, depersonalization, and the social distance between residents and staff.

IV.—THE IMMEDIATE SOCIAL AND EMOTIONAL ENVIRONMENT

Residents of old people's homes and long-stay hospital wards are there because they are deemed to need the care and attention that such settings can provide; they are unable to continue living 'in the community'. As Hunt (1978) has shown, the older and frailer are the persons living in the community, the less likely they are to have a range of social contacts that younger people take for granted such as visits, phone calls and letters from friends and relatives. Taking social contacts with people outside the household as a whole, the housebound and bedfast are undoubtedly the most severely isolated. Other groups who are badly off in this respect are people aged 85 and over, and divorced persons. The increasingly likelihood of death with advancing age inevitably means that those surviving lose friends, relatives, and most important, spouses. The average woman can expect ten years of life as a widow, but the death rate among men and women in the year after they are widowed is ten times higher than that among people of the same age who are married. About half the over seventy-five-year-olds in the UK live alone, although this does not necessarily mean they feel lonely. Friends and *confidants* seem increasingly important for the mental wellbeing of older people, yet they too inevitably die leaving the survivor increasingly dependent upon their own inner resources and upon help from younger relatives or the State.

Often, however, younger relatives are themselves old. Sanford (1976) describes an incident which prompted him to investigate the support that 'the supporters' needed: a despairing telephone call from a sixty-year-old daughter who, after being up three times in the night to help her mother to the commode, had left the old lady for twenty minutes and returned to find her lying, immovable, on the kitchen floor. The daughter had come to the end of her tether and phoned to ask if her mother could be admitted to hospital just so that she herself could have some rest. Sanford notes that this was the third request of its kind he had had that day, and there were no beds available. The main support many supporters appear to need is a 'night sitter'; someone who can come in and look after the older person during the night so that the younger carer gets some sleep. Sanford (1975) notes that some 12% of all geriatric admissions to hospital may simply occur because relatives just can no longer cope.

Although there is a range of statutory services geared to supporting old people in their own homes in the community (doctors, health visitors, district nurses, home helps, council welfare officers, social security and supplementary benefits officers, meals on wheels or similar 'outreach' provisions), as well as friends, relatives and volunteers, some 5–6% of persons aged 65 plus live in institutions of one kind or another. Often the reason for a person entering a home will be a mixture of increasing infirmity and social isolation, and a 'support network' that has been stressed to the limits. Homes and hospitals should be designed to minimize the effects of infirmity, to provide a support service that is 'on tap', and to improve the quality of a resident's life through the provision of opportunities for social interaction, and the expression of choice, independence and autonomy.

When homes for old people were created after World War II, they were modelled on the concept of a 'hotel', where residents would be 'guests'. Implicit (though not explicit) in such a model is the notion that guests pay for services, and have the 'whip hand' in so far as they can withhold payment if they consider the service to be unsatisfactory or substandard. In this respect the hotel model was fallacious from the beginning, since the 'power' was never in the hands of residents, but always in the hands of staff. Townsend's (1962) book *The Last Refuge* revealed that the quality of life led by a substantial number of residents of old people's homes was a long way from anything one could describe as desirable. A similar critique was done on hospital accommodation for old people by Robb (1967) in a book aptly titled *Sans Everything*.

What both these books demonstrated, and subsequent ones (see, for example, Meacher, 1972), was that institutionalizing forces had taken over, and produced institutionalized residents. Barton (1966) coined the term 'institutional neurosis' for this phenomenon: a state in which persons become detached and isolated, passively 'adjusted', rigid in behaviour, and suffer a general impoverishment of personality. The institutional environment tends to be one in which residents go to bed and get up at fixed times, take their meals at fixed times, go to the toilet at fixed times, and receive visitors at fixed times; that is, it offers a rigidity of routine. After getting or being dressed residents may have to wait around, they may have to queue for meals, wait in line to have a bath, queue up for the toilet, go to the toilet in groups, sit waiting at tables before meals are served; that is, residents get block treatment. They may find their clothes 'get lost' and they are dressed in someone else's, their private possessions may be handled as a matter of routine (tidying up) by staff, they may have very few private possessions, they may not be able to personalize their physical environment, they may be served meals in standard portions; that is, residents suffer depersonalization.

Residents may have no access to kitchens and clothes washing facilities, they may find little privacy when using the (public) toilet, they may be assisted to bath whether they require or want it or not, they may seldom interact socially with staff over meals or whilst watching television, they may not mix with staff outside the institutional premises; that is, they may be kept at a marked social distance from staff. Readers may care to imagine what it would feel like to have to live their daily lives under such an institutional regimen!

Not all institutions accommodating old people present a depressing picture of residents sitting all day long in their chairs spread around the walls of lounges in a way that makes social interaction difficult, with a television switched on all the time while no-one pays the slightest attention; but many do. The problem is that both staff and residents perceive the way the institution is organized as being *the only way* in which it could be organized, and evaluate quality of life solely in terms of 'care' and cleanliness. Some institutions present a much more positive picture, with residents helping each other, making snacks, doing their own washing, making soft toys, playing darts, and having a drink at the bar; but many staff believe such a way of life is impossible to achieve given the level of frailty of residents coupled with the constraints on staffing and finance currently in existence.

V.—THE WIDER SOCIAL AND ORGANIZATIONAL ENVIRONMENT

Most people would want a good quality of life for themselves in old age as long as this does not necessarily mean foregoing too many pleasures along the way. However, having a good quality of life in old age is intimately tied up with two key factors; health and finance. Many of the jobs that ultimately damage one's health are also underpaid. This does not imply that the somewhat naïve notion of simply providing more money, often a panacea preventing one from seeing what is really wanted, is the answer. More money may bring more of the same and, in terms of service provision in particular, the psychologist often needs to persuade people to accept a change in type of service rather than more of what went before. Nevertheless, poor housing, poor diet, lack of rest, and preoccupation with finding the wherewithal to get by, tend to preclude such niceties in planning for a good old age as developing various hobbies and interests, taking exercise, cutting out fatty foods, making sure you are up-to-date with all the benefits and services that are rightly yours. Thus a substantial number of people, as they get older and their health begins to fail, find that aspects of the physical environment with which they have hitherto coped become more of a problem: the toilet at the bottom of the garden; the Post Office at the top of the hill; getting up stairs to bed; getting on and off a bus (when a bus stop is near enough); and crossing roads.

Other aspects of daily living may also become more problematic: finding shops that will sell just one sausage and one rasher of bacon; cutting toenails; getting out of the bath; keeping warm; doing household repairs; and gardening. To the extent that such difficulties accumulate, the older person becomes increasingly at risk, and dependent upon others for assistance. As was suggested earlier, there is a variety of services in existence to provide assistance. The task for older people is first to find out to what services (or benefits) they are entitled, how to go about obtaining them, and how to coordinate or orchestrate the variety of available services so that they complement each other.

Finding out about one's 'rights' is a straightforward matter in Britain if one can write to 'Age Concern' for their helpful information sheets; but getting one's 'rights' is another matter. Often a bewildering variety of forms have to be completed, a substantial proportion of which are difficult to understand. Not surprising, then, that many benefits are not claimed. But how *does* one get someone else to come and cut one's toe-nails? On the financial benefits and allowances front, social workers are the older person's most likely source of common-sense information and assistance. For medical and paramedical treatment, the person's general practitioner or the health visitor or district nurse should provide the help and advice. In theory, having all these services available sounds wonderful but in practice it can be a different story, and this is precisely why voluntary organizations have stepped in not only to fill the information gap, but to provide volunteers to undertake services not available statutorily (the 'Street-warden' scheme, for example).

What older people have to face up to, then, apart from finding the energy to manipulate the available resources, is that they can begin to feel a nuisance or a burden. Most people at any age do not want 'to be a burden', and it is this stance that on the one hand inhibits some older people from asking for services, and on the other prevents their questioning the services that are offered: it is not gracious to bite the hand that feeds you. Thus, many older people may end up, for example, having repeat prescriptions for some medicinal remedy because it is less trouble for themselves and for the doctor than having another check-up. Consequently many older people have too many drugs over too long periods, the side-effects of which may then require treatment through further medication!

Whereas the various services mentioned are available for people of all ages, but are used to a disproportionate extent by elderly people, some provisions in the community have been set up solely for older people: there are forms of sheltered accommodation, and a variety of other domestically-scaled accommodation schemes run by charities such as Anchor Housing. This provision, in the form of physical fabric appropriate to older people (small groupings of bungalows or flats that are self-contained, communal rooms and service areas, often with a 'warden') is seen as a preventative measure, easing the burden on individuals living at home in the community, and hopefully forestalling their entrance into institutional forms of accommodation.

Resources are scarce, and waiting lists for sheltered accommodation, like waiting lists for hip-replacements or consultations concerning arthritis and rheumatism, are long. All too often, this might mean that whereas the provision of sheltered accommodation or a place in a home should be a well-planned thought-through affair, frequently it is the case that a 'crisis admission' ensues. As noted earlier, relatives often just cannot cope any longer and they themselves receive little assistance, so the support network for the older person collapses. Whereas the realization that this is what has happened might be depressing enough, what follows, namely the displacement of older people from their homes, to some other form of accommodation, can be even more of a trauma (Shultz and Brenner, 1977).

Such forms of provision have varied historically and continue to vary in different industrialized societies. In the past, old people who could not look after themselves and who had no relatives to look after them, would find themselves in Workhouses, and 'to end up in the workhouse' was something to be dreaded indeed. A select fortunate few with certain professional or religious backgrounds would be cared for in charitable almshouses or hospices. The predominant form of institutional care in Britain, the old people's home, differs from its European and North American counterparts largely in terms of its size. In the UK a home with 60 residents would be considered quite large, whereas homes in Canada, the USA and Holland, for example, might have 300 residents and be considered of average size.

The UK seems behind in developing both retirement communities and residential complexes which have on hand the full range of services old people might need as they get even older. In the UK sheltered accommodation, residential homes and geriatric hospitals are provided by three different administrative institutions: housing authorities, social services departments, and hospital authorities, and consequently are rarely to be found on the same site. In the USA and Europe it is more common to find facilities which provide the same range of services (plus nursing homes) if not in the same building then at least in very close proximity. Provision in the UK is largely made by the State, but elsewhere often by commercial agencies or charities. Those that appear most desirable are often those where old people pay large fees for the services they themselves say they want.

VI.—TYPES OF INTERVENTION

Non-psychological, physical forms of intervention, largely involve the use of drugs. Drug induced confusion, disorientation and sensory defects are not rare (Simon, 1970). Anyone working with older people with behavioural problems needs to be aware that a large variety of symptoms can themselves be drug induced. Eisdorfer and Stotsky (1977) have given a comprehensive account of drug intervention with older people. Another form of intervention may be termed 'environmental'. This is the provision in the person's home of equipment (e.g., aids to help people get in and out of bed, on and off the toilet) or external modifications such as the provision of ramps and grab rails. Specific strategies of psychological intervention mainly focus on three areas: fostering sociability amongst residents and between residents and staff in institutional settings (this is presumed to increase the general level of the residents' quality of life); increasing residents' levels of awareness for their surroundings (often termed 'reality orientation'); and modifying forms of behaviour that are deemed to be a problem (e.g., trying to reduce levels of incontinence).

The first area, *fostering sociability*, may be illustrated from a study by Galliard (1978). A time-sampled observational study on a geriatric psychiatry ward revealed very low levels of social interaction between residents (although staff claimed they followed a policy of encouraging patients to be mobile and to talk to one another, and considered that they were, in the main, successful at this).

> As our observations had shown an unsatisfactory social environment we attempted to alter the social environment to increase interaction. Tea-time in the afternoon was just a time for ingestion of liquid. Cups of tea were handed out, drunk, and cups handed back. It had none of the social significance that beverages usually have. We therefore tried to get tea-time viewed as a social activity, to be served in the dining-room, with patients grouped round tables so that conversation became possible. To do this required the agreement of the nursing staff (who were apparently enthusiastic) and the domestic staff. The latter raised some objections because the dining-room then required extra cleaning. However, after two months' discussions it was finally agreed, and tea was served round tables with a pot per table, and it was a great success, becoming a social event rather than just fulfilling a physiological need . . . (Galliard, 1978).

We shall continue the quotation in the next section to see the ultimate outcome of Galliard's study. A second quotation from Galliard is worth reproducing here because it illustrates what can be revealed through observational research techniques, and how intervention may follow:

> Another example is a problem that was presented initially as a complaint from nursing staff of a high level of nocturnal restlessness. On investigation, we found the evening shift change was at 8.30 p.m. In order to reduce the night shift's work, the day shift got all the old people to bed before the night shift came on, everyone in bed by 8.30 p.m. This meant that by 3 o'clock in the morning many of the patients had had all the sleep they needed and were wandering about. They would be given sedation and put back to bed, only to awaken at between 6 a.m. and 8 a.m. when the sedative was still active. They would then sit in a chair and doze the rest of the day, building up a vicious circle. After much persuasion and discussion, we altered the system to the night shift putting them to bed and the day shift getting them up. . . . (Galliard, 1978)

Reality orientation (RO) is an intervention strategy used with elderly people having a moderate to severe degree of memory loss, confusion or time-place-person disorientation (Holden and Woods, 1982). The backbone of RO is the repetition and learning of basic information such as the patient's name, the place, the time of day, day of the week and date, what the next meal is, the time for bathing, and so on. This essential repetition is conducted formally in classes and informally by staff having regular contact with the residents. RO classes may take place at a set time each day, but informal RO should be conducted on a 24–hour basis. An 'ordinary' verbal exchange might involve 'Do you want a cup of tea or coffee?'. An RO equivalent exchange might be 'Good morning Mrs. Brown, it's nearly 11 o'clock, time for a drink. Do you want tea or coffee this morning Mrs. Brown?'. The effects of RO are discussed in the next section.

Behaviour modification or reinforcement therapy operates on the simple level of systematically rewarding desired behaviours and ignoring undesired ones. Rewards, often tokens, should follow the desired act quickly. Tokens can be exchanged for something of significance to the resident. Hopefully token rewards can be replaced by a verbal reward system which might itself then be phased out when the desired behaviour is thoroughly established. Reinforcement systems in a home or on a ward may vary extensively in their levels of sophistication, but the significant factor is that staff learn the psychological principles involved.

Barns, Sack and Shore (1973), in reviewing treatment approaches for older institutionalized people, suggest that behaviour modification may be appropriately applied to a variety of aspects of self-care (such as dressing, brushing teeth and combing hair), of ward care (making one's bed, cleaning one's room) and of social behaviour (helping others and talking to others). They list a series of 12 steps to be followed in setting up an individual programme of reinforcement therapy. These range from choosing a resident who has a particular need or one in whom staff have a particular interest (step 1), through observing the resident's current behaviour carefully for several days (step 4) in order to describe in simple words the specific behaviour to be selected for modification (spitting, hitting, or screaming, for example). Step 4 also includes obtaining a baseline by recording the time and frequency of occurrence of the behaviour and any factors that seem to precipitate the behaviour or to increase or decrease it; listing the desirable behaviours of the resident in terms of what he is doing right and what are appropriate behaviours; and finding out what is meaningful to the older person that could be used conveniently and effectively as a reward or reinforcer for the behaviours to be encouraged. Step 8, for example, involves informing team members and others involved in order to get consistency in the reinforcement regime. Step 12 includes summarizing the resident's behaviour at the beginning of the study and at the end, indicating what progress has been made in the particulars studied, the specific treatment actions taken, and making an evaluation of the study, particularly including suggestions for improving the techniques employed.

VII.—IS PSYCHOLOGICAL INTERVENTION SUCCESSFUL?

The first of the above quotations from Galliard continues . . . 'Two months later the old system had returned'; that is, no more 'social' tea-times. The second quote continues . . . 'However, again without constant vigilance the system slipped back.' Constant vigilance is also required for reality orientation to operate successfully. This author recalls only too well a visit to an USA psychogeriatric ward where the Reality Orientation Board (a large board in the ward, with large lettering showing the date, the day, the name of the place, etc.) was completely inaccurate: it wasn't Monday; the weather was not clear and hot; yesterday was not Sunday . . .! Schwenk (1979) in a review of RO studies noted that serious methodological problems invalidate the results of most studies, but that the few adequate studies suggest that RO can sometimes help reduce confusion, although it does not seem to increase autonomy or happiness among the elderly. Reality orientation may be perceived by staff and visitors to be beneficial because it is evidence that something positive is actually being attempted. However, like colour television receivers donated by well-wishers which remain perpetually on and perpetually ignored by residents, unless reality orientation and other techniques can be demonstrated to increase residents' life satisfaction, one must question their utility.

The lack of success reported by Galliard in changing ward routine reflects the great difficulty facing anyone attempting change in such settings—*institutional inertia*. This is, in a sense, an aspect of the practical problem facing applied psychologists that we return to in the next section—namely operating in the 'real world'. Galliard pointed out that any major change in ward routine could involve as many as ten groups of staff with up to eight different levels of administration and two different levels of union representation. But, even when such changes had been implemented, without the continuous active involvement of the psychologist (as change agent), the new programme lapsed, and the ward reverted to its previous routine. Either the change agent must be in some sense a permanent feature of the situation or the situation must be so changed that it *can* and *will* continue to operate in its new mode; but this is far easier said than done.

Clearly, though, applied psychologists must have an understanding of organizational psychology if they are going successfully to implement change in organizations. This implies taking a systems approach to the situation. Focusing attention on residents alone, or on staff alone, without attempting to understand the constraints the wider organizational context imposes on their relationships (for example, union views and management views of desirable outcomes, which inevitably influence the attitudes and values of all involved), may produce short-term change but seldom produces accommodation (in the Piagetian sense) of the underlying structure so that the change becomes part of an evolved system.

Though success with behaviour modification programmes for psychogeriatric patients has been reported, they too depend on an organizational system of individuals all of whom should be interacting purposefully with clearly specified goals in mind. Intervention is likely to be successful and continued to the extent that it can be shown to staff that it is indeed achieving its aims. This implies the need for baseline measures and follow-up measures and an understanding of all the situational factors that impinge on desired outcomes. Measures should be valid and reliable in order to answer questions like, 'Does this drug improve cognitive performance?'; 'Has this change in ward routine increased the life satisfaction of residents?'; and 'Has the dementing process been slowed down by the provision of stimulation and activity?'.

VIII.—METHODOLOGICAL AND PRACTICAL PROBLEMS

One practical problem has already been mentioned, namely the difficulty of instituting change in a large organization. An associated problem for applied psychology researchers is getting access in the first place to organizations they may wish to study. To conduct a simple survey of the extent of personalization around hospital beds may require the permission of a committee which might be less malleable than an individual. To conduct observational studies in which the resident or patient is the focus of attention, nevertheless may be seen by staff as 'spying on them', and to a certain extent it often is. Other practical problems may concern the duration of any study: it may need to be conducted and monitored over a period of months if not years; and it may require the sort of stamina that the more laboratory-oriented psychologist is seldom required to face; for example, working shifts to obtain baseline data on ward activities (not something a university lecturer would find easy to accommodate into a teaching/research timetable). In the early stages of a project research workers may feel it is useful to conduct participant observation studies and actually live and work, for example, in an old people's home for a period of a few weeks.

Methodological issues can be more specifically focused on the problems involved in the clinical assessment of older people. Schaie and Schaie's review (1977) points to the difficulties inherent in using psychological tests on older people, be they designed to aid diagnosis, ascertain the effects of therapeutic intervention, or assist in counselling. Baseline determinations in the elderly are problematic because many may be functioning closer to their marginal limits, and increased variability in performance means more behaviour sampling is needed. Responses in older people unfamiliar with testing may reveal more reaction to the test itself than to its content.

Most norms found in the literature, even if 'age corrected', are developed from cross-sectional studies, and are hence cohort specific; that is, measures are taken at one point in time of people in different age groups. Difficulties arise in interpreting results because one cannot hold environmental inputs constant; for example, older people will probably have had poorer nutrition as children, and have experienced the stresses of a World War. Since groups of older people tend to have had less education, be at a lower socio-economic status and in worse health, controlling for such variables is necessary if one is attempting to examine ageing effects.

In testing situations the older person's auditory and visual acuity may well affect performance on tests designed to measure other capacities; few questionnaires have alternative large type-face versions. Tests which differentiate between normal and pathological functions among young people cannot be assumed to do so with older people too and most of the currently used tests of intelligence assess the intellectual competence of old people with respect to constructs defined for the young. Tests designed to estimate criteria relevant to the lives of old people are yet to be developed and validated. Presently many tests contain items of little relevance to older people (e.g., statements of the 'Do you like riotous parties?' variety) which may bias their response to other statements, and behaviour samples gathered in an assessment setting may not accurately reflect the older person's capability at home.

Another range of problems that have practical methodological ramifications are conceptual in nature. Consider the notion of 'adjustment'. Burton (1966), referred to earlier, uses the phrase 'passive adjustment' to refer to a symptom of institutional neurosis. Yet many administrators in charge of old people's homes, for example, would consider that 'well adjusted' residents do not complain, do as they are asked, are no trouble or bother, and are grateful for what is done for them; while others have taken instances of arguments and hostility in social intercourse in such settings as evidence of more positive adjustment. Essentially at the heart of the matter are almost diametrically opposed conceptions of adjustment, based on different value judgements, where being assertive is seen as positive adjustment by some, and being acquiescent is seen as positive adjustment by others. Nor is the dilemma necessarily resolved by appeal to research evidence in this area. More assertive residents may rate themselves as having less 'life-satisfaction' (and this is another 'measure' often used in studies of older people's assessment of their quality of life) than do acquiescent residents. Conceptions of 'morale', 'adjustment', 'life-satisfaction' and suchlike are embedded in notions of 'positive mental health' which themselves are difficult to define, let alone measure in a truly reliable and valid way.

The situation is well summarized by Schaie and Schaie (1977) who note that assessment of the aged still tends to be a problem because (a) very few psychologists have been trained to work with the aged; (b) with some few exceptions adequate norms are not yet available for most of the techniques found useful with young adults; and (c) new techniques specifically constructed for clinical work with the aged are sparse and, where available, lack clear-cut demonstration of acceptable psychometric characteristics.

IX.—PROBLEMS OF ETHICS AND CONFIDENTIALITY

Despite the growing emphasis on the rights of the older person in society, the time seems far off when we can expect any British equivalent of the National Convener of the Gray Panthers (an American old people's organization campaigning for their rights) to write an open letter to a respectable gerontological journal stressing, amongst other things that:

> There is an urgent need for new research methods, particularly to demonstrate the interaction between the individual and society and to make full use of the experience of old people to form the widest possible data base for radical social analysis. Gray Panthers press for studies action/research which move beyond developmental psychology to economic political factors and present viable alternatives to the current styles of research.

> The new subjects of research should focus on the power elites, the knowledge definers, pharmaceutical houses, the media or the heads of the granting agencies. More studies are urgently needed to evaluate the extent to which old people can control and/or provide input in the formulation and implementation of policies and services which purport to 'serve the elderly'. (Kuhn, 1978, pp. 423–424)

In other words, older people want a say in what research workers should be doing, and maybe, even, in how they should be doing it.

Brocklehurst (1974) noted in connection with visiting regulations that:

> For those who are not relatives . . . and to whom the old person, if at home, would have the option of either allowing or refusing entrance to their own home, access to people in institutions may prove much more difficult. This is important to bodies carrying out scientific research and, in particular, to those who wish to further the amenities which old people should be receiving by discussing with them their own estimate of the quality of the service available to them. (pp. 8–9).

Brocklehurst suggested that old people living in their own homes have the option 'of either allowing or refusing entrance'. Is this a right that should be extended to those living in institutions—those people for whom an institution has to substitute as home? A particular problem here concerns research with people who are 'confused'. Under what circumstances should people be permitted to make decisions on their behalf about their participation in research? Who decides if the research is morally justified? Who performs what Reich (1978) calls the 'risk-benefit analysis'? Who decides that there is equity in the selection of subjects, rather than 'captive populations' being discriminated against in this respect? Who decides if the subject has given *informed* consent to being researched upon? Taking informed consent as an example, it would be reasonable to assume the notion means that the person has the capacity or competence to give consent, has sufficient knowledge on which to decide, sufficient comprehension of the information to make an enlightened decision, and freedom, both internal and external, as regards the choice to be made. How many research workers seek such informed consent from their older subjects?

Butler (1975) has claimed that research involving the aged has concentrated primarily on studies of the 5% of older people who reside in institutions. It is certainly clear that residential homes, nursing homes, and hospitals have been and continue to be the setting for both biomedical and behavioural as well as social research. Of course, persons resident in such settings are 'captive populations' subject to exploitation in general and diminution of freedom and voluntariness in particular. The circumstances here are especially insidious. Institutionalization fosters dependence and offers inducements to conform to institutional expectations. These are, in effect, inherently coercive constraints and, as such, are obstacles to both voluntary and competent consent. More often than not, residents want to please the very staff upon whom their well-being depends and are thus highly vulnerable to the granting or withholding of institutional privileges, privileges which may in form be subtle or not so subtle. This often means that privacy is a very scarce commodity and confidentiality is something to which lip-service may be given but which in practice may go by the board (Slater, Lipman and Harris, 1977).

X.—THE ROLE OF OTHER DISCIPLINES AND PROFESSIONS

Many of the professional groups listed below will have received varying amounts of psychological input into their basic training. Increasingly, psychologists involved in teaching medical and paramedical professions have been able to tailor their material to the needs of those being taught, as more psychological interest in and research pertinent to their work has developed.

The Social Worker   In the hospital context the social worker contributes by assessing and advising in two contrasting areas: (a) how the person and his or her family are likely to adjust to the problem situation and their motivation to resolve the problem; and (b) the extent of the availability of resources they may need. Personal motivation is probably the most important element in rehabilitation because of the hard work, courage, shift in attitudes, and perhaps pain that can be involved during the attempt to regain independence. Hospital-based social workers will often need to liaise with community-based social workers who should know all the community services, their quirks and limitations.

The Nurse   The traditional role of the nurse has been one of caring *for* and doing things *for* the patient, who was seen in a dependent, passive role. In dealing with the rehabilitation problems of older people a different attitude is needed, one which looks for ways in which individuals can do things for themselves, perhaps at first with some assistance, but later unaided. This does not mean that the rehabilitative role precludes the caring supportive role, just that the latter should be judiciously not gratuitously performed.

The Health Visitor   Because of health visitors' roles in general practice and contacts within the community, they are in a good position to detect disability in older people at an early stage and give appropriate advice and support to older people and their relatives. The health visitor should also be skilled at liaison between the various service agencies.

The Speech Therapist   Dysphasia (any impairment of language function due to brain lesion) is a common accompaniment of strokes, and is a symptom of dementia in its later stages. It is all too easy, however, to assume that because a patient's speech is confused, the patient is confused. Speech therapists give advice about the best way of communicating with a person with dysphasia, show the dysphasic person how to communicate what he or she means, and demonstrate ways in which family and friends may help with language work or may learn to use an alternative system of communication.

The Physiotherapist   Assessment of a patient by a physiotherapist focuses on five areas: functional activities (e.g., can the patient get into bed, stand up from a chair, get up off the floor, walk?); balance; joint mobility; muscle strength; and coordination. Following a thorough assessment, the physiotherapist will form a plan of action, exercises and activities, to help restore the functional activities that have been found to be lacking.

The Occupational Therapist   Although still conjuring up the inappropriate image of someone who shows you how to make wickerwork baskets, the occupational therapist working with older people is concerned with furthering the improvement made through physiotherapy to basic functional activities, so that the activities of daily living, such as getting dressed, cooking, making a bed, and doing light housework, remain within the patient's behavioural repertoire.

The Doctor   Mental and physical disorders commonly occur together in later life and psychological difficulties are more often present, but less obvious than in earlier years. Social and environmental considerations become of more critical importance in a treatment regime, so the doctor has to be aware of the increased importance of relatives, social workers, therapists, psychiatrists and others.

The Voluntary Worker   Given adequate guidance, voluntary workers can extend the activities of other groups (such as nurses, physiotherapists and occupational therapists), particularly if individuals confine themselves to one specific disorder, such as strokes, or arthritis.

These eight groups of 'carers', operating as they do in homes, day-hospitals, residential homes, and hospitals, may present a somewhat confusing array of people who may look more likely to pull the older person apart than help him or her to stay together. The older person may feel like a football the 'care team' kicks around. This is why *coordination* of effort, teamwork directed at specific goals, is so important.

XI.—FUTURE PROSPECTS

Bromley (1977) remarks that it is difficult to be both a gerontologist and an optimist. One speculation that makes Bromley's view of future prospects for ageing and for older people a little bleak is the notion that older people have 'aversive properties'—something less talked about, suggests Bromley, even than euthanasia. Many people who have little direct contact with the elderly experience some kind of aversion on encountering a physically and mentally deteriorated old person, just as many have the same feelings, akin to revulsion, for profoundly handicapped children. From whence such feelings may spring we do not know, but there is certainly some element of 'fear of the unknown' in the process. We feel comfortable when we know our behavioural repertoire can cope with the situations in which we find ourselves. We feel insecure when interacting with individuals whose behaviour we find odd, different, not easily understandable.

For many centuries people with odd forms of behaviour have been made outcasts and scapegoats, and it is only relatively recently that people with physical handicaps have become increasingly a part of the community in which they live. Segregation would seem to lead to stigmatization and stereotyping, to an increase in inaccurate perceptions of and about older people and their capacities of the kind referred to at the beginning of this chapter. If the future holds more segregation for older people (from the world of work and from the community into special homes and hospitals), then their prospects do indeed look bleak. But if increased segregation does not come about, and it may not because it appears to be too costly (at least in terms of social and health services provision), then a community forced to come more directly to terms with its ageing population may be one that serves them and itself better.

Increased unemployment will give people more time on their hands. In order that such time may be willingly spent helping others (not only the elderly), sharing expertise and skills, providing mutual support and counselling, rather than wasted in purposeless and ultimately unrewarding egocentric activities, applied psychologists must turn their attention to meshing the needs of unemployed people to do something useful and rewarding with those (amongst whom may be numbered many elderly persons) who need the services and assistance the state increasingly seems unable (or unwilling) to provide. Not only must applied psychologists be able to produce change in a structured institutional context, but if the future prospects of every person who is ageing are to be better served, they must also turn their attention to community psychology.

XII.—ANNOTATED READINGS

Bromley, D. B. (1974). *The Psychology of Human Ageing*. Harmondsworth: Penguin.

This remains the most thorough and comprehensive British book on ageing, and it has dated very little since the second edition. It includes a good technical appendix on research designs and associated problems.

Carver, V. and Liddiard, P. (1978). *An Ageing Population*. Sevenoaks: Hodder and
    Stoughton.

This is an unusual collection of papers and is the Reader for the Open University's course 'An Ageing Population'. It brings together a useful compendium of material from diverse fields, and its refreshingly practical overall orientation makes many of its papers particularly interesting to read.

Puner, M. (1974). *To the Good Long Life*. New York: Universe Books.

This is a good, amusing, interesting 'easy read', that also manages to remain reasonably well referenced and documented.

Meacher, M. (1972). *Taken for a Ride*. London: Longman.

This book focuses on the position of confused old people in residential homes. It makes absorbing reading, is well referenced, and highlights the problems inherent in labelling someone as 'confused', as well as the subtle processes of institutionalization.

Birren, J. E. and Schaie, K. W. (1977) (Eds.) *Handbook of the Psychology of Aging*.
    London: Van Nostrand Reinhold.

One of the three handbooks (the others being on Aging and the Social Sciences, and the Biology of Aging) presenting 'state-of-the-art' chapters, with voluminous references.

Brocklehurst, J. C. and Hanley, T. (1976). *Geriatric Medicine for Students*. London:
    Churchill Livingstone.

Although aimed at undergraduate medical students this 250-page paperback is not too difficult for other students to follow. Anyone with an interest in ageing and older people needs some medical information, and this book provides a digestible guide to the 'basics'.

XIII.—REFERENCES

Barns, E. K., Sack, A. and Shore, H. (1973). Guidelines to treatment approaches. *The Gerontologist*, **13**, 513–527.

Barton, R. (1966). *Institutional Neurosis*, Bristol: John Wright.

Bergmann, K. (1978). Psychogeriatrics. In: V. Carver and P. Liddiard (Eds.) *An Ageing Population*. Sevenoaks: Hodder and Stoughton.

Brocklehurst, J. C. (1974). *Old People in Institutions—Their Rights*. Mitcham: Age Concern England, Manifesto Series No. 10.

Bromley, D. B. (1977). Speculations in social and environmental gerontology, *Nursing Times*, **73**, 53–56.

Butler, R. N. (1969). Aging: another form of bigotry. *The Gerontologist*, **9**, 243–246.

Butler, R. N. (1975). *Why Survive? Being Old in America*. New York: Harper and Row.

Eisdorfer, C. and Stotsky, B. A. (1977). Intervention, treatment, and rehabilitation of psychiatric disorders In: J. E. Birren and K. W. Schaie (Eds.) *Handbook of the Psychology of Ageing*: London: Van Nostrand Reinhold.

Galliard, P. (1978). *Difficulties Encountered in Attempting to Increase Social Interactions Amongst Geriatric Psychiatry Patients*. Paper presented to the British Psychological Society, Annual Conference, York, April 1978.

Goffman, E. (1961). *Asylums*. New York: Doubleday Anchor.

Holden, U. P. and Woods, R. T. (1982). *Reality Orientation: Psychological Approaches To The 'Confused' Elderly*. London: Churchill Livingstone

Howarth, C. I. (1980). The structure of effective psychology: man as a problem-solver. In: A. J. Chapman and D. M. Jones (Eds.) *Models of Man*, Leicester: The British Psychological Society. (Hillsdale, NJ: Lawrence Erlbaum, 1982).

Hunt, A. (1978). *The Elderly at Home*. London: Her Majesty's Stationery Office.

Kuhn, M. E. (1978). Open letter. *The Gerontologist*, **18**, 422–424.

Meacher, M. (1972). *Taken for a Ride*. London: Longman.

Palmore, E. (1977). Facts on ageing: a short quiz. *The Gerontologist*, **17**, 315–320.

Pattie, A. H. and Gilleard, C. J. (1979). *Manual of the Clifton Assessment Procedures for the Elderly (CAPE)*, Sevenoaks: Hodder and Stoughton.

Plutchik, R., Conte, H., Lieberman, M., Bakur, M., Grossman, J. and Lehrman, N. (1970). Reliability and validity of a scale for assessing the functioning of geriatric patients. *Journal of the American Geriatrics Society*, **18**, 491–500.

Puner, M. (1974). *To The Good Long Life*. New York: Universe Books.

Reich, W. T. (1978). Ethical issues related to research involving elderly subjects. *The Gerontologist*, **18**, 326–337.

Robb, B. (1967). *Sans Everything*. London: Nelson.

Sanford, J. R. A. (1975). Tolerance of debility in elderly dependents by supporters at home: its significance for hospital practice. *British Medical Journal*, **3**, 471–473.

Sanford, J. R. A. (1976). Ebbing lives: the rising tide. *Concord*, **5**, 57–64.

Schaie, K. W. and Schaie, J. P. (1977). Clinical assessment and aging. In: J. E. Birren and K. W. Schaie (Eds.). *Handbook of the Psychology of Aging*. London: Van Nostrand Reinhold.

Schultz, R. and Brenner, G. (1977). Relocation of the aged: a review and theoretical analysis. *Journal of Gerontology*, **32**, 323–333.

Schwenk, M. A. (1979). Reality orientation for the institutionalized aged: does it help? *The Gerontologist*, **19**, 373–377.

Simon, A. (1970). Screening of the aged mentally ill. *Journal of Geriatric Psychiatry*, **4**, 5–17.

Slater, R., Lipman, A. and Harris, H. (1977). Problems of research in homes for old people. *Long Term Care and Health Services Administration Quarterly*, Winter, 293–299.

Townsend, P. (1962). *The Last Refuge*. London: Routledge and Kegan Paul.

Zipf, G. K. (1965). *Human Behavior and the Principle of Least Effort*. New York: Hafner.

SUBJECT INDEX

Note that a number of very important topics (for example, individual assessment, types of intervention, problems of ethics and confidentiality, and so on) appear in *all* chapters. Therefore, full and complete reference is not given in the Index. Similarly, items marked with an asterisk (*) appear too frequently within the text to be fully indexed.